THE BP BOOK OF
INDUSTRIAL
ARCHAEOLOGY

Neil Cossons

David & Charles

The Author

Neil Cossons is the Director of the Science
Museum, London and an English Heritage
Commissioner. In 1971 he was appointed
the first Director of the Ironbridge Gorge
Museum, a post he held for over 12 years
before becoming Director of the National
Maritime Museum at Greenwich. For many
years a leading advocate of industrial
archaeological conservation, he is a past
President of the Association for Industrial
Archaeology and the Museums Association
and was the first Chairman of the Association of Independent Museums of which
he is now President. He has broadcast
widely on radio and television and written
a number of books and numerous papers
on industrial archaeology, conservation
and museums. He is married and lives in
Shropshire.

A DAVID & CHARLES BOOK

© Neil Cossons 1975, 1987, 1993

First published 1975
Second edition 1987
Third edition, paperback 1993

A catalogue record for this book is
available from the British Library.

ISBN 0 7153 0134 9

Typeset by Typesetters (Birmingham) Ltd, West Midlands
and printed in England by Butler & Tanner, Frome
for David & Charles
Brunel House   Newton Abbot   Devon

CONTENTS

FOREWORD

The wealth and diversity of our industrial heritage remind us that Britain was the world's first industrial nation. This helps explain today's widespread interest in industrial archaeology and makes the safeguarding of the evidence of the origins of modern industrial society well worthwhile.

These reminders of dynamic past industrial activity underline the fact that economies constantly evolve and that further change in the industrial landscape will continue for as long as we have a thriving manufacturing sector.

As one of Britain's leading industrial concerns, BP is very much part of that landscape. That is why we are delighted to support the publication of this updated edition of *The BP Book of Industrial Archaeology*.

Since its original publication in 1975, the book has become a respected standard work on the subject and I very much hope that this new paperback edition will help encourage a still wider interest in Britain's proud industrial heritage.

Lord Ashburton
Chairman
The British Petroleum Company plc

PREFACE

Indulging oneself in reminiscence is something that occurs all too infrequently, so this preface affords an opportunity to lapse into anecdotage for which I make no apologies. In looking back at the emergence of my own interest in industrial archaeology there are several quite specific events which I remember with vivid clarity. The germ came without doubt from my father whose interest in turnpike roads led him and later both of us to seek out bridges and tollhouses and those remaining milestones that had not been buried or destroyed in the war. A journey by Barton's bus (were Barton's buses *really* all different?) from Beeston near Nottingham to Shardlow to see the flood-damaged remains of Cavendish Bridge brought me into contact, for the first time consciously, with a place which breathed the atmosphere of the Industrial Revolution and of past prosperity and activity, the inland port on the Trent & Mersey Canal with its superb warehouses and basins. There was a magic about deserted Shardlow. Here was a *place* where things had happened but where nothing happened now. On the line of the Ashby & Ticknall Tramway or the Charnwood Forest Canal, at King's Mills on the edge of Donington Park, beside the remains of the Morley Park blast furnaces at Heage or the great mills at Cromford, this sensation of place became overwhelming, the essential ingredient that brought alive for me the men and horses, the boats, wagons, flames and smoke of a period which was otherwise as distant or unreal as that of Ancient Egypt or Rome. There were also from time to time interminable Sunday afternoons which then passed me by completely, when my father's smoke-filled study was full too of

J. D. Chambers or W. E. Tate or, on occasion, both. They were decrying the desecration of Nottingham in a period before a conservation movement existed, and so the threatened extinction of the beautiful Collin almshouses in Friar Lane became an inevitable reality. Who could stand in the way of progress?

Much later, with Michael Rix at Preston Montford in Shropshire, I realised there were others with broadly the same sort of interest and that it was gaining identity as 'industrial archaeology'. But by then I was already in the business myself and the opportunities to practise were broadening rapidly. The diversity of the interest in industrial archaeology is astonishing and has undoubtedly been one of the great aids to its rapid evolution over the last thirty years, to the growth of a broad base of popular interest and to the awakening of an active appreciation that the remains of industrialisation in Britain are the tangible marks of the beginnings of a new civilisation which a thousand years hence the archaeologist and historian will identify, categorise and certainly revere in the same way as we do the ancient cultures of the Mediterranean. With the remains of the Industrial Revolution, however, we have the opportunity to keep them alive because we are close enough to identify with the people who were involved. This book is largely concerned with the physical remains as such, with their historical and technological origins and with guiding the visitor to the *place* where imagination may be stimulated.

Since the first edition was published in 1975 immense changes have taken place in the industrial landscape and in our attitudes towards it. There has been a virtual extinction of many of those traditional industrial heartlands based on coal and steam, iron, steel and textiles – the so-called smokestack industries – and the growth of a service economy often based on leisure and supported by tourism. These have fuelled a boom in industrial archaeological preservation and museums. At the same time redundant industrial landscapes are increasingly seen as developable; for example, derelict waterfront or dockland areas. The change in attitude is reflected in how places see themselves and their future prosperity; for the first time a Bradford or a Glasgow can effectively and successfully market itself as a place to visit. Britain's industrial archaeology is becoming a form of national asset and never before has the need to reconcile the voices of the past with the needs of the future been so real.

In compiling this work I owe thanks to many people who have offered encouragement and given me active help and advice. My wife and children have entered very much into the spirit of industrial archaeology; their support has been invaluable. My colleagues at Ironbridge and latterly at the Science Museum have made many useful comments and brought to my notice innumerable sites of interest. To Brian Bowers, Ivor Brown, Robert Bud, Keith Gale, Charles Hadfield, John Iredale, Kenneth Major, John Powell, Stuart Smith, Michael Stratton, Barrie Trinder and George Watkins I am particularly grateful, for their kindness in reading sections of the draft text and giving invaluable comment and criticism. I am deeply indebted to Peter Stoddart, who prepared the line drawings, for his painstaking attention to detail and his sensitivity to the problems of interpreting mechanisms in what we both hope will be a comprehensible manner. Brian Bracegirdle, John Cornwell, John Hume and Gordon Stacey were also of very great assistance with the visual aspects of the book and in making available to me photographs from their collections. Angus Buchanan, whose friendship I have enjoyed over many years, has been of great help and encouragement, and to Kenneth Hudson I have been continually indebted for preventing those lapses of self-indulgent antiquarianism into which anybody involved in archaeology is so easily inveigled. Gordon Payne deserves my special thanks for his numerous and helpful suggestions and his comments on the original draft manuscript.

Above all, my thanks are due to British Petroleum plc, without whose enlightened initiative and support for the concept this book would not have been originally published in 1975. It is through their continued generosity that this revised, paperback edition has been possible.

Many people have kindly supplied me with information and offered suggestions, and without their help this book could not have been written. In recording their names here I am both expressing my gratitude and dissociating them from any errors of fact or of emphasis, for which I am wholly responsible: David Anderson, Owen Ashmore, Frank Atkinson, Kenneth Barton, Jonathan Bryant, John Butt, John Cockcroft, John Corin, Arthur Corney, Glenys Crocker, John Crompton, Joan and Roy Day, Paul Elkin, Keith Falconer, Bill Gilmour, Patrick Greene, Douglas Hague, Bob Hawkins, Kenneth Hawley, Tony Herbert, Dan Hogan, Tony Hirst, Derek Janes, Michael Lewis, Jeremy Lowe, Pamela Moore, Marilyn Palmer, Michael Rix, John Robinson, John Sawtell, David Sekers, Michael Stammers, Paul Stephens, John Stengelhofen, Donald Storer, Jennifer Tann, Michael Thomas, Rex Wailes, Mark Watson, Margaret Weston, Peter White, Catherine Wilson, Michael Wright and Christopher Zeuner.

The engravings used throughout the text are taken, with their original captions, from Charles Tomlinson, *Illustrations of Useful Arts, Manufactures and Trades*, 1858.

Neil Cossons
Ironbridge
January 1993

A NOTE ON USAGE

The location of sites is by National Grid Reference, presented in the standard form with the grid letters followed by a six-figure reference. Where an area rather than a specific point is referred to, a four-figure reference is given indicating the kilometre square within which the site comes.

Where appropriate, sites are located by county. In the case of England and Wales the present, post-1974, county boundaries apply. In Scotland, where the administrative areas are now regions and districts, the old county names have been retained within each region in order to give a more precise location.

As the buildings and machines referred to in the text were built to imperial standards, the imperial measurements used in the first edition have been retained. The following conversion tables will assist in reconciling these measurements with their metric equivalents:

Table of weight equivalents
1 oz	28.35 g
1 lb	0.4536 kg
1 stone	6.3503 kg
1 cwt	50.803 kg
1 ton	1.016 tonnes

Table of distance equivalents
1 in	2.54 cm
1 ft	30.48 cm
1 yd	0.9144 m
1 mile	1.6093 km

Table of £sd/£p equivalents
£	s	d	£p
		1d	½p
		2d	1p
		3d	1p
		4d	1½p
		5d	2p
		6d	2½p
		7d	3p
		8d	3p
		9d	4p
		10d	4p
		11d	4½p
	1s	12d	5p
	2s		10p
	3s		15p
	4s		20p
	5s		25p
	6s		30p
	7s		35p
	8s		40p
	9s		45p
	10s		50p
	11s		55p
	12s		60p
	13s		65p
	14s		70p
	15s		75p
	16s		80p
	17s		85p
	18s		90p
	19s		95p
	20s		100p

CHAPTER 1

A PERSPECTIVE ON THE NATURE OF INDUSTRIAL ARCHAEOLOGY

The Industrial Revolution in Britain, which gained momentum during the middle years of the eighteenth century and dominated the nineteenth, was a unique phenomenon in the history of mankind, the repercussions of which have spread throughout the world. It was much more than a revolution in technology – in the techniques of making things; it was a revolution whose cultural, social, economic and environmental implications radically altered the way in which people thought and lived. We live today in a society which is essentially industrial, our prosperity is based on the fruits of industrial activity, and our surroundings, both urban and rural, are largely the result of over two centuries of progressive industrialisation. But not only has the Industrial Revolution left us a physical legacy in the form of the world's first industrial landscapes, it has left us with an overwhelming emotional ambivalence that dominates our attitude towards this most important period of our past and which for over a century has shaped a broad spectrum of cultural expression hostile to industrialism and economic growth based on what we perceive industry to represent.

Only in the last twenty years or so has our view of the Industrial Revolution period, and in particular of the physical remains of industrialisation, begun to assume a more rational equilibrium, helped in part by the perspective of time but also by a distaste for much of what happened to our surroundings in the 1950s and 1960s. Our understanding of the Industrial Revolution has been greatly enhanced by the study of the evidence surviving on the ground – the archaeology – of blast furnaces, mills, factories and warehouses, of canals and railways, and of whole industrial landscapes combining all these things and many more with the houses in which the new industrial population lived, their pubs, chapels, churches and shops. Today we recognise the importance of these industrial monuments and landscapes as part of the national estate and attempt to record and preserve them. We may not yet accord the Iron Bridge in Shropshire, the Elsecar engine in Yorkshire or Brunel's great railway terminus at Temple Meads, Bristol, the same reverence as Hadrian's Wall or Winchester Cathedral but we are right to see them in the same context, as the supreme symbols of their age and all it represented. Unlike the Wall however, or even Winchester, these great industrial monuments derive little from cultures overseas. They represent the achievements of a completely new epoch when Britain, for a brief period of perhaps five generations, held the centre of the world stage as the first industrial nation, birthplace of the Industrial Revolution.

As a technique of history, archaeology illuminates the past through the examination of its physical remains. Typically, archaeologists have defined the broad divides in man's progress by technology – the sort of tools he used – or by the overwhelming geographical dominance of a culture like that of Imperial Rome. Industrial archaeology is a cultural archaeology, the study of the culture in which industry has been dominant and in particular its physical manifestations and the light they shed upon our understanding of industrial society. This book is thus primarily concerned with the eighteenth and nineteenth centuries, with the age in which a largely home-grown process of industrialisation began to dominate people's lives, and with the evidence of it that survives so profusely on the ground. By the beginning of this century Britain's industrial pre-eminence was being usurped and this is reflected in the changing nature of the industrial economy and landscape. Thus, although almost everything that was happening in the Britain of, say, the 1830s was the result of indigenous innovation and self-initiated economic growth, a century later that was manifestly not the case. Once again our fortunes and our culture owed more to forces outside than anything we generated for ourselves. The first Industrial Revolution was over.

The Industrial Revolution period provides then the core area, the mainspring, of industrial archaeology. But there is a diffuse penumbra too, into which the industrial archaeologist, like the archaeologist of any other period, must inevitably venture to provide a perspective and a context for the main area of study. Industrial archaeology spreads out chronologically, in terms of subject area and technique, well beyond its obvious centre. Like any other archaeologist, or historian, the industrial archaeologist must have an understanding of the antecedents of his particular area of study. Thus the evolution of wind and water power in the eighteenth and nineteenth centuries can only be fully appreciated in the context of much earlier developments. But to regard industrial archaeology as being concerned with only *industrial* activity within the last two centuries or so is also to reject the cultural definition. The industrial archaeologist, if he is to have any real understanding of the sites and artefacts of the Industrial Revolution, must look at the landscape in its entirety. Industrial archaeology is in part a landscape study and cannot be restricted to a wholly thematic approach.

The period of the Industrial Revolution is a most significant one in terms of what we are today and this provides in part the key to the remarkable growth of interest in industrial archaeology in recent years. Industrial archaeology was born not out of a detached or academic interest but on a wave of emotional enthusiasm and a less defined but clearly deep-seated feeling that a vital part of the past was being destroyed. The ambient conditions of the 1950s were exactly right for the growth of this new interest. The postwar years, dominated by a preoccupation with renewal and a new foundation for future prosperity, saw also the destruction of much that was old. The reaction was perhaps inevitable – the birth of an environmental movement based on the increasingly widespread appreciation that the landscape was a delicate organism sensitive to uninformed meddling. The Industrial Revolution itself had provided the awful warning and, while most people recognised that the worst excesses of industrialisation had to go, there was an increasing awareness that the industrial landscape itself contained unique elements as worthy of care and attention as those of more traditionally accepted cultural, historical or aesthetic value.

This apparent paradox, the conflict between a conservation movement interested in sweeping away the remnants of industrialisation in the interests of aesthetic objectives, and those who saw in old industrial landscapes elements that were desirable was not the only one however. There was a growing disenchantment with contemporary planning philosophies which also had their origins in a previous generation's reaction to the problems of industrialisation and urbanisation. Town planning arose in response to social distress, a condition that could be alleviated, *inter alia*, by improvement of the physical environment. The concept of amenity promoted by advocates of pleasantness, civic beauty and visual order like Octavia Hill and William Morris, had as its objective the creation of sylvan and genteel suburbs which were soon to evolve into white towers in green parks. It was a direct response to the worst excesses of the Industrial Revolution and yet nearly a century later we have seen a widespread loss of confidence in these basic planning tenets and in our ability to create new urban environments in which people can live.

Instead a new attitude has emerged which may perhaps provide a more satisfactory reconciliation of society's demands for 'amenity' with the economic realities of a so-called post-industrial society largely devoid of ritual expectations of growth. Increasingly, the decayed urban or industrial landscape is seen as an exploitable asset in its own right with intrinsic social and economic value. The nature of the British landscape, dominated as it is by eighteenth- and nineteenth-century developments (some 70 per cent of the built environment dates from the period of the Industrial Revolution), means that it will inevitably be the physical remains of industrialisation that provide the building bricks, so to speak, for the future. This places special responsibilities upon us in terms of how we view their conservation, an issue that is addressed later in this chapter.

THE GROWTH AND STUDY OF INDUSTRIAL ARCHAEOLOGY

Industrial archaeology has thus grown into a broad-based study encompassing more than the words 'industrial' and 'archaeology' would seem to imply. It is already inconceivable that another, more appropriate, term will emerge to supplant it. 'Industrial Archaeology' is obscure in origin but it may have been coined in Manchester in the early 1950s. Its first appearance in print occurred in 1955, when the late Michael Rix published an article in *The Amateur Historian* emphasising the need to record and preserve the remains of industrialisation before they disappeared. As a study it draws its life-blood from a wide variety of disciplines, demanding on the one hand an appreciation of economic or social history or geography and on the other a knowledge of mechanical or civil engineering, metallurgy or architecture. Like the other archaeologies, it has attracted a wide variety of people from many backgrounds and walks of life. Unlike traditional archaeology, however, it has not yet developed a caucus of trained professionals.

This broad sense of awareness which enabled industrial archaeology to gain ground so rapidly has been both its strength and its weakness. Lacking respectable academic origins, it has been the subject of considerable criticism, its interdisciplinary nature and absence of accepted technical standards making it unpalatable to many traditionally based academics. Nevertheless the problems and opportunities of industrial archaeology have caught the imagination of large numbers of people, who as amateurs or professionals, have gained the skills necessary to achieve the right sort of standards. It has developed, generally speaking, outside the orbit of traditional archaeological activity, and only recently have industrial archaeologists begun to pick up the well-established techniques of the traditional archaeologist and apply them to this new study. There are few practical techniques peculiar to industrial archaeology, although some, such as the recording of machinery and various aspects of conservation, pose specific problems which will undoubtedly provide the foundation for considerable industrial archaeological research in the future.

It is increasingly clear that there is a truly 'archaeological' element of study, the potential of which has hardly been developed. Not only is the industrial archaeologist, in his role as a fieldworker and interpreter of the landscape, in a position to provide an extra dimension to the findings of historians who have relied predominantly on documentary sources, but there are a number of areas of investigation where field evidence is itself the primary source. For example, no documentary information exists to provide a detailed explanation of the development of iron railways, or plateways, from the mid-eighteenth century onwards. Archaeological evidence alone reveals the regional differences between various types of plateway, the technology of their track systems, rail and sleeper design and earthworks.

Similarly, industrial archaeological investigation has provided conclusive evidence of the evolutionary stages in the transition from timber to iron-framed factory buildings. Again, no extraordinary techniques have been used, merely those already developed by historians of architecture; but without the availability of the physical remains of the buildings themselves our understanding of this fundamental advance in structural engineering would be incomplete. Metallurgical analysis applied to the slags of early blast furnaces provides another example of physical remains yielding evidence of value. Although by no means restricted to Industrial Revolution sites, slag analysis enables the historian of metallurgy to gain a more complete picture of the raw materials used and their sources, the temperatures at which the furnace operated and the nature of the finished product.

A completely different approach to site evidence is the area surveying and mapping of industrial installations, workers' housing, water mills or mine shafts as a means of establishing distributional patterns. Here the techniques of the geographer and statistician are required, coupled, as always, with an understanding of the underlying framework of economic activity. Relations can be established between types of waterwheel and the gradient profile and consistency of flow of streams, between blast furnace design and the qualities of the raw materials' charge, between topography and the flue arrangements of lead smelters or between surface geology and road turnpiking. These are all simple examples of the role field evidence can play in the assembly of information.

The artefacts of industrialisation can in other ways also provide an appreciation of the evolution of technology which would be impossible from documentary sources. Many of the innovations which formed the basis for progress in the eighteenth and early nineteenth centuries were brought about by craftsmen whose contribution was rarely, if ever, documented. Frequently the situation arises of a company with substantially complete commercial records being unable to provide information on the manufacturing processes which provided the foundation of its existence. The key to the understanding of these processes is often in the surviving artefacts, which may take the form of the manufacturing equipment or the products that were made with it. They often also provide an insight into the lives and intellects of the people who made and worked with them far more potently than

any written evidence could do, even supposing it existed.

The craftsman as an innovator as well as a producer, personally and physically involved in the manufacturing process, intuitively applying the craft skills acquired through apprenticeship in his everyday work, was fundamental to the progress of industrial technology. James Nasmyth, himself an inventor of some stature, wrote of that great craftsman, entrepreneur and innovator Henry Maudslay, with whom he worked for a time as an assistant:

> To be permitted to stand by and watch the systematic way in which Mr Maudslay would first mark or line out his work, and the masterly manner in which he would deal with his materials and cause them to assume the desired forms, was a treat beyond all expression. Every stroke of the hammer, chisel or file, told as an effective step towards the intended result. It was a never-to-be-forgotten lesson in workmanship in the most exalted sense of the term.

Herein lies what much of industrial archaeology is all about – an appreciation and understanding of the genius of innovation and the skill in making things, combined with recognition of the practical and aesthetic qualities of workmanship. For this the original object is essential.

The physical remains of industrialisation thus far transcend in importance their role as historical evidence, and this has provided the primary motivating spirit behind the widespread interest in industrial archaeology as a study. To an increasing number of people the engines and machines, factories, mills and warehouses, canals and railways which came to dominate the landscape in the last two centuries have become profoundly significant as part of our cultural heritage; they are implanted in the subconscious of innumerable ordinary people who, with no background of scholarship or training in artistic or architectural appreciation, find themselves responding aesthetically to the sweep of a railway curving through a wooded valley, to the triumphant striding of a viaduct, to the sound and smells of a perfectly running mill engine or the rhythm and symmetry of an eighteenth-century textile mill. Not only do these monuments to industrialisation represent a functional perfection of design but their heroic scale excites the imagination and stimulates the senses. They represent the skill and inventiveness, adventurousness and suffering of the first Industrial Revolution. Their study and preservation is the justification for industrial archaeology.

As we have seen, industrial archaeology is relatively new, but the preservation of industrial artefacts has been going on for at least 150 years. As early as the Great Exhibition of 1851 it was appreciated that there were technologically important machines dating from the early years of the Industrial Revolution that were worthy of presentation to the public. The beginnings of what is now the Science Museum in London were a tangible expression of this, and items such as early stationary steam engines and railway locomotives were collected and preserved. Indeed, the importance of preserving locomotives was recognised at a remarkably early date, with the result that Britain, the birthplace of the steam railway, possesses a very complete series of early examples including, in the Science Museum's collection alone, *Puffing Billy* of 1813, and *Rocket, Sans Pareil* and *Novelty* of 1829, all three of which were competitors at the Rainhill Trials. Museums in Edinburgh, Newcastle and York also contain pre-1830 locomotives. The original York Railway Museum, opened in 1928 by the London & North Eastern Railway in the aftermath of the Stockton & Darlington Railway Centenary celebrations of 1925, was the first large museum of its type, and another exhibition, in Newcastle-upon-Tyne, led to the opening there of the Museum of Science & Engineering in 1934 and provided the initial collections. These were all museums of the traditional type in which exhibits were collected and brought into a building where, space permitting, they were exhibited to the public. The justification for most of these early collections was that the items in them represented outstanding contributions to the development of engineering and technology. In many cases they were world 'firsts'. Little if any recognition was given to the social or economic context of the material collected.

Active study of at least the technological aspects of industrialisation is also much older than industrial archaeology and centres largely around the work of the Newcomen Society, which was formed as a result of the James Watt Centenary celebrations held in Birmingham in 1919. Its object is to support and encourage study and research in the history of engineering and technology, and the preservation of records, both technical and biographical. Although the society takes its name from Thomas Newcomen (1663–1729), the father of the steam engine, its interests cover all aspects of industrial, and in some cases pre-industrial, technology. The *Transactions* form an invaluable source of information, and to these and the dedication and enthusiasm of Newcomen members over more than fifty years, industrial archaeology owes a great debt.

The spontaneous growth of industrial archaeology in the 1950s and 1960s manifested itself in a variety of ways. Evening classes and new local societies provided the focus of activity, much of the work being concerned with the recording of industrial sites and monuments on a record card system initiated by the Council for British Archaeology (CBA). This eventually grew into the National Record of Industrial Monuments (NRIM), based after 1965 at the Centre for the Study of the History of Technology in the University of Bath, under the direction of Dr R. A. Buchanan.

In 1959 the CBA established an Industrial Archaeology Research Committee as a means of extending into this new field the role it had played since its inception in 1945, of co-ordinating the work of regional archaeological societies. Subsequently an Advisory Panel was set up as a subcommittee of the Research Committee to ensure that industrial monuments received the right sort of legislative protection. The then Ministry of Public Buildings and Works – later to become part of the Department of the Environment (DoE) – also recognised the need for an active policy towards recording and preserva-tion and in conjunction with the CBA launched the Industrial Monuments Survey (IMS) with Rex Wailes, a retired engineer and past President of the New-comen Society, as its consultant. He un-doubtedly played an important role, by his travels throughout the country, in stimulating industrial archaeological work at a local level. Later, the Survey was transferred to the CBA to whom the DoE made a cost-covering contribution. From the outset the Department's Ancient Monuments Board – its main source of independent scholarly and professional advice – had backed the IMS and this support continued, an important sign that the distant and the more recent past shared a common godparent.

When Rex Wailes retired in 1971, to be succeeded by Keith Falconer as Survey Officer, much had been accomplished but it was also clearer how much more needed to be done. The Survey Officer, carrying out his work county by county and in con-sultation with innumerable local field-workers, reported to both the Research Committee and the Advisory Panel, en-abling the CBA to recommend many hundreds of industrial monuments for scheduling under the Ancient Monuments Acts and buildings for Listing under the planning legislation. Thus in most re-spects industrial archaeological sites came into line in law with those of other periods.

But it was not until 1974 that a national organisation – the Association for Indus-trial Archaeology (AIA) – was established in order to represent the interests of industrial archaeology, to assist and co-ordinate the work of existing regional groups and to continue the well-estab-lished pattern of annual conferences, begun at the University of Bath in 1966, and out of which the association had itself grown. These conferences had provided the focal point for British industrial archaeology but no longer was this enough. There was a vacuum which was not filled either by the CBA's Industrial Archaeology Research Committee or the Newcomen Society, which as we have seen is concerned primarily with the field

of engineering history. In other areas of archaeological activity national, member-ship-based organisations represented most periods and a number of specialist areas. In addition there are such organisa-tions as the Georgian Group and the Victorian Society, concerned mainly with architecture but to some extent impinging upon industrial archaeology too. The AIA has not competed with or replaced the co-ordinating role of the CBA, but neither has it gained the consultative recognition from government, allied with financial support towards its casework costs, that the other major national archaeological and amenity bodies enjoy. Through its Endangered Sites Officer the Association maintains a 'watchdog' surveillance throughout the country over sites threat-ened with destruction or irreversible alteration and makes representations where appropriate. A *Bulletin* is published quarterly and a journal, *Industrial Archae-ology Review*, twice a year.

With the reorganisation after 1983 of the Ancient Monuments & Historic Buildings Directorate of the DoE into the Historic Buildings & Monuments Commission for England, operating under the name English Heritage, the opportunity was taken to rationalise the respective roles of the new Commission, the long-standing Royal Commission on Historical Monu-ments (England) and the National Monu-ments Record. The Royal Commission's primary remit is to record, and so on the basis of both logic and expediency it now embraces the National Monuments Record and has taken over the residual responsibility for the Industrial Monu-ments Survey, together with the employ-ment of the Survey Officer, Keith Falconer, who has been fully absorbed into its establishment.

Under the National Heritage Act 1983 which set up the Historic Buildings & Monuments Commission, the Ancient Monuments Advisory Committee (AMAC) (successor to the Ancient Monuments Board) and the Historic Buildings Ad-visory Committee (HBAC) (successor to the Historic Buildings Council) are statutorily enshrined and both process casework relating to industrial archaeology and advise the Commission accordingly. But as we shall see later, such is the problematic nature of industrial archaeology, often falling between the stools of the legislative framework, that some co-ordinated means of handling industrial archaeological matters and of providing expert advice was needed. Consequently, in 1985 a joint Industrial Archaeology Sub-Committee was established to advise both AMAC and HBAC on all matters relating to Scheduled or Listed industrial monuments or buildings and to make such other recommendations as are deemed necessary to ensure that the industrial landscape receives appropriate care and protection. By these apparently cumbersome means industrial archaeology, the cuckoo in the nest of the archaeological and historic buildings establishment, commands at least a reasonable amount of responsible advice and legislative attention although still only a minute proportion of the total cash and staff resources of the Commission.

In Scotland and Wales things are different. When English Heritage was devolved from government, as a Commission, Scotland did not change so Ancient Monuments and Historic Buildings are still dealt with in the traditional manner through the Scottish Development Department. Wales did devolve on a somewhat different basis, to a new agency called Cadw. In both Scotland and Wales the respective Royal Commissions carry on their work of recording sites, monuments and buildings. It is also worth noting that, despite the transfer of many of the nation's archaeological and historic buildings responsibilities to Commissioners, the specific responsibility for Scheduling and Listing and matters related to, for example, consents to demolish or carry out alterations, still rests with the appropriate Secretary of State.

As we have seen the acceptance of industrial archaeology took place against a background of radical changes in attitude towards the landscape. Growth of interest in past industrial environments was, in effect, just one of many manifestations of a broader landscape movement which developed from the early 1960s. Reaction

against air and water pollution, threats to wildlife, loss of trees and hedgerows, destruction of historic buildings and town centres for road or office building, all combined to fuel the fires in the bellies of the new environmentalists. Conservation trusts, civic societies, new museums, all sprang up as part of this popular movement. Enormous activity, backed in some cases by new legislation, followed: the Civic Trust, the Civic Amenities Act 1967, the First International Congress on the Conservation of Industrial Monuments held at Ironbridge in 1973, the Association for Industrial Archaeology, Rescue and the new archaeology movement, European Architectural Heritage Year 1975 and the Heritage Education Group, the Association of Independent Museums, SAVE Britain's Heritage – all reflected a world in which people saw their surroundings through different eyes and wanted to ensure its more desirable qualities were nurtured. The term 'Victorian' ceased to be a pejorative and assumed a new connotation initially of delight in newly discovered eccentricities and presently a firm respectability born of imperial wealth and traditions. The move to use old buildings for completely new purposes which had swept North America rapidly assumed importance in Britain and was seen, not always rightly, as the only means by which most historic industrial structures might be retained. A new tourist industry has grown up too, heritage tourism, fostered and encouraged by the tourist boards and there has been a boom in the history of work and in labour history, often exploiting new techniques of oral and visual history. Local history and urban history, subjects which, like industrial archaeology, lend themselves to cooperation between amateurs and professionals, reflect the participative nature of much of this new history and archaeology and the demands of its adherents. It occurs in the opportunities to learn craft skills and in the courses run by new museums like Styal in Cheshire or Ironbridge in Shropshire. History and archaeology – in particular industrial archaeology – have generated a new clientele – a new market – for the past

which radio and television, book pub-
lishers, museums and the environmental
preservation movement in general have all
sought to satisfy.

Such has been the rapidity with which
this moving threshold of public taste and
attitude has advanced that it is already
difficult to realise that less than twenty
years ago the destruction of the shot tower
in Bristol – the first in the world, built in
1782; the great Cornish engines at Sudbrook that drained the Severn Tunnel
(Illus 1), or the magnificent Sailors' Home
in Liverpool could take place with hardly a
murmur. As for the earlier loss of the
Euston Arch, Philip Hardwick's triumphal
entrance to the London & Birmingham
Railway, its destruction can be seen as
clearly marking a turning point; it was the
initial sacrificial offering necessary to save
succeeding generations of structures
threatened by redevelopment. What is
also particularly pertinent about the
Euston disaster is the subsequent realisation that the arch would have had even
more relevance and monumentality had it

1 Beams of the Cornish engines installed at
Sudbrook, Gloucestershire [ST 508874] in 1886 to
drain the Severn Tunnel; demolished in the
early 1970s   (Neil Cossons)

been allowed to perform its original function for the new station. Today's architect
or planner would savour with delight an
opportunity to exploit the development
potential afforded by something so distinguished. But even distinction is not necessarily a prerequisite; the mere patina of
age, the presence of a few cast-iron
columns or window frames, an old factory
yard or proximity to a waterfront can be
enough to turn the most unprepossessing
of late nineteenth-century warehouses
into a highly developable asset. This is not
archaeology for its own sake, nor even
archaeology at all, but an understanding
that in certain circumstances there can be
a strong market demand for the rehabili-
tated industrial building for new office or
residential use. The question now to be
asked is: can those industrial archaeological sites and monuments that sur-

2,3,4 Death of a mill. 'Juteopolis' as Dundee was nicknamed has its most spectacular monument in the Camperdown works in Methven Street [NO 383317]. Its great clock tower and Italianate brick chimney – 283ft high – still dominate the city's skyline but most of the mill is being demolished for building materials. The fate of what is left is still to be decided *(John R. Hume, Neil Cossons)*

vived the years of neglect now survive the period of rampant rehabilitation?

We have already touched on the early involvement of traditional museums in industrial conservation in the period before industrial archaeology was born. The Science Museum, London, officially the National Museum of Science & Industry, has collections of outstanding importance, many more than it can adequately present to the public. In Edinburgh, Cardiff and Belfast each of the national museums has established departments covering broadly the fields of industry or technology and including transport. But the nature of industrial archaeological material makes it difficult for traditional museums of this type to respond in an appropriate manner. The gas or heavy chemical industries, for example, do not lend themselves to conventional museum treatment. These traditional museums have also tended to be conservative in their collecting policies – prime movers often preserved but rarely the machines they drove, is a typical example. In many cases on-site preservation is the only answer and this has led to the setting up of outstations. The National Museum of Wales, for example, runs the Welsh Slate Museum in the former workshops of the Dinorwic slate quarry in Llanberis, Gwynedd [SH 586603] and the Museum of the Woollen Industry at Drefach Felindre, Dyfed [SN 355385]. The Royal Museums of Scotland administer Biggar gasworks in Lanarkshire [NT 040378] as a site museum, one of only two preserved gasworks in Britain – the other is at Fakenham in Norfolk [TF 919293].

Non-national museums have also responded to the needs of industrial archaeology and here overwhelmingly the trend has been towards the development of a museum around the nucleus of an industrial site which has its own intrinsic qualities and value. Thus the Leicestershire Museum of Technology [SK 589066] occupies the site of Abbey Pumping Station, a former sewage works with four Woolf compound beam engines of 1891. Similarly at Kew Bridge pumping station, Brentford [TQ 188780], which houses the most important *in situ* group of beam

pumping engines in the world, ancillary buildings are being developed into a museum of water supply. Similar trends and themes can be seen at Papplewick pumping station north of Nottingham [SK 582522] and Ryhope pumping station near Sunderland [NZ 403523]. In Hove, East Sussex, Goldstone Pumping Station [TQ 286066] is the home of the British Engineerium, a centre devoted to presenting examples of good engineering practice in the form of real machines and of models, and providing training in engineering skills.

The motives for this mixing of museums and sites are many and complex and raise fundamental issues of how far the integrity of an important, original and perhaps substantially complete industrial archaeological site may be compromised. Sometimes the incentive is to provide something to keep volunteers occupied, elsewhere to make sufficient of a show to generate a reasonable number of visitors, who pay for the operating costs. Given careful planning and sensitive design no harm need be done. What is without question however is that, particularly in the field of large stationary steam engines, an enormous amount of preservation activity has taken place over the last twenty-five years, of a high technical standard and almost invariably with strong emphasis placed on operation.

In many respects then the development of industrial museums is a form of adaptive re-use, little different in principle from the re-use of buildings for wholly new purposes, although of course access to the public is provided. There is in fact a continuous spectrum of conservation treatment ranging from the site of prime archaeological importance Scheduled and perhaps in the guardianship of the nation or another responsible authority, through those sites, such as those above, which are themselves important but which may also sustain a museum element, to buildings that may have features of archaeological or historical interest but are preserved primarily to house a museum collection. Moorside Mills, Bradford, home of Bradford Industrial Museum [SE 186357] is a good if not outstanding example of a textile mill which now houses an important collection of textile machinery. Moorside House, nearby, originally the home of the mill owner, has been furnished to show the domestic life of a late Victorian middle-class family. In the case of the National Museum of Photography, Film & Television, a part of the Science Museum and also in Bradford [SE 163329], the 1960s office and cinema complex which it occupies had no real use until the museum moved in.

Thus, the careful mixing of the *in situ* conservation of an important industrial site with the re-use of the available buildings for museum and interpretive purposes is proving a successful formula. Fuelled by the imperative to retain archaeologically or historically important buildings on the one hand and the opportunities of 'heritage tourism' on the other, the industrial and transport museums movement has flourished in recent years. At Styal in Cheshire [SJ 835829] the great eighteenth-century Quarry Bank Mill complex owned by the National Trust is now a thriving and expanding museum; at Ellesmere Port the Boat Museum [SJ 405775] occupies much of the canal interchange area between the Shropshire Union Canal and the Manchester Ship Canal including the site of the great Telford warehouse destroyed by fire in 1970. The museum's former plans to rebuild the warehouse have now been shelved (Illus 208).

Perhaps the the most ambitious project of museum-based urban rehabilitation is Albert Dock in Liverpool (Illus 5), [SJ 342898] where Jesse Hartley's great quadrangle of warehouses enclosing some 7 acres of water is the focal point of a major dockland revival programme. Completed in 1845 the five-storey brick and iron fireproof warehouses afford thousands of square feet of potentially re-usable space in a city plagued in recent years by the rundown of its docks, high unemployment and urban decay. Massive capital investment, mainly through the medium of a government-funded dockland development corporation, is being directed towards the re-use of derelict waterfront areas and part of the key to this revitalisation is the maritime museum based on Albert Dock, nearby graving docks and the dock ofices. Here the museum is the catalyst which has set the tone for the area, attracted substantial numbers of people into it, and provided the essential encouragement for commercial users to occupy neighbouring buildings.

This formula of heritage-led rehabilitation is being applied all over the country. It is most noticeable in urban waterfront environments where the stimulus to keep what is there stems not from archaeological or historical imperatives but from commercial development potential – the opportunity to use derelict industrial landscapes as the raw material from which

a new environment can be created (Illus 8–11). Warehouses in proximity to water and the opportunity for ship preservation have proved to be potent ingredients for commercially based rehabilitation in North America. The same formula is being applied in the docklands of London and Liverpool, in Bristol's Floating Harbour, Swansea and Hull and will undoubtedly spread still further.

In parallel with this enthusiasm for adaptive re-use there has been a blossoming of preservation societies, trusts and new museums created specifically to preserve industrial archaeological sites and monuments, usually *in situ*. On the one hand the threat of decay or destruction, on

5 Albert Dock, Liverpool [SJ 342898] now converted to a maritime museum, art gallery, shops, offices and apartments
(*Royal Commission on Historical Monuments, England*)

the other the initiative, ingenuity and prodigious energies of volunteer enthusiasts have generated a boom in industrial archaeological preservation and museum projects. Awareness of the past on the part of an increasingly mobile population with disposable time and disposable income has produced the demand which in terms of heritage tourism in general amounts to well over 100 million visits a year in Britain. Industrial archaeological projects

6   Abbey Mill, Bradford-on-Avon [ST 826609], the last major woollen factory to be built in Wiltshire. Dating from 1875, the technology of its construction has contributed towards a sympathetic conversion into offices for the Avon Rubber Company. Earlier mills often prove more difficult   (*Neil Cossons*)

7   Lewis Merthyr Pit, now preserved in the Rhondda Heritage Park [ST 036910]   (*Neil Cossons*)

represent an increasing proportion of this total. In addition hundreds of miles of canals and navigable rivers have been restored for leisure boating whilst the railway preservation movement sustains innumerable working railways throughout the country.

Of specific sites preserved, wind- and watermills are the most numerous and stationary steam engines – particularly beam engines – are exceptionally well covered. Early metal mining and working sites include numerous blast furnaces, mainly preserved as field monuments, together with non-ferrous mining sites like Wanlockhead in Dumfriesshire [NS 873125], now the Museum of the Scottish Lead Mining Industry; Magpie Mine in Derbyshire [SK 173682]; Laxey on the Isle of Man [SC 432851]; Aberdulais Falls, West Glamorgan [SS 775994]; the Tolgus tin works near Redruth [SW 690438] and numerous other sites in Devon and Cornwall associated with the tin and copper industry. Coal mining is represented by preserved collieries at Chatterley Whitfield, near Stoke-on-Trent [SJ 885534] and Big Pit, Gwent [SO 239088], Lewis Merthyr pit in the Rhondda [ST 036910] and Caphouse Colliery near Wakefield [SE 253165].

Preserved textile mills in which machinery is operated, include Higher Mill, Helmshore, the Museum of the Lancashire Textile Industry [SD 777214], Queen Street Mill, Harle Syke, Burnley [SD 868349]; Styal in Cheshire [SJ 835829] and Coldharbour Mill, Uffculme, Devon [SJ 062122]. A framework knitter's shop has been preserved at Ruddington in

8   The last tram of coal raised in the Rhondda, 30 June 1986   (*Neil Cossons*)

Nottinghamshire [SK 572329].

Open-air museums reflect on a larger scale the need for a more comprehensive approach to preservation. At Beamish in County Durham [NZ 212549] the North of England Open Air Museum is developing a 200 acre site to preserve and present aspects of the way of life of the north in the early part of this century, at the peak of its industrial prosperity. Reconstructed houses and shops, a colliery, street tramway and railway create a vivid picture of the past which is accessible to many who might otherwise have no knowledge of or interest in their own history. At Dudley in the West Midlands the Black Country Museum [SO 948917] is engaged on a similar project while at Amberley in West Sussex [TQ 028118] the Chalk Pits Museum is developing a 36 acre site around the theme of local industries. At Singleton, also in West Sussex [SU 875129], the Weald & Downland

9,10,11,12 Station to supermarket: Bath Green Park station [ST 745647], northern terminus of the Somerset & Dorset Joint Railway, is now a restaurant and a covered car park for Sainsbury's store   (*Neil Cossons*)

Museum and near Bromsgrove, Hereford & Worcester, the Avoncroft Museum of Buildings [SO 953683] – open-air museums of a rather different type – preserve buildings, mainly of rural origin, as examples of building technology.

An altogether different sort of project is the Ironbridge Gorge Museum in Shropshire [SJ 6703] established in 1968 to preserve, mainly *in situ*, the remains of early industrial activity scattered along three miles of the Severn valley between Coalbrookdale and Coalport. Here, centred on the Iron Bridge of 1779, a 'network museum' embraces the Old Furnace in Coalbrookdale, where iron was first smelted using coke, together with the houses of iron-masters and their employees; wharves, warehouses and blast furnaces along the river, the Coalport china factory and the great tileworks at Jackfield. In addition, at Blists Hill Open Air Museum, buildings and machines which cannot be preserved *in situ* are being reconstructed. A colliery winding engine, a foundry making iron castings and a sawmill, printers, candlemakers and locksmiths are in regular operation.

A wrought-iron works in which iron is puddled and rolled is also demonstrated from time to time (Illus 83 and 84).

Obvious trends in the presentation of industrial sites and landscapes include moves towards improved techniques and quality of interpretation and facilities for visitors together with an increasing interest in the social history of industrialisation. Many succeed through their good scholarship and displays, in presenting a balanced and authoritative picture of industry with occasional glimpses of real people too. Others purvey nostalgia – a warm and cosy fondness for what was often awful at the time, a view of quaint industrial peasants, equivalents of the mythical rosy-cheeked yokels whose idyllic rural domain they were supposed to have replaced. It is often easier to present a picture of the past that accords more with the folk myth of the local resident or visitor than the facts of history.

The museum approach to preservation has its obvious limitations. In the North of England, Pennine Heritage, a charitable trust engaged on an ambitious programme to encourage regeneration of the area, promotes the re-use of industrial buildings for a variety of purposes, the objective being not merely to preserve the physical structures themselves but the social and economic fabric too. Through Pennine Heritage Network, publications, displays and residential courses, usually produced on a partnership basis, further promote the cause of revitalisation based on the re-use of the intrinsic assets of the Pennine region. In the North East the Tyne & Wear Industrial Monuments Trust engages in the *in situ* preservation and management of sites throughout the area while SAVE Britain's Heritage acts as a national pressure group in support of the re-use of industrial buildings, commissioning economic, architectural and planning studies as part of the persuasion process.

The issues facing industrial archaeology have thus widened immeasurably since the mid 1970s. On the one hand the necessity to conserve the evidence of the Industrial Revolution – the archaeological imperative – has gained ground only

slowly. On the other, the belief that adaptive re-use is the universal panacea has been too readily accepted. There are indications however that these views are changing. The voices of the past must be reconciled with the needs of the future, and clearly for the large majority of industrial buildings that future must lie in their adaptation to new and economically viable uses. Many of them are important enough to demand a standard of treatment

which reflects and enhances their intrinsic qualities; for others a more liberal approach is inevitable if a financially attractive formula for rehabilitation is to be devised. But within the broad canvases of these great industrial landscapes, in which the remnants of the Industrial Revolution will increasingly provide the foundation for new economic growth, lie the key sites and areas of international significance – the essential monuments of

13 Manchester Central station [SJ 837977], shortly before closure; after years of decay the great train shed now houses the city's exhibition centre   (*Neil Cossons*)

the world's first industrial society. For these we carry a special and unique responsibility, to afford them the most thoughtful attention and conscientious care. Their future has still to be secured.

CHAPTER 2

THE INDUSTRIALISATION OF BRITAIN

The industrial archaeologist, as we have seen, is primarily concerned with the examination and analysis of the physical remains of the age of industrialisation, accepting that there are specialist antecedents, within various branches of technology for example, which must be understood first. Before considering the areas of specific interest to the industrial archaeologist industry by industry, it is important to consider the historical, social, economic and technological framework within which something as complex as an industrial revolution could occur. The term 'Industrial Revolution' itself has been in common usage now for over a century and was coined at least as early as the 1830s. What was the Industrial Revolution? Why did it happen in Britain first?

Historians have been arguing for three generations over the causes of the Industrial Revolution, but the accumulated literature is largely the literature of disagreement. What appears to have taken place is that at some point, probably in the second half of the eighteenth century – although some would put it slightly earlier – Britain reached a point of 'take-off into self-sustained growth' based on radical changes in methods of production. These changes, occurring over a relatively short time, had widespread repercussions throughout society, the national economy and the landscape. The changes were rapid and their results were there for everyone to see. The rate of change was indeed 'revolutionary'.

The early period of the Industrial Revolution, therefore, is marked by the beginning of a rapid rate of change in the economy. In quantitative terms it might be possible to pinpoint the start of the Industrial Revolution by identifying when the gross national product, representing the national income or the total value of goods and services produced in the economy, first began to increase by about 2 per cent per annum. Any pre-industrial economy would be growing at less than 1 per cent per annum. This take-off point occurred in Britain somewhere between 1740 and 1780.

One of the problems of using the term 'revolution', and it was taken from what started in France in 1789, is that it implies instant upheaval, an overturning of old values and their immediate substitution by new, a dramatic change whose beginning can be precisely dated. It appears that this apocalyptic element of comparison is unreal, and this has led many to criticise the use or relevance of the term at all. But if one looks, from the standpoint of the second half of the twentieth century, at the changes wrought by the French Revolution and by the British Industrial Revolution, the comparison is perhaps more valid. The eighteenth century in Britain saw changes which produced similar long-term political effects to those created by the bloody revolution in France. There was as much, if not more, of a difference between pre- and post-industrial Britain as between pre- and post-revolutionary France. The watershed between the essentially medieval and the essentially modern economy, if not marked by a sharp ridge, was nevertheless a real one.

Britain was the first country in the world to undergo an industrial transformation of its national economy. This transformation occurred spontaneously, without any outside direction, without any conscious policy of stimulating industrial growth, without any momentum being directly imparted through taxation or by capital being made available. Indeed the state showed no interest in promoting industrial activity or encouraging new skills. The revolution happened, and we can only surmise the reasons why.

No *single* factor brought the economy to this point of take-off. A whole complex of interrelated movements, some with their origins as far back as the Middle Ages, reacted one with another to produce a situation in which the economy went critical in the second half of the eighteenth century. Once the chain reaction had begun, growth became more or less automatic. What factors were involved? There were the direct economic forces of population growth, of agricultural improvement, of increasing trade and the growth of markets, of capital accumulation and the development of a flexible banking system, of the breakdown of medieval conditions of control and regulation and their replacement by those of competition, of business enterprise, of improvements in communication and of technological innovation. There must also have been many subtler influences resulting from deep-seated stirrings within society – changes in religion and conditions of religious tolerance, scientific advances and a political situation in which government, if not giving active support to industrial enterprise, was at least acquiescent. Conditions of relative stability in Britain must also have been important. The country became a haven for political and religious refugees, many of whom brought with them manufacturing techniques and the enterprise necessary to put those techniques into practice. There were also natural advantages in the availability and, in some cases more importantly, the close proximity to each other of raw materials such as good quality sheep pasture, iron ore and coking coal and consistently flowing streams for power. Also to be considered must be those entirely fortuitous occurrences such as the succession of good harvests in the 1730s, which contributed to general prosperity and the creation of surpluses, and thus helped to generate a climate within which the other components of change could interact more satisfactorily.

We are not here primarily concerned with the origins of the Industrial Revolution but more with the fact of its occurrence and its physical effects on society and the landscape. Nevertheless it is worthwhile looking a little deeper into causes in order to gain some understanding of the enormous changes brought about by industrialisation, and to follow them through into the period of the Industrial Revolution itself. Firstly, population. This was increasing at the end of the seventeenth century in parallel with a gradual increase in food supplies. The population of England in 1700 was probably slightly more than 6 million; it had increased to 6½ million by about 1750 and then started climbing rapidly to reach just over 9 million by 1801, the date of the first census. Economic expansion in the first half of the eighteenth century was facilitated by two decades of good harvests after 1730. The increase of real incomes provided a market incentive, a stimulus to producers of goods and imported commodities. The increase in foreign trade, in addition to the new home demand, was opening up overseas markets to home manufacturers. Population growth, therefore, was only one of the features of this first phase of industrial growth. But was it in fact a cause or a consequence of the economic changes? The dramatic growth rate after 1770 may have been a result of the rise in birth rate, itself resulting from the demand for labour leading to earlier marriage and therefore earlier parenthood. On the other hand social and economic factors such as improved food supply and better clothing and housing substantially reduced the death rate, a trend accentuated by the beginnings of smallpox inoculation and improved medical knowledge applied to the feeding of children. In the middle of the eighteenth century, however, the initial growth took place before the period of rapid economic expansion and must therefore be regarded as one of its causes. What is also certain is that once the balance had been tipped in favour of self-sustained growth, an increase in consumers and workers became a necessary condition of further industrially based economic advance.

Population growth was by no means evenly distributed and, once industrialisation had got under way, the effects of a reorientation of the population axis were, in terms of landscape changes, of great importance. Illus 14 shows population distributions at the beginning and end of the eighteenth century. In 1700 the population was thickest along a line running south-west to north-east through the fat agricultural lands of lowland England. By 1800 that axis had been turned through 90 degrees and there it still lies today. The areas in which industry was centred saw a more rapid population growth than predominantly rural counties, which, although in a few small areas suffering an actual decline, continued to grow but at a less rapid rate. The growth in the new industrial areas was not generated entirely from within; there were massive migrations from the countryside.

By 1831 about one-third of England's population was engaged in industry, a proportion, but not of course a total number, which remained more or less stable throughout the rest of the century. The 'new population' was predominantly concentrated in towns and cities in the Midlands and North. Previously towns, particularly in lowland England, had been evenly spread nodal points with primarily market functions. (The area of densest population on the 1700 map, Illus 14, still has this essential character today.) After the axis had shifted, enormous urban concentrations grew up. London had always been much larger than all other towns. In 1800 it had nearly 900,000 inhabitants but there were only fourteen other towns with populations of over 20,000. By 1851 London had a population of over 2¼ million; by then, however, there were fifty-four towns and cities with a population between 20,000 and 100,000 and seven (Birmingham, Bradford, Bristol, Leeds, Liverpool, Manchester and Sheffield) with over 100,000 inhabitants. Of these only Bristol lay outside the new axial belt of economic and population growth.

There were two major factors in the increased agricultural output which went hand in hand with population growth throughout the eighteenth century. The first was enclosure, the second the superior methods of husbandry and of farming technology introduced by the great improvers. Both were closely interlocked, enclosure being the essential prerequisite for the introduction of new techniques. Much of the new equipment introduced after 1750 would have been useless on the old strips of the open-field system. Similarly, introduction of new crops or rotations and methods of animal breeding was out of the question in an essentially feudal agricultural system where custom, tradition and the standards of the poorest quality cultivator were dominant. In other European countries, where enclosure lagged behind Britain, the introduction of new methods was slower and confined to large estate farms. Enclosure then was the largest single movement affecting land use, and therefore output, because it made possible all other innovations. Enclosure increased the cultivable area by eliminating the commons and wastelands which had been essential rough grazing areas under the old system, and bringing them into active agricultural use on the regular sequential basis of the new rotation farming.

By 1750 perhaps half of England (and the open-field system was confined almost entirely to lowland England) was enclosed. In some areas open fields had never existed and in others they had been long outmoded. These areas lay around the edges of a core of unenclosed land with counties such as Northamptonshire at its centre. The south-west and the grass counties of the Welsh marches, the north-west and the south-eastern counties of Suffolk, Essex, Sussex and Kent were all substantially or completely enclosed by the middle of the century. For the remainder of England the major period of the enclosure movement was 1760–1815, when most enclosures, in contrast to the earlier period, were made as the result of Parliamentary awards. Over 1,000 Acts covering 7 million acres were passed between 1760 and 1800, with a further 800 by 1815. The first batch related generally to areas where grazing and cattle-fattening were the dominant forms of husbandry, and the latter mainly to arable land where

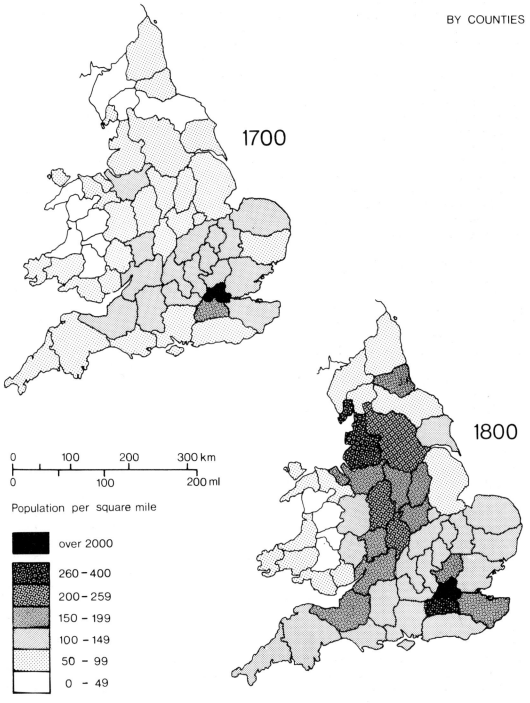

DISTRIBUTION OF POPULATION
IN ENGLAND AND WALES

BY COUNTIES

1700

1800

0   100   200   300 km

0   100   200 ml

Population per square mile

over 2000

260 – 400

200 – 259

150 – 199

100 – 149

50 – 99

0 – 49

Illustration 14

enclosure was stimulated mainly by the rise of grain prices during the Napoleonic wars. These enclosures took in most of the remaining open fields. Today one or two areas still survive – Laxton in Nottinghamshire and Portland in Dorset, for example – where traditional practices are continued.

The sequence of events, therefore, was firstly the introduction of new theories and new crops in the seventeenth century, such as Townshend's turnip-fed stock, followed by the first stages of mechanisation promulgated by men like Jethro Tull. Diffusion of these ideas on a wide scale came later with enclosure and with the increased demand resulting from a growing population, particularly in towns.

Capital availability was significant to this 'agricultural revolution', but it was much more important to the new industrial entrepreneurs. The early growth of banks, not only in London but in country areas too, made short-term credit available for agriculture, industry and transport. By 1780, when there were 100 banks outside London, a network of credit extended throughout the country, facilitating the transfer of funds, the settling of debts and the obtaining of cash. By the late 1820s there were 554 country banks, after which numbers declined as they were absorbed into the big joint-stock banks with their networks of branches.

The banks did not, however, provide the key to the much larger quantities of capital required by industrialists to launch their enterprises. Most manufacturing industry was in the hands of family businesses or partnerships in the middle of the eighteenth century. This was to some extent inevitable, as without the protection of Limited Liabilities Acts (which did not come in until 1855–62) each partner in an unincorporated business was totally liable for its debts, however little he had invested in it. The 'South Sea Bubble' Act of 1720 had limited the number of shareholders to eight, so unless the company was set up by Act of Parliament, as a few large enterprises like canals and later railways were, the corporate responsibilities carried by those in industry were considerable. Partners

tended, therefore, to be found within the framework of a family or a church where the ties of trust were strongest. With some sectors of the community, such as the Quakers, family and faith were often inextricably interwoven, and the fact that they were debarred from political positions made them turn to those avenues which were open to them – industry and commerce.

Most of the capital that financed the early phase of the Industrial Revolution came from two main sources. Firstly, there was accumulated capital, the result of the more or less continuous expansion in the economy in the middle years of the eighteenth century before industrialisation really got under way. Accumulation of capital in the hands of landowners and merchants, for example, was considerable, and much of this found its way into industry, often industry within the family network. 'Outside' capital was the other source, the investment by many sectors of the community of relatively small sums in an industrial enterprise. The landed aristocracy, traditional holders of wealth, were frequently energetic investors and in many cases financed new industries directly themselves, but the savings of the professional classes, craftsmen and working men, often through their friendly societies, found its way into industry also. One of the great strengths of industry in Britain, and conversely one of the greatest heartaches when a company failed, was the broad base of industrial investment, seen at its extreme in the capitalisation of the railways.

Another important factor was that, for many industrial enterprises, the cost of the initial fixed assets was relatively low, so it was possible to start on a small scale and expand almost entirely on the reinvestment of profits. Technology was relatively simple and the cost of buildings and equipment not inordinately large. Given technical expertise in the process, perhaps the most valuable single asset in setting up a new manufacturing firm, it was not too difficult to make a start. The number of skilled craftsmen who left established organisations to set up on their own with no more than the traditional 'life's savings' was considerable, and an almost typical feature of some sections of industry.

We have mentioned population increase as an important factor, representing both a new source of labour and also a new market for manufactured goods. Of increasing significance throughout the eighteenth century also was the development of Britain's overseas trading connections. In the 1570s England had one major export commodity in woollen cloth, which accounted for some 80 per cent of the value of her trade, nearly all of which was with North Sea ports or the Atlantic seaboard of Europe. By the 1770s she had a wide range of manufactured exports, of which wool still constituted the largest, and a big re-export trade in colonial and export goods. Her trade extended not only throughout Europe but to America, Africa, India and China. Indeed the century after about 1660 has been titled the period of the 'Commercial Revolution', so important was it to the development of merchant organisation, to capital accumulation and investment and to the market opportunities which were provided to the new industries.

Firstly, the collapse of Antwerp in the late sixteenth century as the entrepot for Europe led, after a period of initial uncertainty, to English merchants having to seek their own connections, by sea, with their European markets. Because the system of money transfer by bills of exchange was not developed in these new markets, merchants were bringing back materials for which there was initially no immediate home sale, including coarse linens, sugar, cotton, silk, flax, hemp and timber. In consequence, a thriving re-export business developed at the beginning of the seventeenth century, but it gradually declined as the home market became more sophisticated and as new, often port-located, industries grew up; these industries sometimes used immigrant labour, as with silk weaving, to absorb these readily available raw materials. London began to assume the position once held by Antwerp, becoming the base for merchants and, as the eighteenth century progressed, for financiers,

bankers, insurance companies and shipping underwriters.

Before 1640 there was little home demand for the products resulting from Britain's small but increasing long-distance trade with Asia and America, which was beginning to thrive on the re-export business. Indeed Europe, by far the largest single market until well into the nineteenth century, had great attractions to Britain, whose direct access to distant ports enabled her to re-export directly or process and then re-export the imports resulting from this trade. The notorious triangular trade with West Africa and the Americas developed in this way, with weapons and 'toys' from Britain being exchanged for slaves in West Africa, and those slaves exchanged for sugar, tobacco, dyestuffs or hardwood in the West Indies. These imports were frequently processed in London, Bristol or Glasgow and then re-exported to Europe. As home demand grew, however, the need to re-export died away, and completely new imports provided the basis for industrial growth. The Lancashire fustian industry and the Nottinghamshire cotton hosiery trade were both based initially on imported Indian cotton. In a city like Bristol a high proportion of the considerable industrial activity became based on imported raw materials for eventual home consumption. Sugar refining, sherry blending and wine bottling, chocolate making, tobacco processing, logwood dye manufacture, even cotton spinning and weaving for a short time, all grew up in or around Bristol because it was the place of import and thus the logical break-of-bulk point at which to carry out processing.

By the latter part of the eighteenth century the 'Commercial Revolution' of the previous 100 years had provided Britain with trading connections throughout the world, had made London the financial and mercantile centre of Europe and was producing an accumulation of capital much of which was finding its way into industrial investment. Much of the profit from trade went into mining and manufacturing industry. Bristol and London merchants helped finance coal-mining and ironmaking in South Wales, and Glasgow and Liverpool merchants put capital into the cotton industries of Scotland and Lancashire respectively.

We have now looked at a number of the major factors which combined to trigger off the Industrial Revolution. One classic prerequisite, however, of the British Industrial Revolution, although not necessarily of others that have come since, remains to be examined – the role of technological innovation. The development of new technologies was such a remarkable and obvious feature of the Industrial Revolution that many people have regarded it as the primary cause. To them the Industrial Revolution was a technological revolution in which new manufacturing machines were driven by new sources of power in new large-scale units called factories. So enthusiastic was Samuel Smiles about this thesis that he wrote in his *Lives of the Engineers*, 'Our engineers may be regarded in some measure as the makers of modern civilisation . . .', and then went on to pose the question, 'Are not the men who made the motive power of the country, and immensely increased its productive strength, the men above all others who have tended to make the country what it is?' To some extent Smiles was right, but for new inventions in technology to be relevant a whole range of other factors, such as those we have already considered, had to be there too.

Given these favourable base conditions, there also had to be a will to generate new ideas and a climate in which new ideas, if not universally acceptable, could find currency amongst other enthusiasts who would implement, multiply and perhaps improve upon them. That climate was growing in Britain throughout the latter part of the seventeenth century and the whole of the eighteenth in the form of a new class of bourgeoisie, intelligent but not always educated, well-to-do but not always wealthy, articulate but not always cultured, who owned property, manipulated money or followed one of the growing professions. These were not often the people who created the new ideas, but they were the ones who were prepared to listen, who were capable of understanding and who were prepared to offer backing.

Another requirement of technological innovation, although not necessarily of the invention which might precede it, was need. Necessity may indeed have been the mother of invention. The steam engines of Savery and then of Newcomen were developed because of the specific problem of draining mines and, at a much later date, Watt was almost forcibly directed into developing a *rotative* steam engine capable of driving machinery because Boulton appreciated that the need was there. In the United States a different sort of necessity in the middle of the nineteenth century resulted in the development of sophisticated production machinery as a means of maintaining and increasing output in the face of an acute shortage of skilled manpower. The finished product was not necessarily any better, but the technique of making it certainly was.

Some inventions relied on intellectual genius, others on the systematic investigation of possible alternatives until the right answer came up, and others still required some almost fortuitous outside factor to intervene. Abraham Darby I was undoubtedly aware of the social and economic need for an alternative fuel to charcoal for iron smelting, although how far that need was being directly felt in Coalbrookdale in 1709 is difficult to assess. The geological accident of the eminent suitability of the Coalbrookdale 'Clod' coal for making coke for smelting purposes must be borne in mind when measuring the significance of the coke smelting technique which he perfected. Over a century and a half later another attempt to find an alternative fuel, in this case the substitution of coal for coke in locomotive fireboxes, was tortuously pursued for years, with innumerable patents and experimental designs, before the perfection of the brick arch in 1859 allowed coal to be burnt successfully. Successful invention and innovation demand a number of prerequisites – a climate of acceptability, perhaps the one feature unique in Britain in the eighteenth century; an obvious need; and an element of genius, perseverance or opportunism, or possibly all three.

Undoubtedly the cumulative effect of innovation in technology was beginning to be felt on a large scale by the end of the eighteenth century. Using the simple indicator of patents, of the 2,600 for the whole of the century, more than half were registered after 1780. We must, however, allow innovation in technology no more than its proper importance, for although the products of many of the great inventive engineers provide much of the inspiration for the study of industrial archaeology, they had relevance only when combined with entrepreneurial ability and the effective organisation of capital, the market and the methods of production. Thomas Telford was arguably an organiser of men first and foremost and an engineer second. The canal network owed little or nothing to advanced technology but much more to the organisation of large numbers of men and the mobilisation of capital. In the textile industry a whole range of closely interlinked inventions provided the baseline from which the industry could free itself from its medieval shackles, though it was in the factory, which was primarily a symbol of organisation rather than technology, that the potential of these inventions was realised. The factory system was being exploited for its organisational advantages by people like Benjamin Gott in Leeds, for example, before the advantages of power applied to a multiplicity of machines were fully realised.

If we accept that the Industrial Revolution had its beginning in the eighteenth century, when, if at all, did it end? Application of the self-sustaining growth theory has suggested that 1830 was the terminal date, the point by which the chain reaction had got going and the economy was in a state of more or less automatic and continuous growth. Certainly some industries had undergone a complete technological change by that date: the textile industry was largely mechanised and power-driven; and the iron industry, where both cast iron and wrought iron were available in quantity, was using coal instead of charcoal and the puddling furnace instead of the finery and chafery.

Canals networked the country and, although not representing any major technological breakthrough, they were an essential ingredient of industrial growth both as an internal transport system and as a means of getting commodities to and from the ports. If 'revolution' in this context only means the period of change from one style of economy to another, the period when growth rate in the economy accelerated, then the choice of 1830 has some validity; but if continuity of growth, particularly growth based on new technologies and new industries, is included, that date is clearly of no significance at all.

The industrial archaeologist needs to take a much broader approach. He is looking primarily at the period of industrialisation beginning in the eighteenth century, but he has to look back beyond that date to find the antecedents, to explain the evolution of the waterwheel, to understand the transfer from charcoal smelting to coke smelting, to discover the scientific ground rules which had been established in the sixteenth century and were implicit in the development of the atmospheric steam engine. Having accepted that industrialisation is under way he must apply archaeological rather than historical criteria when trying to settle how far he goes chronologically. The period of take-off as seen by the economic historian is quite unsatisfactory for the industrial archaeologist, who is looking at the remains of industrial activity over a much longer period. To him the obsolescence of a process or of a social or economic demand for an industry must form the terminal criteria; absolute date is almost irrelevant.

Let us consider 1830 as a terminal date in relation to the whole period of industrialisation. Railways were only just beginning to be accepted, the Liverpool & Manchester Railway opening in that year. The shipping industry was still largely traditional and pre-industrial in character, although steam power was beginning to be applied. There were no iron ships, let alone steel ones. Cheap steel was still more than a quarter of a century away, with Henry Bessemer and the converter. Michael Faraday, in 1831, produced a continuous electric current, the beginnings of one of the most fundamental developments in power for industry of the latter part of the century. These events and many that have come since are the valid concern of the industrial archaeologist.

Let us examine the magnitude of the effects of industrialisation on Britain. The economic consequences are measurable and staggering in their scale. National income in England and Wales was £130m in 1770; in Great Britain as a whole in 1800 it was £230m, in 1830 £350m and in 1850 £525m. This shows a doubling of average income per head. By the end of the nineteenth century the national income had increased by a factor of about fourteen and real income per head had roughly quadrupled. Despite the traditionally pessimistic view of the horrors of industrialisation seen in terms of poverty, of appalling living conditions and of periodic heavy unemployment, the real wages of the majority of workers in British industry were rising and their living and working conditions, *on average*, were improving.

The statistics of growth for individual industries provide some of the most startling indicators of the effects of industrial activity. There were less than twenty blast furnaces in 1760. By 1790 this figure had increased to over eighty and in 1797 England became for the first time an exporter of iron and iron goods. There were 177 blast furnaces in 1805, 372 in 1830 and 655 in 1852. The majority were coke-fired after 1800. Pig iron output increased from 30,000 tons in 1700 to 250,000 tons by 1805, 650,000 by 1830 and 2 million tons by mid-century. In the cotton industry growth was still more spectacular, largely as the result of the improvements made in machine spinning by James Hargreaves, Richard Arkwright and Samuel Crompton with the introduction of the jenny, the water frame and the mule respectively. Import of raw cotton, which was less than 8 million lb per year in 1780 had risen to over 25 million lb by 1790, 37.5 million lb by 1800 and nearly 60 million lb in 1805. The 100 million lb point was reached in 1815, 250 million lb in 1830 and 620 million in 1850. The number of cotton spindles increased similarly from less than 2 million in 1780 to 21 million by the middle of the nineteenth century. Mechanisation in weaving of cloth developed slightly later but, once under way, the results in terms of production were no less remarkable. With hardly any power looms in 1820 the industry grew to have 50,000 in 1830 and 250,000 in 1850. The cotton industry as a whole employed about half a million people in 1830, of whom about half were working in factories. Over 50 per cent of total production was exported, representing in value about 40 per cent of all British exports.

'Good roads, canals and navigable rivers, by diminishing the expense of carriage, put the remote parts of the country nearly on a level with those in the neighbourhood of the town; they are, upon that account, the greatest of all improvements.' So wrote Adam Smith (1723–90) in the late eighteenth century and, without doubt, good communications provided the basis for the factory growth of the iron, the cotton, and many other industries. In 1750 there were about 1,000 miles of navigable river in England. In the following century over 4,000 miles of canals had been built, linking the main industrial areas with the rivers, ports and coalfields. What is more significant, however, is that nearly three-quarters of that canal mileage had been completed by 1800, thus providing, at the beginning of the Industrial Revolution period, the consolidation and unification of the English market that was so essential for growth. The significance of railways was still greater, and in the decade between 1840 and 1850 5,000 route miles were built, more than the whole of the country's total canal mileage. The effects of railways were felt in many fields beyond those connected directly with the transport of goods. Besides reducing the time and cost of travel and extending the communications system over a wider area than that covered by the canal network, the railways increased the mobility of labour and further encouraged concentrations of population, gave an enormous boost to the iron and engineering industries with their demand for rails and locomotives and were largely responsible for the new and widespread habit of investment in industry. By 1850, for the first time ever, a nation was devoting at least 10 per cent of its total income to capital accumulation in one form or another.

In addition to communications, coal was essential to the development of industry, and the discovery of ways of using coal where once wood had been essential was a decisive technological factor in allowing many industries to 'take off'. The use of coal to generate steam removed industry still further from its reliance on nature by reducing dependence on water power. As early as the beginning of the eighteenth century England had been unique in Europe for its large consumption of coal, probably then about 3 million tons per year. By 1800 it had grown to 10 million tons, almost entirely as the result of increased industrial activity. Coal (in the form of coke) began to replace charcoal for iron smelting and later for puddling of wrought iron, it was the primary fuel of the rapidly expanding brick industry and, of ever-increasing importance, it powered the new steam engines. By 1800 there were perhaps 1,000 steam engines in use in England, the large majority pumping water from mines. About 250, however, were driving machines in the cotton industry and, as the nineteenth century progressed, steam engines increasingly replaced human, animal, wind and water power. Thus, by 1838 the cotton industry was using 46,000 steam hp and the woollen industry 17,000. By 1850 the textile industry as a whole was using nearly 100,000 steam-generated hp. All of this was provided by coal, the first raw material in history to be measured in millions of tons. From 10 million tons produced in 1800 output grew to 25 million tons in 1830 and 50 million tons in 1850.

These statistical indices of growth tell only a small part of the story of industrial development in Britain during the eighteenth and nineteenth centuries, covering up at a single sweep the subtleties of social change and enormities of social cost which can never be fully documented. The remains of the landscape changes wrought by industry are still there to be seen and studied by the industrial archaeologist, but the effects on ordinary people of those changes, the most radical changes of environment which any society had ever experienced, can only be pieced together from fragmentary evidence. Much of this evidence results from the observations of outsiders not directly involved themselves in industrial activity – in the diaries of travellers, the reports of commissions of enquiry, and the essays of political writers, all of which reflect to a greater or lesser extent the particular axe which their authors had to grind. Moreover, those artists who did not regard it as beneath their dignity to portray industrial subjects, provide a startling and perhaps slightly less biased insight into the nature of Industrial Revolution Britain. But despite these conscious attempts at documentation, objective or not, the real magnitude of the change in the way of life of ordinary people as industrialisation gathered momentum and eventually became a tide carrying all before it can never be assessed. They rarely documented themselves, although songs have sometimes survived, and possessions – few at the time – are almost non-existent today. Only the houses in which they lived and the factories in which they worked provide a widespread, tangible and emotive source of evidence which can be analysed, in association with oral and documentary sources, to gain some insight into their way of life, attitudes and aspirations. The industrial landscape is the *place* where all this happened and therefore represents one of the closest contacts we have with the people who made it happen.

CHAPTER 3

WIND AND WATER POWER

The twentieth century has witnessed the virtual extinction in Britain of the use of wind and water power for commercial purposes. Man's earliest engines, the first mechanisms to release him from the slow and tedious labour of grinding corn by hand, have almost ceased working. The crafts of milling and millwrighting, passed on without interruption through many centuries, have also now almost disappeared, and only our nostalgia and the respect in which we hold these reminders of the beginnings of civilisation have led us to preserve both windmills and watermills in considerable numbers. A few of them are still working, and in this way we

15   The Cat and Fiddle windmill, Dale, Derbyshire [SK 438398], a preserved post mill of 1788 with a brick roundhouse, c1844   (Neil Cossons)

can keep alive their techniques of operation.

The earliest application of the power of water was perhaps in the first century BC, probably in Greece. The earliest known record of a watermill in England is much later, in a charter granted in AD 762 by King Ethelbert of Kent to the owners of a monastic mill east of Dover. The use of wind power on the other hand is more recent, and although early windmills were known in Persia and Asia Minor well before the tenth century AD, they do not seem to have been used in north-west Europe until the twelfth century. The earliest known in England appears in a documentary reference of AD 1158 recording a corn mill in the village of Weedley in Yorkshire. It is just conceivable that such early English mills, which are recognisable from illustrations as post mills, were the first of their type, for there was a noticeable spread of them eastward through Europe during the thirteenth century, suggesting that they may have developed quite independently of the primitive windmills of Persia. If this is so, it represents a significant reversal of the prevailing flow of ideas from the East, and may be the first example of West European technology to find widespread use.

Wind power had nothing like the impact water had on the growth of industrialisation, for while the waterwheel developed into a reliable, controllable and powerful prime mover for driving a wide variety of machinery, often in very large factories, the windmill kept very much to its traditional role of grinding corn and draining low-lying land. Considerable efforts were made to improve its efficiency, but the inherent unreliability of the wind prevented it being used to drive manufacturing equipment where regular hours of work and continuity of output were essential. It is worthwhile therefore considering the windmill first, as the story of its evolution and decline is outside the mainstream of events that led up to and carried forward the large-scale industrialisation of Britain during the eighteenth and nineteenth centuries. Indeed the improvements made to the windmill, all of which came after the waterwheel and steam engine were well established, may be regarded as *products* of the new technology, used to increase the efficiency and reliability of existing capital equipment in an area where investment potential was low.

The question of availability of capital was an important one, as a major obstacle to the use of power during the sixteenth and seventeenth centuries had been cost, a factor which remained relevant in some agricultural areas almost to the end of the nineteenth century. The capital involved in a windmill or watermill relative to the power generated was fairly high, so there was a tendency to perpetuate man- or, more frequently, animal-powered equipment. At a later date the same factors militated in favour of the waterwheel when it came to the question of its replacement by steam power. A number of disused horse-powered mechanisms still survive, mainly those employed for driving farm machinery, but also a few used to raise coal or water. More often the building alone remains. In a county like Durham, where horse gins were exceptionally numerous, a typical feature of many of the farms is an octagonal building with a pointed roof; such buildings once housed a horse walking endlessly around a central spindle coupled by drive shafts to machinery.

WINDMILLS

The earliest type of windmill in England was the post mill (Illus 15); its body, which contained the machinery and on which the sails were mounted, stood on a central post about which it could be rotated to bring the sails into the wind. The absence of a dominant wind in Britain

16 The body or 'buck' of Danzey Green post mill being lifted into position at the Avoncroft Museum of Buildings near Bromsgrove, Hereford & Worcester [SO 953683]; the mill was moved from Tamworth-in-Arden
(*Avoncroft Museum of Buildings*)

meant that the simpler type of uni-directional mill which originated in east and south Europe could not be adopted. None of these medieval mills survive, but illustrations are profuse, all showing the post mill in a form almost identical to those existing today. St Margaret's Church, King's Lynn, Norfolk [TF 617197], has a mid-fourteenth-century memorial brass depicting a post mill, and representations carved in wood can be seen on a fifteenth-century misericord in Bristol Cathedral [ST 584726] and on a sixteenth-century bench end in the parish church of Bishops Lydeard, Somerset [ST 168298]. This last example clearly shows the sails in their earliest form, symmetrically mounted on the stocks.

The post mill, even today, is remarkable for its technical ingenuity, representing one of the medieval carpenter's greatest achievements in design and construction. It consisted of a small timber-framed building designed to balance and pivot on a single vertical post. The post was held in position by diagonal quarter bars resting on a pair of oak crosstrees that were arranged at right-angles to each other and provided the base for the whole structure. The weight of the body or 'buck' of the mill was borne by a transverse beam, the 'crown tree', which rested across the top of the post and was free to rotate on it (Illus 16). Originally an oak pintle would have provided the centre, but later an iron gudgeon was usually fitted. The end of the crown tree carried the frame of the mill, mortice and tenon jointed and dowelled together, with timber diagonal braces providing rigidity. Very little iron was used. From the back of the buck projected a tail pole that was used like a tiller to orient the mill towards the wind (Illus 16). The pole was moored to wooden posts arranged around the circumference of the circle described by its tip. In some cases, such as in Chillenden Mill, Kent [TR 268543], a wheel on the end of the tail pole helped support some of the weight of the tail ladder.

Early post mills, like Bourn Mill, Cambridgeshire [TL 312580], had a simple pitched roof, but most have the familiar curved shape, providing greater clearance for the brake wheel, and are generally clad in horizontal weatherboarding. From the eighteenth century it became common to enclose the underframe in a roundhouse, usually built of brick, with a conical roof. This provided useful storage and protected the frame timbers from the weather. Holton Mill, Suffolk [TM 402776], has a very typical roundhouse.

The earliest surviving post mills in England probably date from the beginning of the seventeenth century, when the first dated inscriptions occur; the date 1627 carved on a timber of Pitstone Mill, Bucks [SP 945157], is perhaps the oldest. By this time a new type of mill had been introduced from Europe – the tower mill, which possibly had its origins in the fifteenth century. In this type of mill the

17 Alford Mill owned by Lincolnshire County Council and open to the public [TF 457766]; it is one of the only three 5-sail windmills (*Lincolnshire County Council*)

grinding machinery was mounted in a fixed stone or masonry tower, circular in plan and usually conical in elevation. On top of the tower was a movable cap on which the windshaft and sails were mounted. Only the cap had to be turned to bring the sails into the wind, and the drive from the windshaft was transmitted to the millstones mounted in the tower by a central vertical spindle, the main shaft. The early towers were squat and cylindrical, like those still to be seen in Spain. In Britain the type has only survived in Somerset where Ashton Mill, Chapel Allerton [ST 414504], is the last complete example. It is maintained by Bristol City Museum and is open to the public. The cap was usually conical and covered with thatch or tiles. A thatched cap survives, also in Somerset, at High Ham Mill [ST 433305].

The first tower mills had tail poles for

rotating the cap and this effectively limited their height. Similarly the cylindrical shape of the tower was dictated by the angle of the windshaft, which was initially horizontal. Later the windshaft was inclined, balancing the weight of the sails and reducing the likelihood of them being lifted out of the mill by a freak wind catching them from behind. Mill towers could then be conical in shape, and much more satisfying structurally (Illus 17). Not all were circular in plan: the tower of Wheatley Mill, Oxfordshire [SP 589052], is octagonal and that at West Wittering, West Sussex [SZ 797972], is circular, though standing on an octagonal base.

The third basic type of windmill in England was the smock mill (Illus 18), its name allegedly derived from its similarity in appearance to a man wearing a smock. It was basically a tower mill, the tower being built of timber, usually on an octagonal plan. At each corner a 'cant post' extended the full height of the mill, its foot resting on a timber cill, its top providing support for the circular curb on which the cap rotated. The sides between the cant posts had horizontal and diagonal framing and the whole was clad in weatherboards, often painted white. The cill was normally set on a brickwork plinth to provide a firm foundation, but in the nineteenth century brick bases as high as one or even two storeys became common and the height of the mill was no longer restricted by the availability of long timbers for the cant posts. The Willingham smock mill in Cambridgeshire [TL 404697] and the very fine Cranbrook Mill, Kent [TQ 779359], the tallest mill in England, are both of this type. The oldest English smock mill is at Lacey Green, Buckinghamshire [SP 819009]. It was originally erected at Chesham about 1650 and moved to its present site in 1821, and although substantially complete, it is now in poor condition. The last mill to be built in England was also a smock mill, in 1929 at St Margaret's Bay, Kent [TR 363435].

Both tower and smock mills were surmounted by timber-framed caps of a wide variety of shapes. The cap was carried on horizontal beams that supported the weight of the sails and windshaft. It revolved on a circular curb of timber forming the top of the tower. In early mills this was greased and the cap simply slid on the smooth surface – a 'dead curb' – but later hardwood or iron rollers were fitted to form a 'live curb'. At the front of the cap the 'weather' or 'breast' beam carried the neck journal of the windshaft, the other end of which was mounted in a thrust bearing on the tail beam. The distinctive shapes of windmill caps seem to have some regional variation, although how far these are significant is difficult to assess. The simplest form is a triangular gable, as at Bembridge, Isle of Wight [SZ 640875], an eighteenth-century stone tower mill, cement-rendered on its weather side. In Kent, Essex, Surrey and Sussex caps are shaped like small post mills with curved gables. Notable examples are at Herne [TR 184665] and Cranbrook in Kent. A variation of this type but curved in both planes to conform more to the plan of the top of the tower is the boat-shaped cap found in the eastern counties and exemplified by Gibraltar Mill, Great Bardfield, Essex [TL 681308]. Simple cones do not occur in England, as they do on the continent, but

18 Smock mill near Great Thurlow, West Suffolk [TL 671499]   (John C. Sawtell)

TOWER MILL

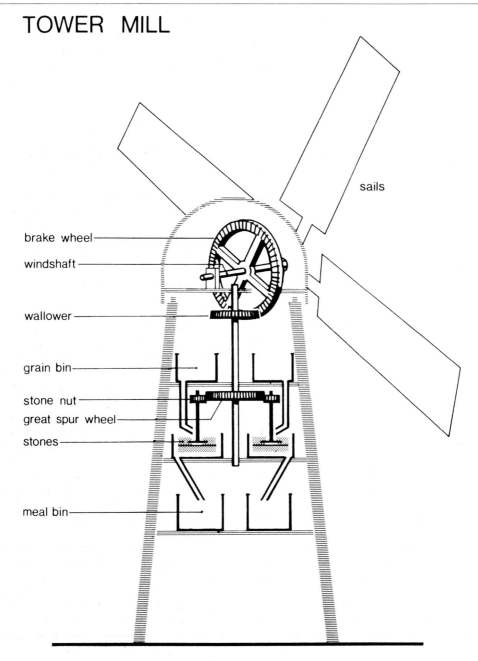

sails

brake wheel

windshaft

wallower

grain bin

stone nut

great spur wheel

stones

meal bin

Illustration 19

domes have a wide distribution, ranging from Polegate [TQ 581041] and Selsey [SZ 843933] in Sussex to West Wratting, Cambridgeshire [TL 604510], and Wilton [SU 276617] in Wiltshire. Far and away the most exotic are the ogee mill caps of Lincolnshire, which are made all the more prominent by the tall brick towers they usually sur-mount. They occur throughout eastern England, however, with subtle variations in shape from one area to another. Some have slightly flared bases, as at Burwell, Cambridgeshire [TL 590665], while others achieve an almost onion shape. Some are boarded and covered in painted canvas, and others have sheet-copper cladding that has often weathered green. Almost all have finials, usually in the form of a ball, though occasionally an acorn style is used.

Early windmills had simple wooden frames on which the canvas sails were spread. These frames were mounted symmetrically on stout tapering beams known as stocks, which were crossed at right-angles and morticed through the end of the windshaft. Lateral support was provided by short 'sail bars', rather like the rungs of a ladder, which were connected at their outer ends by light longitudinal 'hemlaths'. By the eighteenth century the symmetrical sail had given way to the 'common sail' seen on many mills today, in which the whole surface area was on the trailing side of the stock. A narrow windboard along the leading edge directed the air flow on to the cloth which was arranged on the front of the sail frame. 'Pointing lines' secured the canvas and were used by the miller in reefing the sails to suit the speed of the wind. As mills grew larger, it became common to construct the sails as separate units on long tapered 'whips' which were strapped and bolted to the stocks. A major point of weakness on early mills was the joint where the stocks were morticed through the windshaft, but the introduction of cast iron provided something of a solution to the problem, the end of the shaft being replaced by a massive casting known as a 'canister' or poll end into which the stocks were secured by wedges.

The common sail was light, simple and aerodynamically fairly efficient, but it suffered a major disadvantage in that a change in wind speed necessitated stopping the mill and rearranging the canvas a sail at a time. In 1772 a Scottish millwright, Andrew Meikle of East Lothian, invented a sail composed of shutters arranged like a Venetian blind and linked by a connecting rod or shutter bar which ran the length of the sail. An adjustable spring at the windshaft end maintained the shutters in the closed position under normal wind pressure but allowed them to open and spill air during gusts. Spring sails controlled by elliptic leaf springs can be seen on Outwood Mill, Surrey [TQ 327456], and Chillenden Mill, Kent [TR 268543].

The miller still had to stop the mill to make adjustments to the spring tension but the automatic regulation was a valuable benefit. In 1789 a Captain Stephen Hooper introduced a roller reefing gear similar to that used on sailing craft but it found little favour.

The most significant step forward in sail design came in 1807 when William Cubitt's patent sail appeared. For the first time in nearly 1,000 years the windmill had become a controllable machine in which the sails could be matched to the wind speed while they rotated. Patent sails retained Meikle's shutters and shutter bars but at the centre the springs were replaced by bell-cranks connected to an iron 'spider'. The spider was mounted on an iron 'striking rod' which passed through the hollow windshaft and emerged at the back of the mill where it terminated in a rack-and-pinion drive controlled by an endless chain hanging down to the ground. Moving the striking rod backwards and forwards operated the shutters. A fully automatic control was achieved by hanging weights on the chain which held the shutters closed against the air pressure but still allowed spillage if wind speed increased or conditions were gusty. Patent sails are found on, for example, Cranbrook Mill [TQ 779359] and Herne Mill, Kent [TR 184665], and at West Wratting in Cambridgeshire [TL 604510] the mill combines two patent with two common sails.

Although most mills had four sails, some were built with five, six and even eight in an attempt to increase sail area and efficiency. Five sails were least common, as the loss of a sail resulted in imbalance and stoppage until a replacement could be fitted. Three five-sail mills still exist, all in Lincolnshire: Maud Foster Mill, Boston [TF 333447], Burgh-le-Marsh [TF 504650] and Alford (Illus 17) [TF 457766] in which the sails are mounted on an iron cross instead of the conventional poll end. Six sails were more satisfactory and a six-sail mill could still operate in balance with only four if necessary. Sibsey Trader Mill, Lincolnshire [TF 345510], is an example. It has been extensively restored by English Heritage and is open to the public during the summer. Of the seven eight-sail mills built in England, only one still survives, the spectacular Heckington Mill in Lincolnshire [TF 145436] dating from the early nineteenth century but fitted with its present cap and sails in 1892. Bought by the then Kesteven County Council in 1953 and subsequently restored, the mill is accessible to the public on enquiry at the adjacent mill house.

As we have seen, it was necessary to keep the mill's sails facing into the wind, and with the medieval post mill, the miller hauled the tail pole around and moored it in a suitable position. He had to keep a constant eye on the wind direction and strength to ensure efficient operation and to avoid possible disaster if the mill was 'tail winded' in a storm. Although some of the Dutch tower mills also have complex tail pole arrangements for moving their caps, in England it became general practice to rotate the cap by continuous chain operating a worm driving onto wooden cogs projecting from the curb. A good example, and one that may easily be seen, is on Bembridge Mill, Isle of Wight, but numerous variations exist, frequently with cast-iron gears and a toothed iron curb cast in segments. Fully automatic luffing of the sails came in the eighteenth century after Edmund Lee's 1745 patent for the 'fantail' or 'fly'. This early example of a servo-mechanism is very simple in principle and heralded the large number of improvements which were to culminate in the highly efficient nineteenth-century tower mills of the eastern counties. The fantail was a small wooden vaned windwheel fitted to the back of the mill at right-angles to the sails and coupled through gears and shafts to a winding mechanism. As the wind veered or backed, the fantail rotated and turned the sails into the wind. With the high gearing ratios used there was great sensitivity to minor variations in wind direction, so typical in England, and the fantail became a characteristic feature in other European countries as well. Generally speaking the fantail drove onto the curb of a tower or smock mill to rotate the cap but a few post mills had them also and in these cases the drive was transmitted to wheels at the foot of the

'tail pole', which ran on a circular track. Post mills with fantails include Saxtead Green, Suffolk [TM 254644], maintained by English Heritage and open to the public, Great Chishill Mill, Cambridgeshire [TL 413388], Holton Mill, Suffolk [TM 402776], and Cross-in-Hand Mill, East Sussex [TQ 558218].

Transmission of power from the sails to the grinding stones was modelled initially on the medieval watermill and the design of gearing passed through similar stages of development in both types. Most early waterwheels, particularly in corn mills, had 'compass arms', that is spokes morticed into the wooden shaft, which was thereby not only weakened but made liable to rotting. An initial improvement was to provide 'clasp arms', whereby the spokes embraced rather than penetrated the shaft, and in the late eighteenth century cast-iron bevel wheels superseded the traditional combination of wooden face wheel and lantern pinion. Timber gears were never entirely displaced, however, and many can still be seen in both windmills and watermills. So too can morticed gears in which wooden teeth, usually of hornbeam or apple, are wedged into a cast-iron wheel which runs against the teeth of an all iron gear. This arrangement runs quietly with the minimum of wear.

In the windmill the general arrangement of the drive was from the great face wheel or 'brake-wheel' mounted on the windshaft to the 'wallower' on the top of the vertical main shaft running down the centre of the mill body or tower. A 'great spur wheel' on the main shaft drove a small 'stone nut' on top of the 'stone spindle', which in turn rotated the upper runner stone. Early mills had one pair of stones, but as post mills increased in size, a second pair were usually included.

Grain was fed to the millstones by gravity. Corn was initially taken by sack hoist, which was usually powered by the sails, to the top of the mill where it was put in the grain bin. A chute took it to a hopper above the millstones and the grain trickled from the bottom of the hopper into a 'feed shoe' which was vibrated by the 'damsel', an extension of the stone spindle in the form of a cam. As the upper or runner stone revolved, grain was fed into the eye to be ground and expelled at the outer circumference of the stones. Only the upper stone revolved, and it did not come into contact with the stationary bedstone below. The space between the surfaces of the stones was carefully controlled to produce the best results. Nevertheless the meal falling away from the rim of the stones into the meal spout and finally into the bin on the floor below is surprisingly warm to the touch, an indication of the considerable power absorbed in the grinding process. Keeping the stones in correct relation to each other is known as 'tentering' and taxed the ingenuity of both millwright and miller to find a means of carrying out the operation automatically. The distance apart of the stones must relate to the speed of the mill, so a number of factors had to be related. As we have seen, the fantail and various automatic patent sails were in effect regulators or servo-mechanisms. Another type, which probably originated in mills, was the centrifugal ball governor in which two bob weights when rotated at speed moved outwards from the drive spindle. This movement could be coupled to brake the speed of the sails or, more commonly, to regulate the distance apart of the millstones. The use of these governors in windmills and watermills almost certainly predates their introduction and patenting by James Watt for regulating the supply of steam to steam engines.

Many mills operated two types of stone and both can frequently be seen today, in mills or standing decoratively in the open, often an indication that a windmill or watermill nearby has gone out of use or been demolished. Derbyshire Peak stones of grey millstone grit were used for barley, but flour was usually processed on the harder French burr stones which were more suitable for finer grinding. These latter stones were not cut from a single piece, as were the Derbyshire ones, but built up out of sections of quartz cemented together and bound with iron bands. The surfaces of the stones had a series of radial grooves in them which facilitated the grinding of the grain and

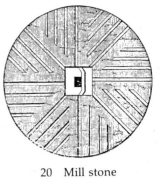

20   Mill stone

encouraged the resultant meal outwards towards the rim. The stones would be dressed from time to time by recutting the grooves using hardened steel mill bits wedged into a mason's maul. Not all stones revolved in the same direction, although millstones which revolved clockwise were easier to dress. This usually implied an anti-clockwise rotation of the sails in the normal post mill. It is always possible to work out which way the sails rotated on a derelict or disused mill by examining the sailstock or whip, which was always at the leading edge of the sails, or by observing the wear on the gear teeth.

Not all windmills were for grinding corn, their other major use being for drainage of low-lying areas such as the Fens. Wind power was used extensively from the sixteenth century onwards in the numerous Fenland drainage schemes and a number of windmills still survive, although no longer working. Naturally enough they derive some of their design features from Holland and many had a distinctly Dutch look, with squat towers, common sails and tail poles. Most early drainage mills were of the smock type but later examples were brick, often tarred. The machinery inside was much simpler than that in a corn mill. A conventional brake wheel on the windshaft drove the wallower on the vertical shaft, which at ground level had a bevel gear that drove in its turn a pit wheel on a horizontal shaft. On the other end of this shaft, usually on the outside of the windmill structure, was a scoop wheel which lifted water up and discharged it at a higher level. Sometimes, as at Horsey, a turbine pump was used.

Today few drainage mills survive intact, their decline beginning quite early in the nineteenth century when large-capacity steam pumps were installed, each one capable of replacing a number of windmills. Fine examples of mills can still be seen, however, at Wicken Fen, Cambridgeshire [TL 562706], belonging to the National Trust; Horsey Mill [TG 457223] and Berney Arms Mill [TG 465051], both in Norfolk. This last mill, said to be the tallest in East Anglia, has a 70ft tower and is preserved by English Heritage. A curious feature is that the scoop wheel is separate from the mill itself and connected to it by a rotating drive shaft. It is also unusual in being used for grinding cement clinker and having access only by rail or water.

Although the traditional mill is now completely obsolete, a much more recent counterpart, which enjoyed considerable popularity down to the 1930s, can still be found fairly commonly. Wind pumps, used for raising water for farm use, are

21   A Norse mill preserved at Southvoe, Shetland [HU 401145]   (*John R. Hume*)

automatic in operation. Most types have a steel wire-braced tower, with a multi-bladed wind vane and driving a reciprocating lift pump by means of a crankshaft geared down from the windshaft. Although relatively modern, operating examples are becoming surprisingly scarce, their role usually having been usurped by electric or internal combustion engine pumps.

There are still some 300 windmills in Britain of which reasonably complete remains survive and many more in the form of derelict towers or conversions into houses. Most are in the Eastern Counties, with notable concentrations in Essex, Kent, Lincolnshire, Norfolk, Suffolk and Sussex. Many of them are preserved. There were isolated pockets of wind power in the west, however, usually in areas where surface water was unavailable or not easily utilised. In England the Somerset levels, Wirral peninsula of Cheshire and Fylde of Lancashire all once had numerous windmills, although little evidence of them now survives. Ashton Mill, Chapel Allerton [ST 414504], is the best

WATERMILL

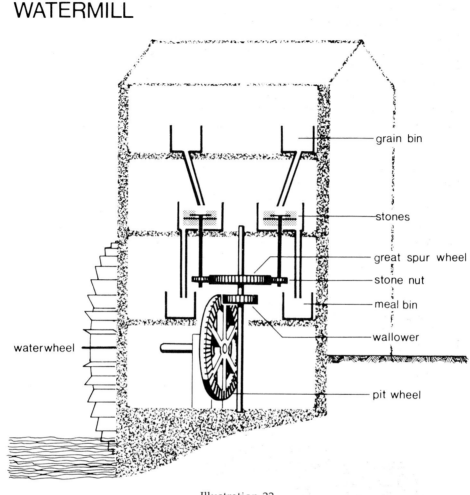

grain bin

stones

great spur wheel

stone nut

meal bin

waterwheel

wallower

pit wheel

Illustration 22

Somerset example; Bidston Mill [SJ 287894] near Birkenhead still has sails and internal machinery, while on the Fylde, Marsh Mill, Thornton Cleveleys [SD 335426], is preserved by the local District Council. On Anglesey, the single area of Wales where windmills were common, only derelict towers survive.

WATER POWER

The first watermills in Britain were for grinding corn and this purpose remained by far the most widespread use of water power. Unlike the windmill, however, water was employed to drive a wide variety of industrial equipment, beginning with the water-powered textile ful-

ling mill that was probably developed during the twelfth century. The earliest types of waterwheel used in Britain, of which examples still survive, were called Norse mills. They had vertical shafts and inclined wooden blades rather like scoops and developed at the most about ½hp. The wheel powers directly a single pair of millstones, the drive being taken through the eye of the bottom stone, which remains stationary, the top stone rotating above it (Illus 22). At least two Norse mills, Click Mill in Orkney [HY 325228], and the lower mill at Southvoe, Shetland [HU 401145] have been preserved (Illus 21).

It is known that the Romans used water power in Britain – three watermill sites have been excavated along Hadrian's

Wall, for example – but no detailed evidence survives. These Roman mills were probably very like the waterwheels used extensively in Britain from the eighth century onwards. Known generally as Vitruvian mills after Vitruvius, the engineer and architect who first described them, they had horizontal shafts with flat buckets that dipped into fast running water of a stream or river. Besides these primitive stream wheels the Romans also used overshot wheels at least as early as the fourth century AD and possibly earlier.

Little is known of the development of water power during the Dark Ages but by the *Domesday Survey*, begun in 1080 and completed in 1086, there were over 5,000 corn mills in England, most of them south and east of the Rivers Trent and Severn. These were probably of both Norse and Vitruvian types, but the latter eventually predominated. A watermill is shown in Illus 22.

By the sixteenth century water was by far the most important source of motive power throughout Europe, and Britain was no exception. Although primarily used for corn milling, water also drove fulling mills, the hammers and bellows necessary for the manufacture of wrought and cast iron, wire drawing equipment, drills for gun barrels and machinery used to hoist, crush and stamp metalliferous ores. The availability of water for driving wheels became an important factor in the location of industry; and in the manufacture of wool textiles, for instance, where manual spinning, carding and weaving had long been carried out as a cottage industry in East Anglia and the East Midlands, the new water-powered fulling mills set up on streams in the Cotswolds, Yorkshire, the Lake District and the West of England drew the other processes to them. Similarly the iron industry, although primarily located near raw materials such as iron ore and charcoal, took advantage where possible of streams to power hammers and bellows. In Kent, Sussex and Surrey where the industry was centred this was not always easy, as streams were inconsistent in flow. In summer men might have to work the wheels like treadmills to keep things going. In the Lake District and Shropshire, however, two other areas where blast furnaces in particular became established, the streams had a more consistent flow, and it is interesting to speculate on how influential this factor was in encouraging the industry to these areas.

By the sixteenth century too a corpus of knowledge on waterwheel technology was being established. John Fitzherbert's *Boke of Surveyinge and Improvements*, published posthumously in 1539, notes that it was common to build corn mills not on large rivers but on a more convenient site served by a man-made millstream to a weir. Fitzherbert also refers to the need for an adequate fall in tailrace to minimise the disadvantages of back-watering, which in time of flood might cause the wheel to slow down through water building up below it. He also confirms that breastshot and overshot wheels produced more power than undershot wheels if their buckets were well filled, and that water should, as far as possible, be prevented from leaving the buckets before they reached their lowest point by the building of a close fitting breast of brick or stone shaped to the profile of about a quarter of the wheel and only an inch or so from it. Types of waterwheel are shown in Illus 23.

As industrialisation got under way in the early years of the eighteenth century, the simple undershot wheel was then the most numerous in Britain. It was cheap and easy to install, needed a minimum of groundworks to arrange its water supply and did the job for which it was required effectively if not efficiently. Mechanical inefficiency was of little importance if there was adequate water in the stream all the year round to drive a low horse power wheel reliably. Only when greater power was demanded from limited supplies of water did other types of waterwheel become necessary. Thus in the eighteenth century eminent engineers such as John Rennie (1761–1821) and Sir Marc Isambard Brunel (1769–1849) used large undershot wheels to drive saw mills at Dartford and Chatham. One important modification in the design of the undershot wheel was made in the early years of the nineteenth century by J. V. Poncelet (1788–1867), and

TYPES OF WATERWHEEL

Stream

Horizontal
or
Norse mill

Undershot

Breastshot

High
breastshot

Low
breastshot

Overshot

Pitchback

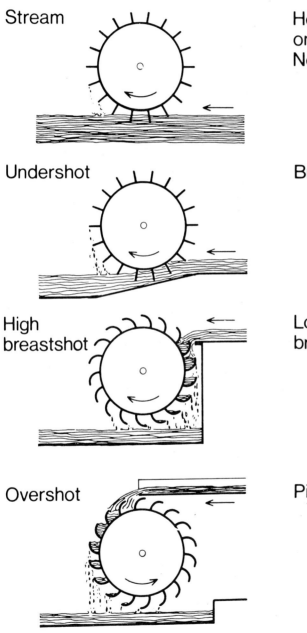
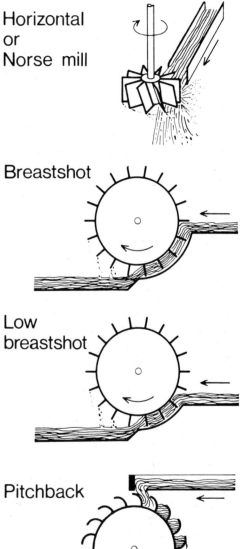

Illustration 23

24 Preston Mill, Prestonkirk, East Lothian [NT 595779], a seventeenth-century watermill preserved by the National Trust for Scotland and open to the public. It has a low-breast wheel driving two pairs of stones and there is a circular drying kiln attached *(John R. Hume)*

became widely adopted where maximum efficiency was required from a small head of water. By curving the paddles or blades of the wheel, as shown in Illus 23, he provided for the entry of water into the compartments without shock, the idea being that water would run up the surface of the vanes, come to rest at the inner diameter and then fall away from the wheel with practically no velocity. This design raised the efficiency of the undershot wheel from about 22 per cent to about 65 per cent.

Between 1750 and 1850 the waterwheel came into its own for industrial purposes, well after the steam engine had become firmly established. Water had been the primary source of power in the early years of the Industrial Revolution and the steam engine was at first as much a product of industrial growth as a contributor to its development. Waterwheels were cheap and easy to install and could drive

machinery which the early non-rotative steam engines could not. Indeed the steam engine was used in the middle of the eighteenth century to pump back the tail water of the waterwheel and even to supply water to wheels which had no stream supply of their own. For example, Bedlam furnaces, built on the bank of the Severn at Ironbridge in 1757, relied on a Newcomen-type steam engine to lift water from the river to drive an overshot and undershot wheel on each of the two sets of bellows. It is significant too that almost all the really high horse power waterwheel installations, developing more than about 100hp, were built between 1820 and 1850, long after the rotative steam engine had become well established.

A major contribution to the improvement of waterwheel design resulted from the experiments of John Smeaton (1724–92), who built and tested models to determine the most efficient type of wheel. He established the principle that there must be considerable losses when a jet of water strikes the flat blade of an undershot wheel, and that it was clearly much better to develop power by filling the buckets of an overshot or breast wheel with water and doing the work by gravity rather than by impulse. Smeaton also introduced the first cast-iron shaft in 1769, which was fitted to the waterwheel of a furnace blowing engine at the Carron Ironworks in Scotland. This in itself was an important step forward as one of the major problems with developing a large-output waterwheel was designing a shaft capable of transmitting the power. Smeaton's iron shafts were strong, and although they did not solve all the difficulties – they were subject to fracture in the region of the flanges – they provided some sort of answer to the problem until better designs were evolved.

Metal construction throughout followed in the early years of the nineteenth century with cast iron replacing wood. Buckets were made of curved sheet iron, with the inlet angle carefully designed to reduce the shock loss of water entering the wheel and the bucket shaped to retain as much water as possible during the descent. As the size of waterwheels increased, both in diameter and width, trouble was experienced with air locks as the water entered the buckets and also, when water in the tailrace was high and the bottom of the wheel submerged, with water leaving. The remedy was found by Sir William Fairbairn (1789–1874) who described it thus:

> It was observed that when the wheel was loaded in flood waters, each of the buckets acted as a water blast, and forced the water and spray to a height of 6 or 8 feet above the orifice at which it entered . . . in order to remedy it openings were cut in the sole plates, and small interior buckets attached, inside the sole . . . The air in the bucket madëits escape through the opening and
>
> passed upwards . . . permitting the free reception of the water . . . The buckets were thus effectively cleared of air as they were filling . . .

Fairbairn claimed an increase of power due to this modification of 25 per cent.

25 Philiphaugh Sawmill, Selkirkshire [NT 450278] has an iron low-breast wheel 12ft wide and 15ft in diameter driving a sawbench through gearing. The nearby corn mill [NT 457282] has power supplied by two water turbines. Until 1972 a twin tandem-compound mill engine was used as a standby. These, together with a Lancashire boiler, are *in situ* (*John R. Hume*)

From the end of the eighteenth century .the use of high horse power waterwheels for driving factories posed new transmission design problems. Wheels developing as much as 100hp were becoming common, and contemporary wheel shafts, even those made of iron, could not transmit this power at the low speeds then employed. The difficulty was overcome by taking the power from the wheel at its periphery where a segmental gear wheel, usually of cast-iron sections attached to the rim or spokes of the waterwheel, drove a smaller pinion wheel. Thus the secondary shaft rotated at a much higher speed and the wheel shaft had only to be strong enough to support the weight of the waterwheel itself. Spokes too could be of lighter section as they no longer transmitted power, the ultimate result of this trend being the suspension wheel in which the spokes, like the spokes of a bicycle wheel, were of thin section and in tension rather than compression. Generally speaking the position of the power take-off on waterwheels with a rim drive was as close as possible to where the power was being generated – immediately below the sluice through which water entered the wheel.

The suspension wheel was developed about 1805 by Thomas Cheek Hewes (1768–1832), an engineer and textile machine manufacturer of Manchester, in association with William Strutt (1756–1830) of Derby. Hewes was an early pioneer in the application of cast and wrought iron and for a short but crucial period in 1816–17 employed William Fairbairn (later Sir William), who later achieved much greater renown. Thwaite Mill, Hunslet, Leeds [SE 318312], rebuilt in 1823 by Hewes and Wren, used water power in the manufacture of putty; it is now preserved. One of the finest suspension wheels still in existence was made by the same firm in 1826 for Woodside Mills, Aberdeen, and is preserved in the Royal Museum of Scotland, Edinburgh. The wheel is 25ft in diameter and 21ft wide. It generated over 200hp with an 18ft head of water, transmitting power by a rim gear of twelve cast-iron segments. There are forty-eight wooden ventilated buckets, twelve wrought-iron spokes of 2½in diameter on each side of the wheel and a similar number of diagonal wrought-iron braces. The shaft, of cast iron with a cruciform section, is of a type known as a feathered shaft. At Quarry Bank Mill, Styal, Cheshire [SJ 835829], a large suspension wheel, designed by William Fairbairn and moved from Glasshouses Mill near Pateley Bridge has been installed in the original wheelpit (Illus 26). It is in regular use to drive textile machinery.

Another large suspension wheel is at Hartlington Mill, Burnsall, Wharfedale [SE 042609]. Unfortunately these most sophisticated of waterwheels, nearly all of which were installed to drive factories, have largely disappeared as the result of the competition from steam engines during the latter part of the nineteenth century. Thus, while many hundreds of relatively primitive wheels in rural corn mills survive, very few high horse power industrial waterwheels still remain *in situ*.

Not all large wheels were of the pure suspension type although a number had lightweight spokes. An example is the 33ft diameter overshot wheel at Killhope lead mill in Weardale, County Durham [NY 827429]. Here the spokes are of flat section wrought iron and rigidity is maintained by cross bracing. The wheel once drove lead crushers, which have now gone, but the wooden launder that supplied its water has been restored. Another large-diameter wheel is at Lothersdale Mill, Keighley, Yorkshire [SD 959459]. Built in 1861 it is 44ft in diameter, 5ft 1in wide and has an unusual arrangement of alternating wooden spokes and wrought-iron tension rods. It is a high breast wheel with U-shaped floats of sheet iron and there is an outside rim drive. It powered cotton spinning and weaving machinery until the 1930s. At Foster Beck Mill, Pateley Bridge, Yorkshire [SD 148664], is a fine external breast wheel 35ft in diameter. It has wooden spokes and rim drive but no bracing, and the 'penstock' from which the water was fed to the wheel through a sliding hatch or 'shuttle' is particularly conspicuous. The wheel drove a hemp mill which has now closed and the machinery has been removed.

The largest waterwheel ever built in Britain is the celebrated *Lady Isabella* installed in 1854 by the Great Laxey Mining Company of the Isle of Man [SC 432851]. It is 72ft in diameter and 6ft 1in wide and was built to pump water from a lead and zinc mine 1,480ft deep. The drive was by means of a crank on the shaft and 600ft of timber connecting rods. The wheel, which has wooden spokes and wrought-iron diagonal bracing rods, is of the pitchback type (see Illus 23) in which the water is reversed in direction at the point of access, in contrast to the conventional overshot wheel where the direction of flow is continuous. This somewhat unusual feature was probably adopted as a means of securing efficient entry of water into the buckets and to avoid the constructional problems of carrying the high-level leat beyond the wheel centre as in a normal overshot wheel. Another possible advantage was that the water leaving the wheel flowed away down the tailrace in the same direction as the wheel was rotating. The

26 Installation of the suspension wheel at Quarry Bank Mill, Styal [SJ 835829] showing the feathered shaft and rim drive   (*Neil Cossons*)

Lady Isabella last worked the mine pumps in 1926, was restored in the late 1920s, and in 1965 was bought by the Manx Government whose Tourist Board now maintains it. During renovation the spokes have been replaced by steel girders, clad in timber to retain the original appearance.

In coastal areas tide mills took advantage of the fact that water could be ponded up in a small estuary or creek at high tide and used to drive a waterwheel – usually of the low breast or undershot type – over the period of low tide. There were two working shifts in each 24 hour period and, because of the successional movement of the tides, the tide miller worked somewhat unusual hours. The last operating tide mill in Britain, on the River Deben at Woodbridge in Suffolk [TM 275487], has been restored and is open to the public. The mill ran until 1956 when the 22in square oak shaft of the waterwheel broke, but since then a trust has been established to raise the money necessary to restore the machinery and timber-framed building. At Carew, Dyfed, the tide mill – French Mill [SN 042038] – has been restored and is open to the public. Also under restoration is Eling tide mill near Totton, Hampshire [SU 365125]. It stands on the seaward side of the causeway that contains Bartley Water. The causeway itself is a toll road and has cabin and tollboard. At Three Mills, Newham, East London [TQ 383828] are two semi-tidal mills, the largest in the country, with seven undershot wheels (Illus 27).

A much less common use of water power was to drive beam pumps used in mine drainage and one incomplete example survives at Straitsteps lead mine, Wanlockhead, Dumfriesshire [NS 873125]. At one end of the beam is a broken pump rod which once went down the mine shaft. At the other end a bucket rod is connected to the beam via a crosshead moving in guides and a connecting rod. The method of operation was for the bucket to be filled from a nearby stream supply until the weight of water caused the beam to fall, raising the other end and the column of water in the pump barrel in the shaft. When the full bucket reached the end of its travel, a valve in the bottom was triggered open, the water flowed out, and the pump end of the beam, appropriately weighted, fell, filling the pump barrel again. The Wanlockhead water-bucket engine, which is thought to date from the 1880s, is preserved by the Wanlockhead Museum Trust and is Scheduled as an Ancient Monument. A restored water-wheel-powered beam pump is situated at Wheal Martyn in Cornwall [SX 004555].

The ultimate application of water power has been through water turbines, initially to drive machinery by gearing, and later for electricity generation (see Chapter 12). Much of the early development took place in France where after 1820 Benoit Fourneyron (1802–67) perfected a vertical-shaft design particularly suited to low heads of water. It might be regarded as an indirect successor of the primitive Norse mill. In the Fourneyron turbine (Illus 28) there are two concentric horizontal

27   Tide mills at Three Mills Lane, Bromley-by-Bow, Newham [TQ 383828]. House Mill on the left, rebuilt in 1776, has four undershot water-wheels; Clock Mill on the right, rebuilt in 1817 has three. The largest tide mills in the country, they occupy a site which has been used for distilling since 1727. Clock Mill is now used as offices   (*Neil Cossons*)

wheels. The inner wheel, or stator, is fixed and water flows from its centre through curved blades which direct it on to the outer wheel, the rotor or moving wheel, which has blades curved in the opposite direction and is attached to a vertical shaft running up through the centre of the machine. From the 1840s manufacture took place in Northern Ireland, apparently illicitly, and it is one of these products, made by MacAdam Brothers of Belfast that was installed in Spicer's papermill at Catteshall, Godalming in 1869 [SU 982444]. The turbine has a rotor diameter of 12ft and produced about 50hp from a 6ft head of water. It has now been removed from the mill, Scheduled as an Ancient Monument and is undergoing preservation by

FOURNEYRON WATER TURBINE HALF-SECTIONED

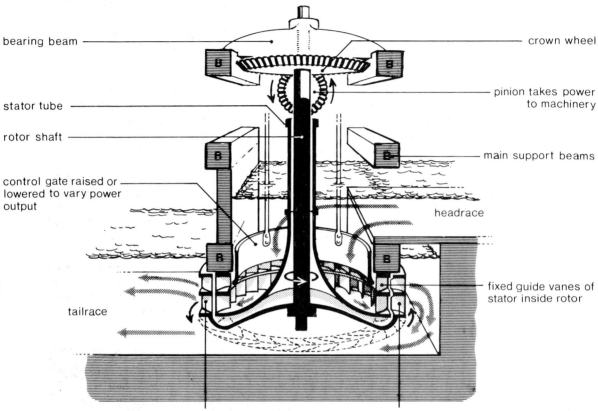

bearing beam — crown wheel

— pinion takes power
to machinery

stator tube —

rotor shaft —

— main support beams

control gate raised or
lowered to vary power
output

headrace

— fixed guide vanes of
stator inside rotor

tailrace

vaned rotor outside stator turns shaft

Illustration 28

the Godalming Water Turbine Trust. Other types of turbine design were also adopted and, although nothing like as numerous as waterwheels, examples can still be found, usually as adaptations of more traditional mills.

The use of water for power provides a fruitful and worthwhile area of study for the industrial archaeologist, as surviving evidence in the form of wheels and the watercourses associated with them is plentiful. There are thousands of sites, in England particularly, where a small weir, a rotting sluice-gate or a dried-up leat pro-

vide the clue to a once thriving water-powered mill or factory. Investigation of these remains is in many cases truly archaeological in nature, as although documentary or map evidence is often available to locate a watermill site, most details of its technology – what type of wheel and transmission gear was used, for example – can only be discovered by fieldwork.

A number of basic principles can be applied to help with these on-site investigations. The requirements of a water-wheel are a head of water to drive it, a consistent and controllable flow of water and avoidance, if possible, of the effects of mild flooding. On a large slow-flowing stream or river with a relatively low gradient the easiest and cheapest mill to build would have a short leat taking water to the wheel which, because only a low head would be available, would have to be of the undershot type. The mill might be susceptible to flooding and a more reliable siting might involve a longer leat and tailrace (to avoid water backing up on the wheel) and perhaps a low weir in the river. By using a long leat a greater head of water would be made available, and a breastshot or overshot wheel might be installed to provide greater power for a given size of wheel. If the stream or river was particularly susceptible to minor changes in level, a long weir placed diagonally across the stream could mini-mise these effects, combining the merits of a long leat in creating a good head of water and an efficient governor for the wheel. The longer the weir, the less varia-tion is there in water level during spates.

If the stream supply was small or the flow inconsistent, water would have to be collected in a millpond and, in certain cases, a type of wheel that would derive maximum power from a limited supply would have to be devised. There are two ways of gaining more power from a water-wheel – increasing its width or increasing its diameter. A good example of a wide wheel is to be found at Claverton (Illus 198) [ST 791644] on the River Avon near Bath, where a waterwheel provided power for a beam pump designed to lift water from the river into the Kennet & Avon Canal. Here the head is low but the supply plentiful, so to obtain the necessary power, this low breastshot wheel was built some 24ft wide. The present installa-tion contains an interesting design modi-fication, as the shaft of the original *c*1810 wheel was not stiff enough, and a cast-

29 High pressure water being used to clean the rotor of the 1869 water turbine from Catteshall Mill, Godalming, Surrey [SU 982444] (*Godalming Water Turbine Trust*)

iron A frame and bearing had to be fitted to provide intermediate support to the shaft, which now carries two wheels in parallel, each one 11ft 6in wide.

In situations where the volume of water was low and water storage impracticable or too expensive, the only way to obtain high power outputs was by building large-diameter wheels. In some cases the supply of the waterwheel would be by a pipe, as at Pateley Bridge [SD 148664] and the *Lady Isabella*; with the latter the pipe approaches at ground level and rises vertically inside a stone tower to feed the top of the wheel. Another large-diameter wheel where water supply is a problem is at Priston Mill in Avon [ST 695615] where an iron overshot wheel is fed from a pond.

The factors which led to the decline of water power are more complex than might

30,31 Rossett Mill, Clwyd [SJ 364572], 1970 and 1985; from derelict mill to attractive dwelling. All over the country, buildings such as this have undergone conversion to new uses

(Neil Cossons)

at first be imagined. The popular notion that the steam engine was immediately responsible for the elimination of the waterwheel is far from true, and many large and successful waterwheels were being installed throughout the first half of the nineteenth century. Indeed it was not until the 1840s that steam engines were being built to exceed the hp of the largest waterwheels. As late as 1834 estimates by the first four factory inspectors indicate that approximately one-third of the power used in cotton mills in Britain was from water. A further factor in the decline of water power during the latter part of the nineteenth century was the steadily increasing diversion of water from higher districts to supply the domestic needs of the new towns, while Fairbairn, writing in 1864, claimed that land drainage schemes had altered river regimes drastically, resulting in rapid run-off, a higher incidence of flooding and subsequent low water conditions, all of which were detrimental to water-power users.

By the latter part of the nineteenth

century, however, steam engines began to replace waterwheels, particularly in large-scale industrial locations where technology was evolving rapidly and power requirements were increasing. The rurally based industry on the other hand often continued to use the waterwheel as its main source of power, perhaps adding a small steam engine or later an oil engine as a supplementary source. There was little incentive to change from water if it did the job. Maintenance costs were low and nothing went on fuel. The major factor in bringing about the closure of the large majority of watermills (those grinding corn) was not directly related to the power source. During the latter years of the nineteenth century the increasing importation of foreign grains and the introduction of roller mills led to very large flour milling complexes being set up at the major ports. The small miller, whether he was using wind or water power, could rarely compete and almost all flour production soon passed into the hands of big companies. Today a few small corn mills are still working, mainly for the production of animal feed.

Nevertheless a surprising number of waterwheels can still be seen in operation, in most cases preserved, but indicating the very wide variety of applications in which water power has been used in very recent years. At Sticklepath in Devon [SX 639940] is Finch Foundry, a water-powered scythe and edge tool works with hammers and grinding wheels. Abbeydale [SK 325820] and Shepherd Wheel [SK 317854] in Sheffield also have preserved and operational waterwheels driving basically the same types of equipment, while in Cornwall the Tolgus Tin Company [SW 690438] uses water to drive ore-crushing stamps. At Redditch, Hereford & Worcester [SP 046686], a needle mill is water-driven; and at Cheddleton in North Staffordshire [SJ 974525] flint grinding mills are water-powered. Working preserved corn mills include High Mill, Skipton [SD 989518], Nether Alderley, Cheshire [SJ 844763], and Preston Mill, East Linton, East Lothian (Illus 24), [NT 595779].

CHAPTER 4

STEAM AND INTERNAL COMBUSTION ENGINES

It is perhaps not generally realised that a high proportion of the total requirements of energy in Britain today is satisfied by steam power in the form of steam turbines, which are amongst the largest and most efficient prime movers employing heat energy, and generate most of the electricity we use. At one time the reciprocating steam engine, that is one employing a piston moving backwards and forwards in a cylinder, held this pre-eminent position, but although it has not been entirely displaced, still finding specialist applications in a number of fields, its use has declined considerably. Steam turbines, diesel engines and gas turbines have superseded it after over 250 years, during which the steam engine was unchallenged for almost two centuries. In those 200 years Britain and many other countries were transformed into highly industrialised, technology-based societies; the significance of the steam engine in bringing about this transformation is inestimable. As a means of draining mines, of powering textile machinery, of driving railway locomotives and ships, and now of generating electricity, the power of steam, harnessed successfully in the early years of the eighteenth century, is without doubt the greatest single technological factor in the huge social and economic changes which we have called the Industrial Revolution. The significance of the steam engine far transcends its purely technical aspects; its evolution was the first major step in the liberation of mankind from toil.

THE STEAM ENGINE

In the late seventeenth century mines had become sufficiently deep to create serious problems of drainage, a difficulty overcome in some instances by the use of water-powered pumps but more often by men and horses. Severe limitations were imposed on further deep mining by the capacity and expense of mine-pumping equipment. It was into this field of outstanding need that the steam engine came as a result of the discovery that the pressure of the atmosphere could be applied to do useful work.

Before examining the evolution of the steam engine proper it will be worthwhile to consider the state of experimental science at the end of the seventeenth century and the extent of knowledge about the atmosphere and the properties of gases at that time. As early as the first century AD Hero of Alexandria had demonstrated that gases expanded and contracted when heated and cooled respectively, but it was not until 1606 that an experiment, carried out by Giovanni Battista della Porta of Naples, used the pressure of steam generated in a flask to force the water out of an enclosed tank. He also described how a flask full of steam and with its neck in a vessel of water would draw up water as the steam condensed, the principle being that 'nature abhorred a vacuum'. The fundamental breakthrough, the realisation that the atmosphere has weight, was made in 1643 by Evangelista Torricelli (1608–47), a pupil of Galileo, when attempting to explain why a suction pump would not draw water from a depth greater than about 28ft. After experiments with mercury he stated that the atmosphere exerted a pressure because of its weight and that this would support a column of water 28ft high or, in the case of the much denser mercury, some 30in in height. It was this discovery that established one of the basic principles on which the first generation of steam engines depended and also, of course, resulted in the invention of the mercury barometer.

The power of atmospheric pressure was further demonstrated in the 1650s by Otto von Guericke (1602–66), of Magdeburg, who succeeded in evacuating a copper sphere, which resulted in its collapse. Later he evacuated the air from a cylinder having an accurately fitting piston and utilised the atmospheric pressure to raise a weight of over a ton. It was the Dutch scientist Christiaan Huygens (1629–95), and his assistant Denis Papin (1647–1712?), however, who in 1690 used the condensation of steam beneath a piston in a cylinder as a means of creating a vacuum, a great improvement on the air pump used by von Guericke. Although Papin never developed his ideas to a larger scale than an experimental model with a 2½in diameter cylinder, he had in his grasp all the fundamentals that were to be applied in practical terms by Thomas Newcomen 20 years later.

The first practical application of steam power and a steam-generated vacuum for mine drainage was, however, not evolved from Papin's work with pistons in cylinders but derived its principles from della Porta's steam pressure and vacuum experiments of 1606. In 1698 Thomas Savery (c1650–1717), a Cornish engineer, patented a machine for the 'Raiseing of Water . . . by the Impellant Force of Fire'. Steam from a boiler was admitted into a closed vessel and condensed by pouring water on its outside. The resultant vacuum caused water to rise up a suction pipe through a non-return valve into the bottom of the vessel. Steam was then admitted again and the pressure drove the water in the vessel through a second non-return valve and up the delivery pipe. The major difficulties encountered with the Savery engine, the so-called 'Miners' Friend' which probably never actually operated in service at a mine, was that boilers capable of withstanding pressures of several atmospheres could not be easily made at that time and that the length of the suction pipe was limited to about 25ft,

making the engine unsuitable for deep drainage work. Certainly Savery's engine never entered widespread use and there are no surviving remains. Savery's work was not completely a dead end, however, as in the late nineteenth century the portable Pulsometer steam pump was developed on very similar principles. The main working part was an oscillating valve admitting steam alternately to two water chambers. The steam pressure acted directly on the surface of the water in the chamber and ejected it through a flexible hose. Pulsometer pumps can still be seen occasionally, their main use being for draining excavations and flooded mines, and ship salvage. Lightweight internal combustion engine pumps have largely supplanted them.

To return to the early development of the steam engine, it was in Papin's piston and cylinder experiments that the germ of the commercially successful machine lay. Papin did not pursue his experiments but Thomas Newcomen (1663–1729), an ironmonger of Dartmouth working on similar principles but almost certainly without knowledge of the Dutch scientist's work, was actively pushing towards a practical application. Newcomen was well aware of the critical drainage problems in the Cornish tin mines, and after pursuing experiments for some 15 years in an attempt to find a solution, he erected his first engine in 1712 (Illus 33). Curiously this was not in Cornwall but at a colliery near Dudley Castle, Worcestershire. It had a cylinder of 19in diameter, a stroke of 6ft and developed some 5½hp. A replica has been built at the Black Country Museum, Dudley (Illus 32) [SO 948917] and is steamed regularly.

The principle of operation was both simple and extremely reliable and, at least as important, no advanced technology was involved in the engine's manufacture or erection. An open-topped vertical cylinder contained a piston connected through a piston rod and chain to the arch head of a rocking beam. The 'piston ring' consisted of a disc of leather cupped upwards and kept pressed against the bore of the cylinder by a layer of water on top. From the end of the beam distant from the steam cylinder the pump rods were suspended. Below the cylinder was mounted a boiler which was little more than a tank of water with a fire beneath it and rather like a brewer's copper in appearance. When steam at slightly above atmospheric pressure was admitted into the cylinder, the piston was drawn upwards by the weight of the pump rods on the other end of the beam. At the same time any air in the cylinder was ejected through non-return valves. Closure of the steam inlet valve was followed by condensation of the steam in the cylinder by a jet of cold water which created a partial vacuum and allowed the unbalanced atmospheric pressure on the top of the piston to push it down, raise the pump rods and thus make a working stroke. The cycle was then repeated, the steam valve and injection cock being opened and closed by a plug rod also hung from the beam.

32 Replica Newcomen engine at the Black Country Museum, Dudley, West Midlands [SO 948917] *(Neil Cossons)*

Newcomen's initial design was thoroughly practical and was little altered for more than half a century. At first royalty payments had to be made to Savery, whose original patent covered all methods of raising water by fire, but after 1715, when Savery died, a group of speculators, including Newcomen himself until his death in 1729, acquired the rights and administered them until they expired in 1733. By the time of Newcomen's death his engine was in use throughout Britain and in Hungary, France, the Low Countries and possibly Germany and Spain. It is doubtful if Newcomen gained much, if any, financial benefit from his invention, which with the possible exception of Abraham Darby's perfection of coke smelting of iron ore, perhaps constituted the most important single technological factor in bringing man into the modern world.

One of the most important surviving memorials to Thomas Newcomen is the Hawkesbury engine, re-erected in the Royal Avenue Gardens, Dartmouth [SX 879515], and opened to the public in July 1964 to commemorate the 300th anniversary of its inventor's birth. The engine probably dates from the mid-1720s and is the oldest steam engine in existence. It was originally installed at Griff Colliery, Warwickshire, later moved to Measham, and in 1821 was installed on the bank of the Coventry Canal at Hawkesbury Junction [SP 363846], where it was used to raise water from a sump into the canal itself. The engine was occasionally worked until 1913 and in 1963 was presented to the Newcomen Society by its owners, the then British Transport Commission. Incidentally the canal-side site at Hawkesbury is in itself still well worth a visit as a relatively unspoilt junction with cast-iron bridges and boatmen's pub.

A number of modifications may be seen on the Hawkesbury engine, the most significant of which is the 'pickle-pot' condenser below the cylinder, an improvement in design to increase thermal efficiency and at the same time avoid an infringement of Watt's separate condenser patent, discussed below. Another surviving engine of Newcomen type stands at

NEWCOMEN'S ATMOSPHERIC ENGINE, 1712

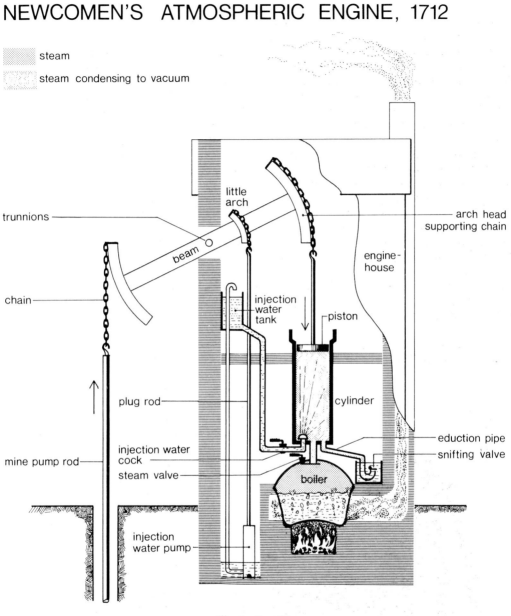

Illustration 33

Elsecar [SK 387999] South Yorkshire, where it was used for colliery drainage from 1787 until 1923. Again numerous modifications have been made from the original, including replacement of the wooden beam by a cast-iron one. Condensation of the steam, however, was effected within the working cylinder by the use of a jet of cold water in almost exactly the same manner which

Newcomen had applied in his first 1712 engine. The Elsecar engine (Illus 34) is now preserved on its original site by British Coal and may be visited by arrangement with the South Yorkshire Area office at Wath-upon-Dearne, Rotherham.

Before leaving the Newcomen type of atmospheric engine it is worthwhile considering some of its constructional details and the improvements which were made in its efficiency. The atmospheric engine was a thoroughly practical machine and the techniques necessary for its manufacture were all well known to the millwrights and similar men who were responsible for its erection. Only the cylinders caused any serious problem. Initially these were cast in brass and, as no means of accurately machining the bore existed, they were rubbed smooth on the inside with abrasives. Small wonder, therefore, that the cylinder was the most expensive single component of the engine, exceeding even the engine house in cost. A 1733 estimate for a Newcomen-type engine near Newcastle-upon-Tyne

34 The Elsecar engine, a Newcomen-type mine pumping engine preserved by British Coal at Elsecar near Barnsley, South Yorkshire [SK 387999]. Built in 1787 and the only eighteenth-century engine in the world on its original site, it worked regularly until 1923, and until 1945 for demonstration purposes. The cast iron beam replaced the wooden original in 1836. Nearby is the planned industrial village of Elsecar   (*British Coal*)

totalled £849, of which £150 was accounted for by the cylinder alone. By the 1740s cast-iron cylinders were becoming common and, although less efficient thermally because of their greater wall thickness, they were significantly cheaper in first cost.

John Smeaton (1724–92) was responsible for bringing about the greatest improvements in efficiency of the Newcomen engine, and a machine which he erected at Long Benton Colliery, Northumberland, in 1772 achieved a duty of 9.45 million foot-pounds of useful work per bushel (84lb) of coal. The average Newcomen engine only achieved 6 million foot-pounds. Despite his improvements, which were largely the result of careful design and manufacture, particularly of the cylinder, Smeaton's engine had a thermal efficiency of less than 1 per cent.

It was James Watt (1736–1819) who solved the problem of the fundamental inefficiency of Newcomen's steam engine. Watt, a first-class craftsman, was employed as an instrument maker in Glasgow University where in the winter of 1763–4 he was responsible for the repair of a model Newcomen engine which was

NEWCOMEN & WATT ENGINES
Showing method of condensing steam

steam

steam condensing to vacuum

NEWCOMEN
condenses in cylinder

WATT
has separate condenser

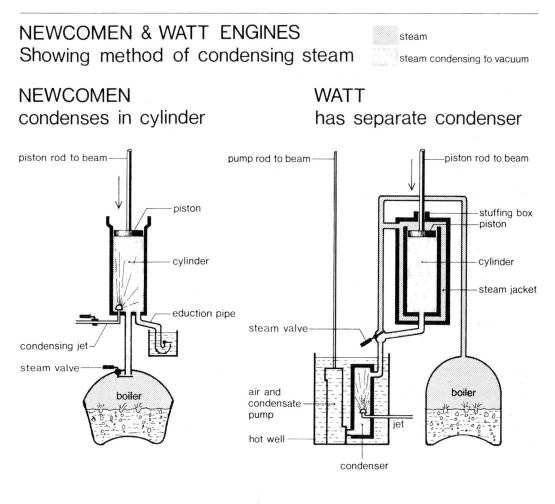

Illustration 35

faulty in operation. His investigations led to the realisation that enormous thermal losses resulted from having to raise and lower the temperature of the cylinder at each stroke, as steam was admitted and subsequently condensed. As he wrote later: 'I perceived that, in order to make the best use of steam, it was necessary – first, that the cylinder should be maintained always as hot as the steam which entered it; and, secondly, that when the steam was condensed, the water of which it was composed, and the injection itself, should be cooled down to 100°(F), or lower, where that was possible.' His solution was to connect a closed vessel, exhausted of air, to the steam cylinder by a

pipe. Steam rushed into this vessel, which was kept cool by cold water injection, and continued to do so until all had condensed. This was the basis of Watt's separate condenser (Illus 35), perhaps the greatest single improvement ever made in the efficiency of the steam engine. In order to keep the condenser free of air and the water resulting from injection and condensation, he used a pump connected to the beam, while the working cylinder was kept permanently hot by means of a steam jacket. To improve efficiency still further, steam instead of atmospheric air was used to press the piston down, the piston rod passing through a steam-tight gland or stuffing box in the cover of the cylinder.

Watt patented his separate condenser in 1769 and in 1773 entered into partnership with the Birmingham entrepreneur and industrialist Matthew Boulton (1728–1809), whose works he had once visited when on a journey to London. There were only eight year to run on the condenser patent but Watt successfully petitioned Parliament for an extension to 1800 and in 1776 completed his first two full-size engines, one for colliery drainage at Tipton, Staffordshire, and the other for blast furnace blowing at John Wilkinson's ironworks near Broseley in Shropshire. At his Broseley works two years earlier Wilkinson (1728–1808) had developed and patented a boring mill, initially for guns and then for steam engine cylinders. The significance of the boring mill in the success of the Watt engine cannot be overestimated as, for the first time, a large-diameter bore could be cut so accurately that 'a 72 inch cylinder would not be further from absolute truth than the thickness of a thin sixpence in the worst part'. A model of a water-powered multiple-spindle cylinder boring mill can be seen in the Science Museum, South Kensington. There too are some of the most important relics of Watt's early career, including the

cylinder and condenser which he probably used in his original experiments and the contents of his garret workshop from Heathfield, Birmingham. The workshop, containing some 6,000 separate items, was left undisturbed from 1819, when Watt died, until its removal in 1924 to the museum, where it has been set up in a replica room. The model Newcomen engine on which Watt carried out his earliest work on steam power is preserved in the Hunterian Museum at Glasgow University. A Boulton & Watt engine of 1779, the Smethwick engine, is on display in the Museum of Science & Industry, Newhall Street, Birmingham 3, and steamed regularly.

The first Boulton & Watt engines were an immediate success, consuming less than one-third of the coal used by the Newcomen types commonly in use, and as a result bringing enquiries from all over the country. The demand was greatest in Cornwall, where coal was expensive, so that within a few years all the atmospheric engines there had been replaced. The basis for installation of a Boulton & Watt engine was to charge a royalty equal to one-third of the saving in the cost of fuel as compared with that of a 'common' or

36   An original Boulton & Watt engine

atmospheric engine. Two engines at Poldice Mine, Cornwall, were tested and used as the standard. To register the number of strokes of the engine, from which the premium payments were calculated, a pendulum-operated counter in a locked box was attached to the beam.

Further improvements were devised by Watt, with the active encouragement of Matthew Boulton who fully appreciated the potential market for efficient and reliable steam engines. In 1782, three important advances in design were patented by Watt. The first was to make the engine double-acting, that is to apply steam alternately on each face of the piston instead of only to the top as had been the previous practice. Thus twice the power could be developed from the same cylinder volume. The second used the steam expansively and, when perfected, resulted in considerable savings of fuel. The principle was that by closing the inlet valve to the cylinder when the piston had completed only a part of its stroke, the steam already in the cylinder would still do useful work by expanding and pushing the piston through the remainder of the stroke, but with diminishing force. Although less work would be done, still less steam would be used, hence the fuel saving. At first the economics resulting were very small, but as steam pressures increased, the practice of expansive working became all-important, forming the basis for the highly efficient compound engines of the late nineteenth century.

Watt's third 1782 patent was a second best, an attempt to circumvent another idea patented two years earlier and possibly stolen from him by one of his own workmen. The idea of developing the steam engine to provide rotary power and thus drive machinery was exercising the minds of several engineers in the 1770s and early 1780s. The far-seeing Boulton was well aware of the huge new market that the 'rotative' steam engine could tap and pressed Watt hard to produce a satisfactory design. It is characteristic of the two that Boulton, the enthusiastic businessman, should write in 1781 '. . . the people in London, Manchester, and Birmingham are *Steam mill mad . . .*' and that

the dour Watt should grumble in the following year '. . . surely the devils of rotations is afoot'. The problem was to adapt the simple reciprocating movements of the beam engine to produce rotary power. Nowadays one would imagine nothing could be simpler than the use of the common crank to connect the end of the beam to a rotating shaft, and even in Watt's time the crank was a well known mechanism in everyday use on the foot lathe and spinning wheel. What was not appreciated, however, was the fact that the variable stroke of the beam engine, which Watt at first feared would wreck any attempt to adapt it to rotary motion, would be controlled and regulated by using a connecting rod, crank and flywheel. Unfortunately for Watt another engineer, James Pickard of Birmingham, patented the crank first in 1780 after using it to replace an unsatisfactory rack-and-pinion drive to a rotating shaft. Watt held numerous patents himself and suffered throughout his life from others infringing them. Instead of contesting Pickard's patent, he thought it politic to devise a substitute. The result was the sun-and-planet or epicyclic gear in which the 'planet' wheel, fixed rigidly to the end of the connecting rod, is made to move round the perimeter of a 'sun' wheel keyed to the driven shaft. A property of this gear is that the flywheel will revolve twice for every double stroke of the piston, something of an advantage with the early and slow-moving engines. The gear was used until 1802 although Boulton & Watt built engines with cranks before and after the expiry of Pickard's patent in 1794.

Two further Watt inventions are worthy of note, particularly as they cover features familiar on almost all the beam engines surviving today. In 1784 Watt solved the problem of a satisfactory connection to transmit the simple up-and-down movement of the piston rod to the end of the beam, which described a segment of an arc. The 'parallel motion' devised by Watt combined the three-bar motion and the pantograph in a most elegant way. Watt himself stated that he was more proud of this invention than any of his others.

37,38 Woolf compound beam engine at the Ram Brewery, Wandsworth [TQ 256747], built by Wentworth & Sons in 1835   (*Neil Cossons*)

To ensure steady motion of the engine under variable load conditions, Watt introduced, in 1787, the conical pendulum centrifugal governor, consisting of two balls which flew outwards as speed increased to move a sleeve which by linkage controlled a butterfly valve in the steam pipe. Watt neither claimed this invention as his own nor attempted to patent it, as it had already been used in flour mills to regulate the speed and distance apart of millstones.

With the advent of rotary power generated by steam, industry was on the verge of a major technological breakthrough. By 1800, when Watt's partnership with Boulton ended and the patent on the separate condenser expired, 496 engines had been built, of which 308 were rotative. A few of these were rated at 40hp but most had an output of between 15 and 20hp, well within the capacities of the major prime mover in use at that time, the

waterwheel. The main advantages of the steam engine, however, were its freedom from siting problems and unreliability of water flow, which restricted the widespread application of water power. Indeed Matthew Boulton's first interest in the steam engine was aroused by the lack of water for driving waterwheels in summer, the 'thirsty season'.

The distribution of Boulton & Watt engines, drawn up from the very full records of the firm's trading now housed in the Birmingham Reference Library, provides an indication of the impact of steam power on industry in the last quarter of the eighteenth century. It shows a wide dispersion both geographically and in terms of the variety of industries in which the engines were used. The poor representation of Watt engines at collieries is to some extent misleading, however, as the coal industry had actively taken up the Newcomen engine for pumping purposes and, as fuel costs were not an important factor, there was little incentive to change. Thus in the Northumberland-Durham coalfield, which had fifty-seven

39 Builder's plate of the 1835 engine at the Ram Brewery   (*Neil Cossons*)

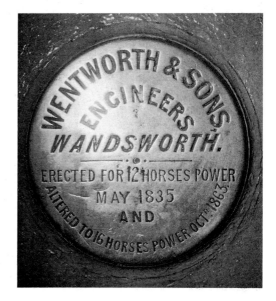

Newcomen-type engines in 1769, only six Boulton & Watt engines were in use by 1800.

Those industries able to take greatest advantage of the rotative engine did so enthusiastically. Cotton mills, woollen and worsted mills, flax mills, textile finishing works, forges and foundries, metal workshops, pot banks and glassworks, corn mills, breweries and distilleries, canals and waterworks were all using steam to some extent by 1800. Over one-third, 114 engines, were in use in the textile industry, and cotton alone accounted for 92 of these. Next were ironworks, with a total of 37 engines, followed by collieries with 33, mainly for pumping, while corn mills, breweries and distilleries together employed 39 engines. As Watt had a virtual monopoly of steam power until 1800, these figures represent fairly accurately the relative degree of penetration of steam power into industrial activity in Britain. The geographical distribution, shown in Illus 40, is just as interesting, illustrating the early establishment and relative importance of the

industrial areas we know today. Only Shropshire and Cornwall, where the iron and tin industries respectively have declined, are over-represented in terms of today's pattern of industrial distribution. A total of fifty-five engines were in use in Lancashire, largely in the cotton industry. The next highest total, of forty-one, was in Middlesex, demonstrating the enormous, and often overlooked, significance of London as an industrial centre.

The beam engine enjoyed greatest popularity for driving machinery between 1800 and 1860, but in both its rotative and non-rotative forms it was in vogue for water and sewage pumping until the early 1900s. Few non-pumping engines are still in active use, although a number are preserved. An early example of a Watt engine, dating from 1788 and complete with sun-and-planet gear, wooden beam and centrifugal governor, may be seen in the Science Museum, South Kensington. A pair of beam engines still in occasional use drive mashing and milling machinery in the Ram Brewery, Wandsworth (Illus 37, 38 and 39) [TQ 256747]. Built by Wentworth &

Sons in 1835 and 1867 these compound engines exhibit all the classic features, including slide valves, lattice eccentric rods (introduced by Murdock in 1799), cast-iron beams, timber-lagged cylinders and the immaculate cleanliness so typical of steam engine maintenance.

The mechanical fascination and tremendous visual impact of the large beam engine has led to numerous examples being preserved *in situ*, although all too few are in steam. At Stretham in Cambridgeshire [TL 517730] one survives for fen drainage. Installed in 1831 by the Butterley Company of Derbyshire, it has a single cylinder of 39in diameter and 8ft stroke and developed 105hp at 13 to 16rpm. A scoopwheel acting, in effect, like a waterwheel in reverse lifted some 30 tons of water at each revolution. The original wheel was 28ft in diameter but this was increased to 33ft in 1848. The engine last operated in 1941 and is now under the care of the Stretham Engine Preservation Trust.

The robust reliability of the beam engine made it popular with water supply companies and for sewage pumping, and in these roles it reached a high degree of development by the latter years of the nineteenth century. Two late engines of this type are preserved at Papplewick, Nottinghamshire [SK 582522]. Built by James Watt & Co in 1884, these rotative engines with their 46in diameter cylinders and 7ft 6in stroke, each raised 1,500,000 gallons of water per day from the Bunter sandstone to supply the city of Nottingham. The iron pillars supporting the engine are covered in intricate decoration, which recurs throughout the interior of the engine house in tilework and stained glass windows. The whole effect is heightened by the landscaped setting and ornamental pool beloved of waterworks companies at this period. Also preserved in the East Midlands are four sewage pumping engines at Abbey Lane, Leicester [SK 589066], built in 1891 by Messrs Gimson, a local firm. They form the centrepiece of the Leicestershire Museum of Technology, Abbey Pumping Station, Abbey Lane, Leicester. In Tyne & Wear, Ryhope pumping station near Sunderland [NZ 403524],

with its two 1868 rotative compound engines by Hawthorns of Newcastle, is under the care of the Ryhope Pumping Engines Preservation Fund, while in Hampshire, Portsmouth City Museums have restored two sewage pumping engines of 1887 at Eastney [SZ 674993].

A specialised, and in many cases very large, type of beam engine was the Cornish pump (Illus 42) developed by Richard Trevithick (1771–1833) from an engine erected in 1812 at Wheal Prosper tin mine at Gwithian in Cornwall. The Cornish engine operated at a much higher pressure than contemporary Watt engines, usually about 50lb per sq in, and used expansive working to gain high efficiency. It was a single-acting, usually non-rotative beam engine in which steam applied above the piston lifted, through the beam, pump rods in the mine shaft. The sequence of operation was then as follows:

With the piston at the bottom of the cylinder the equilibrium valve was opened, allowing steam to be transferred from the upper to the lower side of the piston as the unbalanced weight of the pump rods caused the piston to ascend.

When the piston was at the top of the stroke the equilibrium valve was closed and steam admitted above the piston.

At the same time the eduction valve at the bottom of the cylinder opened to the condenser.

Thus the power stroke was effected using steam pressure on top of the piston and a partial vacuum below caused by condensation of steam in the condenser.

Cornish engines were extensively used for draining mines and also found widespread favour for water supply pumping and other drainage applications, as in the Severn railway tunnel. The increase in thermal efficiency over Watt engines was enormous with 125 million foot/pounds per bushel claimed in 1834 from an engine with an 80in diameter cylinder as compared with the 20 millions normally attained by the low pressure engines.

As their name suggests, they were most

DISTRIBUTION OF BOULTON & WATT
STEAM ENGINES, 1775-1800

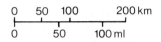

Each dot represents 1 engine

Illustration 40

numerous in Cornwall, where five engines were preserved by the Cornish Engines Preservation Society and are now in the care of the National Trust. These include one of the largest, built in 1892, with a 90in diameter cylinder, at Taylor's shaft, East Pool [SW 674416], and an early rotative winding engine of 1840 at Levant Mine [SW 375346], six miles from Land's End. In Scotland the Cornish engine at Preston-grange Colliery, East Lothian [NT 374737], built by Harvey & Co of Hayle, Cornwall, in 1874, is being restored to form the centre of a historical site devoted to the Scottish coal industry. Last worked in 1954, this pumping engine has a steam cylinder 70in in diameter with a stroke of 12ft.

Newcomen atmospheric beam engine

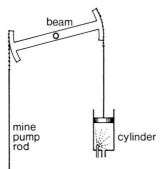

Developed for mine pumping, the Newcomen engine used the pressure of the atmosphere for its power stroke. A partial vacuum was created in the cylinder beneath the piston by condensing the steam with a cold water jet

Watt single-acting beam engine

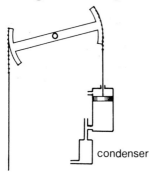

In Watt's engine the efficiency was improved by condensing the steam in a separate vessel – the separate condenser – thus avoiding the alternate heating and cooling of the cylinder. The engine was still only for pumping

Watt double-acting rotative beam engine

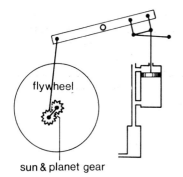

In the rotative engine – the first heat engine to drive machinery – a number of new features were introduced. The piston had steam pressure applied to both top and bottom, making the engine double-acting. A linkage – the parallel motion – connected piston rod to beam. The other end of the beam drove a flywheel through a connecting rod and sun-and-planet gear

Illustration 41

Single-cylinder rotative beam engine

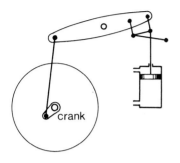

After about 1800 the Common crank was almost universally used for the drive from the beam and connecting rod. Beam engines of this type were built in large numbers for driving all types of factory machinery down to the 1880s

Woolf compound beam engine

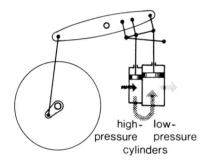

high- low-
pressure pressure
cylinders

Efficiency was still further improved by compound expansion using a high- and low-pressure cylinder both at the same end of the beam. Woolf compound engines were widely used in water pumping stations and to a lesser extent in small factories

Cornish beam engine

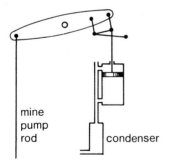

mine pump rod

condenser

The Cornish engine was a highly efficient single-acting development of the non-rotative beam pumping engine, and was used extensively in tin mines. Developed by Richard Trevithick it used high-pressure steam, expansive working and condensation to obtain maximum economy

Illustration 42

McNaught compound beam engine

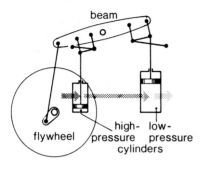

Patented in 1845, the McNaught principle consisted initially of the addition of a high-pressure cylinder to the flywheel end of an existing beam engine, thus deriving compound expansion and reducing stress. Later many large beam engines were built in this form

Grasshopper engine

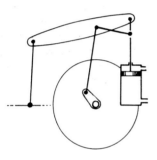

The grasshopper engine was usually small and compact, based on a single bed-plate, allowing easy installation. The beam was pivoted at one end instead of at the centre, and the drive to the connecting rod was taken off at an intermediate point near the piston rod end

Maudslay table engine

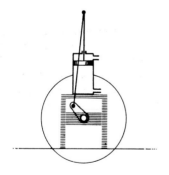

Maudslay's table engine also had the advantage of compactness and ease of installation. The beam was dispensed with altogether and a direct connection made between the vertical piston rod and the crankshaft mounted at a low level below the cylinder. It was widely used as a small factory power unit

Illustration 43

Single-cylinder vertical engine

In the single-cylinder vertical engine the drive was similar but the crankshaft was mounted vertically above the cylinder. The type was used in factories and mills and for colliery winding particularly in the North East

Single-cylinder inverted vertical engine

The inverted vertical single-cylinder engine, introduced in the 1840s, was rarely large. The type was particularly common for small factories and, with reverse gear, for marine applications. Later versions had enclosed crankcases and forced lubrication

Single-cylinder horizontal engine

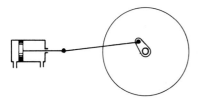

Perhaps the most common simple type of steam engine, the single-cylinder horizontal was built in large numbers in the second half of the nineteenth century. Most had slide valves, were non-condensing and the compact cast iron bed made them easy to install

Illustration 44

Horizontal tandem-compound engine

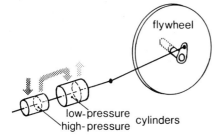

A logical development from the single-cylinder horizontal was the tandem-compound in which high- and low-pressure cylinders were mounted one behind the other on the same piston rod. Highly sophisticated, tandem compounds of medium power output were built for textile mills

Horizontal cross-compound engine

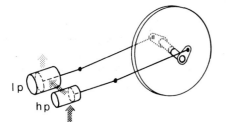

Another means of compounding the horizontal engine was to have high- and low-pressure cylinders side by side driving each end of the crankshaft. Many mill engines were of this type, the drive being taken off the flywheel rim between the two cranks

Horizontal triple-expansion engine

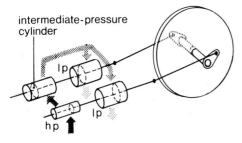

A development of the compound principle involved three stages of expansion. Steam passed from a high-pressure to an intermediate-pressure cylinder on the other piston rod and thence to a pair of equal diameter low-pressure cylinders, one on each side of the engine

Horizontal twin tandem-compound engine

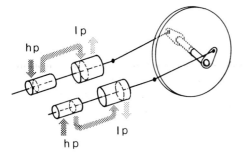

The twin tandem-compound consisted simply of two tandem compounds driving a single crankshaft. Like the other compound and multiple expansion engines, this type became highly developed for powering textile mills

Illustration 45

Vertical compound engine

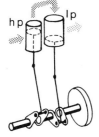

In its simplest form the vertical compound was used mainly in ships, but a small enclosed-crankcase high-speed type, developed from the end of the nineteenth century, became popular for generating electricity

Vertical triple-expansion engine

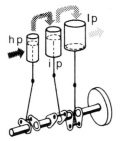

Vertical triple-expansion engines were almost universally used in large ships before the introduction of steam turbines. On land they became the generally accepted successors to beam engines for water and sewage pumping

Twin-cylinder oscillating engine

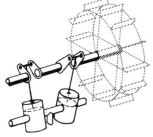

The oscillating engine, in which rocking cylinders were mounted on trunnions formed from the steam inlet and exhaust pipes, had no connecting rods, the piston rod being attached directly to the crank. Their compactness made them particularly suited for use in paddle steamers

Side-lever engine

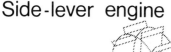

The side-lever engine with its low centre of gravity was designed for marine application and was used extensively in paddle steamers before 1850. It was basically a beam engine with the beam pivoted at a low level

Illustration 46

Illustration 49

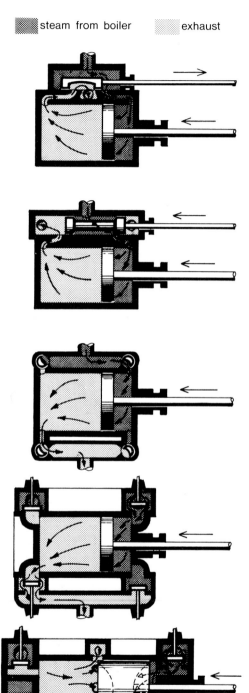

47   Valves of the 1838 Maudslay beam engine at Kew Bridge Waterworks, Brentford [TQ 188780] (*Neil Cossons*)

48   Parallel motion of the Maudslay engine at Kew Bridge   (*Neil Cossons*)

STEAM ENGINE VALVES

Slide valve

The slide valve, invented in 1799 by William Murdock (1754–1839), consisted of a metal box sliding on a flat face in which were cut the steam inlet and exhaust ports. Steam was usually admitted at the ends and exhausted through a central port under the hollow box valve, as shown in the example illustrated. Steam pressure thus helped retain the valve in contact with the face.

Piston valve

Like the slide valve, the piston valve was a single unit controlling steam inlet and exhaust. It consisted of a pair of pistons on a single spindle moving in a cylindrical bore that had inlet and exhaust ports in its sides. As the valve spindle moved backwards and forwards in the steam chest, the appropriate ports were uncovered to admit and exhaust steam. Both slide and piston valves had the disadvantage of steam being admitted and exhausted through the same channels, with consequent loss of efficiency resulting from alternate heating and cooling.

Corliss valve

The Corliss valve had none of these disadvantages, as a separate inlet and exhaust valve was provided at each end of the cylinder. Developed by the American George H. Corliss (1817–88) and patented in 1849, this type of valve became widely used on large mill engines. Each valve consisted of a barrel that partially rotated in a bored chamber to uncover the steam port. The inlet valves were opened by the valve rods against a dashpot. At the cut-off point the valve was released by trip gear to be closed rapidly by the dashpot.

Drop valve

Drop valves had turned circular faces fitting into valve seats in the steam chests. Valve and seat were ground together to ensure that they were steamtight. There were four valves per cylinder, the inlet valves being raised to admit steam and dropped by a trip gear to provide instantaneous admission cut off. Both Corliss and drop valves gave very economical steam consumption and steady governing, essential in driving textile machinery.

Uniflow engine

In the uniflow engine only admission valves were provided, as exhausting the steam was achieved by the piston at the end of its stroke uncovering a ring of ports in the wall of the cylinder. Although there were manufacturing difficulties with the uniflow type, it was highly efficient because there was no alternate heating and cooling of the cylinder ends by steam being admitted and exhausted through them.

TYPES OF BOILER
CUT OPEN TO SHOW INTERIORS

Haystack

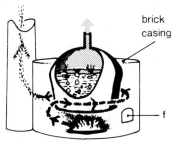

brick casing

f

▢ steam

▢ water

➤ flow of hot combustion gases through boiler

➤ flow of hot combustion gases in brick flues along outer surface of boiler, giving extra heating

➤ smoke to chimney

f   firehole door(s)

Wagon

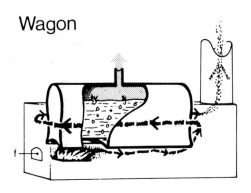

f

Cornish
1 furnace tube

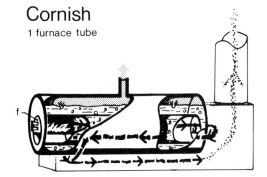

f

Lancashire
2 furnace tubes

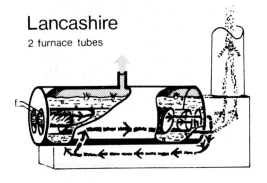

f

Fire-tube

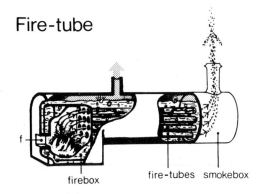

f

firebox   fire-tubes smokebox

Illustration 50

Crofton on the Kennet & Avon Canal in Wiltshire [SU 262623] has the oldest engine in the world still to operate on steam (Illus 52). The pumping station was begun in 1803 and designed to supply the 35 mile section of the canal between Bedwyn and Seend with water lifted 40ft out of Wilton Water. The first engine began pumping in November 1809. It was built by Boulton & Watt in 1801 for the West India Dock, London, but was diverted to the canal company in 1802. On the initiative of John Rennie, the engineer for the canal, a more powerful engine was ordered from Boulton & Watt and began work in 1812. Originally both engines were of the single-acting atmospheric type operating at about 5lb per sq in steam pressure and using Watt patented separate condensers, but in 1844, in an effort to increase efficiency, they were converted to the Cornish cycle of operation by Messrs Harvey of Hayle, Cornwall, with new boilers providing steam at 20lb per sq in. Later, in 1844, a Sims Combined Engine was installed to replace the 1801 machine, but this gave considerable trouble and was rebuilt in 1905 as a simple condensing engine, with a new 42in cylinder. The 1812 Boulton & Watt engine has been restored to working order and is doing the work for which it was originally installed. It can be seen every Sunday and is in steam on selected weekends throughout the year. Restoration of the second engine is in progress.

The higher steam pressures at which the Cornish engine operated demanded stronger boilers (Illus 50) than the 'haystack' or 'wagon' types which were used with Newcomen and Watt engines. The earliest haystack boilers were made of copper with a lead top, but after about 1725 hammered wrought-iron plates were used. The wagon boiler used by Watt had a similar cross-section to the haystack but was elongated to give more heating surface. Its rectangular shape was also easier to make. Neither was suitable for pressures in excess of 10lb per sq in, so about 1812 Trevithick developed a cylindrical boiler with a grate set at one end of an internal tube running through its length. At the rear the hot gases divided and

passed forward in brick flues along each side before returning beneath the bottom to the chimney. These Cornish boilers, as they came to be called, generated steam at some 50lb per sq in and were widely adopted as high-pressure steam engines spread. They remained popular until the introduction of the Lancashire boiler (Illus 52) after 1844. In that year William (later Sir William) Fairbairn (1789–1874) and John Hetherington of Manchester patented a cylindrical boiler with two flues, devised, as Fairbairn stated, 'with a view to alternate firing in the two furnaces in order to prevent the formation of smoke', but also, of course, providing a substantially increased heating surface. Lancashire boilers are still in common use and examples may be seen in association with most of the preserved engines already mentioned. The Cornish boiler has almost

51 East Pool winding engine, Camborne, Cornwall [SW 675416] built in 1887 by Holman Bros and one of the last of its type built; the engine is preserved by the National Trust

(Ray Bishop)

52   Crofton pumping station [SU 262623] on the Kennet & Avon Canal   *(Neil Cossons)*

completely disappeared, but Trevithick's 1812 original is preserved at the Science Museum, South Kensington. Many boiler shells of both Cornish and Lancashire types may be seen converted for use as oil storage tanks.

The opening years of the nineteenth century saw several alternatives to the beam engine introduced to achieve greater thermal and mechanical efficiency, higher speeds and simplicity of erection. This last factor was of some importance as the cumbersome beam engine required skilled engineers to assemble it on site, was not easily adaptable to the often rapid rate of development of factories, could not easily be resited and took up a lot of space. Thus relatively portable self-contained direct-acting engines, dispensing with the heavy rocking beam between connecting rod and crankshaft, began to appear in increasing numbers. An early form was the table engine (Illus 43) introduced in 1807 by Henry Maudslay (1771–1831) and this was followed after about 1825 by numerous designs of the soon to be popular horizontal engine having a single cylinder, slide bars and crankshaft bearings on a cast-iron bedplate of box-girder section. In the table engine the vertical cylinder of the beam engine was retained but the piston rod drove a crankshaft beneath by means of two return connecting rods. Its portability made it popular until the middle of the nineteenth century for driving workshops, but it has now almost completely disappeared. An example may be seen at the Science Museum.

The horizontal engine was introduced as early as 1802 by Richard Trevithick as one of a number of his experimental designs using high-pressure steam. Another high-pressure design by Trevithick, but employing a vertical cylinder, is preserved in the Science Museum. The horizontal engine (Illus 44) was little exploited until after 1830 and did not become widespread until the 1850s. After this date, however, simple single-cylinder horizontal engines were produced in large numbers for use in breweries, saw mills, small engineering shops and many places where an easily maintained power unit was required. Firms such as Tangye of Birmingham made standard designs in a variety of sizes which could be installed either as a single cylinder version or with two identical cylinders, one on each side of the flywheel. An example of this latter type dating from 1885 used to power the Port of Bristol Authority workshop at Underfall Yard, Bristol [ST 572722] and is now preserved *in situ*.

The direct-acting vertical engine (Illus 44) with the crankshaft above the cylinder was patented in 1800 by Phineas Crowther of Newcastle-upon-Tyne but its only widespread application seems to have been for colliery winding in the Northumberland and Durham coalfield. One remaining example is preserved at Beamish [NZ 212549] under the care of the North of England Open Air Museum. The inverted vertical engine (Illus 44) with its crankshaft immediately below the cylinder was introduced in the 1840s by James Nasmyth (1808–90) as a logical derivation of his steam hammer design of 1839. It achieved considerable popularity as a small power source, particularly in the marine application of driving screw propellers. Various types of supports for the cylinder can be found, ranging from a single-side cast-iron frame with or without a turned steel column at the open side to a symmetrical 'A' shaped casting. Later versions, built in large numbers well into this century, have the connecting rod and crankshaft completely enclosed, in the same manner as a motor car engine, and operate at high speeds with pressure lubrication.

Despite this profusion of new engine layouts during the nineteenth century, the beam engine continued to be built with various modifications and one or two ingenious adaptations. One of these was the grasshopper engine (Illus 43) patented in 1803 by William Fremantle, the same principle being employed by Oliver Evans

in America at about the same time. In this design the piston rod was connected by a pin to one end of the beam while the other end was supported on two long back links which allowed it to rock backwards and forwards. The centre of the beam was constrained by radius arms and the drive to the connecting rod taken off at a point between the centre and the piston rod link. The major advantage of the engine was one of compactness. Another beam engine variant, introduced in 1805 by Matthew Murray (1765–1826), had the beam centred below the cylinder and crankshaft. Side rods connected the piston rod to one end of the beam while the other had a connecting rod driving upwards on to the crank. Its low centre of gravity made the engine (Illus 46) popular in paddle steamers, and an example may be seen in the tug *Reliant*, built in 1907 by J. T. Eltringham & Co of South Shields, and on view in the Neptune Hall of the National Maritime Museum at Greenwich.

By far the most significant advance in steam engine design in the nineteenth century was the introduction of the compound or multiple cylinder expansion principle, initially applied to the beam engine and later providing the basis for a wide variety of highly efficient direct-acting engines. As early as 1781 Jonathan Hornblower (1753–1815) had patented an engine with two cylinders in which the steam was introduced to the first direct from the boiler and was exhausted into a second cylinder of larger diameter where it continued to expand and do useful work on the piston. It was not found to be significantly more efficient than the contemporary Watt engine, but in 1804 Arthur Woolf (1776–1837) revived the idea using high-pressure steam. Although reasonably successful, Woolf's engines (Illus 42) were not widely adopted, being more expensive and complicated than the Cornish engines of Trevithick with which they were compared. In 1845, however, William McNaught of Glasgow introduced an ingenious and highly successful method (Illus 43) of compounding by adding a smaller diameter high-pressure cylinder on the crank side of the beam of a conventional beam engine, between its centre and the connecting rod. This avoided overstressing the beam and, by replacing the old low-pressure boiler with a high-pressure one, both power and economy were improved without the need for a completely new engine. By the 1860s compound beam engines were widespread and new engines were being built in the Woolf manner with cylinders side-by-side driving on to the same end of the beam. Compounding enabled steam to be expanded in the cylinders to many times its original volume with minimal losses from condensation and leakage. The Ryhope engines mentioned above are typical compound beam engines.

With high-pressure direct-acting engines, compounding (Illus 45) was still more successful, eventually being achieved in three and even four stages through cylinders of successively increasing volume. The triple-expansion type with three cylinders mounted vertically and driving on to the crankshaft below found favour for marine use and also as a replacement for beam engines in water pumping stations. Two of the largest land-based triples ever built are at Kempton Park Waterworks, Hounslow [TQ 110709], now out of use but to be preserved. They were built by Worthington Simpson of Newark and date from the 1920s.

By the end of the nineteenth century the big textile mills of Lancashire and Yorkshire were demanding even higher horse-powers to drive their vast numbers of machines and a specialised type of engine, the mill engine (Illus 45) was developed to satisfy this need. These engines were almost invariably horizontal compounds and some were designed to produce as much as 4,000hp. The two most popular layouts were the tandem-compound in which the high- and low-pressure cylinders lay one behind the other with a common piston rod, and the cross-compound in which the high-pressure cylinder drove one end of the crankshaft and the low-pressure the other. Between the two was the flywheel with its broad face cast in grooves for the cotton drive-ropes that powered the mill. The engine of Dee Mill, Shaw, near Rochdale [SD 945093], is an example of the ultimate in mill engine design. It is a twin tandem-compound, that is it has two piston rods, each with a high- and low-pressure cylinder driving each end of the crankshaft. Built in 1906 by Scott & Hodgson Ltd of Guide Bridge, the 'Dee' engine has two 18in diameter high-pressure cylinders with Corliss semi-rotary valves and two low-pressure cylinders of 42in with piston valves. Between 1967 and the sale of the mill by Courtaulds in 1982 the engine was cared for and regularly steamed by the Northern Mill Engine Society, an organisation that has done more than any other to ensure the survival of the breed. But despite being Scheduled as an Ancient Monument, removal of the boilers, followed by demolition of the mill itself in 1983, leaves the future of the engine uncertain.

The society also runs the Bolton Steam Museum in the engine house of No 3 mill, Atlas Mills, Chorley Old Road, Bolton [SD 701101]. The museum is a monument to the enterprise and enthusiasm of a small group of people who since 1966 have dismantled and saved from destruction more than twenty stationary engines from mills in Lancashire and Yorkshire. Amongst them are an 1840 twin beam engine from Crosfield Mill, Wardle, near Rochdale, two horizontal tandem-compounds of 1896 and 1902, an 1884 twin tandem-compound from Fern Mill, Shaw, near Oldham, and a beam engine compounded on the McNaught principle in 1919. Several of these engines are in steam at the museum on selected days throughout the summer. At Trencherfield Mill [SD 579052] the society has assisted Wigan Borough Council to preserve and steam one of the largest surviving steam engines in the country, a 2,500hp horizontal four-cylinder triple-expansion engine (Illus 45) built in 1907 by J. & A. Wood of Bolton. It is open to the public as part of the Wigan Pier project. On a smaller scale, but in steam five days a week is the 1894 tandem-compound by Roberts of Nelson which powers the looms of Queen Street Mill, Harle Syke, Burnley [SD 868349]. Mill engines are also in steam at the Science Museum, South Kensington, the Greater Manchester Museum of Science & Industry and the

Birmingham Museum of Science & Industry.

In the 1880s a new demand arose for engines to power electrical dynamos. At first slow-speed engines were used to drive dynamos by belt but the advantages of direct coupling led to the introduction of a specialised type of engine capable of running at speeds in the region of 500rpm. A number of these were made single-acting to avoid the reversal of load on the crankpin and thus eliminate the knocking which would develop unless impractically small bearing clearances were used. The most successful and widely adopted design of this type resulted from patents taken out in 1884 and 1885 by Peter William Willans (1851–92) for a central valve engine in which the steam was distributed by a piston valve inside the hollow piston rod. The valve was worked by an eccentric on the crankpin and the engine, which was a vertical, had a totally enclosed crankcase with splash lubrication. Simple, compound and triple-expansion types were made in large numbers and ultimately in sizes up to 2,500hp. Although extremely economical, they have almost completely disappeared from use and examples are much more difficult to find than are beam engines. Willans engines can be seen in the Science Museum, South Kensington and the Guinness Museum, St James's Gate, Dublin.

The introduction of the steam turbine in the 1880s and its rapid development in the following years rendered the Willans engine obsolete by the early 1900s, but another type of high-speed reciprocating engine was also rivalling it by that date. This came from the Bellis & Morcom company of Birmingham, which introduced a double-acting enclosed vertical engine in the mid-1890s in both compound and triple-expansion form, largely

53 Crossness sewage pumping station [TQ 484811]. Steam power was used extensively for water and sewage pumping in the great Victorian sanitary improvement schemes *(Royal Commission on Historical Monuments, England)*

for powering small generators. It had forced lubrication and was extremely efficient. Large horse power versions were built, up to 2,500hp, but these could not compete with turbines. In small sizes, however, the Bellis & Morcom type of engine, made by a variety of manufacturers, is still used particularly in hospitals and laundries where low-pressure steam is required for heating or process work. By generating steam at a high pressure and feeding it first through an engine, electricity can be generated at very small additional cost.

Before turning to the steam turbine and its development, let us consider a number of other types of reciprocating engine that may frequently be encountered by the industrial archaeologist in a variety of applications. So far we have dealt mainly with large engines designed for powering factories or major installations such as water pumping stations, but numerous steam engines were produced after about 1870, and well into the present century, to provide relatively small amounts of power at almost any point where it was needed. The most popular of these was based on the locomotive type of boiler on which the engine itself was mounted. Its most mobile form was the traction engine, consisting of a single-cylinder, or twin-cylinder compound, horizontal engine providing power both to move the engine and to drive machinery such as threshing machines. A similar type, known as the portable engine, was not self-propelled but had to be towed to where it was needed by horses or a traction engine. It was used mainly for powering saw mills and electricity generation at fairgrounds. A semi-portable form, although without wheels, consisting of a boiler with the engine mounted on it, found favour in saw mills as well as flour mills and in small, often rurally situated factories, where a cheaply run engine of moderate horsepower was needed. A variation, known as the undertype, had the engine placed beneath the boiler in the same position as the cylinders of a railway locomotive. Rarely did these portable types of engine exceed 150hp.

The patenting of a practical steam turbine in 1884 by C. A. Parsons (1854–1931) was one of the most significant events in the evolution of heat engines as prime movers, and marked the beginning of the end for the reciprocating steam engine. It also brought to fruition the dreams of scientists and engineers over many centuries who had been fascinated with this problem of rotary power. Between 1784 and 1884 nearly 200 patents were taken out in Britain alone for steam and gas turbines, some of them anticipating in principle designs which were ultimately to be successful. In the turbine the steam, instead of being used under pressure against a piston, is set in motion, and the conversion of this pressure energy into velocity or kinetic energy produces the rotation of the turbine shaft. Parsons* success lay in his appreciation of the problem of expanding the steam effectively through the turbine, a problem which he solved by dividing the pressure drop into many small stages, at each of which was an elemental turbine. Each of these turbines consisted of a ring of blades mounted on a long shaft, the rotor and the stator, which carried similar rows of blades projecting inwards between the rows of blades on the shaft. Steam admitted at one end of the stator flowed parallel to the axis of the turbine, that is axially, between the blades of the rotor and stator alternately, eventually exhausting to atmosphere. In order to eliminate end thrust on the rotor bearings Parsons arranged a central admission point for the steam, whence it flowed through two identical sets of blades towards each end of the turbine.

The incentive behind the development of the steam turbine, like that behind the high-speed reciprocating engine, was the need for an effective power source for electricity generation, and in this role it proved an immediate success. Indeed Parsons first turbine was direct-coupled to a 7.5kW dynamo using steam at 80lb per sq in and running at a speed of 18,000rpm. The rate at which improvements were

*Parsons issued instructions that the apostrophe should be omitted in cases like this, preferring to offend those who knew than suffer those who did not.

made by the original inventor was remarkable, and by 1900 1,250kW units were in service, rivalling in power output and efficiency the best reciprocating engine generators. In 1897 the first practical marine application of the turbine was made by Parsons in the experimental *Turbinia* fitted with three axial flow turbines direct-coupled to three screw propellers. Steam from the boiler was led first to the high-pressure turbine on the starboard side, then passed to the intermediate-pressure turbine on the port side and next to a low-pressure turbine placed amidships before being exhausted to the condenser. A separate turbine on the central shaft drove the vessel astern. The spectacular introduction of the marine turbine to the assembled navies of the world at the 1897 Spithead review, when *Turbinia* raced up and down between the ranks of ships at an unprecedented 34.5 knots, established beyond all doubt its supremacy over the reciprocating engine. Exactly ten years later the Cunard liner *Mauretania* of 38,000 tons attained 26.04 knots powered by steam turbines of 70,000hp.

Two important Parsons turbine generating units are preserved in the Science Museum, South Kensington. These are his original 1884 unit with bipolar dynamo and the first condensing turbo-alternator of 100kW built for the Cambridge Electric Lighting Company. Other Parsons turbines may be seen at Abbeydale industrial hamlet, Sheffield; Glasgow Art Gallery & Museum, Kelvingrove; and, appropriately, Newcastle-upon-Tyne Museum of Science & Engineering, where *Turbinia* is also preserved. Also at Glasgow Museum are an early De Laval turbo-generator and a high-pressure and low-pressure turbine from the Clyde steamer *King Edward* of 1901, the first commercial turbine-driven vessel in the world.

The steam engine, as we have seen, was the first effective power source to release man from his reliance on natural agencies – on his own muscles, the use of animals or on windmills and watermills. Power was available in almost unlimited quantities for the driving of machines, and the early application of steam to transport in the form of ships and railways means that this one prime mover occupies a fundamental position in the expansion of industry and the development of industrial society in the last 250 years. Over this period the reciprocating steam engine has come to command a respect quite unique among machines, from a wide range of people who gain some aesthetic satisfaction from the sight, sound and smell of a steam engine in action. Today the industrial archaeologist, in tracing the evolution of the steam engine, can find numerous examples preserved which illustrate many of the major stages of development, although beam engines of one type or another are by far the most numerous. So far very few of the last generation of large steam engines have been kept and, although a number of mill engines, colliery winding and pumping engines are still in regular use, their numbers are decreasing rapidly. Similarly the steam turbine, much less interesting visually, does not have a wide enthusiast following, and only a few small and early examples have been preserved, as static exhibits in museums.

THE INTERNAL COMBUSTION ENGINE

The significant history of the internal combustion engine lies mainly in the period between the 1850s and the present day, although the experimental beginnings go back much further. Indeed the concept of burning fuel in the working cylinder is older than that of the steam engine itself, being ascribed to the Dutch scientist Christiaan Huygens (1629–95) who devised a machine using burning gunpowder to provide the expansive forces necessary to raise a piston. Cooling of the gases created a partial vacuum and atmospheric pressure forced the piston down. It was the substitution of gunpowder by steam, using an external heat source, that was to lead to the development of a practicable engine in the early eighteenth century.

It was not until 1859 that an engine burning its fuel within the cylinder was devised to operate continuously under industrial conditions, but by then the steam engine was universally established and in an almost unassailable position. Earlier experimental machines had been built and an engine made in 1820 by the Rev W. Cecil of Cambridge using hydrogen as a fuel was perhaps the first internal combustion engine to work in Britain or, for that matter, in the world. Nothing came of it, however, nor of the dozens of patents for 'gas exploding' engines taken out in the first half of the nineteenth century.

Success was finally achieved by a Frenchman, Etienne Lenoir (1822–1900), who in 1859 introduced a gas engine resembling in appearance a double-acting horizontal steam engine. A gas and air mixture was admitted alternately to each end of the cylinder but there was no compression. The mixture was introduced during the early part of each stroke, then fired by an electric spark and expanded during the remainder of the stroke. There were thus two combustion phases per revolution of the crank, one on each side of the piston. While induction, ignition and expansion were taking place on one side of the piston, burnt gas was being exhausted at the other. Although small, ranging between ½ and 3hp, and consuming rather large quantities of gas, Lenoir's engine achieved a considerable measure of success, 300–400 being in use in France by the mid-1860s. An example can be seen in the Science Museum, South Kensington.

In 1862 another Frenchman, Alphonse Beau de Rochas (1815–91), obtained a patent for a gas engine employing what we now call the four-stroke cycle. He laid down a range of conditions for good efficiency, namely: the cylinder should have the greatest volume with the least possible cooling surface, there should be the greatest rapidity and ratio of expansion, and the maximum possible pressure in the cylinder at the beginning of expansion. These conditions led to the following sequence of events in his engine:

1 Suction or induction of the gas-air mixture during a complete outward stroke of the piston.
2 Compression during the following inward stroke.

3 Ignition at or near the dead point followed by combustion and expansion during the third stroke.
4 Exhausting of the burnt gases from the cylinder on the fourth and final inward stroke.

The cycle is then repeated. Beau de Rochas did not follow up his theory and it was left to a German engineer, Dr N. A. Otto (1832–91), after whom the four-stroke cycle was for many years named, to put it into practical operation.

During the 1860s Otto had developed an 'atmospheric' free piston gas engine bearing striking resemblances in its principles of operation to the Newcomen steam engines of a century and a half earlier. The piston, mounted in an open-topped vertical cylinder, was raised by the expansion of gases ignited beneath it. Cooling and contraction of these gases resulted in the atmospheric pressure on top of the piston forcing it down. This was the working stroke, and a toothed rod, or 'rack', attached to the piston engaged in a gear wheel on a shaft converted its reciprocating motion into rotary power suitable for driving machinery. Fuel consumption was substantially less than in Lenoir's engine and, after its introduction by the firm of Otto & Langen in 1867, it had soon driven almost all competitors off the market. In Britain Crossley Bros Ltd of Manchester produced the engine under licence in a variety of sizes and a number have been preserved in museums. Examples of the 2hp type may be seen at South Kensington and Glasgow Art Gallery & Museum, while Bristol City Museum has a 4hp version in store.

By 1876 Otto had produced a still more successful engine operating on the four-stroke cycle proposed by Beau de Rochas. The 'Otto Silent Engine' without doubt marked a milestone in the progress of the internal combustion engine, being the first really strong competitor to the steam engine and, in proving the practicability of the four-stroke cycle, forming the basis for the motor car engine of today. Crossley's took up this new Otto engine and produced a variety of sizes under licence. Large numbers have found their way into museums, as have similar slow-speed single-cylinder horizontal gas engines made by other British manufacturers. A number of types and sizes may be seen in the Birmingham Museum of Science & Industry, where a Tangye engine is usually running on gas.

In all these early four-stroke gas engines, steam engine practice was followed to a large extent. They were usually slow-speed horizontals with admission of gas and air controlled by a slide valve. Although some engines used electric ignition, others relied upon a continuously burning flame inside a chamber in the cylinder wall. When the firing point arrived, the slide valve opened a slot exposing the flame to the mixture in the cylinder. Ignition of the gases, however, extinguished the flame itself so it was necessary to have a second one outside the chamber in order to re-ignite the internal flame. At the moment of ignition the external flame was shut off from the internal one. A later idea was the hot tube kept at bright red heat by an external flame.

The fuel used in most of the early gas engines was town gas, but gas from coke ovens, blast furnace gas and producer gas were also employed. By the end of the nineteenth century special gas producers, using coal, were being made for direct coupling to gas engines, thus making them independent of piped gas. In most designs the main piston of the engine was used to draw air into the producer. In the 1870s a number of engineers, notably in Austria and the United States, were experimenting with engines using an oil fuel instead of gas but little success resulted, largely because of difficulties in getting the oil into a sufficiently divided or atomised state to be easily combustible. The first really satisfactory design was the Priestman engine of 1886, which used paraffin (kerosene) as its fuel. The liquid was atomised by compressed air and vaporised in a vessel heated by exhaust gas before being drawn into the cylinder with the fresh air charge and ignited by electric spark. The Hornsby horizontal oil engine had a vaporiser at the end of the combustion chamber, on the cylinder head, and a special portable oil lamp was used to preheat it before starting, while in Crossley engines vaporisation was achieved in a spiral pipe encircling the oil lamp chimney. Once the engine was started and had reached its operating temperature, the lamp was no longer required. All these early oil engines were slow-running single-cylinder water-cooled horizontals similar in general arrangement to both gas and steam engines of the period.

About 1890 a very different type of oil engine was designed by Herbert Ackroyd-Stuart (1864–1927), who owned an iron foundry at Bletchley where he conducted experiments with the advice of Professor William Robinson of University College, Nottingham. The engine had a combined vaporiser and combustion chamber forming part of the cylinder head. The vaporiser, which was in the shape of an elongated bulb, was maintained by the heat of combustion at a temperature high enough to vaporise the oil which was injected directly into it, and high enough to cause ignition of the fuel/air mixture at the end of compression. For starting purposes the vaporiser was heated with a blow lamp.

The Ackroyd-Stuart engine exhibited two features of great importance. It required no devices for igniting the inflammable mixture, once it had started, and the fuel was injected 'solid', that is, without the use of atomising air. These two features are characteristic of the modern high-speed oil engine, but it must be emphasised that the modern engine is fundamentally one of high compression, whereas the Ackroyd-Stuart design deliberately avoided high compression and provided auxiliary means for reaching the necessary ignition temperature. Lack of capital prevented Ackroyd-Stuart from carrying on his experiments and in 1891 he sold a licence to manufacture his engines to Ruston & Co of Lincoln, who made them successfully for a number of years.

Rudolph Diesel (1858–1913), a German engineer born in Paris, was responsible for taking the final step of developing an engine in which ignition took place solely by the heat generated by compression. His principal aims were to circumvent the two main sources of heat loss in an internal combustion engine – by controlling the maximum temperature, through the gradual introduction of the fuel, and by lowering the temperature of the exhaust gases. To these ends he designed an engine working on the four-stroke cycle in which air only was compressed by the piston to a very much higher degree than the mixture in any former type of oil engine. An injector pump then forced a minute but accurately determined quantity of oil into the combustion chamber, where it ignited spontaneously on contact with the compressed air. It was found that its maximum thermal efficiency was some 11 per cent higher than that of any other form of prime mover and that the engine worked well on a wide variety of petroleum oils. Initial disadvantages resulted from high weight, as the engine had to be solidly built to withstand pressures of up to thirty-five times atmospheric, but improved construction techniques had, by the 1920s, put the Diesel engine into a strong competitive position for both stationary and automotive uses.

It was Gottlieb Daimler (1834–1900) of Württemberg who successfully developed the small lightweight high-speed engine running on liquid fuel, in this case light petroleum spirit. In 1885 he patented a single-cylinder vertical engine with enclosed crankcase and flywheels. From this design all subsequent Daimler engines were derived and in two- and eventually four-cylinder versions this type of engine formed the basis for the evolution of the motor car. A suction-operated inlet valve was used with a mechanically worked exhaust valve, a governor being arranged to prevent the latter opening when engine revolutions exceeded a predetermined speed. Introduction of the fuel was not such a difficulty as with the oil engine, as petrol vaporises readily in the presence of air. Wick feed carburettors were soon to give way to jet feed types, particularly for road vehicles.

Almost exactly contemporary with Daimler's introduction of the high-speed engine in 1885, Karl Benz (1844–1929) was building his first motor vehicle. This incorporated a horizontal engine using petrol as a fuel and operating on the 'Otto' four-stroke cycle but at the slow speeds of a gas engine. It was the high-speed engine pioneered by Daimler which eventually triumphed, however, and although a number of ingenious variations and layouts were tried in the period before World War I, the general arrangement of vertical water-cooled cylinders and enclosed crankcase is still by far the most popular type of motor car engine throughout the world. Numerous early motor cars are preserved in museums and often their engines can be examined closely. Notable collections include those of the National Motor Museum at Beaulieu in Hampshire; the Science Museum, South Kensington; the Herbert Art Gallery & Museum, Coventry; and Glasgow Transport Museum. For a real appreciation of the early motor car engine in operation, however, the London to Brighton road on the first Sunday in November, the occasion of the Veteran Car Club Run, enables one to see, hear and smell the faltering post-natal beginnings of the machine which has had such a fundamental effect on the lives of us all. The Historic Commercial Vehicle Club Run takes place over the same route on the first Sunday in May each year.

Despite the fact that the internal combustion engine is so familiar, and indeed commonplace, in the everyday world, its origins and early years are as much the province of industrial archaeological enquiry as are those of the steam engine. The rate of development of internal combustion engines has been such that almost any example dating from before 1930 and still in use is a rarity. Paradoxically it is often the Otto-Crossley gas engine of the 1880s, slow-running and slow to wear out, that has survived to be preserved.

CHAPTER 5

COAL

Coal did not become a really important fuel until the sixteenth century, and in terms of industrial development it was not of major significance until the middle of the eighteenth. From then on, however, coal was far and away the most important of all the natural resources of Britain, providing heat for both the smelting and fashioning of metals and the generation of steam. Initially coal was not a popular fuel and for domestic use wood and charcoal were generally preferred. Only poor people living near the workings burnt coal. The impurities in coal which caused the noxious fumes so distasteful to the domestic user in a house with inadequate ventilation also caused problems to industry, so it was in a purified state, as coke, that coal was first used on a really large scale for industrial purposes. Thus coke was the first successful replacement of charcoal for iron smelting in 1709. Similarly, it was not until 1859 that the introduction of the brick arch into the fireboxes of railway locomotives enabled coal to be burnt satisfactorily. Previously coke had been used in all except small and relatively inefficient engines working in or near collieries.

This does not mean that coal had no industrial uses. Limeburners, bakers, brewers and glassmakers, for example, all adapted their processes to burn coal and, as the huge forested areas of England became decimated, the price of timber, coupled with the strategic timber requirements of the Royal Navy, stimulated an increase in the use of coal wherever possible. By the 1760s the coal industry was growing at a rapid rate, and it reached its peak in 1913; since then it has suffered a steady decline in the face of oil, and more recently natural gas and nuclear power. It is worth remembering, however, that most of the electricity generated in Britain still comes from coal-fired power stations.

The first access to coal was at outcrops where it could be picked up on the ground, and on beaches where coal in cliffs was being constantly eroded. By the twelfth century small quarries and ditches were being dug, and in the thirteenth century, in addition to such opencast methods, coal was also being won from shallow drifts and bell-pits. Drifts were usually found in hilly districts and consisted of more or less horizontal tunnels or galleries cut into the hillsides and following the seams of coal. Several hundred privately owned drifts are still being worked under licence today, and although they are small by twentieth-century standards, they are much larger than their thirteenth-century predecessors. In areas such as the Forest of Dean in Gloucestershire there has been a continuous history of drift mining, and the 'free miners' of the Forest still exercise their medieval rights to mine coal. Their workings, although involving some modern equipment, are little altered from those of five centuries ago and include many of the basic techniques of mine operation. Reconstructions of small drift mines can be seen at Blists Hill Open Air Museum, Ironbridge, Shropshire and the North of England Open Air Museum, Beamish. British Coal has built a number of new large drift mines, notably in South Wales and Yorkshire.

Problems of ventilation and drainage limited the size of the early drift mines, but where coal lay at only a shallow depth below the surface, it was won by sinking bell-pits, a simple process involving little equipment and no drainage or ventilation gear. Bell-pits are so called because, when viewed in section, they have the shape of bells. A pit was sunk like a well shaft to a shallow coal seam and the coal at the foot of the shaft was then taken. Next, it was cut away around the pit bottom in all directions until the sides were in danger of collapse. The pit was then abandoned and a new one started nearby. Bell-pits were rarely more than 30ft deep, usually circular in plan, and often dug very close

together. Very frequently they collapsed after their abandonment, so that areas of bell-pit working can now be recognised by a characteristic pock-marked surface to the ground made up of numerous circular depressions 20–30ft in diameter. Evidence of bell-pits can be found on many of the older worked coalfields, particularly in Derbyshire at Stretton, Wingerworth and Shipley, in Lancashire at Castercliff near Nelson, in Shropshire on Brown Clee and at Rudland Rigg in North Yorkshire (Illus 54).

Where seams lay deeper than 30ft, bell-pits were wasteful of labour, so headings were cut out horizontally into the coal for

54 Bell pits, Rudland Rigg [SE 654936], North Yorkshire   (*Royal Commission on Historical Monuments, England*)

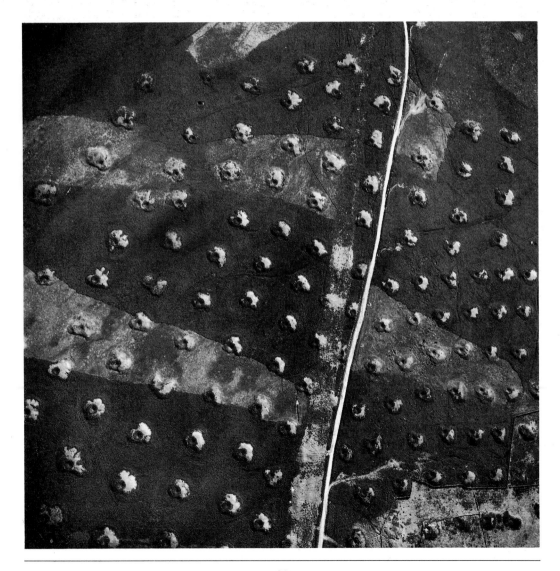

PILLAR-AND-STALL
1 Working in the whole   2 Working in the broken

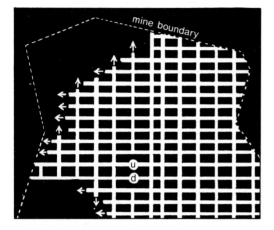

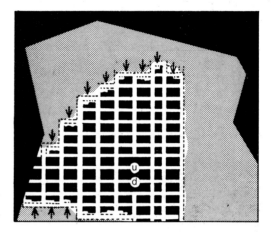

LONGWALL

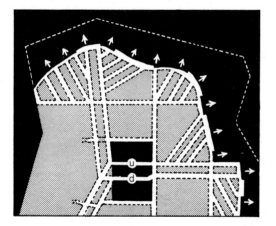

■ uncut coal

□ coal removed, roof still supported

▨ 'goaf' or 'gob'- all coal removed, roof allowed to settle down gradually

▨ workings kept open with props

⊟ u upcast shaft - foul air drawn out

⊟ d downcast shaft - fresh air drawn in

N B Circulation of fresh air round the mine is controlled by air doors and ducts which have been omitted for clarity

Illustration 55

a short distance from the shaft bottom. Between these headings wide pillars of coal were left to support the roof. The arrangement was at first irregular in pattern, resulting in as much as half the coal being left behind, but it was soon recognised that it was both practicable and economical to divide the seams up into large pillars by roads driven at right-angles, and subsequently to follow up by extracting the pillars. This method of mining is known as bord-and-pillar or, more commonly, pillar-and-stall working (Illus 55). There were two distinct stages in the cutting of coal in this way. Initially, when the bords or stalls were being driven as working advanced from the pit bottom, the process was known as 'working in the whole'. The second stage, of extracting the pillars while retreating back towards the shaft was called 'working in the broken', although most miners would call this 'robbing the pillars on the retreat'. The method of removing pillars was to take slices off one side, the roof meanwhile being supported by timber props. When the whole of the pillar was cut away, the timber supports were withdrawn and the roof allowed to collapse.

Pillar-and-stall working became the standard method of coal extraction in all the major coalfields of Britain, and in Northumberland and Durham in particular continued well after nationalisation of the coal industry in 1947. The miner of the North East, with his highly developed tradition of craftsmanship and skill, tended to be rather slow in adopting new mining techniques. The system of working, in which an individual miner or small group of men worked a stall also engendered a craft approach and perpetuated this system of mining long after it had been replaced elsewhere by other techniques.

Pillar-and-stall working was a two-stage operation ideally suited to workings where there was not more than about 900ft of rock lying above the coal. Where depths were greater, there was a tendency for the overlying rock to crush the pillars as, or sometimes before, they were removed. There were also frequent problems of ventilation. To overcome these drawbacks, extraction in one operation was developed. Known as the longwall method, it originated in the late seventeenth century, probably in Shropshire, but did not come into widespread use until after 1850. In this system a wall of coal about 100yd long is won out and removed bodily in line. As the coal is taken away, any stone available is built into dry stone walls or packs 6–20ft wide arranged in parallel lines at right-angles to the advancing wall or face. The purpose of these walls is to support the roof after the layer of coal is removed and thus preserve it in a largely unbroken state. Longwall working is particularly suited to mechanical coal-cutting methods in seams which have layers of stone or shale within them,

although in modern mechanised working packs are no longer built, the roof is left unsupported and total caving takes place.

Once mines had grown beyond the scale of the early drifts and bell-pits, the cutting of the coal itself became a relatively minor problem compared with those of shaft sinking and winding, ventilation and drainage. Indeed the finding of a solution to these last two difficulties was the major preoccupation of miners and engineers from the end of the sixteenth century onwards. Until answers could be found, there were specific limits to the depth at which mines could be sunk and the distances to which workings extended from the pit bottom. The early miners on the exposed coalfields were working in known conditions. They could see where the coal was and assess the problems of working as they went along. Once mines away from the outcrops developed, shaft sinking became speculative and some means of discovering the presence of coal and any undesirable stratigraphical conditions above it became a necessity. As early as 1606 Huntington Beaumont, one of the first of the great coal entrepreneurs, who had extensive interests in Nottinghamshire and the North East, was demonstrating his 'art to boore with iron rodds to try the deepnesse and thicknesse of the cole'. This of course was much cheaper than digging trial shafts. In 1708 the cost of boring was said to be 15–20 shillings a fathom, while sinking a shaft cost 50–60 shillings a fathom. In 1804 James Ryan invented a boring technique which allowed cores to be extracted, and the application of steam power, first tried by Richard Trevithick, both speeded up and cheapened exploration.

Shaft sinking was usually carried out by hand picks and shovels and wedges for splitting rock. Later, boring rods were employed, and in 1749 occurs one of the earliest references to the use of explosives, for a 210ft shaft near Halifax. Shafts were generally circular in section, 5–12ft in diameter, with about 7ft being the most common, though one shaft at New Rock Colliery, Somerset [ST 647505], in use until recently, was only 4ft 6in in diameter. Square or rectangular shafts were frequent

COLLIERY WINDING GEAR

Windlass or Jack Roll

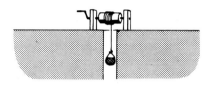

Cog and rung gin

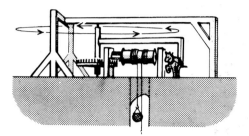

Whim-gin

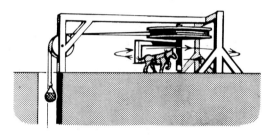

Steam whimsy

flat chains

Vertical steam winder

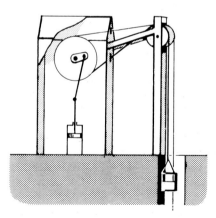

Horizontal steam winder with tandem headgear

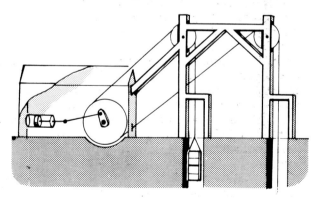

Illustration 56

on some coalfields as they could be easily and cheaply lined with wooden boards. Small rectangular shafts can still be found in the Forest of Dean, although often the timber lining has deteriorated, making them very dangerous to enter. Where water was a problem in a shaft, it was held back with 'tubbing' consisting of wooden planks arranged like the staves of a barrel or tub. The first cast-iron tubbing used in the Midlands was at Snibston Colliery in Leicestershire [SK 417145], sunk by George Stephenson in 1841–3. This can still be seen in the upcast shafts. Elsewhere brick lining was used, mostly with mortar but occasionally without. It was cheaper to lay bricks dry, and they could be used again when the shaft ceased production. A drylined shaft can be seen below the headgear from Farm Pit, Heath Hill, reconstructed at Blists Hill Open Air Museum, Ironbridge [SJ 694031].

There were various methods of raising coal up the shaft (Illus 56), of which the earliest was a simple hand winch or wind-lass, sometimes known as a 'jack roll' and similar to that used on a domestic well. The barrel of a windlass of this type, found in 1969 at the bottom of a shaft exposed on Stainsby Hag opencast site in Derbyshire, may be seen at the Chatterley Whitfield Mining Museum, Tunstall, Staffordshire [SJ 885534].

To improve the performance of the hand windlass, horse-driven cog-and-rung gins were introduced in the early seventeenth century. A vertical spindle was geared to the horizontal barrel of the winch, and the horse, attached to the spindle via a wooden pole, walked round the mouth of the pit to raise coal in small baskets known as corves or corfes.

Towards the end of the seventeenth century, further improvements were effected with the whim-gin, horse-whim or whimsy. This new winder had the rope drum mounted on a vertical shaft, which was erected some distance from the pit shaft. The horse walked round rotating the drum as in the cog-and-rung gin and the rope passed over a vertical pulley mounted on a wooden headgear over the shaft itself. Depending on the size of the mine, one, two or more horses were employed.

Whim-gins were used until the early twentieth century in some places and a reconstructed example may be seen at the Nottingham Industrial Museum, Wollaton Park [SK 531393].

The use of water power for winding purposes occurred to a limited extent in Britain, initially with waterwheels mounted on horizontal shafts round which the winding rope was wound, and later using water balances. A waterwheel for winding coal was installed at Griff Colliery, Warwickshire, by John Smeaton (1724–92) in 1774, and in the North East non-rotative steam engines were used to raise water which was also used to power 'water gins'. No evidence survives of waterwheel winders but in South Wales, where water balances were used, a well preserved balance tower can be seen at Blaenafon, Gwent (Illus 57) [SO 250094] and there is a headgear at Cwmbyrgwm, Gwent (Illus 58) [SO 251033]. In a water balance coal was drawn up the shaft in a cage by the weight of a tub, filled with water at the pithead, which descended in a parallel shaft. When the water tub reached the bottom, the water was drawn off through a valve, a tram of coal was placed on top of the empty tub and then drawn up the shaft by the weight of another descending water-filled tub. An example from the Forest of Dean is displayed in the National Museum of Wales, Cardiff.

The earliest use for the steam engine, at the beginning of the eighteenth century, was for mine drainage, but it was not until 1784 that the first steam winder, a Watt engine, was erected, at Walker Colliery on Tyneside. The early steam winding engines were primitive and somewhat unreliable which encouraged the persistence of horse-gins at many small and poorly capitalised pits. One of the problems in tracing the introduction of steam winding in the late eighteenth century and early nineteenth results from the use of the word whimsy to describe a steam engine or a horse-gin, so that it is often difficult, if not impossible, to distinguish one from the other. What is certain, however, is that steam power was rapidly adopted, particularly in the large collieries

of the Midlands and North East and that it remained the primary means of winding both coal and men until well after nationalisation in 1947.

Electric power, introduced about 1906, has since 1947 become universal, and there are now no steam winders working in Britain, although a number of dead engines survive, some *in situ*. Some have been preserved and others recorded on film. Some steam winding engines, as at Caphouse, West Yorkshire [SE 253165] and Chatterley, Whitfield, Staffordshire (Illus 64) [SJ 885534] have been renovated and are open to the public.

Many of the early engines worked on the Newcomen atmospheric principle with open-top cylinders and timber beams, and by the end of the eighteenth century large numbers were being made, notably by the Coalbrookdale Company. A Newcomen-type winder used at Farme Colliery, Rutherglen, Scotland, between 1810 and 1915 is preserved at Glasgow Museum but is not on display at the time of writing. It has a 42in diameter cylinder with a stroke of 5ft 8in. By the mid-nineteenth century a standard layout of

57 Water balance tower at Blaenavon, Gwent [SO 250094]. In the foreground are the remains of Blaenavon Ironworks, founded in 1789 and in production until the 1860s. The blast furnaces and associated casting houses have been consolidated in recent years   (*Neil Cossons*)

58 Water balance headgear, Cwmbyrgwm, Gwent [SO 251033]; the last headgear of its kind *in situ*, over a shaft sunk in 1820   (*John Cornwell*)

59 Engine house of Jane Pit, Workington, Cumbria [NX 995277], built c1843 (*John Cornwell*)

winding engines had developed. It comprised a drum on a horizontal shaft at each end of which was a crank; two horizontal cylinders, usually mounted on separate cast-iron bedplates, which also supported the crankshaft bearings, drove this shaft. The engineman had a control platform mounted above the cylinders, whence he could survey the whole engine house and in many cases see the pithead too. Most engines that survive today are of this twin-cylinder horizontal type. Notable among these is the engine from Old Mills Colliery near Radstock in Somerset, built in 1861 by William Evans at Paulton Foundry and now preserved by Bristol City Museum. This engine, which is not on display, has cylinders of 26in bore and 5ft stroke, with a rope drum 12ft in diameter. A small horizontal engine with one cylinder and its crankshaft geared to the winding-drum shaft instead of the more normal direct drive has been re-erected and is running on steam at the Blists Hill Open Air Museum, Ironbridge. The engine comes from Milburgh Pit near

Broseley, Shropshire.

Of generally the same layout as twin-cylinder types is the large twin-tandem compound engine at Astley Green Colliery, Tyldesley, Greater Manchester [SJ 705999], built by Yates & Thom in 1908. In many ways it resembles a contemporary mill engine, with Corliss valve gear and a white tiled interior to the engine house. The engine is now out of use and may be scrapped, but there are hopes of preserving a twin-cylinder horizontal capstan engine once used in connection with maintenance of the shaft. The headstocks at Astley Green are typical of those built at larger collieries early this century, with four legs of lattice steel construction standing astride the top of the shaft.

A notable regional variation from the standard horizontal winding engine occurred in North East England, where vertical winding engines were common on the Northumberland and Durham coalfield. The direct-acting vertical engine with crankshaft mounted above the cylinder, patented in 1800 by Phineas Crowther of Newcastle-upon-Tyne, formed the basis for engines built by Thomas Murray and James Joicey for pit winders. One example, from Beamish Colliery [NZ 212549], is preserved by the North of England Open Air Museum. Built in 1855 by J. & G. Joicey of Newcastle-upon-Tyne, the engine occupies a tall stone-built engine house, and the timber headstocks have two vertical legs astride the shaft and two almost horizontal members running back to be supported in the front of the engine house. Other surviving vertical winders are at Elemore, Tyne & Wear [NZ 356457], and Old Glyn Pit near Pontypool, Gwent [ST 265999], where there is also a beam engine of 1845 that was formerly used for pumping. Both the Pontypool engines were built by Neath Abbey Works.

The introduction of steam engines for winding resulted in new types of winding rope being used. Those originally employed were round and made of hemp that consisted of several strands wrapped to form a composite rope. Flat ropes, in which the strands were stitched together side by side, were also extensively used, and had the advantage that during winding the rope could be wrapped layer upon layer on a narrow drum, thus varying the leverage. At the beginning of winding, with the load at the bottom of the shaft, the rope was wrapped around the smallest circumference of the drum and the empty basket or cage on its own rope at the top was wrapped round the largest. A similar form of continuously variable gearing can be seen on the winding drum at Astley Green Colliery, where a scroll on the side face of the drum feeds the cable from the small diameter at the beginning of the wind to the full diameter of the drum when the load is moving. In early coal mines, baskets or corves were wound up from the trams at the foot of the shaft on free-hanging hemp ropes, but owing to the twist on the rope they tended to spin round and sway from side to side. Thus the speed of winding had to be slow. To overcome this swaying, shaft guides were introduced in 1787, and baskets were attached to cross-bars which slid in wooden guides attached to the sides of the shaft.

The introduction of stranded iron wire ropes after about 1840 led to their being widely adopted for winding and also as shaft guides, two cables being hung down each side of the cage and stabilised by heavy weights in the shaft sump. In Shropshire particularly, with its local chain industry, flat wrought-iron chain was extensively used for winding purposes. Known as 'rattle chain', it was used in much the same way as flat hemp or wire rope, and wound on to a narrow drum. Despite the fact that wear in chain was difficult to detect and breakages were sudden and unexpected, rattle chain continued in use throughout the nineteenth century. Lengths can still be found all over the East Shropshire coalfield, used for a wide variety of purposes, including fencing.

In the late 1840s cages were introduced to replace corves for lifting coal up the shafts, and by 1860 most collieries of any size had them. Even so, corves were used as late as 1875 at William Pit, Whitehaven. One may be seen at Chatterley Whitfield

60,61 Engine house of Wynnstay Colliery, near Ruabon, Clwyd [SJ 294433] c1855

(Neil Cossons)

Mining Museum. The introduction of the cage, which was basically an open-sided box running on guides in the shaft, brought about the end of the primitive and dangerous methods of man-riding practised in many collieries. Often colliers merely clung to the rope to get up or down the shaft. The cage greatly improved the efficiency of coal winding in mines, as a load of coal could travel on rails in a truck or tram from where it had been cut at the coalface to the bottom of the shaft, run on to rails in the floor of the cage, be safely hauled to the surface and there be emptied while the cage returned underground with an empty truck. A typical small cage can be seen at the preserved Heath Hill Pit at Blists Hill Open Air Museum, Iron-bridge.

Having considered methods of mine operation, we must examine the two major problems facing the coalminer from the sixteenth century onwards – drainage and ventilation. The hand windlasses and horse-gins used for raising coal could also lift water, but there were obvious limita-tions to their capacity. By the end of the seventeenth century the size of coal mines and, for example, tin mines in Cornwall, was limited by the ability to keep them drained although in some collieries and lead mines quite effective use was made of underground ditches or drainage tunnels known in the North East as 'water gates', in the south as 'adits' and in parts of the Midlands, such as Derbyshire, as 'soughs'. These were clearly of little use for deep mines, and although wind and water power were used, it was the introduction of the steam engine after about 1712 that broke the deadlock. The steam engine was developed specifically for mine drainage and for the first half century or so of its existence did little else. The details of its development are considered in Chapter 4, as are some of the surviving examples which were used for mine drainage. These include the Hawkesbury engine now pre-served at Dartmouth [SX 879515], which was originally installed in the 1720s at Griff Colliery, Warwickshire, and is the oldest steam engine in existence, and the atmo-spheric drainage engine at Elsecar [SK 387999] South Yorkshire. The Elsecar engine

is preserved on its original site by British Coal. Adjacent to the engine house is a timber headstock over a small shaft. Another atmospheric engine, of 1791, from Pentrich Colliery, Derbyshire, was acquired in 1917 by the Science Museum, London, where it is now preserved.

One of the most spectacular colliery sites and drainage engines is at Preston-grange, East Lothian [NT 374737], on the B1348 road east of Musselburgh. At the centre of the site is the Cornish beam pumping engine by Harvey's of Hayle, Cornwall, which pumped water from the mine from 1874 to 1954. The beam weighs approximately 30 tons, is 33ft long and 6ft 4in deep at the centre. The single cylinder is 70in in diameter with a stroke of 12ft. The site is now part of the Scottish Mining Museum of which the other part is the Lady Victoria Colliery, Newtongrange, Midlothian [NT 336636].

Elsewhere it is difficult to find surface evidence of colliery drainage works, although here and there an engine house survives. The massive house of Calcutta Colliery pumping engine near Thring-stone, Leicestershire [SK 421169], is one example, and another, of rather Cornish appearance, may be seen at Nailsea in Avon [ST 479691]. In some coalfields engines were installed away from the collieries themselves to drain whole areas in which the various mine workings were con-nected by levels. An example was the scheme to drain the Fitzwilliam Barnsley Bed in South Yorkshire, of which the Elsecar engine was part. Similarly the Lloyds engine, Madeley Wood, near Iron-bridge [SJ 690031], of which recognisable remains survive, drained a number of mines in the area.

Before turning to mine ventilation, we should mention an unusual form of coal extraction at Worsley in South Lancashire, which combined drainage levels and soughs with the mine workings them-selves. The site has considerable historical significance in the early development of

62 Lewis Merthyr Colliery, Trehafod, Mid Glamorgan [ST 036910] sunk in 1864 has been preserved and is open to the public

(Neil Cossons)

63 Experimental firing of a restored mine ventilation furnace in the Golden Valley, north of Bitton, Avon [ST 690710]   (*John Cornwell*)

trations of 5–15 per cent methane it is highly inflammable. By the late eighteenth century colliery explosions, often of great violence, were common, especially in Northumberland, Durham and South Wales. There were 643 explosions in the North East between 1835 and 1850, even after the introduction and widespread use of the safety lamp devised by Humphry (later Sir Humphry) Davy (1778–1829) in 1815.

The Society for Preventing Accidents in Coal Mines, formed in Sunderland in 1813, largely as a result of the Felling Colliery disaster of the previous year in which ninety-two men and boys died, approached Davy, who expressed interest in the problem. He discovered the true nature of firedamp, the conditions under which it explodes and the rate of passage of flame through tubes of varying diameter. He found wire gauze in the form of a sleeve around the flame to be the most effective barrier. The gauze was made from iron wire ranging from $\frac{1}{40}$ to $\frac{1}{60}$in in diameter containing twenty-eight wires to the inch, or 748 apertures to the square inch. Two other men, Dr W. R. Clanny (1776–1850) and George Stephenson (1781–1848), the steam locomotive engineer, also devised safety lamps at about the same time. Miners' lamps are common in most industrial museums, but a particularly fine collection may be seen at Salford in the Museum of Mining in Buile Hill Park on Eccles Old Road. Safety lamps reduced the incidence of explosions somewhat, but when they did occur in the bigger mines, the results were often catastrophic. In 1860 145 men died in the Risca Mine at Newport; in 1867 178 lives were lost at Ferndale Colliery in the Rhondda Valley. The causes of these two have since proved to be the ignition of coaldust; today this is combatted by spreading stone dust in the mine workings.

canals and is readily accessible to the visitor. The entrance to the Worsley Mine is north of Worsley Road and west of the Delph [SD 748005]. For further details of these extensive workings, see p 255.

As mines grew in size, problems of ventilating them increased. In small workings the only gas with which the miner had to contend was 'stythe' or 'dampe', known now as blackdamp or chokedamp. It is a mixture of carbon dioxide and nitrogen which in large quantities will suffocate those coming into contact with it. Later, as mines became deeper, firedamp, a mixture of methane and air, was encountered and the era of the serious mine explosion began. Another explosive element in mines – the concentration of fine coaldust – was not known about until much later. Firedamp is produced during the decay of vegetable matter and its conversion into coal; it remains in the cleavage planes of the coal and the nearby rocks and is released as soon as the seam is worked. In mixture with air at concen-

Most early mines relied on convection currents or natural air flow through two shafts for their ventilation. With increased size a forced ventilation system became necessary, and in the mid-seventeenth century the first reference to the use of a fire basket occurs, at Cheadle in North Staffordshire. Fire baskets and later ventilation furnaces were usually underground at the foot of the 'upcast' shaft. The upward movement of air due to the chimney effect of hot gases induced a downward flow in the 'downcast' shaft and the fresh air, circulated throughout the workings and controlled by trapdoors operated by boys, prevented dangerous concentrations of gas accumulating. A reconstruction of a surface ventilation fire and chimney may be seen at Blists Hill Open Air Museum, Ironbridge, and Brinsley Colliery, Nottinghamshire, still has the flues and furnace underground, though they have not been used since the nineteenth century. In Lancashire ventilation chimneys for underground furnaces could recently be seen at Clifton Colliery, Burnley, and Pewfall Colliery, Garswood. A surface ventilation furnace and chimney can still be seen at a drift mine at Trehafod, Mid Glamorgan [ST 036910]. The last recorded use of a fire basket was at Rock Pit, Shropshire, in 1965, and a surface furnace was used at Broseley Deep Pit, nearby, until 1941. Near Bitton, Avon [ST 690710] on the old Bristol Coalfield a ventilation furnace and chimney have recently been restored (Illus 63).

These survivals were anachronisms, however, and various types of air pump were being installed at the larger collieries from the 1830s onwards. One of the most widely adopted in the 1870s was the Waddle fan, a centrifugal fan of up to 45ft in diameter powered by steam or later electricity at the relatively low speed of 70rpm. The fan consisted of two parallel discs separated by backward curved blades. The centre of the disc was hollow and connected by a large-diameter pipe to the top of the upcast shaft. As the fan rotated, air was sucked in at the centre and expelled along the periphery. Between 1871 and 1896 220 Waddle fans were installed and a few still remain, though not now working. One was at Annesley, Nottinghamshire until recently, and another, from Ryhope Colliery, County Durham, is preserved in the North of England Open Air Museum at Beamish. A Waddle fan at Abergorki Pit, Mountain Ash, Mid Glamorgan [ST 050990], is also preserved.

Before mechanisation began in the latter part of the nineteenth century, and in many collieries years after then, the miner relied on pick, shovel and crowbar to get the coal. By about 1800 explosives were being used in shot-holes made with a chisel-ended iron bar, or, later in the century, by a hand drill. Loose gunpowder was poured into the hole and tamped with clay, using a tamping bar. A pricker or needle left in the hole when the clay was tamped in would then be withdrawn to allow a straw full of priming powder to be inserted. This was lit and burned for long enough to give the shot-lighter time to retire. A slow-burning fuse was invented by William Bickford in 1831 but many miners would not use it on grounds of expense.

A good selection of miners' tools is preserved in the North of England Open Air Museum, Beamish, which also has crackets or working stools and various types of protective headgear. Below ground mechanisation came slowly, and the steam engine, so valuable for pumping or winding, was out of the question as a source of power for coal-cutting machinery. The use of machinery in mines grew with the development of compressed air and electricity, particularly the latter, as sources of motive power. A compressed-air-powered coal cutter, using a toothed disc, was introduced in 1863 by Thomas Harrison, and established the principle of the rotary or continuously moving cutter which applied until relatively recently. Three major types of cutting machines emerged, the first using a disc with teeth on its periphery, the second a continuous chain carrying cutters, similar to the chain saw used today for tree felling, and the third a rotating bar armed with cutters throughout its length. A variety of cutter-loaders have been tried in this century. The Meco-Moore was a widely adopted type, but it is now extinct; it travelled along the face cutting coal with two horizontal gibs, collected it and transferred it to a conveyor running parallel to the direction of the traverse.

The coal-mining industry, perhaps more than any other, has undergone massive change in recent years leading to the closure of dozens of pits and the end of mining altogether in several coalfields. Nevertheless there have in recent years been a number of important initiatives to preserve aspects of the history of the coal industry. Preserved *in situ* are a number of collieries where visitors may go underground, either into original workings that are maintained in a safe and accessible condition or into reconstructed galleries. At Chatterley Whitfield Colliery, Tunstall, Staffordshire [SJ 885534], an extensive surface complex has been preserved including a steam winding engine (Illus 64). Access is provided to a series of demonstration workings. At Big Pit in Gwent, however,

64 Twin-cylinder horizontal steam winding engine at Chatterley Whitfield Colliery, Tunstall, Staffordshire [SJ 885534], built by the Worsley Mesnes Company of Wigan in 1914
(*John Cornwell*)

(Illus 65) [SO 239088] ex-miners guide visitors down the 300ft shaft for a tour which includes coal faces, haulage engines and workshops and the underground stables for pit ponies. Also in South Wales the Lewis Merthyr Colliery at Trehafod (Illus 66) [ST 036910], the last pit to raise coal in the Rhondda, has been preserved as the focal point of the Rhondda Heritage Park, a major land rehabilitation, preservation and interpretation project run by Mid Glamorgan County Council. In West Yorkshire Caphouse Colliery [SE 253165], between Huddersfield and Wakefield, forms the nucleus of the Yorkshire Mining Museum where surface workings are preserved, including the steam winding engine, and there are displays on the social history of the coalfield, a mining library and photographic archive. Here too visitors may descend the shaft for guided tours underground. Further north, in Scotland, the

65 A plough on the Garw seam at Big Pit, Blaenafon, Gwent [SO 239088] in 1979. In the foreground is the armoured conveyor which carries the coal from the face to the main conveyor. The Garw seam was the last to be worked at Big Pit: its maximum thickness was 28–30in *(John Cornwell)*

66 A rotary coalcutter, props and bars, Lewis Merthyr Pit [ST 036910], 1978 *(John Cornwell)*

Scottish Mining Museum has preserved two sites, the Lady Victoria Colliery [NT 336636], at Newtongrange in Midlothian and the remains near Prestonpans [NT 374737], East Lothian, of the 1874 Prestongrange Cornish pumping engine (Illus 42, p 71).

Mining equipment, mainly from the

COAL DROP AT SEAHAM HARBOUR, COUNTY DURHAM

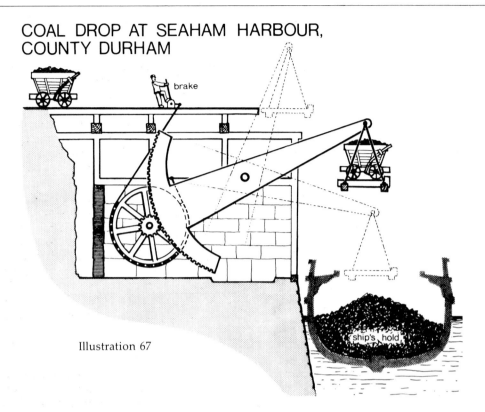

brake

ship's hold

Illustration 67

Lancashire coalfield, is preserved at the Salford Mining Museum, at Buile Hill Park on Eccles Old Road in Salford, and there is an extensive mining collection held by the National Museum of Wales in Cardiff. In addition Ironbridge, with a winding engine in steam every day at the Blists Hill Open Air Museum [SJ 693033], and the North of England Open Air Museum, with the re-erected Beamish Colliery winder and surface buildings, a drift mine and furnished pitmen's cottages, present mining in a wider social context.

No study of the industrial archaeology of the coal industry would be complete without mention of the transport systems which developed to service it. Detailed consideration of canals and railways is given in other chapters, but it is worth remembering that the exploitation of coal was fundamental to the evolution of both. Canals in the Midlands and South Lancashire, for example, developed as a means of opening up coalfields. Associated with the canal were horse-drawn tramway systems connecting individual pitheads with canal basins. In the North East and

South Wales tramways or plateways networked the coalfields, encouraged by the generally favourable gradient downhill from colliery to river or coastal wharf. Late in the nineteenth century, railway companies such as the Bowes Railway in County Durham, the Hull & Barnsley in Yorkshire and, for example, the Taff Vale, Rhymney, Barry and Cardiff railways in South Wales, were built primarily to carry coal. As many as four separate railway companies occupied some valleys in South Wales in their anxiety to share in the carriage of coal to ports such as Penarth, Cardiff or Barry. The most dramatic remnants of the coal trade are to be found in the North East where there are still a few of the wharves, known as 'staithes', by means of which coal was shipped from wagon to vessel. The banks of the Tyne, later the Wear, and eventually such ports as Seaham Harbour, were the shipping points to which the wagonways led. The staithes originally served not only as gangways for loading, but also as storing places for the coal as mine owners found it desirable to keep a large part of their stock on the staithes, ready for immediate shipment, rather than at the pitheads, as shipmasters did not like delaying sailing while small wagon loads were brought from the colliery. The three distinctive features of the coal shipment industry were the staithes themselves, of which the best are at Seaham Harbour [NZ 435495], the chaldron wagons which ran on the wagonways and the coal drops which lowered the wagons over the holds of ships so that the coal could be discharged. A number of chaldron wagons and the last surviving coal drop, from Seaham, are preserved by the North of England Open Air Museum (Illus 67). More modern staithes may be seen at Amble [NU 269049] and Blyth [NZ 3280], and on the canals of West Yorkshire a new coal staithe, the Caroline Staithe, is under construction at Methley near Leeds.

The landscape changes wrought by the coal industry are of an infinitely broader scale than the effects of collieries and pit tips alone, and recognisable regional variations can still be seen. In South Wales the industry, crammed into the confines of narrow valleys, resulted in long straggling colliery villages of terrace houses, rarely more than three or four rows deep, strung out along the valley floors. Row upon row of Welsh slate roofs punctuated by tall nonconformist chapels lay among railway lines, many of which are now closed. In the North East the mining village was a new and distinct nucleated settlement generally fairly compact, well endowed with public houses but with perhaps fewer places of worship than in South Wales. Scotland and the Furness coast northwards to Whitehaven are noted for a preponderance of single-storey dwellings often rendered or pebble-dashed and invariably slate roofed. The colliers of the Black Country or East Shropshire, however, where pits were often small, usually lived in semi-rural surroundings, their tile-roofed cottages scattered in little groups among smallholdings, overgrown waste tips and the dwellings of workers in other industries. Rarely is it possible to pick out the coalworker's house from that of the foundryman, iron puddler or chainmaker.

The North of England Open Air Museum has complete interiors from pitmen's cottages which can have changed little in half a century, but the same cannot be said for other mining areas. Miners' clothing, both working and best, is almost unrecorded. Similarly, material evidence of the living and working conditions of the population of mining areas is surprisingly scarce.

68   An immense block of coal

CHAPTER 6

IRON AND STEEL

Iron and its alloy steel are at the root of our material civilisation. Bridges, railways, ships, motor vehicles, tall buildings, machinery, canned foods and reinforced concrete are just a few aspects of life today in which iron and steel play a fundamental role. The evolution of techniques for making iron and later steel in quantity are therefore of overwhelming significance in the development of industrialisation. From the industrial archaeological point of view the remains of the iron and steel industry present certain problems. Many early sites are often only physically identifiable by the waste products left behind, and analysis of the slags and a detailed knowledge of the ironworking process is needed before any indication can be gained of what originally went on. The Historical Metallurgy Society is devoting itself to the history, not only of ironmaking but of many non-ferrous metal processes also. The eighteenth century and the first part of the nineteenth, a period in which rapid advances in iron- and steelmaking took place, provide rather more in the way of physical evidence readily open to interpretation, though remains from, say, the 1860s onwards, have been to a great extent obliterated by recent advances in the industry. In this respect the iron and steel industry is typical of a number where evidence of earlier processes is much more complete than that of later; age is not necessarily of special significance in determining the relative importance of sites.

The three commercially important forms of iron, in order of antiquity, are wrought iron, cast iron and steel. Wrought iron, for nearly 2,000 years the only form of the metal which was used, is an almost pure iron, ductile and easily shaped in the hot state by hammering or rolling. It is fibrous, has a high tensile strength and a resistance to corrosion far superior to the modern mild steel which has replaced it. Small quantities of slag in the iron contribute to these properties and act as a flux in welding which can be done when the iron is heated to the right temperature, and hammered or squeezed. This process is known as fire welding.

Cast iron, containing a much higher proportion of carbon than wrought iron (up to 3–4 per cent), is the product of melting iron to a completely liquid state and pouring it into moulds, where it solidifies. It has a crystalline structure, making it weak in tension but very strong in compression. It too is resistant to corrosion.

Steel has a wide variety of different forms but is basically an alloy of iron and carbon, but with less carbon than cast iron and more than wrought iron. Mild steel, the commonest form, contains not more than about 0.25 per cent carbon; it is ductile, strong in tension and can be forged, rolled and worked in much the same way as wrought iron. By varying the carbon content and subjecting it to heat treatment processes, steel can be hardened and tempered to give it additional strength and toughness. The addition of carbon to the outer surfaces produces a hard skin, a process known as case hardening. Today there are hundreds of different steels, each designed for a specific purpose and containing other elements such as manganese, nickel, chromium, molybdenum and tungsten. These alloy steels include high-speed steels, stainless steels and die steels.

Although iron is one of the most abundant elements in nature, it almost always occurs in association with oxygen in the form of iron oxides. There are two main types of commercially worked ores in Britain: stratified ores laid down on sea-beds in the Carboniferous and Jurassic periods, and unstratified ore found as nodules. Carboniferous ores occur in association with the Coal Measures; these are the clayband and blackband ores found in the Lowlands of Scotland, South Yorkshire, Derbyshire, the West Midlands and South Wales. They are of medium quality with about 30 per cent iron content and formed the basis for the iron industry of the eighteenth and early nineteenth centuries. Today most of the easily accessible Coal Measure iron deposits are worked out. Jurassic ores occur in a broad band stretching from the Cleveland Hills in North Yorkshire through Lincolnshire where the most important quarries are today, to Leicestershire, Northamptonshire, Oxfordshire and the Cotswolds. They are of low quality, with often as little as 20 per cent of iron content, but are particularly easy to extract. An isolated pocket of richer Jurassic ore in the Weald of Kent formed the centre of the medieval iron industry and was important until the seventeenth century, although the last blast furnace worked until 1810 and the last forge as late as 1820. The most important unstratified ore is haematite, which occurs in the Carboniferous as purple nodules of high iron content (50 to 60 per cent) and has been worked in Cumbria, Lancashire, Glamorgan and the Forest of Dean. The last haematite mine, at Beker-met in Cumbria, closed in 1980.

Evidence of iron ore extraction is very widespread, particularly in North Yorkshire, the East Midlands and the haematite areas of North West England. In the Cleveland Hills mining was the normal technique, beginning in 1836, reaching a peak output in 1883, and declining gradually after World War I to cease completely in 1964. The largest mine, at Eston [NZ 560186] was opened by Bolckow, Vaughan & Company in 1851 to work the Main Seam, and formed the basis for the initial growth of the iron and steel industry of Teesside. It closed in 1949. The Main Seam was also worked from 1872 at North Skelton [NZ 675184], the last mine to work in Cleveland and, at 720ft to the shaft bottom, the deepest. At Boulby [NZ 760181] the Skinningrove Company operated a drift mine from 1903 to 1934, erecting for their workers a shanty town of corrugated-iron houses which became known as 'The Tin City'. The remains of the foundations and floors are still visible. In Rosedale [SE 723946] magnetic ironstone from the Kitchings and Garbutts deposits was worked from the 1850s until 1885. Up to the opening of the Rosedale branch railway in 1861 nearly 40,000 tons of ore had been taken from these mines by packhorse to the railway at Pickering, the last large-scale use in Britain of this form of transport.

In the East Midlands the Jurassic ores are at relatively shallow depths and have generally been worked by opencast methods. The early workings, dating from the 1850s, were located close to the outcrops, but as these became worked out, steam shovels, introduced in the mid-1890s, had to be used to move the increased depth of overburden. By 1916 dragline excavators capable of stripping 25ft of overburden were being used, to be followed in 1933 by electrically operated shovels which could handle up to 55ft. In 1951 the first British walking dragline capable of removing 100ft of overburden was introduced. Initially, no attempt was made to reinstate the worked-over areas and evidence of the first large-scale workings can still be seen in the form of ridges and furrows, with an amplitude of up to 20ft, resulting from the dumping of the overburden after the ore had been removed. Today the quarry areas are levelled and the top soil replaced, leaving an open landscape of large fenced fields devoid of trees and hedges. A steam excavator is preserved in working order by the North of England Open Air Museum, Beamish, County Durham.

The technique of ironstone quarrying has altered little over the last half century. An aspect which has changed, however, is the calcining of ore. The calcining process removed the volatiles, mostly carbon dioxide and water, thereby raising the percentage of iron in the ore. It was

69 Roasting the ironstone in heaps, Dudley, West Midlands

carried out on the floor of the quarry by burning coal mixed with ore before loading it for transport to the ironworks. Coal costs have made this process uneconomic in recent years and it is now no longer carried out. The sequence of events in Illus 71 shows how ironstone was worked in the 1920s. A dragline excavator travelling parallel to the ironstone face (1 and 2) removes the topsoil and overburden. The overburden is dumped opposite the place from which it is taken on ground from which the ironstone has already been removed. Topsoil is replaced and levelled, and the land restored to agricultural use. Having stripped a length of ironstone, the dragline dumps coal slack on the newly exposed surface. A steam navvy following behind digs out the ironstone and deposits it, with the slack intermingled, on lump coal spread out on the ground behind it. The whole heap is fired at intervals as the excavator advances. Calcination is complete in about eight weeks (4), after which the ore is lifted into railway trucks and taken to the ironworks (5). At the end of the working face the excavators return to the starting point for another cut and the railway track is moved laterally forward to the edge of the new face. Today ore, which is usually blasted with explosives, is lifted straight from the bed of the quarry into railway trucks or lorries.

The principle of all conventional iron-making processes involves the removal of the oxygen from the ore by reduction. Carbon in the form of charcoal or coke combines with the oxygen of the ore to release metallic iron and gases. In modern blast furnaces oil is also injected. Wrought iron was made by heating a mass of iron ore in a charcoal fire to create a spongy lump or bloom which could then be hammered into tools or weapons. The iron was not melted, the hammering or forging process being fundamental in the removal of many of the final impurities. This direct process was the only way of converting iron ore into metal until about the fifteenth century when furnaces of sufficient size, using hand or more often water-powered bellows, to increase the temperature, could melt the iron into a liquid state. This new iron, or cast iron, was probably at first an accidental by-product resulting from the overheating of a bloomery furnace. It could not be shaped by hammering and its hard, brittle nature meant that there were at first no obvious uses to which it could be put. It was soon realised, however, that the production of cast iron could be a short cut to larger quantities of good quality wrought iron, and in this manner the iron smelting industry, based on the charcoal-fuelled

70 Roasting the ironstone in kilns, Coalbrookdale

IRONSTONE WORKING IN THE EAST MIDLANDS

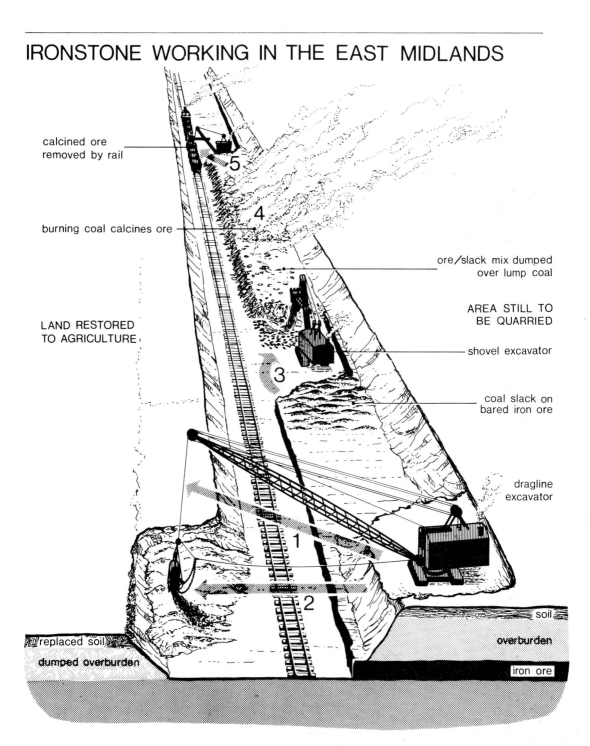

calcined ore
removed by rail

burning coal calcines ore

LAND RESTORED
TO AGRICULTURE

ore/slack mix dumped
over lump coal

AREA STILL TO
BE QUARRIED

shovel excavator

coal slack on
bared iron ore

dragline
excavator

soil

overburden

iron ore

replaced soil

dumped overburden

Illustration 71

72 Craleckan furnace, Argyll [NN 027001], a substantially complete charcoal blast furnace with the date 1755 cast into one of the lintels of the tuyere arch; in the foreground is the casting shed (*John R. Hume*)

blast furnace, came into existence.

The origin of the blast furnace is obscure but it is generally thought to have developed in what is now Belgium before AD 1400. The blast furnace enabled much larger quantities of iron to be produced than the old bloomery, as much as a ton in 24 hours as compared with a few pounds previously. Cast iron from the blast furnace was run as a liquid into depressions in a bed of sand, the main runner being the sow and, for obvious reasons, the side branches being called pigs (Illus 73). Pig iron is still made, although now by machines, the size of the pig being determined by convenience of handling. By the sixteenth century objects such as fire-

backs, cannon and cannon balls were being cast, but cast iron remained of relatively minor importance until the early eighteenth century when it was to become the most vital of raw materials to the civil and mechanical engineer.

The primary object was still the production of wrought iron, which was achieved in two stages in the finery and chafery. During the smelting process the pig iron had absorbed a number of impurities, notably carbon, and, if the temperature was high enough, silicon. The finery was a charcoal-fired hearth, similar to a blacksmith's hearth, in which the iron was stirred at high temperature under a blast of air from bellows. The oxygen in the air blast combined first with the silicon, which was driven off in the form of SiO_2, and then with the carbon to form CO and CO_2. As the iron became purer, its melting-temperature would rise, resulting in the coagulation of a spongy mass of

CHARCOAL BLAST FURNACE   CUT OPEN TO SHOW INTERIOR

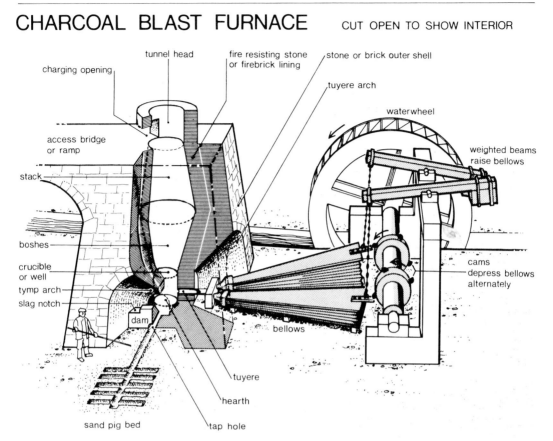

Illustration 73

iron in the hearth. This was hammered into a rectangular block weighing about ½cwt before being transferred to the chafery. The chafery, unlike the finery, had no secondary blast of air and was simply for reheating the iron to forging temperature so that it could be fashioned into a shape suitable for marketing. The iron was not melted and no change in its chemistry occurred. Charcoal was the normal fuel in the chafery, but as iron absorbed very few impurities when in the solid state, it was in the chafery that the relatively 'dirty' fuel, coal, was first adopted. The finery and its ancillary equipment, of which the hammer was the most important, was known as a forge, a term which is still used today for any works where iron is fashioned. Strictly, the term originally applied only to the building containing the finery where wrought iron was manufactured.

The bloomery furnace, and the later finery and chafery, all needed hammers, both to beat the impurities out of the iron and to shape it. From the fifteenth century these were water-powered tilt hammers, each consisting of an iron hammer head on a wooden haft working on to an anvil. The tail of the haft was depressed by a series of cams on the axle of the water-wheel and, as the head was raised, it was pressed against a wooden spring beam which ensured that, when the cam released the hammer, it would fall with a considerable and consistent force. None of these early hammers survive in complete form, although the Weald & Downland Museum near Singleton in West Sussex [SU 875129] has a hammer head and wheel shaft. Later, forging hammers known as helves were introduced for fashioning metal and some of these operated on the same basis as the early tilt hammers (Illus 86).

The importance of a supply of water for working tilt hammers applied equally to the blast furnace, where bellows had to operate continuously for weeks at a time. Indeed, water to power the bellows which blew the air into the furnace was a primary resource of the iron smelting and wrought-iron-making industries, and an important factor in determining the general location and detailed siting of a furnace or forge. This significance can be fully appreciated from the fact that for every ton of iron smelted 5 tons or more of air were required. Today the pools which supplied the water-powered bellows and hammers of early iron works are often the only tangible evidence of their existence, particularly in the South East, where the so-called 'hammer pond' is a familiar feature. Good examples, all in St Leonard's Forest, Sussex, are Hawkins Pond [TQ 217292], Hammer Pond [TQ 219289] and Slaugham Pond [TQ 248281]. At each of these sites the earth dam survives intact, now carrying a minor road, and the drop necessary to provide adequate power and the quantity of water which had to be stored to ensure continuity of operation of the forge are well demonstrated.

The production of cast iron in blast furnaces expanded considerably during the sixteenth and seventeenth centuries, spreading from Sussex to the Midlands after 1561 and reaching the Lake District in 1711. The principle on which the blast furnace operated was relatively simple, although some of the chemical changes occurring within it during the smelting of a charge of iron ore are quite complex and were probably not understood in any detail until the beginning of the nineteenth century. An early type of charcoal blast furnace is shown in Illus 73. In cross section it is shaped rather like a chimney with a narrow top to the stack widening gradually to the top of the boshes. The walls then slope inwards and become vertical in the hearth. There were numerous variations in this shape but the basic arrangement has been maintained down to today and still applies to modern steel-cased furnaces.

The blast furnace operated continuously with iron ore and charcoal charged in at the top and gradually descending through the stack. In the upper part water and other volatiles such as carbon dioxide would be driven off and in the lower section the ore was reduced to metallic iron. The increase in diameter of the stack from top to bottom lessened the tendency for the charge to stick. At the top of the boshes the earthy impurities in the ore fused to form a slag, and molten slag and iron were funnelled down into the hearth where the denser metal lay at the bottom with the slag floating on top of it.

At the same time water-powered bellows blew air into the hearth through the tuyere (pronounced 'tweer') and this reacted with the charcoal to give carbon dioxide and heat and the carbon monoxide which reduced the ore by combination with the oxygen in it. As the iron trickled through this hottest part of the furnace around the tuyere, it would dissolve carbon out of the unburnt charcoal, which accounted for the high carbon content of the resulting cast iron. At intervals the slag was drawn off through the slag notch at one side of the fore arch, and when sufficient iron had accumulated in the bottom of the hearth, the clay plug in the tap hole was broken and the molten iron flowed out down a channel to the pig bed. During the sixteenth and seventeenth centuries most of the iron was run into pigs for eventual conversion into wrought iron, but if objects such as cannon were required, they were cast direct from the blast furnace. The direct technique of casting remained common until the latter part of the eighteenth century.

A typical site for one of these early furnaces would be on a fairly steep slope so that an access bridge or ramp could easily be built from the hillside to the top of the stack for charging. The side of an existing watercourse was particularly suitable. At the foot of the slope there had to be ample space for the pig bed which was often covered by a casting shed, and the bellows which might be 20–25ft long and 5ft wide at their outer ends. Other buildings associated with such a blast furnace were the charcoal store, which was usually a large barn-like building, and often an iron ore store. A particularly good example of an eighteenth-century charcoal blast furnace, where remains of many of

74 The restored Moira blast furnace, Leicestershire [SK 314152] built c1804 alongside the newly opened Ashby Canal, remains of which can still be seen (*Neil Cossons*)

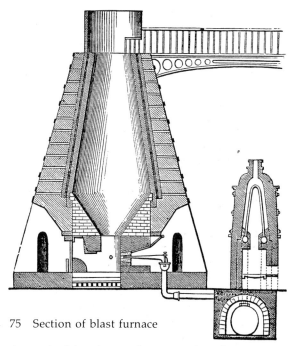

75 Section of blast furnace

the ancillary buildings still survive, is at Duddon Bridge in the Lake District [SD 197884]. The furnace was begun in 1736 and finally abandoned in 1867. Numerous other furnaces can be traced in the same area, including one at Newland [SD 299798] where the casting shed survives complete, and another on Leighton Beck, south-east of Arnside [SD 485778] where, although the furnace itself has disappeared, a large barn that was almost certainly the charcoal store can still be seen. At Charlcotte in Shropshire [SO 638861] is a well preserved blast furnace with an almost complete lining and cast-iron beams over the fore arch and tuyere arch supporting the stack. There are no ancillary buildings surviving on the site. Another good example, pre-served by the Scottish Development Department is at Bonawe in Argyllshire [NN 009318].

Charcoal was used exclusively as the fuel in all early blast furnaces, and this led to huge areas of the country being almost completely denuded of trees. Some fur-naces consumed the wood from over 150 acres of forest in a year with the result that the nation's timber resources, particularly in the South-East where there were the competing strategic needs of the Royal Navy, became seriously depleted. Before

the end of the sixteenth century legislation was introduced to control the consump-tion of woodland and so, as the Wealden industry gradually died, ironmasters were driven to more remote sites in the border country of the River Severn, in Wales itself, the Lake District and Scotland, always seeking the vital combination of iron ore, wood for fuel and water for power.

What was to prove one of the major technological breakthroughs of the early Industrial Revolution occurred in the first decade of the eighteenth century with the perfection of a technique for smelting iron using coke as a fuel instead of the tradi-tional charcoal. There had already been

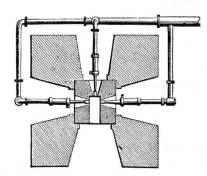

76 Arrangement of tuyeres

77 Morley Park blast furnaces, Heage, Derby-shire [SK 380492], date from 1780 and 1818 and remained in use until 1874 (*Neil Cossons*)

numerous attempts to use coal, of which the unsuccessful efforts of 'Dud' Dudley (1599–1684) are the most notorious, but in none of these experiments was the fundamental problem of contamination of the iron by impurities in the coal overcome. The coke smelting process was developed in Coalbrookdale, Shropshire, in 1709 by the Quaker, Abraham Darby (1667–1717), who had recently come from Bristol to take over an existing charcoal blast furnace set up about 1638. The geological circumstances which led to Darby's success are significant and undoubtedly contributed greatly to the establishment of Coalbrookdale as a major centre of ironfounding technology by the second half of the eighteenth century. The key lay in the local 'clod' coal, which, although not a coking coal in the modern sense of the term, was ideal for iron smelting. The process of coke manufacture was essentially similar to that of charcoal burning in that coal was burned in conditions starved of oxygen in low mounds or clamps, thus driving off the volatile components. The clod coal of Shropshire is of relatively low rank, with a carbon content of 78–79 per cent, and will not 'cake' like normal good quality coking coal. It can, however, be successfully coked in large lumps and, of particular importance for iron smelting, it has an extremely low sulphur content. Thus clod coal produced a coke closer in its resemblance to charcoal than almost any other coal in Britain. It was indeed a fortunate coincidence that Darby should come to a place where an eminently suitable fuel occurred in close proximity to good quality clayband ironstones from the Coal Measures. An additional, although less significant factor was the availability of limestone, which was essential to the coke smelting process as a fluxing agent. It is likely that limestone was added to the blast furnace charge as early as the sixteenth century, and certainly by the beginning of the eighteenth the technique was well known. The object of the flux was to assimilate the various impurities in the iron ore, which could then be easily run off as slag.

Darby's technique was of immediate benefit to him, as the major output from his Coalbrookdale furnace consisted of cast iron domestic products rather than pig iron for conversion to wrought iron. There were initial difficulties, however, in using coke-smelted iron for this purpose, and the new smelting technique did not become widespread until the 1760s. By that time Coalbrookdale was thriving, using coke-smelted iron and also developments of foundry techniques patented by

Abraham Darby in 1707. The patent for 'casting Iron-bellied Pots and other Iron-bellied Ware in Sand only without Loam or Clay' contains no technical details but it may be assumed that Darby had devised what is basically the modern method of dry-sand moulding in conjunction with multi-part moulding boxes. The bellied pots for which Darby obtained a patent were three-legged cauldrons with a maximum diameter in the middle, and they were to become a typical early product of the Coalbrookdale Company which he formed.

By the second half of the eighteenth century Coalbrookdale's ironfounding expertise was widely known. As early as the 1720s Coalbrookdale had been casting cylinders for Newcomen steam engines in iron instead of the traditional brass. The first iron rails were cast there in 1767 and at the end of the following decade the components for the first iron bridge, the first civil engineering work in the world in which cast iron, or indeed iron of any type, played a structural role. By the end of the eighteenth century cast iron was accepted as the major raw material of the civil and mechanical engineer, to be used for steam engines, the columns and beams of mills and warehouses, tramway plates, bridges and aqueducts and innumerable smaller machinery components. Coke-fuelled blast furnaces were being built by the dozen, and in areas where the iron industry had hitherto been non-existent. Indeed the distribution of the iron industry was essentially a reflection of that remarkable geological coincidence which contributed so much to the Industrial Revolution in Britain and the nation's industrial supremacy in the succeeding century – the occurrence in the same series of measures, and often very near the surface, of ironstone and coal admirably suited to the available technical processes of coke manufacture and iron smelting. Coal of the clod type occurred in South Staffordshire in the famous 'Ten Yard' seam, in West and South Yorkshire, and in South Wales, where a denser and less reactive coke resulted in blast furnaces being generally taller than elsewhere. North Wales, Derbyshire and to a lesser

extent Scotland also developed coke-based iron smelting, although in Scotland the 'splint' coals gave a rather lower yield coke and the great expansion of the iron industry there had to await further technological developments after 1820.

In 1760 there were perhaps ten blast furnaces using coke throughout Britain at sites including Cumberland and South Wales and the famous Carron foundry in Stirlingshire. Fourteen more were erected in the 1760s and early 1770s, but the greatest increase took place from 1775 onwards. By 1790 only twenty-five charcoal blast furnaces were still in operation compared with eighty-one working on coke, of which thirty-five were in the Midlands (twenty-four in Shropshire and eleven in Staffordshire). The best results from coke smelting were not obtained until a stronger blast could be developed than that provided by the old water-powered bellows. In 1757 Isaac Wilkinson introduced cast-iron box bellows, to be followed in 1760 by John Smeaton's invention of the cast-iron blowing cylinder, which was basically a piston moving in a large diameter cylinder to provide blast. Both these devices were water-powered, however; it was not until the introduction by James Watt in 1775 of a steam blowing engine at John Wilkinson's Willey furnaces in Shropshire that the coke blast furnace became really efficient and, for the first time, was freed from its stream or riverside site.

78 Blast furnaces, Hanley, Staffordshire

Evidence of this vital period in the development of ironmaking is readily visible in the Coalbrookdale area of Shropshire. In the Dale itself the now modified furnace in which Darby first smelted iron using coke as a fuel [SJ 667047] is preserved by the Ironbridge Gorge Museum Trust, and nearby is the Museum of Iron illustrating the evolution of the iron industry and displaying examples of the Coalbrookdale Company's products. The furnace itself, which is one of Britain's primary industrial monuments, has cast-iron beams supporting the fore arch, the lower two being from the original charcoal blast furnace, one dated 1638. The two upper beams date from 1777 and were added by Abraham Darby III (1750–91), probably to increase the capacity of the furnace sufficiently to cast the ribs of the Iron Bridge. Lower down the valley of the Severn at Ironbridge are the Bedlam furnaces [SJ 677034], which have been excavated and preserved. These furnaces date from 1757 and were some of the first to be built specifically for coke smelting. Originally there were two furnaces side by side, with bellows powered by waterwheels in wheelpits behind. Water supply was extremely poor, however, and a steam engine was employed to lift water from the nearby river to run the wheels. In every other respect the Bedlam furnaces were a model of efficient layout with tramways running down-slope to the charging platform to feed in iron ore, coke and limestone, and a pig bed stretching almost to the banks of the Severn where there was a wharf against which the Severn trows (sailing barges) could tie up. Like the Coalbrookdale Company, Bedlam was dependent on water transport as a means of getting its iron – in this case good quality foundry iron – away to market.

At some date after their construction the Bedlam furnaces were modified to use a steam blowing engine, and today evidence of this can be seen in the form of the three tuyere arches, each of which still contains its cast-iron tuyere pipe. Air was conducted from the engine via the blast main, part of which remains at the back of the furnace, to the tuyeres by iron pipe. Although no tangible evidence of the engine can now be seen, two nineteenth-century blowing engines are preserved by the Trust at the Blists Hill Open Air Museum about ½ mile downstream from Bedlam [SJ 694033]. One consists of a pair of beam engines driving a common crank-shaft and flywheel. Known as *David* and *Sampson* (sic) these engines were built in 1851 by Murdock, Aitken of Glasgow for the Lilleshall Company of Oakengates, Shropshire. They worked until the 1950s and were eventually saved from destruction and re-erected at Blists Hill. Also at the Blists Hill museum are the remains of three mid-nineteenth-century blast furnaces, with the houses that originally held two steam blowing engines. A vertical blowing engine, one of the last generation of reciprocating steam blowing engines to be built before the introduction of modern electric turbo-blowers, has been reinstalled in one of these houses. It provided the blast for Bessemer converters at the works of the Lilleshall Company.

By the time these blowing engines were in use another major development in blast furnace technology had occurred, although, largely as a result of prejudice, superstition and old habits dying hard, it took a number of years to become universally accepted. All blast furnaces until the 1820s had depended on atmospheric air blown through tuyeres by water-powered bellows or steam blowing engines. In 1828, however, James Neilson (1792–1865) of Glasgow patented the technique of pre-heating the blast air using stoves with coal grates, which were installed and operated successfully on a furnace at the Clyde Ironworks in the early 1830s. They raised the air temperature substantially, achieving in due course a saving of 20 per cent in furnace fuel. In 1857 the process was further developed by E. A. Cowper, who applied successfully the regenerative principle used today. In the Cowper stove, air on its way to the blast furnace is blown through and heated by checker-work columns of firebricks which have previously been heated by the combustion of waste gases from the same blast furnace. Using two or more stoves, heat is generated in one while air is blown through another. Alternation of the flow assures a constant supply of hot air for the blast, which reaches a modern furnace at about 1,350°C. Cowper stoves, introduced for the first time at Ormesby near Middlesbrough in 1860, are still used today, and their cylindrical forms with convex tops are a typical feature of most modern ironworks.

The application of hot blast, which was perhaps the greatest single improvement made to the technology of the blast furnace, resulted in a great increase in iron output and efficiency of fuel utilisation. It also meant that with the much higher temperatures involved, certain types of raw coal could be used instead of coke, and notably the blackband ironstones of Scotland with their splint coals. In South Wales anthracite firing was used extensively after 1837 in the Swansea area when George Crane introduced the process at Ynyscedwin. On-site evidence of cold and hot blast furnace practice is usually easy to find. Cold blast slag is of a glassy nature, has a conchoidal (shell-like) fracture, is usually blue and green, and is hard and valuable as hardcore or road metal. Hot blast slag on the other hand is a dull whitish grey and shaly, with a tendency to slake down to a fine mud when wet, although today it is also used extensively for aggregate and railway ballast. The coke smelting technique developed by Darby was acceptable when a perfect combination of raw materials was used, but there were distinct disadvantages when this was not the case. With a few exceptions, coke furnace pig when converted into *wrought* iron produced metal so brittle that it crumbled under the hammer. Much *cast* iron produced by coke furnaces also had a low strength, with a pronounced tendency to crack. The reason was that coke contained more impurities than charcoal, the quantity of ash was higher and sulphur and phosphorus were often present. In Britain the presence of phosphorus was a particular disadvantage, as many of the iron ore deposits which were being worked in the eighteenth century were themselves also phosphoric. In addition, not all the coal being used for coking had the same sulphur-free characteristics of the clod coal of Coalbrookdale.

The answer to the problem of poor quality cast iron was the remelting furnace in which coke-smelted pig could, in effect, be refined, thus improving its purity and homogeneity. The first remelting furnaces developed in Britain in the early eighteenth century were of the reverberatory type in which the iron did not come into direct contact with the fuel, which was usually coal. The name 'cupola' was given to these furnaces which were similar in general arrangement to puddling furnaces (Illus 79). The modern cupola, which became the standard means of remelting iron, was devised in the 1790s by John Wilkinson (1728–1808) and consisted of a vertical shaft rather like a miniature blast furnace. It was used for melting iron, not for smelting, and in its smallest form often consisted of a barrel perhaps 3ft in diameter and 10ft high made of cast-iron staves held together with wrought-iron hoops. It was lined with refractory bricks or cement and fired with coke. A very early example, possibly dating from the 1820s, is on display at the Museum of Iron, Coalbrookdale.

A large late nineteenth-century cupola furnace is shown in Illus 82. It has a shell of rolled steel plates and a firebrick lining, and is similar in most respects to the modern cupola that is such a typical feature of foundry areas like the Black Country. Broken pig iron, scrap cast iron and coke were fed in at the charging level, and molten iron drawn off in small quantities at the tap hole as required. The iron would be either run down channels to moulds in a sand bed or caught in hand ladles and taken direct to the moulds. Although direct casting from the blast furnace continued for certain applications, the cupola almost completely replaced this technique by the end of the nineteenth century. Initially blast was provided by water-powered or even hand bellows, but now electric blowers are employed. A typical small nineteenth-century foundry has been erected at Blists Hill Open Air Museum, Ironbridge [SJ 694034] and is in regular use (Illus 80 and 81).

The other difficulty of making satisfactory *wrought* iron with coke-smelted pig was finally solved in the 1780s. Experiments with reverberatory furnaces using

IRON PUDDLING FURNACE CUT OPEN TO SHOW INTERIOR

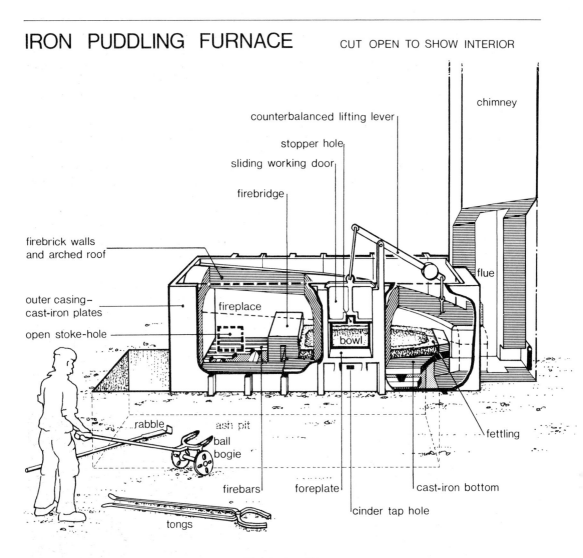

Illustration 79

coal as a fuel were being conducted in Coalbrookdale in the 1760s by the brothers Thomas and George Cranage, who took out a patent for 'making pig or cast iron malleable – in a reverberatory or air furnace, with raw pit coal only' in 1766. For reasons unknown, this process and a similar one patented in 1783 by Peter Onions, were not brought into commercial use. Final success was achieved by Henry Cort (1740–1800) of Funtley, Hampshire, who patented a workable puddling furnace in 1784. Cort's process consisted essentially of stirring molten pig iron on the bed of a reverberatory furnace until, through the decarburising action (removal of the carbon content) of the air which circulated through the furnace, the pig became converted into malleable iron. In this process contact between the molten metal and the raw coal which was used as a fuel was avoided and blowing machinery could be dispensed with. An important contributory factor to Cort's success, however, was his use of grooved rolls which he included in his patents despite their previous use. The combination of the puddling furnace and the use of grooved rolls to produce iron bar led to an immediate and spectacular increase in the output of wrought iron and provided an additional stimulus to the changeover from charcoal to coke smelting of iron ore. Watercourses, a wheelpit and slag can still be found at Cort's Funtley site [SU 550082] but no buildings or equipment survive.

There was, however, one major short-coming of Cort's puddling process: it was wasteful of iron, which tended to combine with the sand floor of the furnace to form a useless siliceous slag. An initial improve-ment was effected by Samuel Rogers of Nantyglo, Monmouthshire, who in 1818 substituted a cast-iron plate and iron oxides for the sand bottom, but the real breakthrough came about 1830 as the result of the 'pig boiling' process devel-oped by Joseph Hall (1789–1862) of Tipton, Staffordshire. Hall used a cast-iron tray for the bottom of the furnace, in which 'fet-tling' of oxidised compounds of iron such as cinder or mill scale was laid. The pig boiling process consisted of the decar-burisation of the pig iron by contact with the molten oxidised compounds. These combined with the carbon in the pig to form carbon monoxide, which burst to the surface of the iron – hence the term boiling – where it burnt with blue flames known as 'puddlers' candles'. Hall's pro-cess, because the iron was molten, became known as 'wet' puddling, in contrast to 'dry' puddling, which was done on sand bottoms. The wet puddling process be-came universal, to the complete exclusion of Cort's and was last practised at Messrs Thomas Walmsley & Sons Ltd, Atlas Forge, Bolton, Lancashire [SD 713084]. The equipment was then transferred to the Ironbridge Gorge Museum where it has been reconstructed at Blists Hill [SJ 695035]. Iron is made there from time to time (Illus 83 and 84).

Illus 79 shows a typical nineteenth-cen-tury wet puddling furnace. Flames from the fireplace on the left were drawn across the bowl of broken pig iron and up the flue. An initial period of melting then took place in which most of the silicon, mang-anese and some of the phosphorus in the

80,81 Foundry at Blists Hill Open Air Museum, Ironbridge [SJ 695935]; iron casting is demonstrated regularly   (*Neil Cossons*)

CUPOLA FURNACE

CUT OPEN TO SHOW INTERIOR

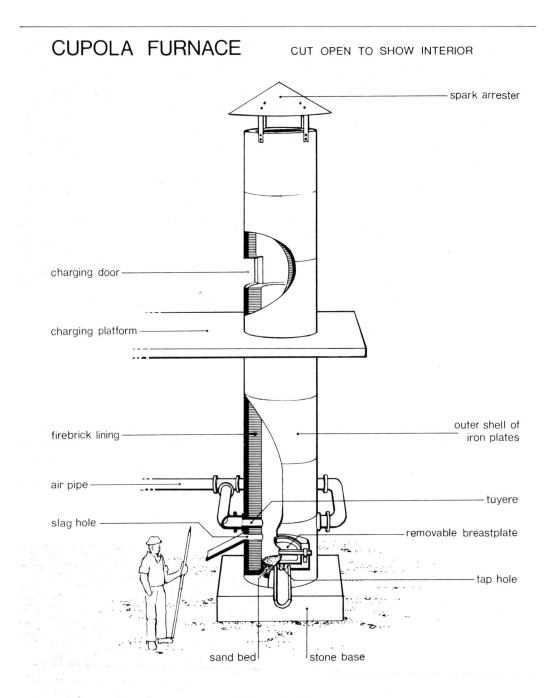

- spark arrester
- charging door
- charging platform
- firebrick lining
- air pipe
- slag hole
- outer shell of iron plates
- tuyere
- removable breastplate
- tap hole
- sand bed
- stone base

Illustration 82

pig oxidised and passed into the cinder fettling. The damper in the flue was then partially closed to 'smother' the furnace while the remainder of the silicon and manganese and most of the phosphorus went into the slag. At this stage 'boiling' began with the carbon combining with oxygen and burning at the surface as puddlers' candles. Throughout this stage the puddler stirred the iron with a rabble until all the carbon had burnt off and the remaining phosphorus was removed. The iron was by now almost pure and, as its melting point rose, it coagulated to be

gathered into four or five spongy balls and removed on a ball bogie to a hammer, where the liquid slag in the interstices would be hammered out and a roughly rectangular lump or bloom suitable for rolling would be formed. Hammering, or shingling as it was called, was initially carried out under a water-powered hammer or helve, of which there were three basic types (Illus 86), all of which were operated by cams on a waterwheel shaft. The type normally used for shingling was the nose or frontal helve, with a head of 5–8 tons in weight. At one end was the fulcrum and at the other the cams. Frequently these nose helves were steam-powered, but after the introduction of the steam hammer in 1839 by James Nasmyth (1808–90) they were gradually superseded and are now extinct. The other types of helve, used primarily for forging, will be considered later.

Once hammered into a rough bloom, the iron was ready for rolling, initially into a puddled bar or 'muck bar', and subsequently into smaller sections. Both the hammering and rolling processes were essential to improving the quality of the

83,84 Puddling furnaces, waste heat boiler (above) and steam hammer (below) in the reconstructed ironworks at Blists Hill Open Air Museum, Ironbridge Gorge Museum, Shropshire [SJ 694034] (*Neil Cossons*)

85   Tilting steel

iron, which was sold according to the number of times it had been rolled. Thus muck bar, cut up, stacked in a pile, reheated in a mill furnace and re-rolled would become crown or merchant bar. The same process applied again produced *Best* iron, a further working resulted in *Best Best* or *BB* iron, and yet another rolling made the highest grade of all – *Best Best Best* or *BBB* iron.

Iron rolling had its origins in Britain in the slitting mills of the sixteenth and seventeenth centuries, which produced iron rod by cutting hammered plate into thin strips. From these developed the grooved rolls of the type patented by Cort in 1784, which produced iron in round or square section, depending on the shape of the grooves. Illus 87 shows the various types of roll, of which the two-high mill was common until the beginning of the nineteenth century. The problem with a two-high mill, particularly for thin section iron, was that, having passed through the rolls in one direction, it had to be returned to the beginning – the dead pass – before it could go through the rolls again, during which time it was continuously cooling. The answer was the three-high mill, in which a third roll, the same size as the other two was mounted above them. Thus a live pass could be made in each direction, the iron going out between the lower and middle rolls and returning between the middle and upper ones, work being done in both directions. Three-high mills

are thought to have been introduced into Staffordshire before 1820, but they were not widespread until the 1860s. Also in the 1860s George Bedson of Manchester developed the continuous rolling mill (Illus 87) consisting of a number of two-high stands placed one behind the other. The reversing mill, in which the hot metal was passed backwards and forwards (Illus 87, stages 1 and 2), was introduced first at Crewe locomotive works in 1866. A very old, probably eighteenth-century, two-high mill for making small section rounds can be seen at Wortley Top Forge [SK 294998] between Deepcar and Thurgoland near Sheffield, while Blists Hill Open Air Museum has a steam-powered rolling mill as part of the wrought-iron works [SJ 694034].

Before leaving the iron manufacturing industry it is worthwhile considering further some of the secondary ironworking processes so closely tied up with it. In both the manufacture of cast iron and wrought iron, continuations of the iron-making process led through to the manufacture of finished articles. In the former case iron castings were initially made direct from the blast furnace and later by melting pig or scrap in a cupola furnace. Thus the foundry industry became separated from the smelting process and is now widely distributed throughout the country. Similarly with the wrought-iron industry, rolled bar or rod of the appropriate quality was the usual end product of a puddling works. Numerous industries, however, used wrought iron as a raw material, some of them employing similar equipment to that found in the ironworks themselves. These are worth considering here.

An example is Top Forge at Wortley [SK 294998], already mentioned. Although parts of the surviving buildings may date from the seventeenth century, most of the machinery is nineteenth century, the period of the forge's greatest prosperity, when wrought iron railway axles were made there. The oldest hammer, or helve, is nearest to the wall of the dam which once supplied the water power for its operation. The helve itself is of wrought iron but originally it would have been of

FORGING HAMMERS

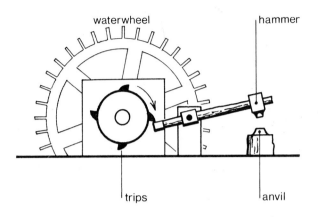

Tail helve

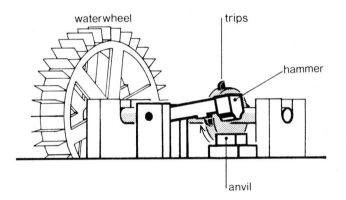

Belly helve

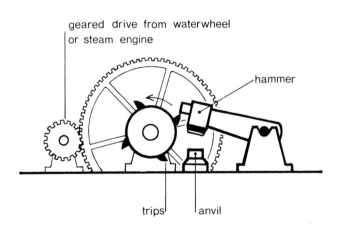

Nose helve

Illustration 86

ROLLING MILL TYPES

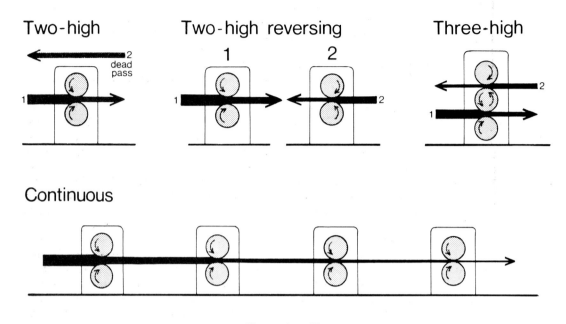

Two-high

2
dead
pass

1

Two-high reversing

1   2

1 → ← 2

Three-high

2

1

Continuous

Illustration 87

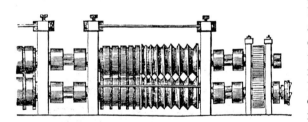

88   Puddle ball rolls

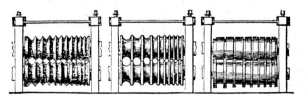

89   Finishing or bar rolls

timber strengthened with iron hoops. It is of the belly helve type (Illus 86) with the cams on the shaft lifting the hammer between the fulcrum and the head. Wagon axles were made from 16in square faggots of iron bars heated to welding temperature and forged to shape under the hammers. A rolling mill was installed in the 1780s and iron puddling may have been carried out slightly later. All work ceased in 1912. The forge, which is being restored by the Sheffield Trades Historical Society is open to the public.

Another preserved site where iron products were made is Finch Foundry at Sticklepath [SX 639940] near Okehampton in Devon. Here from 1814 until 1960 agricultural tools such as scythes, billhooks and shovels were made by successive generations of the Finch family. The machinery, most of which is still in place, was powered by the River Taw and includes a pair of hammers of the tail helve type (Illus 86). A second waterwheel drove a fan to provide air to the various forges, while a third powered grinding wheels where the tools were sharpened. The foundry has been restored by the Finch

Foundry Trust and much of the equipment can be seen in operation.

The availability of wrought iron in quantity from the end of the eighteenth century was almost as fundamental in its effects as that of cast iron produced by coke smelting a century earlier. The reputation of South Staffordshire bar, for example, became well established in the early years of the nineteenth century when Captain, later Sir, Samuel Brown (1776–1852) persuaded the Royal Navy to use iron chain cable instead of bulky hemp anchor cable. In 1813 he made a testing machine to measure the breaking stress of the iron and of the cable made from it. Today the remnants of the numerous chain shops linger on in the Cradley Heath area near Dudley where until a few years ago one or two works, such as those of Noah Bloomer [SO 959867] still hammer-welded chain links by hand. A reconstructed chain forge can be seen at the Black Country Museum, Dudley [SO 948917], where demonstrations are given. Another chain shop is at the Avoncroft Museum Buildings, Stoke Prior, near Bromsgrove [SO 950684].

Samuel Brown developed further his interests in wrought iron, which he used for the chains of the Union Bridge near Berwick [NT 934510], and soon Telford was also using chains for his great suspension bridge at Menai. So great was the increased efficiency of production and volume of use of wrought iron in the early years of the nineteenth century that it dropped in price by 60 per cent between 1806 and 1830. From the mid-1820s rolled iron rails for the new steam railways were introduced. By the 1840s Brunel was using wrought-iron plate for his *Great Britain* steamship, and Stephenson was using wrought iron for the Britannia tubular bridge, the first of a whole generation of large wrought iron railway bridges. About the same time the first wrought iron girders were being fabricated from rolled flats, tees and angles riveted together, and these were making their appearance in large buildings by the late 1850s. A surviving example is in the Sheerness boat store of 1858 [TQ 910753]. As a constructional material, wrought iron reigned supreme down to the end of the nineteenth century, almost completely ousting cast iron. It was itself soon to be superseded, however, by steel, which

90 The forge, Coalbrookdale Company's works at Horse Hey

91 Crucible steel furnace, Abbeydale industrial hamlet [SK 325820], Sheffield (*Sheffield City Museum*)

Mushet and another by John Hawkins as late as 1836.

The first reasonably successful means of producing anything more than the minutest quantities of steel was in the cementation furnace introduced early in the seventeenth century, probably from continental Europe. The process consisted of carburising wrought iron by sealing it in fireclay pots with a carbon-rich mixture, largely of charcoal, and heating it in a coal-fired cementation furnace. The main improvement over earlier techniques was that the pots were sealed, thus ensuring good carburisation. The resulting steel, known as 'blister steel' because of its surface appearance, was generally of rather poor and inconsistent quality and lacked uniformity of composition through a section of the bar. A better quality was achieved by binding a number of bars into a 'faggot', heating and then forging and welding to give 'shear steel'. If the process was repeated, an even better 'double shear' steel was produced. After 1682 high quality Swedish iron was imported to Britain for conversion to steel, and cementation furnaces became established around Newcastle, the main centre of importation. It is in the North East that one of the few surviving early cementation furnaces can be seen – the Derwentcote furnace north-west of Hamsterley, County Durham [NZ 131565], built in the eighteenth century and used until 1880. The only complete example – and the last to work in Britain, closing in 1952 – is at Hoyle Street, Sheffield [SK 348880] in the premises of the British Iron & Steel Research Association.

It is possible that the cementation process was brought from the North East to the Sheffield area, where in about 1742 Benjamin Huntsman (1704–76), a clockmaker from Doncaster, improved upon it with the 'crucible' technique in order to achieve a more uniform steel for springs and pendulums. After many failures, he finally found a method by which steel could be produced in a molten state. He melted bars of blister steel and subsequently iron and even scrap, with the addition of fluxes, in closed clay crucibles; the intense heat necessary was generated

became available in quantity towards the end of the century and is almost universally used today.

Steel possesses a carbon content ranging from 0.1 to 1.7 per cent, depending upon its various applications, which initially were all related to its ability to take and keep a sharpened edge. These qualities were recognised from early times and it was made in very small quantities for such purposes as edging swords and tipping arrowheads. The first processes consisted of heating pure wrought iron in contact with charcoal so that it would absorb carbon. Subsequently numerous but not very successful attempts were made to manufacture steel direct from iron ore. In 1791, for example, Samuel Lucas heated a mixture of iron ore and reducing material such as charcoal, powdered bone or cow horn in a sealed crucible with the intention of producing steel. A similar process was devised in 1800 by David

BESSEMER CONVERTER

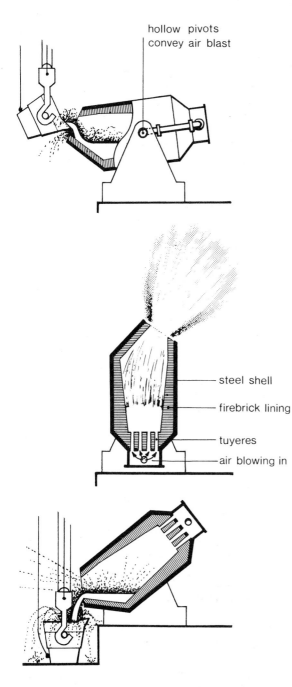

hollow pivots
convey air blast

steel shell

firebrick lining

tuyeres

air blowing in

1 Charging with
molten pig iron

2 Blowing air through
the molten iron

3 Pouring out
molten steel

Illustration 92

93 Blowing-engine house, 1847, Dalmellington Ironworks, Ayrshire [NS 442083], now part of a brickworks and the subject of a preservation project   (*John R. Hume*)

by coke. A crucible was placed in a chamber lined with firebrick, and the top of the furnace closed by a cover of the same material, which was level with the floor of the melting house. A vaulted cellar gave access to the ash pit. Huntsman's process was far superior to those previously used and produced a uniform slag-free steel. In addition costs were reduced and output increased.

Crucible steel was made at Abbeydale, near Sheffield, well into the present century [SK 325820] on a site now maintained by Sheffield City Museums (Illus 91). Here it is possible to trace the manufacture of steel edge tools from the raw materials to the finished product. The crucibles in which the steel was produced were made here and the workshop where the clay was kneaded with bare feet before being made into 'pots', as they were called, is still extant. The high quality steel was made from a charge of iron and scrap, and sometimes steel scrap or blister steel, which

was heated in the pot for about four hours before the carbon was added. The pot was then lifted from the furnace and, after any slag had been skimmed off, the fluid metal was teemed into moulds and allowed to cool to a red heat before removal. When cold, the quality of the ingot was tested before being reheated and forged. At Abbeydale the reheating hearth has water-powered blowing cylinders and hammers under which the steel was sandwiched between outside layers of wrought iron. Thus great strength and reliability was given to the central cutting edge. There are various hand forges once used by craftsmen to temper and straighten the blades and also to manufacture other articles from bar steel made under the hammers. The grinding machinery was driven by an 18ft waterwheel, and during the nineteenth century a horizontal steam engine was added to provide power during times of water shortage. Adjacent to the grinding shop is the hafting and boring shop, which uses a further waterwheel to drive its machinery. In addition to this unique assemblage of workshops there is a large warehouse (now containing museum exhibits), offices, a row of workmen's cottages, and a manager's house built about the middle of the nineteenth century.

Not until the second half of the nineteenth century was steel made in quantities sufficient, and at prices cheap enough, to replace wrought iron for structural purposes, but after the introduction of the Bessemer converter in 1856, less than fifteen years elapsed before the new material was beginning to be used extensively, firstly for railway rails and later for boiler plate and shipbuilding. The converter developed by Henry (later Sir Henry) Bessemer (1813–98) was extremely simple in construction and in the essential principles of its operation (Illus 92), being a trunnion-mounted container with a perforated bottom through which air was blown. The converter was first inclined to receive a charge of molten pig iron and then, with air blowing through the bottom, turned upright for air to pass through the iron to oxidise the carbon, silicon and manganese. As heat is given out by this reaction, the temperature of the iron actually increased. The progress of the reaction

could be judged by the colour and character of the flames issuing from the mouth of the converter. When the process was completed, the blast was turned down and appropriate additions made to achieve the correct alloy composition. The steel was then poured into a ladle and into ingot moulds. An improvement of the Bessemer process was devised by Robert Mushet (1811–91), the pioneer of modern alloy steels such as high carbon, tungsten and manganese steel. He suggested the addition of manganese to remove the excess oxygen which had previously made Bessemer steel difficult to work.

The major disadvantage of the Bessemer process was that it could not remove phosphorus from the pig and, as the phosphorus in the ore accumulates in the iron, only very low phosphorus ores could be used, ruling out many of the chief sources of supply in Britain. The problem was eventually solved in 1879 by Sidney Gilchrist Thomas (1850–85) and his cousin Percy Gilchrist (1851–1935). It was known that lime would react with phosphorus to give calcium phosphate and so remove the

PRINCIPAL STAGES IN THE EARLY MANUFACTURE OF IRON AND STEEL

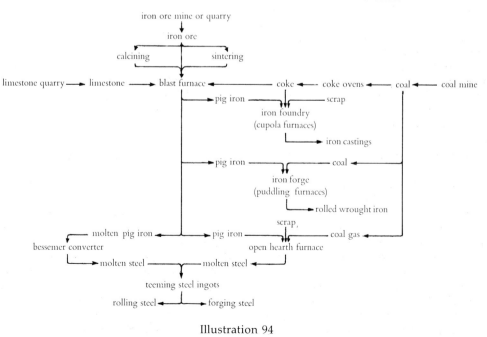

Illustration 94

phosphorus from the iron but, unfortunately, lime attacked the firebrick lining of the Bessemer converter. This problem was overcome by substitution of calcined dolomite bonded with fireclay as a lining for the converter. This new process was known as the 'basic' Bessemer process (because a chemically basic lining was used) to distinguish it from the original 'acid' Bessemer process. The terms 'acid' and 'basic' are still used for modern furnaces and refer still to the nature of the refractory lining.

The final major development in steelmaking technology during the nineteenth century occurred in the 1860s when C. W. (later Sir William) Siemens (1823–83), a German who became a naturalised British subject, introduced the regenerative open hearth furnace which was adapted for converting pig iron into steel, using ore to assist in oxidising the excess carbon and other impurities. The furnace was in some ways similar to the puddling furnace, with flames being directed across the hearth, but the hot gas passes through checker brick regenerators before going up the chimney. The direction of combustion air and gas flow was reversed at intervals so that the incoming combustion air and producer gas were heated in the regenerator before being mixed and burnt in the hearth. Cold or molten pig iron, scrap or a mixture of all these could be charged into the open hearth furnace, which flexibility, together with its greater capacity, led to its replacement of the Bessemer converter.

Later oil fuel replaced producer gas.

Throughout the whole period of the evolution of iron- and steelmaking techniques the fundamental principles have been those of achieving reduction and oxidation, carburisation and decarburisation, and they apply today as strongly as they did for the Wealden ironmasters of four centuries ago. For nearly 200 years, from the beginning of the eighteenth century until the 1870s, almost every new stage of development occurred in Britain, which by the early nineteenth century had achieved a degree of supremacy over all others in the field quite unprecedented and unrepeatable. The technological innovations of that period, besides giving Britain this commanding world position, had important effects inside the country by creating new regional concentrations of industry. Thus Darby and Cort transferred the iron industry to the coalfields, while Neilson influenced the establishment of the industry in Scotland. Much British innovation assisted competitors too, so that by the end of the nineteenth century the output of the German iron and steel industry had surpassed that of Britain, helped to a great extent by the use of the Gilchrist and Thomas process for converting the rich phosphoric ores of Lorraine. The archaeology of the iron industry is therefore the archaeology of one of the most important aspects of Britain's past, of a period and of a range of technological processes fundamental to the growth of industrialisation throughout the world.

95   Iron Bridge crossing the Severn in Coalbrookdale

CHAPTER 7

ENGINEERING

The Industrial Revolution was to a great extent a revolution in the techniques of making things, a revolution in methods of shaping wood and metal to produce machines which themselves were used to carry out other processes. There were, in effect, two stages in machine making, indeed two types of machine, which might be regarded as primary and secondary. The steam engine, as developed by Newcomen and, later, Watt, was a primary machine designed to carry out a specific function – initially the driving of a pump to lift water out of a mine. The limits on the efficiency of this primeval steam engine were twofold: firstly the theoretical concept which provided the basis for its design, and secondly, but at least as important, the practical limitations of available technology that applied to the way in which its components were made and assembled.

Early steam-engine making was the province of the millwright whose skills, developed over centuries in the building of windmills and watermills, were the most appropriate ones available. A Newcomen engine, built into a brick or masonry engine house, using a massive timber beam as the link between steam cylinder and pump rods, was, generally speaking, within the already existing capacities of the millwright. The cylinder, and perhaps the boiler, were the parts of the engine that demanded the most of available technology. As the theoretical concept on which the steam engine was based became more sophisticated, so the demands on technology grew, and so too did the proportion of the total inefficiency of the engine which derived from the way in which it was built. Thus in 1774 when John Wilkinson (1728–1808), the cele-

brated ironmaster, patented his boring mill, initially used for guns but soon after for steam-engine cylinders, he was making a major contribution to the efficiency of the steam engine. Up to this time an engine cylinder had been cast in brass or iron and its bore smoothed by a man rubbing it with rags and sand or by running the roughly cast barrel on a trolley over a boring head mounted on a rotating pole. Any irregularities in the cast bore were inevitably reflected in the finished section, as the flexibility of the pole allowed the cutter head to follow the path of least resistance. By mounting a cutter on a rotating bar which had bearings at each end, and devising a means of moving the cutter head along the bar, Wilkinson was able to bore a perfectly cylindrical barrel in the casting, which was bolted firmly to the bed of the machine. This boring mill was at least as important in the development of the steam engine as any of Watt's specific and recognised improvements; indeed the double-acting engine, depending as it did on a closed cylinder with a stuffing box around the piston rod, could not have been made without an accurately machined bore, and that could only be achieved on a boring mill.

Wilkinson's boring mill falls into the category of a secondary machine – one used to make other machines. It was also what would now be called a machine tool. The evolution of the machine tool was fundamental to the development of better and more efficient machines, and the men who built and used them were engineers rather than millwrights. In engineering a machine tool is a mechanical device concerned with the removal of metal or wood by turning, drilling, boring, milling, planing, shaping and grinding. During the nineteenth century machines were developed to carry out all these processes, sometimes automatically, that is, they could produce a complex sequence of cutting actions using information built into them rather than fed into them by a human operator. This growth of automatic machines and machine tools provided the basis for much of present-day manufacturing industry, saving not just on the numbers of men necessary to carry out a particular process but, much more important, saving on the number of *skilled* men required. The large-scale growth of manufacturing using automatic or semi-automatic tools was a phenomenon initially peculiar to the United States, where there was a great shortage of skilled manpower. It is no accident that the processes developed initially in the manufacture of small arms, which were to culminate in the introduction of production lines for making sewing machines, typewriters and motor cars, should occur first in the United States. The benefits in terms of cheap mass production were obvious, and already industrialised European countries, including Britain, took up these ideas enthusiastically. It is arguable whether these techniques were truly applicable in the context of a British labour force in view of the degradation of skill which they imply, and the first moves away from a production line system where each operative carries out a repetitive but unskilled task to a 'workshop' type of production environment are now being made, notably in Sweden and Holland.

The engineers who developed the first generation of machine tools during the eighteenth and nineteenth centuries were, in a very real sense, paving the way for the massive scales of production that we take for granted today, and the social and economic implications resulting from their innovations are at least as far-reaching as those deriving from other better recognised aspects of technological advance pioneered in the Industrial Revolution period. The machines they produced enabled other machines to be made more efficient, they enabled them to be made in quantity by making possible the large-scale production of identical components, and in doing this they were instrumental in establishing sets of engineering standards, relating to screw threads, for example, which allowed interchangeability of parts between one machine and another.

It is specifically with machine and production tools that this chapter is concerned; unfortunately they represent a much more difficult area of study for the industrial archaeologist than, for example, steam engines, canals or railways, not only because tools such as these were used in factories and workshops where they are often inaccessible but because they became obsolete relatively quickly and were easily scrapped. Many of the best examples of machine tools can now be found only in museums, while production equipment, which is generally very poorly documented, has tended to disappear almost completely. An added problem which applies particularly to production machinery of the last 80–90 years is its often highly sophisticated nature. Thus, appreciation of the significance of a particular machine is confined within the industry where it has been used; if there is no will to preserve it there, it is unlikely that any outside interest will have either sufficient knowledge or influence to secure its retention. Museums of technology tend to collect prime movers and easily understood pieces of manufacturing equipment which can be operated, or their method of operation simulated, in an easily comprehensible way. Rarely do they venture into the fields of complex production machinery, which makes the need for historical awareness in industry itself all the more critical.

As we have seen, machine tools are primarily concerned with cutting metal, taking on the processes previously carried out laboriously and imperfectly by a craftsman using hand tools. The earliest machine tools were the bow drill and the lathe. In the former a simple drilling bit was rotated by means of a string wrapped around the spindle of the drill and with each end fastened to the ends of a bow. Rapid oscillation of the bow resulted in a high speed backwards and forwards rotation being applied to the drill bit. In the early lathes rotation was provided in a similar manner, a string or cord wrapped round the workpiece being held by a bow or, more frequently, connected to a treadle beneath the lathe and a springy pole above. The advantage with the pole lathe was that the operator was left free to use both hands to hold the cutting tool against the work. String-operated drills and lathes are of pre-Christian origin and have been used until surprisingly recently in Britain. Bow lathes were used in watch and watch-case-making workshops in the Clerkenwell area of London at least until 1970, and examples may be seen in a reconstruction of one of these shops in Liverpool Museum. Similarly the larger pole lathe in its most primitive form was the standard equipment of the chairmakers or bodgers active in the beech woods of Buckinghamshire around High Wycombe.

The first major improvement on the pole lathe came with the introduction of the mandrel lathe in the late sixteenth century. The drive was removed from the workpiece and fixed instead to a mandrel or spindle connected to a live centre which supported and rotated one end of the work, the other end running in a fixed centre. This type of drive also made possible the chuck in which work unsuitable for turning between centres could be held. By the early eighteenth century the mandrel, made of iron, was running in bearings cast of lead-tin alloy, although the frame of all but the smallest watch and instrument makers' lathes was still made of wood. Later in the century screw threads could be generated on a mandrel lathe in which both mandrel and workpiece were moved laterally across the cutting tool held stationary on the toolrest by the operator. A guide screw on the mandrel itself was engaged by a fixed key to drive the mandrel forward at a constant rate. To enable screwcutting to be carried out, an alternative to the intermittent drive afforded by a pole or bow had to be found, and two forms were applied to the mandrel lathe. The most common was a treadle-operated crank connected to a large flywheel which was grooved to take a drive cord, the advantage being that the

operator could run the lathe himself. For larger lathes, however, such as those used by wheelwrights for turning wagon-wheel hubs, a separate drive wheel turned by one or even two boys was used.

The primitive screwcutting made possible by moving the mandrel and workpiece was greatly improved upon about 1770 by Jesse Ramsden (1735–1800), an instrument maker. The basis of Ramsden's lathe was to mount the cutting tool, ground to the profile of the thread, in a slide rest and propel it along the workpiece by means of a leadscrew connected to the mandrel by a series of gear wheels. The number of threads per inch depended on the rates of the gears connecting the mandrel to the leadscrew and on the number of threads on the leadscrew itself. The first large-scale practical application of the screwcutting lathe resulted from the work of Henry Maudslay (1771–1831), an engineer who was to have a profound effect on the development of precision engineering and an overwhelming influence over his own and the succeeding generation of mechanical engineers. Indeed, much of the evolution of machine tools can be traced through the personal connections forged between Maudslay and his own employer Joseph Bramah (1748–1814) and those who subsequently worked for Maudslay Sons & Field, the firm he established in London. Born in Woolwich and employed in various workshops of the Arsenal from the age of twelve, Henry Maudslay rapidly gained a reputation for skill as a metalworker, a reputation which about 1790 gained him a position in the workshop of Joseph Bramah, already well established as a maker of permutation locks that, in improved form, are still made today. The influence which this brilliant Yorkshire inventor had on the young Maudslay must have been enormous, and the benefits which Bramah himself was later to derive from the ideas sparked off by his pupil represent a classic example of the cross-fertilisation on which much inventive genius is based. Bramah, besides inventing the lock on which most of his fame rested, also patented a rotary pump, and developed a highly successful hydraulic press, a beer pump and a machine for consecutively numbering banknotes which enabled the Bank of England to dismiss 100 clerks! His interest in hydraulics – as early as the 1770s he had designed a successful water closet which was standard for a century – led him to propose the transmission of hydraulic power from central generating stations by means of mains pipes under the streets to which customers could be connected, an idea later taken up in almost every large port in the country.

In this atmosphere of ideas Maudslay thrived and, probably jointly with Bramah, developed his screwcutting lathe. This comprised a slide rest mounted on a bed of two triangular-section bars, and a headstock carrying the live spindle or mandrel which was connected to the leadscrew by a pair of gears. This leadscrew drove the slide rest, referred to for many years as 'Maudslay's Carriage', on which the tool was clamped. The lathe was equipped with several leadscrews having different numbers of threads per inch so that screws of different pitch could be generated. By 1800 Maudslay had conceived the idea of using change wheels to avoid the need for alternative leadscrews. His screwcutting lathe of 1800, on view in the Science Museum, London, has twenty-eight change wheels, giving a range of 16 to 100 threads per inch.

After the introduction of the slide rest by Maudslay subsequent improvements in the lathe included the development by one of his pupils, Richard Roberts (1789–1864), of the four-step pulley and back gear which gave eight spindle speeds, and the self-acting traverse which enabled the tool to pass smoothly and automatically along the workpiece, driven by a long screw additional to the leadscrew and driven from the main spindle by a type of bevel gearing. Perhaps the most radical improvements, however, came as the result of American inventions, starting in the 1840s with the turret lathe in which a clamp holding as many as eight tools could be rotated to bring any one of them to bear on the workpiece by the simple operation of a locking lever. This was followed in 1873 by the automatic lathe,

introduced by Christopher Spencer (1833–1922), in which movement of the cutting tools and turret was controlled by adjustable cams known as 'brain wheels'. The machine could be fed with bar stock and automatically manufactured components such as screws. A British automatic screw machine, patented by C. W. Parker in 1879, is in the collection of the Science Museum, London, while a similar machine is operated from time to time in the Birmingham Museum of Science & Industry. Other American contributions to lathe development in the late nineteenth century included the multi-spindle automatic lathe in which a number of components could be made simultaneously, and the Norton quick-change gearbox which eliminated the need to slip the drive belt from one pulley to another to change speed. At about the same time the introduction of high-speed steel for cutting tools greatly increased the productivity of the lathe and other machine tools and, because of the greater feed rates which were possible, resulted in much heavier and stiffer methods of construction.

To return to Henry Maudslay, his further contributions to the development of engineering and of machine tools were not concerned only with lathes but with standardisation and automatic machine tools, and in their own way anticipated American inventions by half a century. His table engine of 1807 was an example of a steam engine designed for standardised factory production and great portability, the first such engine to be produced in large numbers and the first widely available form of small steam power unit for factories that did not necessitate the complex installation procedures demanded by the house-built beam engine. Maudslay also pioneered the use of the surface plate as a contribution to accurate work by his employees, a carefully ground slab of cast iron being on every man's bench.

Far and away his most advanced pieces of work, however, were the forty-four machines he made to the designs of Marc Isambard Brunel (1769–1849) for manufacturing pulley-blocks for the Royal Navy. At the instigation of Sir Samuel Bentham (1757–1831), Inspector General of Naval

Works, Brunel was commissioned in 1801 to design equipment capable of producing at least 100,000 blocks per year at a critical period in the war with Napoleonic France. The machines, designed by Brunel, were built by Maudslay, who doubtless contributed to their design. By 1808 the plant was in operation at Portsmouth, perhaps the first installation in the world in which machine tools were used for mass production. Output per year was 130,000 blocks, produced by ten unskilled men doing the work of 110 skilled men and saving the Admiralty £17,000 per annum for a capital outlay of £54,000. Driven by line-shafting from a 30hp steam engine, the machines carried out the whole carefully programmed sequence of operations from sawing sections from elm logs, through the stages of mortising and drilling and turning the lignum vitae sheaves, to recessing for the metal bushes. Many of the machines remained in use for 145 years and several are preserved *in situ* in Portsmouth dockyard [SU 630005]. Eight others are on view in the Science Museum, South Kensington.

The Portsmouth blockmaking machinery established Maudslay's reputation beyond doubt, brought him a most valuable collaborator in the person of Joshua Field (1786–1863), a dockyard draughtsman who eventually became his partner, and, perhaps more important in terms of the long-term development of machine tools, made his firm the focal point for any aspiring young engineer anxious to train in an atmosphere of invention and innovation.

The most eminent of the engineers who worked for Maudslay were Richard Roberts (1789–1864), James Nasmyth (1808–90) and Sir Joseph Whitworth (1803–87). Roberts, as we have seen, made important contributions to lathe design but he was also responsible for making the spinning mule self-acting and for inventing a device for punching rivet holes in wrought-iron plate at exact intervals, in response to a request in 1847 from

96 The smithy, Glengarnock steelworks, Kilbirnie, Ayrshire [NS 324530] in 1978, now demolished   (*John R. Hume*)

97 The heavy turnery of Penn & Son's engine works in the early 1860s; Penn's boiler shop can still be seen at Payne's Wharf, Deptford [TQ 37278], where the engine of HMS *Warrior* was fitted in 1861 (*Science Museum*)

the builders of the great tubular girder bridges at Menai and Conwy.

James Nasmyth was born in Edinburgh, son of a landscape artist and engineer. His early interest in ironmaking, brassfounding and engineering led him at the age of 21 to visit Maudslay at his Lambeth works, where he was taken on as an assistant, a position he held until shortly after Maudslay's death in February 1831. He set up on his own account at Edinburgh later that year and then moved to a small factory in Manchester. As his business expanded, he needed more space and took a 6 acre site at Patricroft, west of Manchester, bounded by the Bridgewater Canal, the Liverpool & Manchester Railway and a good road. There his engineering works grew up. In 1836 he invented the shaper, in which a piece of metal secured to a table is cut by a tool clamped to a horizontal ram that moves backwards and forwards over the workpiece, which in turn is traversed by a screw drive,

either hand-operated or driven from the main shaft. Nasmyth's shaper in basic form is still used today, although there have been detail improvements. It is particularly suitable for planing small surfaces, cutting key-ways or producing any face which can be formed of straight-line elements. Nasmyth's most celebrated invention was the steam hammer, devised in response to the need for a 30in diameter paddle shaft for Brunel's *Great Britain* steamship. In the event the *Great Britain* was built with a screw propeller and Nasmyth's design of 1839 was not implemented until two years later. The only forging hammers available previously had been the water-powered tilt or trip hammers (Illus 86) which were severely limited in that they could only be lifted a relatively small height, and the force of their blows under gravity was not great nor could they be controlled. Nasmyth's hammer consisted simply of a vertically mounted steam cylinder supported on a type of A-frame with a hammer head fastened to the end of the piston rod projecting through the bottom of the cylinder. The anvil lay between the legs of the frame. Initially steam was used only to raise the hammer, which then fell under its own weight, when the steam was allowed to escape, but later versions were double-acting, the steam being applied above the piston to produce a more powerful and controllable blow. Later steam hammers, particularly those for fairly intricate forging work, had only one supporting pillar. There is a steam hammer of this latter type in the Underfall Yard workshops of the Port of Bristol Authority [ST 572722].

The third of Maudslay's eminent employees to make a name for himself in the machine tool field was Joseph Whitworth, a Mancunian who at the age of 22 left his work as a mechanic to come to London. In 1833 he rented a workshop in Manchester and set up as a toolmaker. By the Great Exhibition of 1851 this most prolific of all the machine tool manufacturers was able to exhibit twenty-three separate machines, in contrast to the two or three of most other makers, and by the 1862 Exhibition one quarter of the total space allotted to machine tools was occupied by Whitworth, the remainder containing the products of more than sixty other firms.

Whitworth was not so much an inventor of completely new tools or techniques as an improver of existing ones, and his work was based on the meticulous standards of precision which his years with Maudslay Sons & Field had inculcated in him and an ability to experiment in a relentless and thorough manner. His initial improvements were made to lathes, and his patent of 1839 covered a split-nut which enabled the leadscrew to be engaged and disengaged at will. He also introduced the hollow box casting for lathe beds which was much more rigid than the triangular bars used by Maudslay and afforded good protection to the leadscrews. He produced a highly efficient planing machine based on previous designs by Richard Roberts and Joseph Clement (1779–1844), both Maudslay protégés, but whereas these early machines were hand-operated, Whitworth's was both power-driven and self-acting. In his 1842 machine the workpiece was clamped on a table which ran back and forth in a horizontal plane while a cutting tool mounted above it traversed the work a step at each stroke. His earliest design had a quick-return mechanism to make maximum use of the total operating time for cutting, but in the 1842 model the tool was mounted in a swivelling box that enabled it to be reversed at each stroke and cut the workpiece in both directions of travel.

Another area in which Whitworth's powers of pragmatically inspired im-

98 Planing machine

provement were put to good effect was in the development of precision measuring equipment, and here again the debt he owed to Maudslay is self-evident. In 1841 at the Institution of Civil Engineers Whitworth was advocating 'the general use of standard gauges, graduated to a fixed scale, as constant measures of size', which he pointed out would enable standard machine parts to be produced. Maudslay had already produced a bench micrometer, taking advantage of his knowledge of accurate screw-thread cutting and Whitworth developed this idea further and to greater degrees of accuracy, demonstrating in 1851 an instrument capable of measuring one-millionth of an inch.

Perhaps the most famous example of Whitworth's work was his standardisation of screw threads, which resulted from his famous paper *On a Uniform System of Screw Threads*, read in 1841. At this date the design of screws was chaotic, with no common formula for proportioning the number of threads per inch to their diameter. Whitworth's answer to the problem was characteristic, highly practical and overwhelmingly successful. Making an extensive collection of screw-bolts, as he described them, from numerous engineering works, he analysed their various characteristics in terms of pitch (the number of threads per inch), depth (the amplitude of the thread), and form (the shape of the thread). These he related to various diameters to discover maximum strength and durability. The depth of the thread in the various specimens he examined varied more than did the pitch, and the angle made by the sides of the thread was taken as an expression for the depth. The mean of the angle in the 1in diameter screws was found to be about 55 degrees, which was also nearly the mean in the remaining screws of all diameters which were examined. This angle he then adopted as his standard and in doing so a constant proportion was established between depth and pitch. The 'Whitworth' threads which resulted from this exhaustive survey were quickly and widely accepted and became the main threads used for engineering work in Britain until 1905, when the British Standard Fine Thread was introduced to cater for the need for finer pitches. The Whitworth, or BSW, thread continued in use alongside the BSF and small BA (British Association) threads as standard until 1949, when a new thread, the Unified Screw Thread, was introduced under BS 1580. Since then something of a return to the pre-Whitworth shambles has occurred, with a whole variety of Unified threads, of American origin, themselves being superseded by the Metric threads advocated by the International Standards Organisation. In addition numerous variations occur in the sizes and depths of hexagons for bolt heads and nuts.

There is no doubt that detailed analysis of screw threads and of woodscrew design can provide the industrial archaeologist with valuable dating evidence as, despite the introduction of standard types, there is enough variation in thread design, bolt head and nut shape and size, and materials used (iron or various types of steel), to enable reasonably accurate chronologies, if not absolute dates, to be worked out. Hand chased or leadscrew threads cut on a lathe can be differentiated from threads cut by tap or die, while the changeover from square bolt heads and nuts to hexagons deserves detailed examination. The use of coach bolts with domed heads of various sizes is yet another area of study. The wood screw, too, has been through numerous stages of development. Other types of specialised threads also had their standards, Whitworth's own work extending to cover pipe threads and spanners, as well as wire gauges.

Another important machine tool of the mid-nineteenth century was the milling machine. Milling is the removal of metal from a workpiece by passing it beneath or across a rotary cutting tool, in contrast to shaping or planing, where the tool is fixed. The concept of milling was certainly understood by the French clockmakers of the eighteenth century, who used small milling machines to cut gear wheels, but the credit for developing the miller as a commercial machine tool goes to a group of American engineer inventors of whom Eli Whitney (1765–1825) was the first and most important. In 1818 he made a small milling machine. This had a power-driven table to carry the workpiece, moving horizontally below the cutter spindle and at right-angles to it. It was not until 1848, however, that a milling machine was manufactured for sale, designed by F. W. Howe (1822–91) for the Robbins & Lawrence Company of Vermont. This was followed in 1855 by the Lincoln miller, of which thousands were sold throughout the world. The problem of machining the helical flutes in twist drills, which began to replace the older flat drills during the 1850s and 1860s, inspired further refinements to the milling machine, the answer being found in 1862 by Joseph Brown of the Brown & Sharpe Company of Providence, Rhode Island. The machine he produced embodied all the basic features of the milling machine as we know it today, and with these features it deserved to be called a universal miller. Vertical adjustment of the workpiece using a screw-operated knee sliding in vertical guides, a spiral head geared to the feed mechanism to enable spirals to be cut, and provision for machining tapered spirals (necessary to make tapered reamers) were all included. Five of the original Number 1 model of Brown's miller were sold in Britain, and one is preserved in the Machine Tool Collection at the South Kensington Science Museum.

One further important machining process has still to be considered – the shaping of metals under abrasive stones, both natural and artificial. The development of the grinding machine was again largely the work of American engineers, although Nasmyth produced a grinder in 1845 with two 7ft diameter cast-iron wheels on which the abrasive stones were mounted. The introduction of artificial grindstones in the 1850s consisting of iron oxide, aluminium oxide or silica grits (emery), bonded with clay or rubber, accelerated the development of the grinder, which culminated in the introduction of a universal machine by Brown & Sharpe in 1876 in which most of the features of modern grinders were incorporated. The durability and cutting power of grinding wheels was greatly improved

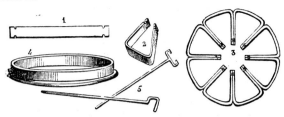

99   Tools and separate parts of a wheel

with the invention by E. A. Acheson in 1891 of carborundum, the name he gave to artificially produced silicon carbide. By the early 1900s grinding had become a well established technique for removing metal and sharpening all types of metal cutting tools.

The failure after about 1870 of the British engineering industry to initiate major innovations in the design and manufacture of machine tools, textile machinery and production equipment is highly significant and marks a distinct terminal point in the hitherto steady progress of industrial growth. Some might say it marked the end of Britain's Industrial Revolution based on new ideas; from the end of the nineteenth century the United States and Germany took the lead in innovation in the manufacturing field. The industrial prosperity of this period in Britain was based on the techniques and skills, tools and equipment that had been used in the previous generation. Markets were easy to find and the incentive to devise new means of doing things had consequently diminished. But a completely new form of engineering industry was developing in the United States, an

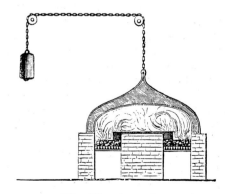

100   Ring furnace

industry geared up to the production of large numbers of identical, relatively small, components, finished to fine tolerances on machines that required little skill from the operator. The significance of this quickly becomes apparent to the industrial archaeologist working in Britain. Firstly he finds machine tools of surprisingly obsolete design dating from the latter part of the nineteenth century. The Port of Bristol Authority's Underfall Yard workshop is an example with an almost complete range of machine tools of the mid-1880s, mainly of Manchester origin and until recently in occasional use. But an examination of the smaller precision mechanisms commonly in use in Britain reveals a different state of affairs. American sewing machines, typewriters, wall clocks and gramophones and German mechanical toys were finding their way into homes and offices. They were made by what came to be called 'The American System' of mass production. Brown & Sharpe micrometers, the ingenious pin tumbler cylinder locks invented by Linus Yale, Jnr, in 1865, and even American agricultural equipment can all be found without difficulty in this country. Eventually the change in approach came in Britain, a change accelerated by the technological demands of two world wars, but not before the demise of much of what the old order stood for. As Henry Ford launched into his 15 million Model 'T' motor cars, firms like Maudslay Sons & Field and James Watt & Company closed their doors for the last time.

101   Bending the tyre for railway carriage wheel

102   Casting the nave of railway carriage wheel

CHAPTER 8

NON-FERROUS METALS

A number of non-ferrous metals were of increasing importance during the eighteenth and nineteenth centuries. Some, such as copper, tin and lead, had been known since antiquity, but others, of which zinc was the most important, were in effect 'new metals' from the point of view of their large-scale industrial application. All these metals were available in Britain, and the industries of mining or quarrying their ores, or in some cases the native metal itself, frequently sustained phenomenal rates of growth and prosperity. Just as often this was followed by total collapse, as deposits were worked out or cheaper foreign ores began to reach Britain in large quantities in the latter part of the nineteenth century. Of the four most important metals already mentioned, and of the less prolific deposits of gold and silver, only tin is mined in Britain today although lead is recovered successfully in Derbyshire and the north Pennines as a by-product of the mining and quarrying of fluorspar (calcium fluoride), used mainly as a flux in the steel industry. As for tin mining, the collapse of world tin prices leaves its fate in the balance and with it the future of South Crofty [SW 669409], the one survivor of this ancient Cornish industry.

The requirements of industrialisation both expanded traditional demands for non-ferrous metals and created new ones. Thus copper, which had been used for coinage both in its pure state and alloyed with tin in the form of bronze, was needed for sheathing the hulls of wooden sailing ships and, of much greater importance, as a component with zinc for the alloy brass. The unprecedented demand for brass created by the growth of the Birmingham metal trades and engine and machine builders led to an enormous expansion in copper mining, quarrying and smelting in the late eighteenth and early nineteenth centuries. Thus copper production rose from about 2,000 tons per annum in 1700 to more than 7,000 tons by the end of the century. Similarly tin, used initially for making bronze, bell metal and solder, came into its own with the growth of the tinplate industry in the early years of the nineteenth century. The expansion of the lead industry, which occurred mainly in the middle of the nineteenth century, was not as rapid, but, like the others, it too eventually fell into decline.

Like iron and steel, the non-ferrous metal industries consist of three basic divisions – the mining of the ore, the conversion of that ore, using a fuel, to produce a refined metal, and the use of the metal to make a finished product. As with iron and steel, developments in technology and the economics of transport resulted in the various refining processes of the industry changing their location. Lead, tin and copper were already being smelted and refined, using mineral fuel, in reverberatory furnaces before the Industrial Revolution period, and, as the industry expanded, there was a growing tendency towards coalfield locations for smelting works. In the 1720s copper smelting was being transferred from sites near the copper mines in Cornwall to Swansea because coal was half the price in Wales, and in the smelting process much more fuel than ore was consumed. The technicalities of smelting also required that ore from different sources be mixed, an additional incentive towards locating on the coalfields. As the main non-ferrous ores, unlike many of the iron ore deposits, tended to be away from coal, considerable transport costs resulted, whichever way the system was worked. Thus Anglesey copper was generally smelted on the Lancashire coalfield, notably at St Helens, but some went as far afield as South Wales. By 1750 over half the total output of British copper was being smelted near Swansea, and it was a similar story with lead. Highly integrated organisations grew up, with partnerships having control of all stages of the process – the ore mining in one area, smelting and perhaps colliery owning in South Wales, and sometimes an interest in a rolling mill or metal manufactory in Birmingham. Thus the whole industry was being controlled by capitalists who had a national, and often international view, could balance the various components of the production process to determine the most satisfactory locations for plant, and determine which ore sources were profitable to work and which were not.

COPPER AND ZINC

Copper was perhaps the earliest metal known to Man, although it was not until it was alloyed with tin to form bronze hard enough for tools and weapons that it became widely used. In the Britain of the Industrial Revolution copper continued to be employed in its traditional role, for making bronze for a variety of purposes, but it was the widespread demand for brass, an alloy of copper and zinc, which resulted in the rapid growth of the industry, and for this reason it is worth considering the two metals together. There were a number of areas where copper occurred in workable quantities, of which parts of Cornwall and Devon, Anglesey and the Lake District were the most important. The ore is generally found in the form of a sulphide requiring a number of processes to convert it into metal. As many as fourteen separate stages were involved but this became simplified to about six during the early nineteenth century as the Webb process became universal. The ore was first roasted and then melted in furnaces with 'metal slag', a by-product from later stages in the process. This gave 'coarse metal'

containing some 35 per cent copper, which was granulated by running it into a pit filled with water. The granulated coarse metal was then calcined (roasted) and subsequently melted with slag or ores rich in copper oxide. This resulted in metal containing about 75 per cent copper and 'metal slag'. The copper was run out of the furnace to make pigs which were transferred to a melting furnace and heated under vigorous air flow. The products of this stage were 'blister copper', about 95 per cent pure, and 'roaster slag'. The blister copper was tapped into sand moulds and further refined in a remelting furnace, where it was allowed to oxidise. The slag was skimmed off and the molten metal had charcoal or anthracite stirred into it with a green wood pole of birch or oak. This resulted in the copper seething as the gases were given off by the wood and becoming exposed to the deoxidising action of the charcoal or anthracite. All these various stages tended to concentrate the impurities in the slag, which was then removed, the final product being very pure copper. Purity was essential, any contaminants seriously impairing the mechanical properties of the metal. Thus even 0.2 per cent of oxygen in the finished copper resulted in brittleness.

Remains of the copper ore extraction industry are numerous although the various refining processes have left little in the way of tangible and comprehensible evidence on the ground. The Swansea valley on the other hand, perhaps one of Britain's most devastated industrial areas, shows what can result from unbridled development and subsequent decline of industries which produce large quantities of toxic or totally sterile by-products. The mining of copper in Britain on a large scale became established through the agency of a government-backed monopoly, The Society of Mines Royal, incorporated in 1568. With twenty-four shareholders, ten of whom were German, and between 300 and 400 German miners, the first workings were started near Keswick in Cumbria. The Crown received one-fifteenth of all copper produced and 10 per cent of any gold or silver. The only very early site identifiable as one worked by the Mines Royal is Goldscope Mine, Derwentwater, although most of the remains are probably of early nineteenth-century date. An adit is visible [NY 228186] and there are shafts nearby [NY 226187]. Over a mile of passages extend beneath Scope End, but these may well have been connected with lead mining as well as copper. Elsewhere in the Lake District more substantial remains can be seen not only of the mines themselves but of the plant used to concentrate the ore before it was taken for smelting. Like so many of these early metal mines, the sites are highly dangerous, with small shafts often completely hidden in undergrowth. Very great caution must be exercised in these areas. Underground workings should *never* be entered except with a local expert in charge.

Perhaps the most rewarding copper mine area is the valley of the Red Dell Beck, where the Coniston mines were established by the Mines Royal in 1599. Most of the present-day traces, however, are of nineteenth-century origin, dating from after 1834. The present youth hostel [SD 289986] is in the centre of the crushing and stamping works area, with the main workings away to the north-west. There are numerous adits, shafts and piles of slag, the remains of smelting carried out at the Low Mill site, 200yd south of the hostel, in the 1890s. Initially the ore was picked over by hand, but by the middle of the nineteenth century mechanical 'jiggers' were being used to sort the grades of ore and there were various types of 'buddle' or separator. Even so, ore processing was a labour-intensive activity and some 600 people were employed, including a number of women and children, when the works was at its peak. Fortunately, water power was available in abundance and there were thirteen waterwheels in use by the 1850s. Before the railway reached Coniston in 1859, about 250 tons of ore a month were carried away to be sent out by ship from Greenodd [SD 315826], then the major port in the area. Subsequently ore was carried to Ulverston by rail. Decline set in soon after the great Rio Tinto mines started large-scale production in 1873, and with further competi-

tion from Chile developing after 1882, Coniston copper mining, like copper mining throughout Britain, soon came to an end. Other remains in the general area include the foundations of crushing houses, wheelpits, and settling beds at Tilberthwaite [NY 306007] built in the 1850s and 1860s.

Although the Mines Royal had interests there in the 1580s, copper mining on a large scale did not begin in Cornwall until the seventeenth century, the ores being shipped in increasing quantities from the 1690s to Bristol, Neath and Swansea, although smaller quantities were smelted near the mines. Between 1700 and 1870 copper was of overwhelming importance in the Cornish economy, reaching a maximum output in the 1860s of 140,000 tons of ore per annum, to be followed by a steady decline as the workings became exhausted and cheaper foreign ores came into the country. Huge fortunes were made out of Cornish copper, both at the mining end of the industry and in the smelting works of Swansea where Cornish entrepreneurs had a large financial stake. There was one major attempt at smelting ore in Cornwall, however, at Hayle, and although the smelting and rolling plant has now gone, the area of Copperhouse [SW 568380] has canal dock walls built from copper slag or 'scoria' blocks 18in × 12in × 8in, which were provided free to the company's employees if they wished to build their own houses. Starting in the 1750s, the Cornish Copper Company's activities at Hayle lasted into the second decade of the nineteenth century, but the idea of smelting in Cornwall was basically unsound, some three to four times its own weight in coal being needed to smelt the copper ore and there being no local coalfield.

The archaeological evidence of copper mining in Cornwall is somewhat confusing, as many mines produced tin as well. The major areas of copper production are clearly defined, however, and included those of Redruth and Chacewater, another west and south-west of Redruth, the Marazion district, the Levant and Botallack mines (Illus 103) north of St Just on the Land's End peninsula, the Porthtowan and St Agnes area and along the coast near St Austell north of Sticker. In the east of the county copper was also mined on Caradon Moor, north of Liskeard, and around Gunnislake and Callington. As the archaeology of the copper and tin industries, consisting largely of engine houses, waste tips, remains of crushing and stamping equipment and a few Cornish engines, is so inextricably intermixed, specific sites will be considered in the tin mining section of this chapter.

Perhaps the most spectacular of all the copper mining sites in Britain is Parys Mountain, Anglesey [SH 4490], which began as a series of small mines in the late 1760s but developed into a vast opencast quarry after the collapse of most of the mine workings. By the 1790s Parys Mountain was being systematically cut away by 1,500 men to form the largest copper workings in Europe, while the nearby hamlet and port of Amlwch [SH 449934] had grown into a small town from which the ore was shipped to Liverpool, Swansea and Holywell. Inferior ore, overcharged with sulphur, was roasted on the spot, the fumes destroying vegetation for miles around. This, together with the great chasm of the quarry itself, evoked descriptions of 'the awful spectacle of sublimity', 'the savage grandeur of the scene' and at the same time 'excited the most sublime ideas intermixed with sensations of terror' from all who saw it. By 1815 the balloon had burst, for copper prices had dropped and the best lodes were worked out. Revivals occurred briefly at intervals down to 1883, when mining finally ceased, leaving the lunar landscape of today surmounted by an incongruous windmill tower [SH 444906] built in 1878 to assist a steam engine in draining the workings. A diorama of the Parys Mountain workings based on J. C. Ibbetston's late eighteenth-century watercolour may be seen in the National Museum of Wales, Cardiff.

Although zinc ores occur, often in association with lead, in a number of places in Britain, notably in Cumberland, Derbyshire, Durham, Somerset and North Wales, nowhere are they found in abundance, nor are they worked today. The most important ore is calamine, the carbonate of zinc, but the sulphide, known as blende or blackjack, has also been of commercial importance. The primary use for zinc found in Britain was for alloying with copper to make brass, but later, from the 1840s, the process of coating sheet iron or steel with the metal, known as galvanising, became increasingly important. The use of zinc for coating grew still further after the development of rolls for producing corrugated iron sheet at West Bromwich in 1844 and the widespread adoption of galvanised wire for fencing, while the development of electric batteries created a demand for the metal in a pure form as anodes.

Evidence of zinc extraction is sparse and difficult to identify, but in one of the major areas of working in Britain – the Mendip Hills of Somerset – 'gruffy ground', as it is known locally, in the neighbourhood of Shipham and Rowberrow is probably the result of calamine working from the late sixteenth century onwards. A stone chimney some 20ft high in a field across the main street from Shipham parish church [ST 445574] could possibly be the remains of a processing plant where the calamine was calcined. Mendip calamine was used for the manufacture of brass, mainly in Bristol, the port where copper was brought in from Cornwall. It was used for wire making, very important for the carding of wool (see p 176); and for sheet brass used in the production of pots and pans known as 'battery ware', the name arising from the fact that the brass was battered under waterpowered hammers.

One of the first brass mills in the Bristol area was set up in 1702 by Abraham Darby at Baptist Mills, and when he moved to Coalbrookdale some six years later, it continued and expanded under the leadership of the remaining Quaker partners. In the succeeding fifty years more mills were established along the River Avon upstream towards Bath and on several of the tributary streams. Keynsham, the most suitable of these new sites, eventually became the headquarters of the company and was the last place in the Bristol region where brass goods were manufactured. Production ceased here in 1927.

In the eighteenth century, however, the Avon valley above Bristol was the technical centre of the brass industry and site evidence can still be seen. At Keynsham itself are remains of the brass mill and its weir [ST 657688], but at Saltford [ST 687671] is a much more complete and very significant site with a waterwheel and the watercourses and pits for three others. The wheels drove battery hammers, a rolling mill and possibly shears. Of particular importance is a substantially complete annealing furnace in which brass battery could be heated to make it malleable again after becoming 'work-hardened' under the hammers. There are also foundations of two others. Although the mill closed in 1908 – the last battery in the country – the rolling mills remained, enjoyed a brief revival in World War I, and closed finally in 1924. Across the Avon, north-west of Kelston [ST 695680], is another important site where the surviving walls and watercourses of a substantial works are dominated by the conical square-section towers of two tall annealing ovens. Much of the Kelston site is now a boat centre.

Another site near Bristol is the Warmley Works [ST 668728] of William Champion, possibly the first place in Europe where

103 Engine houses at the spectacularly sited Botallack tin and copper mine near St Just, Cornwall [SW 364333], consolidated and partly restored by the Carn Brae Mining Society in 1985. The lower engine house contained a 30in pumping engine of 1823; the upper one, built in the late 1850s, was for winding *(John Corin)*

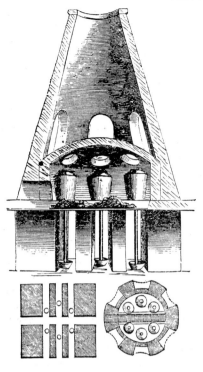

104   Zinc furnace

dry bed of the millpond protrudes the remains of a seated statue of Neptune constructed entirely of slag blocks! Grottoes and ornamental walks separate the lake from Warmley House where Champion lived. The house is now used as council offices.

Although the brass industry of the Bristol region has become obsolete, with no Cornish copper being brought into the city docks and calamine mining on Mendip extinct, the area has continued to have associations with the production of zinc, which in its pure form was being used in Bristol in quantity for galvanising flat and corrugated sheet iron in the middle of the nineteenth century. Today zinc is produced in a modern plant developed at Avonmouth by the Imperial Smelting Corporation, in which a blast furnace is charged with roasted zinc ore concentrates and the vaporised zinc condensed on a continuously circulating stream of molten lead. By feeding lead-zinc concentrates into the furnace, lead also can be recovered.

metallic zinc or spelter was extracted on a commercial scale. It was established at Warmley about 1740, but had earlier origins in Bristol where Champion took out a patent for deriving spelter from calamine. This was a breakthrough of some importance, as previously brass had been made by heating metallic copper and calamine together under a layer of powdered charcoal in a crucible. From 40lb of copper and 60lb of calamine (or blende) some 60lb of brass could be produced.

Champion's ability to separate metallic zinc, which was liable to volatise very readily during the extraction process, led to the manufacture of very fine brass, 'by the direct union of copper and zinc, care being taken to prevent the access of air to the materials while in fusion'. There is little on the Warmley site today which provides evidence of the technical aspects of Champion's activities, but several surviving buildings incorporate black scoria blocks as quoins. The site of the dam which impounded water for the water-wheels can still be traced, while from the

TIN

Tin for alloying with copper to form bronze and with lead to produce pewter and various solders has been mined in Britain, mainly in Cornwall, for over 2,000 years, and tin ore, after iron, has perhaps been the most extensively worked metal-bearing mineral in the country. In the early nineteenth century successful experiments using tin-plated iron sheet to make cans for preserving food led to an enormous demand for tin, and today nearly half the world output of the metal goes into the making of 'tinplate'. Tin, of all metals, is one of the most familiar to everybody, although what is invariably called tin today is in fact tin-plated sheet steel. Tin is highly resistant to corrosion but is expensive and lacks strength. The result of coating a sheet of steel about 0.01in thick with a layer of tin perhaps only 20 millionths of an inch thick is a combination of sterility and strength ideal for food canning.

As was the case with much of the copper from Cornwall, so too the tin mined extensively in the Duchy found its way across the Bristol Channel, to the tinplate works of South Wales. Tinplate making was established there, at Pontypool and Cydweli, in the early eighteenth century and the process continued, but with steel replacing wrought iron, virtually unaltered down to the 1950s. Then the old hand mills finally gave way to modern strip mills, and an electrolytic tinning plant was set up at Ebbw Vale in 1948. A number of buildings used for the manufacture of tinplate can still be seen at Swansea, Pontardulais and Llanelli, for example, but most are now used for other industrial purposes and are of little interest to the industrial archaeologist. The site at Cydweli [SN 421079], however, is worthy of examination if only for the plaque on the wall above the door indicating that the works, 'the oldest in the Kingdom', were rebuilt in 1801. Cydweli was in fact preceded by Pontypool, but the site is nevertheless of considerable note and surprisingly complete, with brick buildings and chimneys still standing,

105 Wheal Betsy engine house on the western edge of Dartmoor, beside the A386 north of Mary Tavy, Devon [SX 510815]   (*Neil Cossons*)

many of early nineteenth-century date. At Aberdulais Falls, West Glamorgan [SS 775994], the National Trust administers a site which was successively used for copper smelting, ironworking and tinplate manufacture although the evidence still remaining belongs almost exclusively to the two final periods of industrial activity – ironworking (c1819–40) and tinplate (c1840–90).

Perhaps the most notable surviving monument of the tinplate industry is the Melingriffith water pump [ST 142801]. The Melingriffith tinplate works at Whitchurch, some three miles north-west of Cardiff, were powered by waterwheels using water from the River Taff, but problems arose as a result of the Glamorganshire Canal Company taking water from the river and causing stoppage of work in dry summers. The final answer, after years of litigation, came when the canal company agreed to take less water from the upper reaches of the Taff and to pay £700 for the manufacture and installation of a water-powered pump to return water to the canal from the river below the works. Although in an advanced state of decay, the Melingriffith pump is still sufficiently complete for its method of operation to be made out. An undershot waterwheel drove, by means of two cranks and connecting rods, timber rocking beams that in turn operated the pistons in two cylinders, the water being drawn up alternately in each. The only other large pump of a similar nature still remaining in Britain is at Claverton near Bath [ST 791644], and that was used for lifting water from the River Avon into the Kennet & Avon Canal (see pp 55 and 265).

Far and away the most spectacular and widespread industrial archaeological remains of the tin industry, however, are in Cornwall, the county which for 2,000 years was Europe's major source of the metal. Reaching its peak in the second half of the nineteenth century, Cornish tin mining then began to feel the effects of overseas imports, mainly from Malaysia, and today, with the exception of those sites mentioned at the beginning of this chapter, the mining industry is extinct. The legacy which tin mining has left the county in the form of derelict mine buildings is dramatic, and the characteristic stone pumping engine house, with its tapering chimney built into one corner, is a trademark of much of the Cornish landscape. The areas where the industry was concentrated were around Wendron, west of Truro, St Ives and, of particular importance, on the Land's End peninsula around St Just-in-Penwith. Tin was also mined in association with copper around Camborne, Gwenapp, St Day and Gunnislake, and even in predominantly copper areas like Redruth and Chacewater, substantial tin deposits were actively worked.

The tin mining industry has an important place in the history of technology, for it was the problems of draining tin mines which instigated much of the work on the development of steam pumping engines, initially by Savery and Newcomen and later in the form of improvements by Watt and Trevithick. Although the Boulton & Watt beam engine was extensively used in Cornish metal mines, it was the refined version of it, the 'Cornish engine' developed by Richard Trevithick (1771–1833), which found the greatest favour and which can still be seen at a number of mine sites today. Several have been preserved as a result of the efforts of the Cornish Engines Preservation Society, set up in 1935 with the immediate objective of preserving the 24in rotative beam winding engine at Levant copper mine near Land's End [SW 375341], the oldest surviving engine in Cornwall. Other engines preserved are the 80in cylinder pumping engine of Robinson's Shaft [SW 669409] within the buildings of South Crofty Mine at Pool and built at Hayle in 1854, the 90in cylinder pumping engine at Taylor's Shaft, East Pool [SW 679419], built in 1892, also at Hayle, and the 30in rotative beam-winding engine built at the Holman Foundry in Camborne in 1887 and preserved *in situ* alongside the A30 (T) at East Pool [SW 674416]. In 1970 the Cornish Engines Preservation Society amalgamated with the Cornish Waterwheels Preservation Society to form the Trevithick Society, an active body dedicated to the preservation and recording of industrial archaeological sites in Cornwall.

106 Tombstone in Calstock churchyard, Cornwall [SX 437693] to Isaac Sleep 'accidentally kill'd in Virtuous Lady Mine by the crank of the water wheel, the 19th August, 1831. Aged 14 years'   (*Neil Cossons*)

These engines, together with the engine houses at Wheal Coats, St Agnes [SW 700501] and Wheal Prosper, Breage [SW 592272], are now administered by the National Trust. In nearby Camborne, once one of the most important centres of the Cornish copper and tin mining industry, a statue of Richard Trevithick (1771–1833) stands in the town centre; half a mile to the south-west, at Penponds [SW 636389], is the cottage in which he was born.

The rich tin oxide ores from the Cornish mines required crushing and concentrating before they could be smelted. Crushing was carried out under stamps consisting of vertical wooden beams shod with iron which were lifted by cams on a shaft and allowed to fall on to the ore fed into a box below. The shaft with its cams was usually powered, through gears, by a waterwheel or, less frequently, a steam engine. Water-powered stamps or their remains can be seen at a number of sites, although the fine set of eight stamps at Nancledra, which were in use until 1948, have been moved to Geevor [SW 375345].

Perhaps the only set of operational Cornish stamps in the world can be seen at the Tolgus works of Kernow Tin Limited [SW 690438] on the left-hand side of the B3300 road out of Redruth to Portreath. Here is a complete and working tin streaming plant which, until 1968, drew most of its raw material from the waste coming from the deep mines of South Crofty and Geevor. Since then, mainly as the result of improved techniques of recovery from these mines, tin has been extracted from waste left at old mines, from beach sand at Gwithian and from ore received from the few surviving 'tributers', or miners working by themselves with the possible help of a son or relative. At the lower works are the stamps, at the upper works a rotary calciner, last used in 1940 to burn arsenic out of the tin ores, together with the rotating tables powered by waterwheels which separated the metalliferous material from the waste. The Tolgus tin works are open to the public during the summer months.

LEAD

Lead, like tin, has been mined and quarried in Britain for some 2,000 years and only in the last half century or so has it ceased to be worked. As with tin, foreign ores coming into Britain in increasing quantities in the early 1900s finally killed the remaining mines, although smelting and processing plants, relying on these overseas sources, have continued in operation. Unlike tin, which was largely concentrated in Cornwall, lead mining was much more widespread, with major working areas in Northumberland, Durham, Yorkshire, Derbyshire, North Wales, Shropshire and Somerset. The main uses for the metal during the eighteenth and nineteenth centuries were for roofing and guttering, water and gas pipes and general plumbing work, shot, and in the very purest form for the lead chambers used in the manufacture of sulphuric acid. It was also used extensively for the oxide (red lead) and the carbonate (white lead), both paint bases.

The most commonly worked lead ore was the sulphide, galena, which could be converted into metal in either specialised types of blast furnaces or in reverberatory furnaces. In some areas, notably the Mendip hills of Somerset, waste materials left behind by Roman lead smelters were reworked during the late nineteenth century, using more efficient processes.

The remains of lead mining and smelting and, to a lesser extent, the sites where lead was used commercially, provide some of the most rewarding areas of study for the industrial archaeologist. The period of working was often over many centuries and carried out within the framework of complex local laws. In Derbyshire and Somerset, for example, the lead working areas were divided into liberties within which miners could seek and mine ore under specific conditions, which included paying dues based on output to the landowner.

Extensive surface remains proliferate in all the main working areas. Headstocks can be found in various states of decay at a number of shaft mine sites, notably George's Shaft, Snailbeach, near Minsterley, Shropshire [SJ 375022]. Further south at Tankerville Mine [SO 355995] are three masonry engine houses, the largest built in 1876 to hold a 40in engine. Magpie Mine, Sheldon [SK 173682], the most complete and extensive leadworking site in Derbyshire, has remains of an engine house and chimney, two winding houses and a modern steel headstock. At Laxey, on the Isle of Man [SC 432851] is perhaps the most spectacular monument of the metal mining industry in Britain, the great 72ft waterwheel, *Lady Isabella*, the largest in the country, built in 1854 to drain local copper, lead, zinc and silver workings. Now preserved, the wheel is at the centre of a mine trail which includes washing floors, miners' cottages and the turbine house of the nearby Welsh shaft.

Elsewhere, in Derbyshire and the Dales of Yorkshire for example, mine remains take the form of almost continuous fissures sometimes stretching for miles where the miners have followed a 'rake vein', as a vertical crevice occupied by the ore was called. The extensiveness of lead mining, coupled with the relative remoteness of many of the sites and their easy accessibility, makes care and precaution in entering them of great importance. Often there are interesting remains underground but a skilled and experienced guide is essential. A number of specialist societies, listed on p361, have detailed knowledge and understanding of many of the workings. Mining tools are abundant in museums such as Derby, Buxton and Sheffield, but the most comprehensive collection is in the Peak District Mining Museum, the Pavilion, Matlock Bath, Derbyshire [SK 293581].

Once the ore was out of the ground, it still had a number of processes to undergo before it was converted into metallic lead. Remains of processing plants or, more correctly, the buildings which housed them, are prolific in many lead mining areas. They exhibit a number of regional differences in arrangement. Ore crushing was usually mechanised, with water-powered crushers. Perhaps the finest surviving lead mill site is in Weardale, County Durham [NY 827429], where the buildings and magnificent 33ft 8in iron waterwheel of the Killhope ore crushing plant are preserved. Before this crushed ore could be fed into furnaces at least a proportion of the impurities had to be removed, so that the material eventually used was reasonably concentrated. This was achieved in a variety of ways, from picking over the ore by hand to various mechanised panning and washing operations. The latter techniques are used today but remains can be found at a number of

sites of the predecessors of this modern equipment. One of the most common types of concentration equipment was the buddle, in which crushed ore in the form of a slurry was fed down a wooden trough or launder into the centre of a circular stone floor. As the ore flowed down and settled on the floor, its surface was brushed by rotating arms sometimes supporting heather. The buddling process relied simply on the fact that the heavy metal-laden fraction of the ore would settle first, near the mouth of the trough in the centre of the buddle, and the concentration would diminish rapidly towards the outer edges. Thus the centre of the

107 Lead concentration flues at Charterhouse-on-Mendip, Somerset [ST 504557], part of the site operated by the Mendip Mining Company between 1850 and 1880 *(Neil Cossons)*

filled buddle could be dug out and smelted, and the material at the outer edges thrown away. Remains of buddle floors can be found on Mendip near St Cuthbert's Lead Works, Priddy [ST 545505]. The almost completely disintegrated skeleton of a jigging table with Archimedean-screw feed, also used for ore washing and concentration, stands on the Snailbeach mining site in Shropshire [SJ 375022].

Perhaps the most distinctive of all the site remains connected with the recovery of lead are those associated with smelting. In 1778 it was shown that lead was sublimed during the smelting of its ore,

galena, and that the vapours settled in the flues and chimneys of the furnace or escaped to poison the surrounding grassland and surface water. It was also appreciated that a substantial proportion of the potentially usable lead in the ore was being lost. As the fumes were very finely divided, they settled slowly, so in order to retain them, very long flues with built-in partitions or obstructions were used to increase the time in the flue and provide sufficient surface area on which the fumes could precipitate. In some cases fine jets of water were tried in an attempt to assist settling. The most satisfactory arrangement seems to have been a long, almost

horizontal flue with a vertical chimney at the end, but return flues and flues with chambers in them were also extensively used. Numerous variations on these themes can be found, defying almost any analysis of the optimum system, even if one was ever discovered. Frequently the nature of the terrain seems to have determined which type of flue was used. The flues have now often collapsed and are readily mistaken for culverts or drainage courses.

In open sites on the Pennines long single flues ran for distances of up to 2 miles from the furnace. One of very great length can be traced at Keld Heads Mill, Wensleydale [SE 077910]. Here a Stokoe condenser was used in the flue about 160yd from the mill, consisting of a chamber filled with brushwood which was constantly sprayed with water. Between 4 and 6 per cent of the lead recovered at the smelt mill came from condensers of this type. Beyond the Stokoe condenser the flue continues for nearly two miles up on the moor beside Cobscar Smelter [SE 060930] and both share a common chimney. At Grassington High Mill [SE 0266] a double arrangement of Stokoe condensers can be found, with the walls of the two compartments substantially intact. At the Surrender smelt mill, Yorkshire [NY 988003], is another long flue extending from the union of two smaller flues from separate ore hearths, and at Lintzgarth Mill, County Durham [NY 925430], two flues are carried on an arched bridge across a stream and a road to enter a condensing chamber. From the far side of the chamber the remains of a single flue run for some 1½ miles across the moor.

On restricted sites flues zigzagged or were banked, grid-iron fashion, with chambers at each return. Flues of this latter type (Illus 107) can be seen at Charterhouse-on-Mendip in Somerset [ST 504557], and there is a zigzag arrangement at Castleside smelter in County Durham [NZ 078485]. The Wanlockhead site in Dumfriesshire [NS 873125] has a curious coiled system of flues nearly 1,000yd long and the remains of a condenser which held racks of pebbles and water-soaked coke filters. Wanlockhead is also notable for the

108 Water-bucket beam pumping engine that drained the Straightsteps lead mine, Wanlockhead, Dumfriesshire [NS 873125]
(*Museum of the Scottish Lead Mining Industry*)

water-powered pumping engine (Illus 108) used to drain the workings.

Associated with these flues were chimneys, often of considerable height, many of which still survive. Some dominate the landscape for many miles, as at Smitham Hill, Mendip [ST 555546], where a chimney of very Cornish appearance has recently been restored. Another 'Cornish' type of chimney of circular section tops the long flue from Langley smelt mill, Northumberland [NY 841611], and there is a square-section stack of squat appearance at Stone Edge Mill, Derbyshire [SK 334670]. Alport, Derbyshire [SK 223648] has a particularly corpulent chimney designed to receive the gases from four separate furnaces.

Before leaving chimneys and flues it is worth mentioning that other metal industries also used them to a certain extent in conjunction with the refining of tin and copper, as at Crews Hole, Bristol, where a copper works chimney survives [ST 625733], and also in the extraction of arsenic. In the latter case the flue played a twofold role in preventing the poisonous arsenious oxide from contaminating the countryside and in providing a means of recovery of the material for commercial use. At the Devon Great Consols mine [SX 425733], which was concerned initially with copper, arsenic had become the main source of income by the 1870s, as the chimney and flue system indicate. In Cornwall the Botallack tin mine [SW 364333] has a complete labyrinth of arsenic flues.

One product for which lead was extensively used – lead shot – required a highly specialised form of industrial building for its manufacture. By a process perfected in Bristol in the 1780s molten lead (mixed with arsenic to make it form hard and spherical globules) was poured through a perforated tray to fall up to 150ft into a vat of water. The droplets solidified as they fell and the water prevented them being damaged by impact. What was probably the first shot tower, built in Bristol in about 1787, was demolished in 1968 for the inevitable road widening, and this great loss, coupled with the destruction soon after of the 174ft Elswick shot tower in Newcastle-upon-Tyne, means that there is now only one in existence in Britain, in the works of Associated Lead at Chester [SJ 415666]. A shot tower that stood near Waterloo Bridge, London, was pulled down soon after the Festival of Britain in 1951.

OTHER NON-FERROUS METALS

Of the other non-ferrous metals which have been worked or processed in Britain, aluminium is perhaps the most important. A relatively 'modern' metal, it was considered semi-precious as recently as the 1890s and a century ago fetched £3 per ounce. The intensive demand for the metal, created particularly by the wartime aircraft industry, has made it the most important after iron/steel. The smelting industry in Britain uses imported bauxite (the ore, hydrated aluminium oxide) and because the process is electrical it is sited near sources of cheap electricity – for instance, in the Highlands of Scotland where hydro-electric generation made smelting more economical than elsewhere. As with the smelting of copper in South Wales 150 years ago, the industry is located near its source of energy.

Although early aluminium smelters may only now be coming within the province of industrial archaeological investigation, gold mining installations in Wales provide a surprising wealth of site evidence. The gold mining industry was largely concentrated in Gwynedd north of the River Mawddach, and in Dyfed. At Dolaucothi in Dyfed, where the Romans had mined gold, there were revivals of activity in 1910 and the 1930s, the site [SN 670410] being finally abandoned in 1940. Although remains of the Roman workings, including an adit and watercourse, can still be seen, the only evidence of recent mining is a concrete capped shaft. At Gwynfynydd [SH 735275] in Gwynedd, however, there are remains of the ore concentration plant, with steel pipes which brought water to a turbine, part of which still survives, and walls surrounding extensive working levels. The mine was worked from a number of levels, and there is a substantial headframe in one of them used for winding up and down an inclined shaft from levels lower down. Near the entrance to one of these adit levels is the strong room [SH 737282] where gold was stored before being transported to the mill. The site was first worked in 1864, reached its peak output in the 1901–4 period and finally closed in 1938. At Ponterwyd, Dyfed [SN 735808] the Llywernog silver/lead mine site has been developed as a museum.

109 Engraved lead plate from the Redcliffe shot tower, Bristol   (*Neil Cossons*)

CHAPTER 9

STONE, CLAY AND GLASS

The iron industry, on which so much of Britain's industrial growth depended, relied on basic raw materials taken out of the ground – iron ore, limestone and coal for coking. So too did non-ferrous metal industries like those of tin, copper, zinc and lead. All these metal extraction industries, and their concomitant processing and refining, underwent radical changes in scale and technology during the Industrial Revolution period, which makes them a legitimate area of study for the industrial archaeologist. There were, however, other extractive and manufacturing industries based on mineral or quarried raw materials, which also gained in importance during the same period. They used non-metallic raw materials, notably stone and clay. The stone industry, based largely on quarrying, was a traditional one which underwent more change as a result of increasing scale of operation than major advances in extractive technology. The products of quarrying in the form of stone for building continued to be used in the traditional manner. The main effects of industrialisation were to create enormous new demands on certain specialised sectors of the quarrying industry – for roofing slates from North Wales, for example – and it is these aspects of the industry on which this chapter will concentrate. Similarly demand for bricks, cement and later concrete was greatly stimulated by the building activity associated with industrialisation. The pottery and glass industries, also based on raw materials out of the ground, expanded enormously and developed new technologies. In the pottery industry, and largely as a result of the organisational innovations of Josiah Wedgwood (1730–95), not only were new manufacturing techniques

introduced but a whole new approach to the basis of employment of workers akin to a 'production line' was devised, with specialist craftsmen each engaged on a limited area of the production process.

STONE AND CLAY FOR BUILDING

Even before the 'transport revolution', which occurred in parallel with the development of industrialisation, stone was carried great distances from the quarry to the place where it was used – Clipsham stone from Rutland to Windsor Castle, Purbeck 'marble' to Durham and many other cathedrals. With the completion of the Avon Navigation in 1727, Bath stone became even more extensively used, in London and Dublin, for example, and in the 1730s Ralph Allen built one of the first railways, to connect his Combe Down quarries overlooking Bath with the River Avon link to the outside world. The nineteenth century saw the real expansion of this long-distance transport of stone. The growth of London alone created enormous demands for stone, as it did for brick and slate also. Dartmoor granite was used for Rennie's London Bridge in the 1820s, Bazalgette's Victoria Embankment came largely from the quarries of Lundy Island, and Portland stone, already well established for the public buildings of the metropolis, became uniquely associated with the imperial *tours de force* of the Edwardian era.

Most stone is quarried, as opposed to being mined, and quarries, both working and abandoned, often yield useful information for the industrial archaeologist. Cranes, primitive railways, rock-sawing equipment, and curious little brick- or stone-built powder houses are among the site evidence to be found in disused stone quarries, which very often contain at least some other abandoned equipment too. A sandstone quarry in Bebington, Cheshire [SJ 315845], for example, possesses fishbelly rails on stone sleepers, thought to be part of the original track of the Liverpool & Manchester Railway.

In contrast to most building stones, Bath stone has since the 1850s usually been mined in underground galleries, many of great size. Only one, the Monks Park mine, is still in operation, but there are remains of others at Box and Corsham. The stone occurs in beds over 20ft thick, which were reached by shafts and inclines. The method of working was, in effect, the 'pillar and stall' technique (see p 91) in that huge stone pillars were left in the workings to support the roof as mining proceeded. The Bath stone was taken out in large blocks which, until the 1940s, were sawn by hand, but today a coal-cutting machine is used (Illus 111).

Of all the building materials quarried in the British Isles, Welsh slate has perhaps had the most geographically widespread use and its extraction has produced some strikingly spectacular landscapes of lunar quality. Before about 1820 North Wales slate was mainly used locally, but with the development of the canal network in England and later of railways, the easily won and highly tractable slate became the cheapest available roofing material over most of Britain. Huge quantities left North Wales on coastal schooners and by rail to cover acres of rooftops in every industrial town and city. Only in areas such as West Yorkshire, Collyweston in Lincolnshire and Stonesfield in Oxfordshire could locally available 'slates' – in fact they are laminar limestone – hold their own. Welsh slates, and to a lesser extent Westmorland slates, were both cheap to quarry and dress and could be provided in accurate sizes of absolutely uniform quality which, in addition to the fact that they were relatively thin, made them ideal for the hundreds of thousands of standardised workers' houses which were being built throughout the nineteenth century.

Several parts of North Wales, even today, are still totally dominated by the slate industry, which once thrived there but is now almost dead. The huge Penrhyn complex [SH 6265] glowers over Bethesda and the entrance to Nant Ffrancon, massive piles of waste spilling over from the working levels high above the floor of the valley, and Blaenau Ffestiniog [SH 7046] is almost surrounded on the north and east by old quarry workings, together with underground mines. Perhaps the most spectacular and, to the industrial archaeologist, one of the most interesting areas of slate working is to the south-east of Llyn Padarn, in the Dinorwic Quarry at Gilfach Ddu, Llanberis [SH 5960]. Here the North Wales Quarrying Museum has been set up, under the care of the National Museum of Wales, in the quarry workshop buildings [SH 586603].

First worked in 1809, the Dinorwig Quarry, like others in Gwynedd, enjoyed its greatest prosperity in the latter part of the nineteenth century, peak output being reached in 1900, when some 3,000 men were employed. The workshop buildings were erected in 1870 around a quadrangle, the main entrance being through a central archway surmounted by a clock with a face of slate. Behind towers the quarry, with terrace upon terrace of workings reaching up from the shores of Llyn Padarn 1,400ft to the top of Elidir. It closed in 1969.

The museum occupies the old workshops or, to be more accurate, the old workshops are the museum, for they are little changed from when they were in use, and contain much of the original equipment. A woodworking shop, pattern shop, foundries, smithies, fitting shops and locomotive sheds made the quarries almost completely self-sufficient, enabling the company to manufacture and maintain almost everything it required for the quarrying, dressing and transport of the slate. All the machines were driven by line-shafting from a single waterwheel of 50ft 5in diameter and 80hp, which was the sole prime mover from 1870 to 1925, when it was replaced by a Pelton wheel that still drives some of the machinery. The foundry, dominated by a huge hand-operated wooden crane of 1872, looks as it did when working, with wooden patterns laid out for gear wheels, locomotive wheels, turntables and numerous smaller castings. At the four blacksmiths' hearths all the hand tools for the quarry were made. The machine shop has lathes, a slotting machine and a drill, most dating from early this century. Slate-sawing tables can be seen and other aspects of the slate-dressing industry are to be included as the museum develops. Outside, what is now called the Llanberis Lake Railway along the shores of Llyn Padarn has been reinstated by a private company to carry passengers. There are a number of other slate working sites open to the public and which afford an opportunity to go underground. In Blaenau Ffestiniog are the Llechwedd slate caverns [SH 708471], which include a slate museum and inclines giving access to some of the sixteen levels of the Llechwedd Deep Mine, and Gloddfa Ganol [SH 698470] where furnished cottages form part of the surface displays. Southeast of Harlech are the Llanfair Quarry slate caverns [SH 596298].

Although Welsh slates were almost universal roofing material for the houses and factories of nineteenth-century industrial Britain, by far the majority of those buildings were built of brick rather than stone. Only in specific areas of Scotland

110 Conical brick kiln, Nettlebed, Oxfordshire [SU 703868]   (*Oxfordshire County Museum*)

and Pennine Yorkshire and Lancashire did stone continue almost throughout, and even here invading terraces of red brick can often be seen. Elsewhere bricks were used for everything – the whole of the Midlands industrial area and most of London. It is in a way remarkable that something as large as a house is built of something as small as a brick but, as a manufactured building unit, the brick had and still has a lot to offer, of which convenience of handling is the most important, being related to what a bricklayer can hold comfortably in one hand. The size of bricks has thus remained remarkably consistent. A curious exception were the bricks made by Sir Joseph Wilkes at his Measham brickworks in Leicestershire during the 1790s in an attempt to beat the brick tax introduced in 1784. Known locally as Wilkes' Gobs, these bricks, almost twice the size of normal ones, can still be seen in a number of houses in Measham [SK 334122] and nearby villages.

Wilkes' Gobs were only successful for a short time, as in 1803 bricks larger than 10in × 3in × 5in paid double the tax. The rate of duty was substantial, starting in 1784 at 2s 6d per 1,000 and reaching 5s in 1803, when tiles were also included. In 1833 the tile tax was repealed but two years later the duty on common bricks was raised to 5s 10d per 1,000. All taxes on bricks were removed in 1850, a considerable sacrifice of revenue by the government, which, in the year before the duty was repealed, collected charges on 1,800 million bricks.

Throughout the nineteenth century brickmaking continued to be the highly localised industry which it had always been, located near its market as the result of heavy transport charges on articles of low unit cost. Clay suitable for brickmaking is widespread and, as these clays are very varied, even in an industrial England where uniformity was almost applauded in ordinary buildings, brick-built houses exhibit a surprising diversity of colour and texture.

Mechanisation of the brick-making process occurred progressively throughout the nineteenth century, although some of

the first improvements, such as the compacting of clay under rollers, were introduced in the middle of the eighteenth. At that date bricks were hand-moulded and often fired in clamps in which the newly dried 'green' bricks were stacked with layers of slack coal under a layer of earth. Later, updraught kilns were used, the bricks being stacked in a chamber with a fire below; temperatures were much higher, greater vitrification of the clay occurred and stronger and more durable bricks resulted. As with kilns for fine china, there is great variety to be found in the types of kiln built for brick and tile firing, both intermittent and continuous. The main problem with brick firing was that it was a batch process, expensive both in fuel and time.

The breakthrough came with the introduction in 1858 of a form of continuous kiln by the German engineer Friedrich Hoffman (1818–1900). The original Hoffman kiln was circular, with a tall central chimney, and consisted of a series of radiating chambers which could be charged, fired and unloaded in a continuous succession. The gas flow was so arranged that the exhaust from the bank

111 Handling stone underground at Monks Park mine, near Bath c 1920. Tools and a crane from the Bath stone mines are displayed at the Bath Industrial Heritage Centre, Camden Works, Bath

being fired dried the 'green' bricks in the next bank and air passing over fired bricks in previous chambers cooled them, while providing preheated air for the chamber being fired. Circular Hoffman kilns are now rare.

What is possibly the earliest surviving Hoffman type of kiln, with sixteen chambers and dating from the end of the nineteenth century, is in Shortwood brickworks, Pucklechurch, Avon [ST 679769]. Also in the South West are the remains of Barham Brothers' brick and tile works in Bridgwater, Somerset [ST 301376] where two kilns survive. Of the really extensive sites however the brickfields of Bedfordshire and Cambridgeshire hold the most evidence. Stewartby, 5 miles south of Bedford [TL 0142], a company town named after its founder, Sir Malcolm Stewart, was planned in the 1920s and is now the centre of the world's largest brickworks with a weekly capacity of 17 million bricks. There are twenty transverse-arch Hoffman-type kilns of which one has eighty chambers. A mile south of Peterborough is Old Fletton, Cambridgeshire [TL 1997] south of which is another huge brickworks which has grown up since the 1880s. The works and their associated clay pits straddle the East Coast main railway line for some 3 miles with more than twenty Hoffman-type kilns of which one [TL 186966] is an early double kiln.

Another aspect of the tile industry which enjoyed enormous markets in the second half of the nineteenth century was the manufacture of decorative wall and floor tiles. Two of the largest makers, Maws and Craven Dunnill, had their works at Jackfield in the Ironbridge Gorge, and although the industry here is now extinct, buildings still survive and the companies' products can be seen in profusion in local buildings. Maws were in fact one of the largest tile manufacturers in the world at the end of the nineteenth century, producing floor and wall tiles which appear in nonconformist chapels, butchers' and game shops and stations on the London Underground. They were responsible for introducing the steam-driven tile press in 1873. Other major tile makers included Minton, Copeland and Doulton although the latter had a greater

113 Strathy limekilns at Farr, Sutherland [NC 852657] were probably built in the 1820s; typical of many in this part of Scotland, they were peat-fired   (John R. Hume)

reputation for making terracotta, a material fired at a high temperature which could be moulded to intricate shapes. Unglazed terracotta and the glazed faience varieties were beloved of architects caught on the crest of the wave of Gothic revival. Without the ingenuity of the Victorian brick and tile makers, we would not have, or would have been spared, the Albert Memorial, Keble College Chapel and the Midland Hotel, Manchester.

One remaining aspect of the building materials industry demands attention – the manufacture of cement and concrete. The huge increase in building works created a need not only for cement for

112 Limestone quarries at Pant, south of Oswestry, Shropshire, were linked in 1779 to the Montgomeryshire Canal by a self-acting incline; this wooden winding drum [SJ 273218] stands west of the A483 at the head of the incline   (Neil Cossons)

114 Limekilns, built in 1842, in the Black Country Museum site, Dudley, West Midlands [SO 948917], before restoration   (Neil Cossons)

115 The same limekilns after restoration
(Neil Cossons)

ordinary constructional purposes but for hydraulic cements which would set in the absence of air. In the early nineteenth century there were numerous so-called 'Roman' cements available, makers being stimulated by the London Building Act of 1774, which encouraged stucco facings for buildings, but more by the demands of canal, harbour and railway engineers. Parker's cement was one of the better patent 'Roman' cements and was used by Thomas Telford in the construction of Chirk Aqueduct, Shropshire [SJ 287372] because of its water-resistant properties. It was also employed by Marc Isambard Brunel (1769–1849) for the Thames Tunnel [TQ 352800].

The first really strong cement came in 1824 when Joseph Aspdin (1779–1855) patented a mixture called Portland cement, the name deriving not from any connection with Portland but probably from a desire to take advantage of the implied quality which the name Portland gave. Portland cement was at once a success. It was made by firing a clay and lime mixture at very high temperature in a type of bottle kiln quite unlike traditional limekilns.

Limekilns are amongst the most familiar and least studied of industrial archaeological sites. The majority were simply for burning lime for agricultural purposes, but these were usually small kilns often only a few feet high (Illus 113). Examination of a large-scale map of an area such as the Mendips reveals a limekiln in the corner of almost every field; exploration on the ground usually produces little more than a pile of rough stones. Coastal sites were quite common, too, and the North Devon and Somerset coasts have numerous limekilns which relied on South Wales coal brought across the Bristol Channel in sailing trows. Some of the Somerset kilns were on the foreshore; the trow ran up onto the beach, stayed there over low water while its coal was unloaded into horse-drawn carts, and left on the following tide. Although many large kilns were built for burning agricultural lime, most were for making lime cement. They are frequently found built into hillsides, in much the same manner as were blast furnaces in the eighteenth century, taking advantage of the high ground at the back for charging in the raw materials and the low front for drawing the burnt lime. Large numbers of this type of furnace can be found associated with limestone quarried along Wenlock Edge in Shropshire. A particularly well preserved group (Illus 114 and 115) are within the site of the Black Country Museum, Dudley [SO 948917], alongside the A4123 Birmingham to Wolverhampton road. These kilns, dramatically depicted by J. M. W. Turner 150 years ago, were served by their own branch from the

116 This 70ft-high split-shaft limekiln, built
c1900, is a prominent feature of the Dorking
Greystone Lime Company's site at Station
Road, Betchworth, Surrey [TQ 208514]. In the
background are the extensive remains of other
kilns with circular brick-built flues and charging towers   (Gordon Payne)

nearby canal, which provided an outlet for
the lime. A much more modern kiln (Illus
116) of the split-shaft type stands at
Betchworth in Surrey [TQ 208514].

Although concrete, consisting of a
cement matrix and an aggregate of stones,
is often regarded as a wholly modern
material, it had its origins at least 2,000
years ago when it was used in Roman
bridges and other engineering works.
Mass lime concrete continued to be used
intermittently for foundations, and in sea
walls and breakwaters, until the nineteenth century, when the first attempts
were made to develop its potential further.
From the 1850s Portland cement was increasingly used instead of the older lime
cements and, although this created problems because setting was so much more
rapid, the vastly improved strength of the
newer material stimulated numerous
experiments in the application of concrete

for building and civil engineering.
Throughout the second half of the nineteenth century attempts were made, particularly in France, to develop concrete
building techniques and eventually two
rival Frenchmen, Edmond Coignet (1850–
1915) and François Hennebique (1842–
1921), perfected concrete construction
systems for commercial use. Coignet
developed the pioneering work of his
father, François (1814–88), who proposed
reinforcing the concrete with iron rods
and beams and from 1890 onwards
patented the use of reinforced concrete for
pipes, tunnels, precast beams and piles.
The Hennebique system was introduced
to Britain when L. G. Mouchel opened an
office in London in 1897 to exploit it under
licence. It embraced columns, beams,
floors and walls, all in reinforced concrete,
and had no rival in Britain until Coignet
introduced his system in 1904.

Early reinforced concrete structures are
surprisingly rare and are seldom appreciated for what they are. One of the first
large concrete-framed buildings, constructed on the Coignet principle, stands
near the entrance to Bristol docks where
three massive brick-clad tobacco bonds
dominate the river [ST 567723], while a very
early reinforced concrete bridge, the Free
Bridge of 1908 [SJ 681033], crosses the Severn
only ½ mile downstream from the pioneer
iron bridge of 1779. What is perhaps the
first concrete bridge in Britain, although
made of mass concrete with no reinforce-
ment, dates from the 1880s and crosses the
River Axe at Seaton in Devon [SY 252899].

POTTERY

As with the manufacture of bricks and
tiles, the pottery industry relies on clays
which are fired in a kiln until vitrification
occurs. The simplest possible classification would group pottery into earthenware, stoneware and porcelain, depending
on the temperature of firing and quality of
the clay and additional ingredients.
Glazes are used for most pottery to make it
impermeable and to produce decorative
effects. Many are based on silica associated with other materials: thus lead glaze
is silica and litharge, while others incor-

porate silica with alumina or felspar. The glaze is, in effect, a thin layer of glass fused on to the surface. Earthenware on the other hand, which is used for drain and sewer pipes among other things, was until recently glazed with common salt thrown into the kiln and allowed to vitrify on the articles being fired.

Clay suitable for pottery making is widespread in occurrence although widely variable in quality. Invariably, however, it requires pre-treatment before it can be used. The first process is usually one of 'blunging' in which the clay is mixed with large quantities of water that is then sieved off from the resulting suspension. When in a stiff plastic form, it is then 'wedged', ie large pieces are thrown on top of each other to remove the air bubbles. Once in a suitable state for working, it may be used in three possible ways to make a pot. Firstly it can be pressed, in its plastic state, into a mould; secondly it can be thrown on a wheel; and thirdly it can be reduced to a liquid sludge and poured into a mould. The finished piece of pottery is then fired in a kiln to produce vitrification of the clay and, at high temperatures, impermeability. At lower firing temperatures glazing is essential.

Although clay for earthenware and stoneware is fairly widespread in its distribution, the raw materials of porcelain, the finest type of ceramic, occur only in limited areas. During the seventeenth century Chinese porcelain was being imported into Europe in increasing quantities, largely as the result of trading connections forged by the Dutch East India Company after its formation in 1609. The properties of Chinese porcelain, fine quality and whiteness, were at that date unattainable in Europe, but by the mid-seventeenth century were being imitated in Delft by the use of a soft clay body covered with tin enamel. By the latter part of the century this was, in its turn, being imitated in England at Bristol, Lambeth and Liverpool. Distinct and independent lines of development are then discernible in the evolution of fine pottery with, on the one hand, the continued production of this glassy, soft paste imitation porcelain,

and on the other the manufacture of true European porcelain. A third quite specific innovation, confined to England, was the making of bone china.

The discovery in Europe of the technique of making real hard porcelain represents one of those curious but by no means unique instances of a technological innovation occurring simultaneously in more than one place as the result of similar, but unconnected, thought processes. Friedrich Bottger (1682–1719), working in Meissen, near Dresden, had pioneered the use of china clay (kaolin) fused with a calcareous flux (marble or alabaster) at temperatures up to 1,400°C and on the basis of his work Meissen porcelain became supreme, and a closely guarded secret. In France the manufacture of porcelain began at Sèvres in 1768 as the result of persistent experiments pursued by P. J. Macquer (1718–84), while in the same year the independent experiments begun in 1745 by William Cookworthy (1705–80), a Plymouth chemist, resulted in the granting of the first English patent for true porcelain. He started manufacture in Plymouth using local timber as his fuel but moved to Bristol in 1770 to take advantage of plentiful coal supplies. By the 1780s the patents, which had been taken over in Bristol by Richard Champion (1743–91), were being challenged and porcelain manufacture began in Staffordshire. One of these Staffordshire potters was Josiah Wedgwood.

The mineral which provided the key to the porcelain secret was kaolin, the product of decomposition of granite. The components of granite are quartz, mica and felspar and it is a decomposition of the felspar (aluminium silicate) by a process known as kaolinisation which produces china clay. Most of the china clay found in Britain has come from the granite massif of Hensbarrow, north of St Austell in Cornwall, but the Lee Moor area on the slopes of Dartmoor above Plymouth has also been important. At first sufficient supplies could be found in small pits close to the surface, but as these became worked out and as demand grew, much larger and deeper clay excavations were carried out, reaching in recent years depths in excess of 400ft. By the mid-nineteenth century huge quantities were being sent to continental Europe, notably Hamburg and Antwerp, but the largest single market was Staffordshire, which by then had become firmly established as the pottery centre of Britain. The siting of the industry here, at such a long distance from the source of clay, is explained largely by supplies of fuel. The pottery industry is to a great extent located near its fuel supplies, which in this case was Staffordshire coal; the additional pull of this area was the already established tradition of pottery manufacture based on locally available clays.

To the industrial archaeologist the china clay area of Cornwall provides perhaps the most extreme example of a landscape of earlier exploitation, with huge pits separated by vast glistening white tips of the quartz and mica waste washed from the kaolin. Despite this, it is a man-made landscape which, perhaps more than any other, has a stark almost ghostly drama and magnificence about it. Like the tin-mine engine houses elsewhere in the county, the clay waste tips of St Austell are now a hallmark of the Cornish landscape.

Evidence of the clay processing can be seen in a number of places but nowhere is the range of equipment as complete as at Wheal Martyn (Illus 117) [SX 004555], west of the A391 St Austell to Bodmin road. Closed in 1966, this was perhaps the last small family clayworking in Cornwall where all the intricate hydraulic processes connected with the separation and settling can still be seen complete. On the site is a 25ft diameter overshot waterwheel which by means of a crank drove a flat connecting rod that operated a pump through a bellcrank. This pump lifted the clay slurry and allowed it to flow through mica drags, from which the refined liquid gravitated to settling tanks and finally kiln tanks. As the water evaporated, the clay thickened and was finally spread on a floor, below which were flues from a coal fire. After drying for some 12 hours the clay was cut from the pan and thrown into a storage shed alongside known as the linhay. The Wheal Martyn site is surprisingly complete, and, in addition to the equipment

noted above, there is a 35ft diameter waterwheel which used to operate, by means of flat rods, another pump 2,000ft away. Shortly before it closed, Wheal Martyn passed from the ownership of the Martyn family, who bought the site in 1790, to English China Clays, and the site is now an open-air museum based on the conservation *in situ* of the surviving remains. In addition a number of other sites are being preserved, including, at Parkandillack clayworks near St Dennis [SW 945568], a 50in beam pumping engine of 1852 complete with Cornish boilers (and dog's pawmarks cast into the iron beam). West of the engine is a 'button-hole launder', or wooden box containing a number of plugs for draining the pit, and an extensive series of micas.

Two other clayworks' pumping engines survive in Cornwall. One, still in its original engine house at Goonvean [SW 947552], is a 50in Cornish beam pumping engine of 1863, and the other has been removed from its original site at Greensplatt Clayworks, Carthew [SW 997554], and re-erected in a park-cum-museum open-air site at Wendron Forge [SW 680315]. Another rare survival at Slip Chinastone Quarry, also at Goonvean, is an overhead aerial ropeway still used for raising clay out of a 250ft deep pit.

Having examined the origins of kaolin, the raw material of the porcelain industry, let us consider the production end of the process and in particular the main centre of pottery making in Britain – the 'five towns' of North Staffordshire centred on Stoke-on-Trent. When in 1782 hard paste porcelain was first made at New Hall near Shelton, Staffordshire was already well established as a pottery-making centre. There was coal, a wide variety of clays and a firm tradition of potting. Even in the late sixteenth century Burslem and Hanley were producing jars, bottles and butterpots, lead-glazed and fired with coal dug by the potters themselves. By the 1680s a second method of glazing became avail-

117 The 25ft overshot waterwheel at Wheal Martyn [SX 004555], showing the launder, balancing box and rod drive to the water pump (*English China Clays Group*)

BOTTLE KILN CUT OPEN TO SHOW INTERIOR

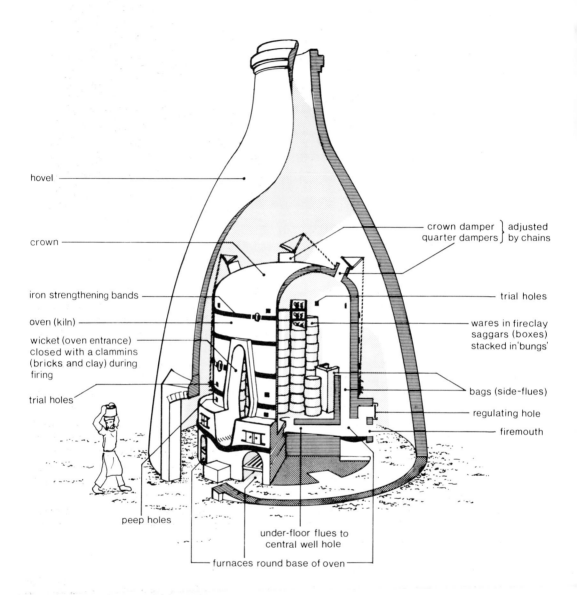

hovel

crown

iron strengthening bands

oven (kiln)

wicket (oven entrance)
closed with a clammins
(bricks and clay) during
firing

trial holes

peep holes

under-floor flues to
central well hole

furnaces round base of oven

crown damper } adjusted
quarter dampers } by chains

trial holes

wares in fireclay
saggars (boxes)
stacked in 'bungs'

bags (side-flues)

regulating hole

firemouth

Illustration 118

able with the introduction of salt glaze from the Low Countries, but neither of these processes, when applied over the common brown clay of the area, resulted in a product with the appeal of Delft. Pale Shelton clays were used in the first steps towards a finer white-bodied ware, and eventually a fine white salt-glazed stoneware evolved from a white-burning clay mixed with fine grit and sand. It enjoyed great popularity during the eighteenth century, being hard, translucent and as near to porcelain as could be reached short of the real thing. John Astbury (1688–1743) was instrumental in developing this ware and also in utilising ground flint (silica) in the body material as a whitener. Initially the flint was ground dry under stamps rather like those used in Cornwall for crushing tin ore, but the problems of silica getting into the lungs of men working the crushers soon resulted in the development of a process for grinding under water.

One of these flint mills is preserved in operational condition at Cheddleton in Staffordshire [SJ 974525]. The original mill on this site was built as a corn mill, certainly before 1694, and probably much earlier. The present North Mill building dates from the 1750s or 1760s, and was probably built by the famous millwright and canal engineer James Brindley (1716–72). In the 1770s the original mill, by now known as South Mill, was converted for flint grinding also. Two undershot water-wheels driven by the River Churnet provide power for the grinding machinery, while set into the bank of the nearby Caldon Canal are kilns for calcining the flint. The Flint Mill Preservation Trust was formed in May 1967 and the mill opened to the public in April 1969. Beside the summit locks of the Trent & Mersey Canal at Hanley, in the heart of the Potteries, a steam-powered mill has also been preserved. The Etruscan Bone and Flint Mill [SJ 872478], built in 1857, has most of its machinery intact together with the small beam engine that powered it.

Despite these attempts during the eighteenth century to produce a superior form of stoneware, it was not until the introduction in the 1780s of real hard-paste porcelain, based on china clay, that Staf-

119 Flint mill

fordshire began to produce wares of the highest quality. Even the introduction of this new technique might not have brought Staffordshire real fame and fortune had it not been for the entrepreneurial skill and organisational ability of Josiah Wedgwood (1730–95).

Brought up as a potter, Wedgwood set up on his own account at Burslem in 1759. One of his initial successes was a fine green-glazed ware, which he followed up by an improved stoneware evolved from earlier creamwares. Having obtained royal patronage, he called it Queen's ware and it was soon being made in dozens of potteries and used all over the country. Wedgwood never looked back. With

120 Flint pan

121 Bottle kilns at the Gladstone Pottery, Longton, Staffordshire [SJ 912434], before its conversion to a museum (*Staffordshire Pottery Industry Preservation Trust*)

122 Throwing

123 Interior of a kiln at the Gladstone Pottery Museum, Longton, Staffordshire [SJ 912434], with saggars, containing the unfired ware, being stacked (*British Tourist Authority*)

newly introduced steam power to drive flint mills and lathes for producing refined shapes, the Staffordshire pottery industry was on the way towards rapid and large-scale expansion. But the expansion was not based solely on mechanisation and increased demand. Wedgwood built a new works at Etruria in which to develop mechanised pottery manufacture, but he realised that to optimise the benefits which powered machinery afforded he had to press the division of labour to the maximum, with each distinct process identified and separated. He aimed at a production line process in which individual craftsmen expressed their skill in a limited field, arguing that this afforded them greater opportunities for developing their latent abilities. The specialisation within the labour force was geared to a graded pay structure ranging from 42s per week for an experienced modeller to 1s a week for the least skilled. There can be little doubt that Wedgwood's friendship with Matthew Boulton (1728–1809), the entrepreneurial half of the partnership with James Watt, stimulated many of the ideas he introduced. By the time of

Wedgwood's death in 1795 the industrial revolution in the pottery industry was in full flood.

To travel through the Potteries only thirty years ago was an experience appalling to the eye and the nose. Hundred upon hundred of bottle-shaped kilns stuck up through the skyline of smoke-blackened terrace houses. Today almost all those bottle kilns have disappeared as the industry has rationalised and adopted new techniques. Tunnel kilns, completely automated in their operation, have replaced the long established 'potbanks' with their bottle ovens and uncomplicated processes. As a result of this change, and in order to preserve something of the old methods, the Staffordshire Pottery Industry Preservation Trust was set up with the specific objective of saving from demolition Gladstone Pottery (Illus 121 and 123) in Longton [SJ 912434]. A museum has been set up in the existing buildings, the best surviving example of a potbank scarcely touched by twentieth-century technology, where the old processes are being carried out. Displays include not only the products but also contemporary

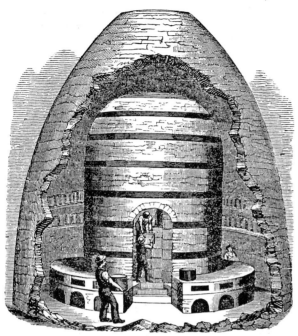

124 Biscuit kiln

information on the supply of materials and distribution of finished wares. A project somewhat similar in concept occupies another early group of pottery buildings at Coalport on the banks of the River Severn in Shropshire [SJ 695024]. Here, in 1976, the Ironbridge Gorge Museum Trust opened as a museum the works, together with their bottle kilns, where Coalport china was made from the late eighteenth century down to the 1920s. The Coalport company moved to Stoke and is now part of the Wedgwood Group, but the original pottery survives substantially intact.

Remains of potteries are surprisingly widespread and include bottle kilns at Portobello, Midlothian, dating from 1906 and 1909 [NT 304742] and at Longport pottery, Kilmarnock, Ayrshire [NS 427387]. At Corbridge, Northumberland [NY 992652], the site of Walkers Pottery, which produced sanitary and domestic ware, has two large bottle kilns, a circular downdraught kiln and two rectangular Newcastle kilns. Wetheriggs Pottery, Clifton, Cumbria [NY 555263] still produces traditionally patterned salt-glaze earthenware and, although modern kilns and machinery are

used the old coal-fired kiln, pug mill, blunger and clay pit survive. Similarly, in Derbyshire T. & G. Green's pottery at Church Gresley [SK 305187] manufactures kitchenware on the original site. In London the most significant relic of the celebrated Fulham pottery on the King's Road, founded by John Dwight in the late seventeenth century, is a bottle kiln [TQ 244761] of much later date. Museum collections of pottery are too numerous to list but there are a number of important museums in pottery sites including the Dyson Perrins Museum, adjacent to the Royal Worcester Porcelain factory [SO 852544] in Worcester and the Wedgwood Museum at Barlaston, Staffordshire [SJ 886397].

GLASS

The earliest man-made glass dates from about 4000 BC, when it was used in Egypt and Mesopotamia as a glaze for beads. By 1500 BC hollow glass vessels were in use; they were probably made around a clay core which was chipped away when the molten glass had solidified. At about the same date small objects, such as pieces of jewellery, were being made in glass by pressing between clay moulds, and finishing by grinding and polishing was also becoming common. The high temperatures necessary to smelt the raw materials for glass were achieved in simple furnaces, the glass being contained in a crucible made of a refractory substance such as clay that had a higher melting point than the glass itself. Possibly in the first century BC mouth blowing of glass, using a blowing iron, was introduced, and this remained the main method of glass forming for nearly 2,000 years. Blown glass vessels of Roman origin are quite common, and it was probably during the Roman occupation that glass was first made in Britain. Traces of Roman glass furnaces have been found at Wilderspool near Warrington and Caistor-by-Norwich. In the first century AD glassmakers had mastered the art of making clear transparent glass, a great improvement over the earlier opaque types, and delicate colours could be consistently achieved by adding a variety of chemical ingredients. Glazed windows were in use by the first century AD also, particularly in the north European areas of the Roman Empire.

Glass is a crypto-crystalline substance solidified from a variety of inorganic materials melted at high temperature, that is its molecular structure does not exhibit a crystalline pattern. Many different glasses, with properties varying according to the raw materials used, are made today. The main ingredients of almost all commercially important glass is silicon dioxide (SiO_2), often found in the form of sand. In its pure state very high temperatures (over 1,500°C) are necessary to fuse silica, but glass which melts at much lower temperatures can be made by adding fluxing agents such as soda ash (Na_2CO_3) to the silica sand. The melting temperature can be reduced to about 800°C by adding 25 per cent of soda ash but the resulting substance, waterglass (Na_2SiO_3), as its name implies, is soluble in water. Addition of a stabiliser such as limestone ($CaCO_3$) results in a non-soluble glass. An ordinary glass bottle or jar contains approximately 55 per cent sand, 25 per cent soda ash and 20 per cent limestone. To assist melting, 15–30 per cent of scrap glass or 'cullet' of the correct composition is usually added to the ingredients, which are known as the 'batch'.

Silica-soda-lime glasses are by far the most important group in terms of tonnages produced and variety of uses. The ingredients are cheap and easily obtained, the glass is well suited to shaping and it has good chemical-resistant properties. The colour of these glasses tends to be greenish, a result of the natural iron content of most sand, and in the case of old bottles where colour was immaterial the iron imparted an almost opaque blackish-green appearance. The cheapest bottle glass of the eighteenth or nineteenth centuries was of this crude and unrefined type. In evidence presented to the commissioners at an excise enquiry in 1831 it was stated that the materials used in common bottle glass were sand, soapmakers' waste, lime, common clay and ground bricks. Flint glass, from which tableware was produced, contained pearlash, litharge or red lead, Lynn or Alum Bay sand (particularly low in iron) or 'Yorkshire stones burnt and pulverised'.

Lead glasses have a high refractive index and electrical resistivity, and consist primarily of silica sand with as little iron as possible, potash and lead oxide. High quality table glass is made of lead glass, which, because its viscosity does not increase at a rapid rate during cooling, is particularly suitable for hand-made production; and also for engraving and cutting, an art that became highly developed in the late eighteenth century. Since the late seventeenth century lead glass has been used and known as 'English crystal'. Its constituents are more expensive than those of common glass, the amount of lead varying considerably – up to 92 per cent of lead oxide in some cases. A modern high-performance glass composed of high-purity silica sand and boric oxide is borosilicate glass. The boric oxide acts as a flux, permitting a reduction in alkali content that results in improved chemical stability and electrical properties. Developed early this century to cope with the problem of rain on hot railway signal-lamp lenses, borosilicate glasses are now widely used where extreme thermal conditions occur, and their low coefficient of expansion and durability makes them ideal for industrial use and for ordinary heat-resistant domestic ovenware. Coloured glass is as old as glass itself but methods of production and knowledge of the chemical additives needed were at first crude and unscientific. Empirical methods, however subject to variation in the quality of the final product, produced some spectacular results, of which the rich glowing blues and reds of medieval church windows are the most notable examples surviving today.

There is little evidence available of the furnaces used by early glassmakers, but Theophilus in his *Diversum Artium Schedula* of the twelfth century AD describes a rectangular furnace divided into two unequal parts; in the smaller section the raw materials were heated to form a vitreous mass known as 'frit', which was broken up and melted in pots sunk in the hearth of the larger part of the furnace.

Agricola in the mid-sixteenth century also describes furnaces in two parts: the oven-shaped fritting furnace, with pots for the molten glass arranged round a central hearth, and the annealing furnace, oblong in shape with a small hearth below the floor. Annealing is an essential stage in the manufacture of most glass. Because of its low thermal conductivity, the surface of glass cools and therefore shrinks more quickly and to a greater extent than the interior. If unchecked, stresses would be set up within the object, leading to breakage, but this can be avoided by slow cooling at a controlled rate. This is annealing, which takes place in an oven or lehr. In a modern glassworks, for example, bottles pass slowly through the lehr on a conveyor belt and over a period of some 2 hours the temperature is gradually reduced from about 540°C.

All early furnaces were fired by wood, the wood ash providing the necessary alkaline flux. One example of a type of wood-fired furnace introduced in the sixteenth century into Britain by French and Flemish glassworkers survives almost *in toto*. It was discovered in 1968 at Rosedale in the North Yorkshire Moors and later moved to the Ryedale Folk Museum, Hutton-le-Hole, near Helmsley, Yorkshire, where it was partially reconstructed and is on view to the public [SE 705900]. The Rosedale glassworkers were perhaps the most isolated group among the numerous glassmaking families who came to England in large numbers in the 1560s and 1570s and set up furnaces in the heavily wooded areas of the Weald, and in Hampshire and Staffordshire.

Other furnaces of this type were set up, mainly in southern England, where timber supplies were reasonably plentiful. Competition from the shipbuilding and iron industries was growing, however, and in 1615 there was a Royal Proclamation forbidding glassmakers to use wood for fuel. Availability of coal now became the chief locational factor, together with suitable sources of clay and the convenience of transport systems.

During the seventeenth century a distinctive and completely new type of coal-fired furnace was developed in England,

125 Glass cone *c*1825 at Alloa Glassworks, Clackmannanshire [NS 881923]   (*John R. Hume*)

using the reverberatory process, in which the burning gases came into direct contact with glass in open crucibles. The English glassworks, consisting of a truncated cone up to 80ft high and with a base diameter of some 40–50ft provided the foundation for the industry on a large scale and was copied in Europe also. So significant was this furnace that it was included in Diderot's *Encyclopedie* in the late eighteenth century, one of the few pieces of British manufacturing technology specifically mentioned. The tall cone fulfilled a dual function, by providing cover for the glassworkers and a high level outlet for the furnace situated centrally on its floor. The grate was at approximately ground level, with a combined flue and ash tunnel running beneath it and extending across the building. The furnace would have between four and ten glass pots, with a flue between each. Immediately abreast of each pot and between two flues was an aperture called the working hole, used for introducing the raw materials and getting out the molten glass.

The furnace was fired by coal shovelled through a square fire hole on to a grate in the centre. The flames or smoke were directed towards the sides, around the glass pots, and discharged up the flues to escape into the central chimney of the cone itself. A ten-pot cone consumed 18–24 tons of coal per week. In addition to the principal furnace around which the glass blowers worked, there was also a small subsidiary furnace or 'glory hole' for softening vessels during fabrication when they were too large to be heated in one of the working holes. A long gallery, the lehr or annealing arch, opened at one end into the cone and the completed glassware was placed in this to cool gradually.

The crucibles in which the glass was melted had to be carefully made to prevent cracking in the intense heat of the furnace and to resist the solvent action of molten glass. They were commonly made of five parts Stourbridge clay, a very pure refractory clay notably free from lime and iron oxides, together with one part burnt clay or 'grog' obtained from old crucibles ground down to a powder.

Some five glass cones still survive in Britain, the most prominent monuments of the eighteenth- and nineteenth-century glass industry. The oldest of these, older indeed than any other cone in Europe, is at Catcliffe near Sheffield [SE 425886]. It is the last survivor of at least six glasshouses known to have been built in the area in the eighteenth century at the height of the prosperity of the South Yorkshire glass industry. The industry became established in the Bolsterstone area in the mid-seventeenth century and by 1696 three glasshouses were in operation – one near

126   Glass pots

Ferrybridge, probably at Glass Houghton, and two near Silkstone. William Fenney, works manager at Bolsterstone, left there in 1740 with a workman named Chatterton to start production in his own works at Catcliffe, 10½ miles to the south-east. Two cones were erected and one of these survives today, substantially complete, 60ft high and with a base diameter of some 40ft. It has recently been restored. Excavation of the flue beneath the cone, which contains no remains of the furnace or ancillary buildings, has revealed that glass bottles were being made there down to the early 1900s when C. Wilcocks & Co owned the works; but flint glass and jugs, vases and flasks, often decorated with opaque white stripes, were known to have been made at least as late as the 1870s.

Of the numerous other glass manufacturers established in South Yorkshire during the nineteenth century little else remains, although a firm originally established at Worsborough Dale in 1828 is still active in Barnsley as Wood Bros Glass Co Ltd. The oldest surviving glass firm in the area, dating from 1751 and now known as Beatson Clark & Co Ltd of Masborough, Rotherham, has preserved many examples of the glassware produced in the nineteenth century, including good examples of glass engraving.

In the North East, at Lemington, near Newcastle-upon-Tyne, is another glass cone [NZ 184646] which, although somewhat later in date than Catcliffe, provides a visual reminder of the industry that became important in the region from the early years of the seventeenth century, attracted primarily by cheap coal. In 1615 Sir Robert Mansel obtained a patent for making glass with coal, and, after trying to start a works in London and elsewhere, 'was enforced for his last refuge contrary to all men's opinion to make triall at Newcastle upon Tyne where after the expense of many thousand pounds that worke for window-glasse was effected with Newcastle Cole'. Glassmakers from Lorraine came to Tyneside about this time also and by the end of the seventeenth century were working at South Shields, where plate glass became important. By the mid-nineteenth century glassmaking had become an important manufacturing industry in the North East, and flint glass, crown glass for glazing, and bottles were produced. The Wear glassworks, established at Sunderland in 1842 to produce a new kind of sheet glass called rolled-plate that was rather like unpolished plate glass, achieved a worldwide reputation after supplying the glazing for the Crystal Palace in 1851.

The Lemington Glassworks, famous in the nineteenth century for flint and crown glass, was founded in 1787 by 'a company of enterprising gentlemen (who) entered into the glass trade in Newcastle under the firm of the Northumberland Glass Company'. They were granted a lease of the site at Lemington and quickly erected their first glasshouse, which was called 'the Northumberland Glasshouse'. Within a short time there were three more, including one which was very lofty and built of brick. This is the cone which still stands at Lemington. The site is now occupied by Glass Tubes & Components Ltd, but the cone is no longer used.

Other glass cones may be seen at Stourbridge, Worcestershire [SO 894865], and Alloa, Clackmannan (Illus 125) [NS 881923], while in Bristol the truncated base of a glass cone of about 1780 has been converted into a restaurant for an hotel [ST 592723]. The incomplete remains of a cone also survive within the works of Pilkington Brothers, St Helens.

Comprehensive physical remains of the glass industry of the nineteenth century, when processes were changing rapidly, are hard to find today, but there are two excellent museum displays which, although they contain little actual manufacturing equipment, go a long way towards explaining the various techniques. The Pilkington Glass Museum at St Helens, Lancashire [SJ 498946], illustrates all the major stages in the development of the industry, concentrating particularly on the production of flat glass. The method of making plate glass of high quality by casting was introduced into Britain from France in 1773, when the British Cast Plate Glass Company, as it became called after 1798, was established at Ravenhead, St Helens. Part of the Ravenhead casting hall

and works still stands within the Pilkington complex, and there are hopes of turning them into a museum to house some of the heavy equipment of flat glass making. Although little glassmaking equipment survives, the everyday products of the industry over the last century and a half, particularly in the form of glass containers and window glass, are commonplace.

Glass wine bottles began to replace leather and earthenware ones in the second half of the seventeenth century. At first wine, like beer, was stored in barrels, and bottles were used mainly for carrying drink from the wine merchants to the tavern, for limited storage and for serving at table. The earliest glass bottles for this purpose were pale green and globular, and of light weight. Having no flat base they were usually 'wanded', that is encased in basketwork, or placed in metal stands on the table. In 1731 wanded bottles were advertised at 42s a gross and common black bottles at 20s a gross. The practice of having bottles embossed with a seal, often dated, grew up in the 1660s, and is a useful aid to tracing the evolution in the shape of wine bottles. Towards the end of the eighteenth century bottles became less globular, acquiring an angular shoulder between body and neck. At the same time the 'kick up', a concavity in the base of the bottle which aided stability and assisted annealing in the days before the development of the tunnel lehr, was increased in size. A fine collection of wine bottles, together with some bottle-making moulds, is exhibited in Harveys Wine Museum, Denmark Street, Bristol [ST 584729].

In the early seventeenth century it was discovered that beer could be kept almost indefinitely in bottles and that with a small amount of secondary fermentation occurring after bottling, it could actually improve in quality. The heavy taxation on glass was an initial restraint to the widespread adoption of bottles, but with the repeal in 1845 of the Excise Acts, which had imposed a tax of 8s 9d per cwt on glass bottles, the industry expanded rapidly.

A major problem with beer and the new carbonated soft drinks was to devise a satisfactory bottle closure. In 1872 the internal-screw stopper was patented by an Englishman, Henry Barrett, and in 1892 the familiar crown cork by an American, William Painter. Louis Pasteur's theories of food preservation were meanwhile put into practice in a Copenhagen brewery, which produced the first pasteurised beer. Earthenware bottles had been used by the early pioneers of soft drinks such as Jacob Schweppe, a Swiss who set up business in Bristol in 1794, but the wired-on cork closures were never satisfactory because they dried out and leaked. The egg-shaped glass bottle was introduced in 1814 to overcome this problem. It had to be stored on its side, thus keeping the cork moist. The egg bottle survived even after the introduction of the crown cork had made the shape and the need for flat storage unnecessary, and was in fact in use until the 1920s.

The best known and most successful internally stoppered bottle, patented by Hiram Codd of Camberwell in 1875, had a glass marble pressed against a rubber ring in the bottle neck by the gas pressure in the drink. Codd bottles were used in Britain from the late 1870s until the 1930s, and between 1890 and 1914 were the most widely used containers for carbonated soft drinks. An exceptional collection of soft drink bottles, together with bottle equipment and gas making plant, from the works of J. B. Bowler of Corn Street, Bath, is now in the Camden Works Museum,

127 Glass-blower at work

Julian Road, Bath [ST 748654]. Also displayed are the contents of Bowler's brass foundry and general engineering works.

Widespread preservation of food in glass containers began in the United States in the 1860s after the invention in 1858 of the screw-topped jar by John Landis Mason. American domestic food-preserving jars are still known as Mason jars. In Britain the similar Kilner jar did not come into general use until the 1920s. Automatic jar manufacturing and filling machinery developed in the 1900s; it was followed in 1923 by the invention of the roll-on closure and in 1926 by the pry-off cap still used today. Bottling of milk began in the 1880s on a small scale, but it was not until the 1920s that pasteurised milk deliveries in bottles replaced milk sold 'loose' from churns in the streets. In 1934 bottled milk with a card disc closure was introduced in schools at a cost of ½d for one-third of a pint. Today the milk bottle has the more hygienic foil cap and the wide-mouthed card-stoppered bottle has completely disappeared. Even the first foil topped bottles of fifteen years ago have now given way to lightweight versions, with carefully contoured shoulders to eliminate internal stresses.

The crown window-glass process was the earlier of the two chief methods of making sheet glass by hand and was in common use until the early years of the nineteenth century. Molten glass on a blowing iron was formed into a large hollow sphere. Then a 'pontil' or solid iron rod was attached to it by a nodule of the molten metal – glass is referred to as metal in a glassworks – and the blowing iron then removed. Reheating the glass on the rotating pontil reduced it to a soft and semi-molten state in which centrifugal force caused it to flash into a disc. The thin fire-polished disc of glass was removed from the pontil for annealing and then cut up into sheets. Every sheet made by this method had a bull's-eye or 'crown' from which it took its name, this being the point where the pontil had been attached. The sizes of pieces of glass made by this method were severely restricted, and after about 1830 the process gave way to hand cylinder-glass making. Crown glass is easy to recognise in window panes by the fine ripples and flow lines which form arcs in its surface. The larger the radius of the arc the nearer the edge of the glass disc was the sheet cut.

The hand-cylinder process of sheet glassmaking was brought to England from Lorraine in 1832 by Lucas Chance. It was essentially a development of the crown glass method, but instead of a sphere and then a disc of glass, an elongated bulb was made 12–20in in diameter and 50–70in long. The ends of the cylinder were removed, it was cut down its long side and, after reheating, the glass was flat-tened in a flattening kiln. The sheets were much larger than those of crown glass, were free from the central boss and were much cheaper to make. In 1839 Sir James Chance (1814–1902) invented a method of grinding and polishing sheet glass, giving it the brilliancy and transparency of plate glass that had been similarly treated.

The third method of making sheet glass was to cast it in plates, a process developed in France in the 1680s and introduced to England in 1773. The great casting hall at the Ravenhead works, St Helens, where the technique became established, still partially survives as one of the largest industrial buildings of its day, 113yd long by 50yd wide. The method of making plate was to pour molten glass on to a flat table, first made of copper and later of cast iron, and when it had cooled and been annealed, over a period of about ten days, the two faces of the glass were then ground and polished. A number of other firms were set up to cope with the enormous demand for flat glass as a result of the building explosion in early nineteenth-century Britain. The St Helens Crown Glass Company was formed in 1825, the Smethwick firm of Chance & Hartley brought continental glassmakers to blow cylinder glass in 1832 and in 1836 the great Union Plate Glass Works was set up at Pocket Nook, St Helens.

All these processes are well illustrated in the Pilkington Glass Museum, St Helens, and the glass technology gallery in the Science Museum, London, but little, if anything, survives of actual equipment. Modern manufacture of float glass and rolled sheet glass can be seen at the Pilkington works; visits for parties can be arranged through the curator of the museum. The float process, developed at St Helens in 1959, is one of the major advances in glassworking of recent years and consists of flowing glass on to a bath of molten tin to ensure a perfect under surface, the heat applied above producing a similar effect on the upper face. Ordinary sheet glass is also now made by a continuous process in which the molten 'metal' is drawn vertically from the melting pot between powered rollers.

128 The glass house

CHAPTER 10

TEXTILES

One of Man's earliest manufacturing techniques was the making of cloth by the spinning and weaving of animal and plant fibres. Before large-scale mechanised industrialisation began in Britain, the making of textiles was widely dispersed throughout the country and was of very great importance in the national economy. Wool, and later various woollen cloths, formed the largest export commodities from the medieval period through to the middle of the eighteenth century. International specialisations grew up between the production areas of Europe, and the fact that English wool was considered to be of the highest quality led merchants, in particular from Flanders and Italy, to come in search of it. English taxation on wool exports led to a change in the trade as dyers and finishers abroad realised they could circumvent the tax by buying un-dyed broadcloth instead of the wool itself. Broadcloth exports from the West of England rose dramatically, as did the lighter fabrics produced in East Anglia, though to a lesser extent, as they were not quite so popular. A large, rurally based cloth industry began to develop in the West of England – in Somerset, Gloucestershire and Wiltshire particularly – based on capitalist clothiers who bought wool, gave it out to hand-spinners and hand-weavers to convert into cloth, then carried out the fulling themselves and finally sent the cloth, undyed and unfinished, to Europe. In Yorkshire, which did not engage in the export market to such a great extent, the structure of the industry was somewhat different, as the clothiers, particularly in the Halifax area, were independent masters in their own right, owning their spinning wheels and weaving looms, buying wool and yarn and

taking their pieces of cloth to the Cloth Hall every week for sale to merchants whom they faced as owners of the cloth they sold. The Cloth or Piece Halls of the West Riding became the symbols of an industry where the structure of production was based on a large number of masters, some of whom would be working in family units and others as employers of labour on a very small scale. Of these the Halifax Piece Hall [SE 095250] is the grandest. Opened in 1779 this magnificent building, with 315 individual selling rooms, represented the crowning glory of the handloom weaver and clothier, but within seventy years it was past its prime. By 1871 it had become a wholesale vegetable market; a century later it has been beautifully restored as a market, museum and visitor centre.

Before the coming of factories, therefore, a proletariat was already developing in many textile regions. Only in the West Riding of Yorkshire did the actual manufacturers have any degree of independence, though theirs was the independence of capital only. Elsewhere – in the West of England, around Norwich, in the worsted area around Bradford, Yorkshire, and in the Nottinghamshire stocking and lace manufacturing districts – the man who organised production and who owned the capital in production was the clothier or 'putter-out' of work, the cloth merchant or the hosier. As most of the capital in the industry was in the raw material and goods in various stages of processing, the merchant was able to control production throughout its course. He owned the materials right through the sequence of processes, paying spinners and weavers for their labour and often renting out the equipment, sometimes to many hundreds of dependent families. The structure of ownership which was later to characterise the factory system, therefore, already existed in several regions of the country in the days of the cottage-based industry, long before the development of modern machine processes.

In order to appreciate the significance of later innovations it is important to look at the processes through which textile fibres went during their conversion from raw material to finished cloth. The stages were substantially the same for all textiles, although here reference will be made mostly to wool, which was dominant before industrialisation. As will be seen later, a development in one branch of the textile industry often had very direct relevance to another, so that from the middle of the eighteenth century onwards the progress of the wool, cotton and to a certain extent flax (for linen) industry went hand in hand.

Wool textiles may be divided into woollens and worsteds. Woollens use short fibre or short staple wool, and worsteds longer staple. In both cases the wool is first washed and cleaned to remove natural grease and dirt, after which there are different techniques for the two fabrics. For woollen textiles the raw wool is 'carded' to lay the tangled fibres into roughly parallel strands so that they can be more easily drawn for spinning. Before the eighteenth century carding was done by hand using two oblong boards, each of which had on one of its sides projecting wires or nails. At first the heads of teasels were used but these were soon to be replaced by brass wire, though the term 'teasing' remained. (The demands of carding in the seventeenth century were, in fact, a great stimulus to the wire-making industry.) Washed raw wool was placed on the teeth of one carding board, and the other was repeatedly drawn over it in one direction, to disentangle the fibres. To get the wool off the cards, one board was turned round and again passed over the other; the teeth being set at an angle, this stripped the wool off the card. Many examples of hand cards survive and may be seen in, for example, Dumfries Burgh

129 Long wool-comb

Museum; the Piece Hall, Halifax; and the Museum & Art Gallery, Peel Park, Salford.

Wool used for worsted cloth required rather more thorough treatment, for the fibres had not only to be laid parallel to each other but also unwanted short staple wool had to be removed. This process was called combing. Two hand combs with tapered metal teeth were used. A small quantity of wool was placed in the teeth of one of the combs, which was held firmly in a bracket while the other was drawn through the fibres, pulling more and more wool out and collecting the longer fibres in its teeth. When most of the wool had become caught in the hand-held comb, the two were changed over and the process repeated. After combing, the long fibres were collected and joined into long slivers known as 'tops', which were sent for spinning. The remaining short staple fibres, called 'noils', were sold for woollens. When spun, combed wool produced a smooth fine worsted yarn, much harder than ordinary woollen yarns. Combing presented considerable difficulties for mechanisation and was the last section of the wool textile industry to be hand worked, remaining so until after 1850. Hand combs may be seen in the Art Gallery & Museum, Cliffe Castle, Keighley, Bradford Industrial Museum, and the Bridewell Museum, Norwich.

After carding or combing, both woollens and worsteds were spun and, although different techniques of manipulating the fibres were employed, both involved the same equipment and went through the same processes. Spinning twists the fibres around each other and draws them together to form a yarn suitable for weaving into cloth. The most primitive technique was to use a spindle and distaff, in which the distaff or stick carrying the wool was held under one arm, often supported by a leather belt around the waist of the spinster. Strands of wool were pulled from the distaff and attached to the spindle, a small stick with a weight at one end. The spindle was suspended from the wool, given a twist with the finger to set it spinning, and the wool paid out slowly. When a length of yarn had been produced, it was wound round the spindle, the end caught in a notch to prevent it unwinding when suspended, and the process repeated.

The spinning wheel, which probably originated in the Far East, was a great improvement over the spindle and distaff and may be regarded as the first example of 'mechanisation' applied to the textile industry. In it the spindle was mounted horizontally in bearings and connected to a large flywheel by a driving band. This produced more consistent rotation of the spindle and speeded up the spinning process considerably. At first the large wheel was turned by hand, but later a treadle, connecting rod and crank on the wheelshaft were used – probably the first use of the common crank for developing rotary motion and at least two centuries before Pickard and Watt 'rediscovered' it for the rotative steam engine. In the early type of spinning wheel known as the 'big wheel' or 'Jersey wheel' a piece of unspun wool was attached to the spindle and the large wheel turned by hand. The other hand holding the wool was pulled back slowly from the spindle paying out at a steady rate strands which were spun into yarn. When a length had been spun, the wheel was turned again to wind the yarn on to the body of the spindle. The process was then repeated.

Later a new type of spinning wheel, the Saxony wheel invented in 1555, largely supplanted the big wheel; it was an improvement as it both spun the yarn and wound it in at the same time, making the whole operation continuous. It was used for the spinning, usually of long fibres, until the late eighteenth century. The main section of the Saxony wheel was the U-shaped flyer that was attached to the spindle. The bobbin ran loose on the spindle shaft and was driven by a separate band from the flywheel. Thus yarn was spun continuously on the spindle and fed from the arms of the flyer to the bobbin rotating at a different speed. With all these methods of spinning, however, there was inconsistency of quality, as the results depended on the skill of the individual spinster, who had to pay out the right amount of wool to maintain an even thickness of yarn. As most of the women in a household learned to spin, this often meant that different qualities of yarn might be found even on the same spindle. This was an inconvenience to the weaver and an important incentive towards devising a machine that would produce consistent yarn. Spinning wheels are perhaps the most common evidence of pre-industrial textile manufacture to be found in museums today. In the Textile Machinery Museum at Tonge Moor Library, Tonge Moor Road, Bolton [SD 728106], both Jersey and Saxony wheels are exhibited, and the Horner Collection in the Ulster Museum, Belfast, contains spinning wheels from a number of countries.

Once a suitable yarn had been spun, the next process was to weave it into a cloth fabric on a loom. The traditional hand loom consisted of a frame carrying the longitudinal or 'warp' threads, which could be separated to allow the transverse 'weft' threads to pass alternately over and under them. This simplest form of interlacing of warp and weft is known as plain weave and was for centuries carried out on simple hand looms. The main obstacle to speeding up the process of weaving was the problem of moving the shuttle containing the weft yarn wound on a bobbin across the loom between the alternate warp yarns. The answer, when it came in the form of the 'flying shuttle', was one of the crucial inventions of the textile industry; it was remarkably simple in principle, cost very little and led to an enormous increase in hand-loom weaving, an increase which was to have tragic repercussions in the 1820s. With the exception of the stocking frame, which produced a knitted as opposed to a woven fabric, and which will be considered later (page 183), it was to be the first move in the sequence of events leading to the fully mechanised textile industry.

From the industrial archaeological point of view the chief features to examine are the textile machines themselves, the prime movers that drove them and the buildings that housed machines and workers. Of the textile machines a reasonably representative range has been preserved in museums, mainly in Lancashire and Yorkshire, but the prime movers – the waterwheels and steam engines that powered those machines – are somewhat harder to find. The technology of these sources of power has been considered in Chapters 3 and 4, but there were variants specific to the textile industry, such as the steam mill engine, which are worthy of additional passing reference. It is in the buildings, however, particularly those dating from the middle of the eighteenth century onwards, that the most prolific archaeological evidence of the industry lies. Indeed, of all the landscape changes brought about by the Industrial Revolution, the textile mill building is one of the most prominent. The evolution of the textile mill, almost from its earliest days, can be traced through surviving examples, in some of which were incorporated important innovations in constructional technique. In examining the industrial archaeology of textile manufacturing we will look first at the development of the machine itself and then at the buildings and power sources.

As we have seen, the bottleneck in the hand-weaving process was the speed at which the weft threads could be passed through the warp. The answer was found by John Kay (1704–c1780) who was born at Park near Bury in Lancashire. He was apprenticed into the weaving machinery trade and spent the whole of his working life involved with textile equipment. His 'fly' or 'flying shuttle' of 1733 consisted of boxes to hold the shuttle at each side of the loom connected by a long board, or 'shuttle race', along which the shuttle ran. Each box had a horizontal metal rod, and on each rod was a freely moving slide known as a 'picker'. Each picker was connected by a string tied to a stick or 'picking peg' held by the weaver. By jerking the picking peg from side to side,

the weaver could throw the shuttle from one shuttle box to the other. Kay fitted wheels or rollers to some of his shuttles but later these were discarded and the term 'flying shuttle' was used. The operation of weaving became not only less tedious but output was often doubled.

There were a number of minor technical difficulties that slowed down the adoption of Kay's flying shuttle, an initial disbelief in its workability and considerable unwillingness by many weavers to pay the 15s per year which he charged for the use of his invention. However, it was widely taken up eventually, and had the effect of speeding up weaving and thereby substantially increasing the imbalance between the weaving and spinning processes. Even before his invention, four or five spinsters had been needed to supply one weaver, and the flying shuttle still further increased the incentive to devise a machine that would spin more than one or two threads at a time. Numerous hand looms, with and without flying shuttles, may be found in museums specialising in textile machinery, including the Piece Hall, Halifax, where they are demonstrated from time to time.

The first attempts at the mechanisation of spinning were made by Lewis Paul (d1759) and John Wyatt (1700–66) and patented in 1738. Their first machine, involving pairs of rollers to draw out the fibres, was unsuccessful, as were a number of variations on it produced in succeeding years, although the roller drawing principle was eventually used with great success. An experimental mill was built in Birmingham about 1741 and another in Northampton, but neither appears to have been very successful.

It was not until the 1760s that James Hargreaves (c1719–78), a weaver of Stanhill near Blackburn, where his cottage still survives [SD 728277], developed a successful mechanism for spinning cotton on multiple spindles – initially eight and later sixteen. This was the spinning jenny, a hand-operated machine that fitted well into the domestically based spinning industry. The term 'jenny' is a simple corruption of the word 'engine', as is the 'gin' used in 'horse-gin', a term used in mining and for the machine that removed seeds from raw cotton. In the jenny a hand-driven wheel powered a number of spindles, and a clasp drew out the spun yarn from each of them at the same time. Having completed the drawing out, the clasp moved forward and the spun yarn was wound on to the 'cop', which, when full, became a cylindrical package of yarn with conical ends. The jenny was, in effect, a mechanised Jersey wheel, as the spinning process was not continuous; but because of the larger number of spindles which it employed, output was very considerable. Jennies to be seen in most museums are of the improved variety, with a large number of spindles, but Higher Mill, Helmshore [SD 777214], now a museum of the Lancashire textile industry, has a jenny built in 1963 to the specification in Hargreaves' original patent. A visitor to Higher Mill can see this and other equipment demonstrated.

There was considerable antagonism in Lancashire towards Hargreaves as a result of his invention, so he moved to Nottingham, where demand for cotton yarn for

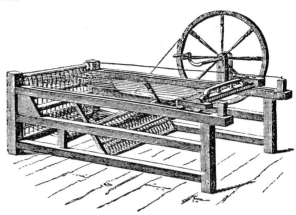

130 Hargreaves's spinning jenny

knitting in the stocking-frame was growing. Here he established a mill and in 1770, several years after his invention of the jenny, he finally took out a patent for it. The fact that Richard (later Sir Richard) Arkwright (1732–92) had patented a new

131 Mule spinning being demonstrated at Manchester Museum of Science & Industry
(Neil Cossons)

device for spinning in 1769 may well have prompted this action by Hargreaves. Certainly Arkwright's machine proved much more suitable than the jenny for producing the fine cotton threads needed in knitting. Yet in Lancashire jennies became more and more popular for the weft yarn of cotton-linen woven fabrics and for all-cotton goods. In the woollen industry, too, the jenny was found to be an efficient means of spinning soft full yarns. Equally as important was the fact that it was cheap and could be used by cottage spinners and small manufacturers alike.

Richard Arkwright was born in Preston, Lancashire, apprenticed to a barber and subsequently set up in business on his own as a barber and wigmaker. He became interested in mechanisms and the problems of a satisfactory spinning machine and, in association with a clock-maker in Leigh named John Kay (not

132 Spinning mule developed by Samuel Crompton, Bolton Textile Machinery Museum (*Bolton Museum & Art Gallery*)

associated with the flying shuttle inventor), Arkwright produced a prototype roller spinning machine for cotton. As with Hargreaves, hostility to Arkwright arose from those people already in the spinning industry who saw the machine as a threat to their livelihoods, so he too went to Nottingham and set up a business providing yarn for the knitting industry. He found a partner in a successful and well established hosiery manufacturer named Jedediah Strutt, and they established a small factory with a number of spinning machines driven by horse power. The yarns produced were most satisfactory for the hosiery industry, so in 1771 Arkwright moved to Cromford on the River Derwent in Derbyshire and there set up a larger mill driven by water power. As a result of the use of this source of power, Arkwright's roller-spinning device became known as the water frame. On it was based the enormous development of factory spinning and the further fortunes of its inventor, who built numerous other mills, was knighted and became High

Sheriff of Derbyshire. Of all the pioneer inventors in textiles during the eighteenth century, Arkwright had the least propitious beginning and derived the greatest benefits. He can really be described as the father of the factory system, an outstanding organiser of labour and machinery processing, ambitious, forceful and persevering.

A still more important advance in eighteenth-century spinning technology was still to come, however. This was the invention of the spinning mule in 1779, in effect a combination of the jenny and the water frame, hence the name 'mule' (Illus 132). Its inventor Samuel Crompton (1753–1827) was born near Bolton, Lancashire, and began spinning on a jenny as a boy. His mule was a great advance on either of the machines from which it derived – if in fact Crompton had any detailed knowledge of Arkwright's invention – and was particularly suitable for making fine yarns for muslin. The first mules had about 30 spindles but soon 130 were common. By moving the driving wheel to the centre, it was possible to operate still longer mules, and 400 spindle machines were built. Later machines carried more than 1,000. In 1792 water power was applied at New Lanark Mills in Scotland [NS 880425] for the

133 Mule spinning with machines that required manual power as well as that from the line shafting; until mules became self-acting the spinner moved the carriage by turning the driving wheel. On the right a piecer twists together broken threads and beneath the frame a child sweeps up waste

first time to drive mules and this established large-scale factory mule spinning. Crompton's house near Bolton, 'Hall-i'-th'Wood' [SD 724116], still stands and is now a museum of the Crompton family. The Textile Machinery Museum in Tonge Moor Road, Bolton, includes water frames, Crompton's mule and other early textile machines. Mules may also be seen at Higher Mill, Helmshore, where there is an original Arkwright water frame from his Cromford mill. A pre-industrial water-powered textile mill in regular operation and open to visitors is the Esgair Moel Mill from Llantwrtyd, Powys, re-erected at the Welsh Folk Museum, St Fagans [ST 118772], in 1951. Here too may be seen a spinning mule, with eighty spindles, together with three hand looms and all the other equipment to convert raw wool into dyed and finished fabric.

Throughout this period of rapid development on the spinning side of the textile industry the hand loom for weaving fabric had remained virtually static, although there was a progressive increase in the use of the flying shuttle. There had been powered looms since the sixteenth century for weaving silk ribbons, but the general opinion among fabric weavers was that the hand loom involved too many independent actions requiring timing and skill to mechanise. The first breakthrough came in 1784 with the invention by Dr Edmund Cartwright (1743–1823), a Leicestershire rector, of a loom which could be powered, although he had never at the time seen a person weave. Cartwright's loom was by no means sophisticated, all its actions being rapid and harsh, particularly that of the shuttle, which was propelled by a powerful spring. Its main contribution was to prove the feasibility of powered looms, and other inventors were stimulated into carrying out further experiments. Cartwright looms of a more highly developed type were in use in Doncaster and Manchester in the 1790s, while in Scotland numerous inventors, including Robert Miller and J. L. Robertson of Glasgow, made improvements. The most significant improvement, however, was devised by William Horrocks of Stockport, who in 1813 introduced a means of varying the speed of separation of the warp threads so as to increase the period for the shuttle to pass through.

Between 1813 and 1820 the number of power looms in Britain increased from 2,400 to 14,150, but even then the bulk of woven cloth was still being produced by hand-loom weavers. The largest spinning mills employed 1,500 people, and almost all the preparatory processes, like carding, had been mechanised for wool and worsted, cotton, silk and flax. By 1820 there were 110,000 workers in spinning mills, but only 10,000 in weaving factories, and some of them were working traditional hand looms in factory buildings. As power looms began to be improved mechanically, their numbers increased rapidly, so that the 2,000 looms per year installed between 1813 and 1820 had become 10,000 a year by the 1830s. Meanwhile the hand-loom weavers sank from

134 Power-loom for cotton

being among the most prosperous workers in the country to some of the most poverty-stricken. The weavers' skills were no longer required, as in the factories the simple work of mending thread breakages and replenishing shuttles could be carried out by women and children. In the 1810s, first in the Midlands and subsequently in Lancashire and Yorkshire, the machine-smashing Luddites responded to these conditions, made all the more appalling by the general depression after the Napoleonic wars.

In other branches of the textile trade, too, mechanisation took place during the late eighteenth and early nineteenth centuries. At the preliminary processing end, carding machines (Illus 135) were developed by a number of inventors; most worked on the roller principle, in which a large cylinder with wire teeth took the fibres round under a series of smaller 'worker' rollers running at a different speed, and they did the carding. Although these early carding machines were developed for cotton, it was not long before they were applied also to wool (Illus 136), where they were called 'scribblers'. Pattern weaving was also greatly improved after about 1800, with the introduction of the Jacquard attachment in which individual warp threads were lifted by a mechanism mounted above the loom and controlled by punched cards. The type of pattern depended on the 'programme' punched into the continuous strip of cards.

In the hosiery manufacturing industry, in which stockings were knitted by the looping together of threads to form an elastic fabric, the basic machine, the knitting-frame, had been developed as early as the 1590s by the Rev William Lee of Calverton near Nottingham. It was one of the most ingenious inventions in the textile industry and formed the basis for the early rise of the East Midlands as a hosiery area. The problem was one of looping threads into each other using a hooked needle, and the answer lay in developing a way of opening and closing the hook automatically to allow the loop to be made and the needle to be disengaged and then withdrawn without re-engagement. The crux of Lee's invention lay in a hook which was normally open but could be closed by pressure. By filing a slot in the shank of the needle, the point of the hook could sink into it upon closure and thus avoid any accidental catching of the loop. This is the bearded needle widely used in knitting machines today. A further development came with the mechan-

isation of rib knitting in 1758 by Jedediah Strutt. Rib-knitted hosiery was more closely fitting than plain-knitted but at the same time more elastic. Strutt's invention consisted of an additional set of needles added to the conventional stocking-frame which, operated in conjunction with the usual needles, had the effect of reversing the loop and producing a rib effect. A more fundamental development came in 1775 when the first warp knitting machine was introduced. Previously loops had been formed in threads running across the width of the fabric (weft knitting), but the new machine, attributed to both J. Crane and J. Tarrett of Nottinghamshire, produced a knitted fabric which could be cut up and sewn into garments. By the 1850s rib knitting was being produced on powered circular machines, thus producing a tubular fabric for stockings, and about the same time M. Townsend of Nottingham patented the 'tumbler' or 'latch' needle, which was to be funda-

135 A card room of the early 1830s with carding engines on the left and a doubling machine to the right

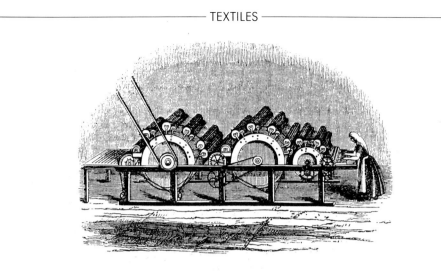

136 Wool-carding engine

mental to the further progress of the knitting industry. Generally similar in appearance to the bearded needle, the latch needle had a hinged attachment to open and close the hook. All these and many more aspects of the technology of knitting can be seen in the large collection of machines on display at the Snibston Discovery Park, Coalville, Leicestershire [SK 419145].

In Chapel Street, Ruddington, Notting-hamshire [SK 572329], a frameshop has been preserved as the Ruddington Framework Knitters' Museum. Open by appointment it is a unique complex of hand-frames, preserved *in situ*, together with the living quarters of the knitters. Other examples of early frameshops can be seen in the main street of Sutton Bonnington [SK 503256], Shepshed [SK 483196] and Hinckley [SP 428943]. Purpose-built three-storey houses with toyshops sur-

137 Bobbin net machine shown at the Great Exhibition

138 Fulling stocks

vive in Stapleford [SK 506279]. The lace industry is also well represented, by machines on display at Nottingham Industrial Museum, Courtyard Buildings, Wollaton Park, Nottingham [SK 531392].

The basic step in the mechanisation of lace making had been made by John Heathcoat (1783–1861) in 1809, when he developed a machine (the bobbinet, later known as the plain net machine) capable of imitating almost exactly the hand-made pillow lace. He used a flat bobbin, resembling a disc, which could pass between the vertical warp threads and thus entwine the weft thread around them. In 1813 his machine was improved by John Lever, who adapted it to make patterned lace, using, if necessary, the Jacquard principle.

One major aspect of fabric production that has still to be considered is the finishing of the woven cloth. One of these finishing processes had been mechanised as early as the thirteenth century, when water-powered 'fulling' mills had replaced manual fulling of wool cloth. The process consisted of pounding the woven fabric in water with fuller's earth to felt it up and shrink it. It was relatively simple to devise water-powered hammers to carry out this work, cams on a shaft raising the heads in much the same manner as the tilt hammers used for ironworking. The effects on location of the industry were similar, too, resulting in an essentially urban-based

craft moving out and dispersing to the fast-flowing streams of north Somerset, central Gloucestershire and west Wiltshire in the South West, and from towns like Beverley and York to the Pennine streams of the West Riding of Yorkshire. A number of fulling mills still survive and at Higher Mill, Helmshore [SD 777214], the waterwheel and fulling stocks can also be seen, as can the tenter hooks on which the cloth was subsequently stretched and dried and the rotary gig-mills containing teasels, which were used to raise the nap on the cloth. This was afterwards sheared, first by large hand-shears and later by a rotary device in action very similar to a cylinder lawnmower.

THE FIRST FACTORIES
The factory system that developed so rapidly in the textile industries at the end of the eighteenth century had its origins in 1702. In that year Thomas Cotchett (b1640) opened a three-storey silk spinning mill on the River Derwent in Derby in which he installed Dutch spinning or 'throwing' machinery. Although Cotchett's business failed and all but a few of the foundation arches of his building have disappeared [SK 356364], his mill has a good claim to the title of the first factory in that it was a single building with complex machinery, a source of power in its waterwheel, and accommodation for a number

of employees. What was perhaps of more immediate importance was that his enterprise attracted the attention of the wealthy London silk merchant Thomas (later Sir Thomas) Lombe (1685–1739), and his half-brother John Lombe (1693?–1722), who worked for a time in Cotchett's Mill. Some years later, possibly after a visit to the highly advanced silk spinning areas of Italy, the Lombes built a much bigger factory in Derby near Cotchett's original building.

Here the three basic operations of converting the silk filament from the cocoon of the silkworm into a yarn suitable for weaving were carried on. The first stages, carried out before the silk arrived at the factory, consisted of unwinding the filament from the cocoon and rewinding it with others to form a skein. This skein was washed to remove the gummy matter known as sericin and was then ready for processing in Lombe's factory. Here it was wound on to bobbins on a winding machine; transferred to a second machine where the strands from several bobbins were wound on to a single bobbin, a process known as 'doubling'; and finally twisted together into a yarn on a third machine, a process known as 'throwing'. If the yarn was to be used for the weft in weaving, only a slight twist was put into it, but if for the warp a stronger twist was applied. The weft yarn was called the 'tram' and the warp the 'organzine'.

The Lombes' factory in Derby was of unprecedented size, the throwing mill alone being five storeys high and 110ft long and accommodating over 300 workers. These were mainly women and children who reknotted the threads when they broke, a very frequent occurrence. A single large waterwheel operated over 25,000 movements in the machinery. The building established the form the textile mill was to take until well into the twentieth century, the name 'mill' itself deriving from the fact that all the early ones were water powered. It remained in active use for silk until 1890, when part collapsed, and after a disastrous fire in 1910 the building was substantially altered. Today the original approach bridge and part of the tower survive, together with

foundations in the river bank. The wrought-iron gates, dating from 1722, were re-sited in 1934 near the Borough Library in Wardwick, Derby [SK 351363].

Why the industry became established in Derby is difficult to explain. The main centre, occupied largely by refugee Huguenot weavers, was in the Spitalfields area of London where, in and around Fournier Street [TQ 338818], a considerable number of their houses with attic workshops still survive. The rise of the Nottingham framework knitting industry is the most likely reason for Cotchett and the Lombes coming to the East Midlands, and Derby may well have been chosen because of the power afforded by the waters of the Derwent. The Trent itself and tributaries like the Leen and Erewash would have been quite unsuitable. From Derby the silk industry spread to other centres after the expiration of the Lombe patent in 1732, and factories were established initially in Macclesfield, Stockport and Chesterfield, and later in Manchester, Salford and Braintree in Essex, where George Courtauld and his son Samuel founded the firm which is now world famous for man-made fibres.

In the first half of the eighteenth century, however, the silk industry's growth rate was relatively slow and, despite the fact that factories had been established, it played no part in the large-scale industrial progress in textiles that came later with cotton and wool. The reasons for this were the shortage of raw silk supplies, which were also expensive, and the competition from continental and eastern silks abroad, which destroyed the chance of appreciable export markets. The cotton industry on the other hand enjoyed unlimited supplies of raw material and, once the plantation system had developed fully in the American South, supplies that fell in price. Cotton fabric, an attractive and cheap alternative to wool, was able to penetrate the enormous and growing home market and at the same time, as a result of the fall in costs and prices because of technological innovations in the industry, to enjoy almost unlimited export demand. Cotton was also a tractable fibre lending itself to machine pro-

cesses more readily than wool. Finally the cotton industry, for reasons which we shall examine shortly, had the good fortune to establish itself in Lancashire, which was not a traditional textile area and had none of the built-in restrictive practices to be found elsewhere. Thus it was cotton which stood in the forefront of industrial progress in the textile industry despite the fact that what might be called the first generation of true factories were for spinning silk.

THE DEVELOPMENT OF THE FACTORY BUILDING

The early silk mills and Arkwright's first cotton mills at Cromford were characterised by the fact that they contained novel machinery in buildings of essentially traditional construction. All the ingenious devices developed to convert fibre into cloth were of a size suitable for arrangement in rows watched over by relatively unskilled operatives. Eventually all could be powered from a rotating shaft that had at its input end a horse-gin in a few early examples, but more often a large water-wheel, and increasingly after about 1800 a rotative steam engine. The requirements of the factory were therefore large numbers of identical spaces, with reasonable

139 Built by John and Joseph Cash in 1857, this model factory in Coventry [SP 335806] was intended to maintain the independence of the individual silk-ribbon workers within the factory system. The two-storey houses with top shops above have recently been renovated (*Neil Cossons*)

natural lighting, arranged in such a way that power could easily be distributed to the machines. The outcome was a new form of building, taking the traditional constructional techniques of brick or stone load-bearing walls and timber beam-and-plank floors as its basis. Typically it was long and thin in plan, rarely more than 40ft deep, rising four to six storeys, and with the line-shafting to carry power for the machines arranged parallel to the long axis and supported at or near ceiling height. This was basically the form the Lombes' mill had taken in 1721, and it was to survive virtually unaltered for two centuries.

Numerous fine examples of early textile mills still exist, although unfortunately Arkwright's Old Mill at Cromford [SK 298569], completed in 1772, has been so substantially altered, with the loss of two storeys, that it is almost unrecognisable. Masson Mill [SK 294573], however, built in 1783, is largely intact, the red-painted

140 The Card Factory, Chester Road, Maccles-field [SJ 909737], like a number of other silk mills in the town, epitomises the translation of the Georgian domestic vernacular into the new textile factories *(Neil Cossons)*

141 Whitchurch silk mill in Hampshire [SU 463479]; recent studies of the building indicate that the red brick exterior hides an inner structure built of chalk-stone blocks *(Hampshire Buildings Preservation Trust)*

walls and white window surrounds a familiar feature on the A6(T) north of Cromford. Arkwright was associated with a number of other mills which, like those at Cromford, were located on streams that could provide power. At Cressbrook [SK 173726] the remains of his 1779 mill can be seen at the west end of the existing 1815 building, the latter a superb four-storey structure built by William Newton, one of the finest examples of the adoption of an enlarged domestic style for mills. It has twelve bays, a centrally placed four-bay pediment, hipped roof and a cupola which held a bell to summon the workers.

An even finer example of this Georgian style may be seen in a number of silk mills in Macclesfield, notably Frost's Mill [SJ 918737] in the centre of the town and the former silk mill on Chester Road (Illus 140), now the card factory of Henry and Leigh Slater [SJ 909737]. This latter building epitomises the large eighteenth-century mill – a rectangular and disciplined brick box for machinery obeying to the letter the architectural rules of the day. The Macclesfield card factory has four storeys and seventeen bays, the centre five brought forward and supporting a pediment with central clock, cupola and wind vane. In Hampshire (Illus 141) the same style on a much smaller scale can be seen in the beautiful red brick Whitchurch silk mill [SU 463479], while in Cheshire, Quarry Bank Mill, Styal [SJ 835829], built in 1784 by Samuel Greg of Belfast on a more complicated plan, has the same graceful rhythm (Illus 142). A number of features typical of most of these early mills are worthy of examination. Firstly the windows, which have small panes and are usually of the

142 Quarry Bank Mill, Styal, Cheshire [SJ 835829], built by Samuel Greg in 1784 as a water-powered cotton spinning mill and later extended to house weaving machinery. Today it is a museum of the factory system (*National Trust*)

sash type, usually have wooden frames. Later, cast iron was used. Generally speaking the smaller window panes are the earlier, good examples being found at Calver Mill, Derbyshire [SK 245744], and Low Mill, Caton, in Lancashire [SD 527649]. In the latter case the mill was built originally in 1784 and rebuilt after a fire in 1838, probably with the original windows. Tie irons of a disc or cruciform shape also are frequent, and in many cases appear to date from the construction of the building. These wall plates are tied by wrought-iron rods that pass right through the building and hold it together.

Inside, the floors consist of timber beams and boards sometimes supported by vertical timber pillars but more often by cast iron columns of circular or cruciform section. The location of original line-shafting, if it has gone, can usually be traced from the positions of brackets or bracket-fixing holes either in the columns or on the ceiling beams. Occasionally the column itself is forked or has a bracket-fixing cast on to it to support the bearing or 'plummer' block. The position and size of watercourses are also worth noting, as they give an indication of the type of waterwheel used. In early mills the wheel

was often centrally placed in the building with a vertical timber shaft taking the drive from the pit wheel up through the building to engage the horizontal line-shafts on each floor. Later, iron shafts and gearing were used. A large iron water-wheel has recently been installed at Quarry Bank Mill, Styal [SJ 835829], now an important museum of the factory system in cotton spinning and weaving.

Although the general form of the multi-storey textile mill had been established at the beginning of the eighteenth century, a fundamental change in its technique of construction evolved in the 1780s and 1790s as a result of what we might now call a research programme. Arkwright's major partner in his Cromford venture was Jedediah Strutt, who had substantial silk interests in Derby and, after the dissolving of the partnership in 1781, took over completely the mills at Belper and Milford. These were greatly extended during the 1790s by Jedediah's son William Strutt (1756–1830), who systematically set about finding an answer to the problem of fire in these timber-floored buildings. Fires were frequent and usually disastrous, the complete destruction in 1791 of the enormous Albion flour mill in London providing the

143 The world's first iron-framed building, the flax mill at Ditherington, Shrewsbury [SJ 500140], completed in 1797; the divided top to the columns housed the bearings for a line shaft (*Neil Cossons*)

144 Cast iron columns and beams, wrought iron ties, brick arches: the fire-proof construction of the Ditherington flax mill

145 Stanley Mill, Stonehouse, near Stroud, Gloucestershire [SO 814043]   (*Neil Cossons*)

final incentive towards devising a solution. The first stage was reached in Strutt's calico mill in Derby, 1792–3, in which the floors were made of shallow brick arches of 9ft span springing from timber beams supported on cast iron columns. The underside of the timber was coated with plaster to ensure that no surface that might catch fire would be exposed. Strutt produced more advanced versions at Milford in 1792–3 and Belper in 1793–5, but it was in fact a friend, Charles Bage, who took the next step by replacing the timber beam with a cast iron one, so producing the world's first iron-framed building, a flax mill in Shrewsbury (Illus 143 and 144) [SJ 500140]. Although all Strutt's early buildings have now gone, the Marshall, Benyon & Bage flax mill, now used as a maltings, still stands at Ditherington, Shrewsbury. The modern factory had arrived and, although it was to be more than another fifty years before it became a completely frame structure and the load-bearing exterior walls disappeared to be replaced by curtain-wall cladding, the Shrewsbury flax mill must be regarded as one of the pioneer structures of the Industrial Revolution. Others quickly followed and, although the immediate descendants have been destroyed, Strutt's own response to the Bage building, his North Mill at Belper [SK 345481], completed in 1804, still survives as the most beautiful, sophisticated and technically perfect structure of its era.

While these giant cotton and flax mills were developing so rapidly in the early years of the nineteenth century, the wool textile industry was stirring, too, although less violently. In the Stroud valleys of Gloucestershire numerous mills, most of them relatively small, were being built in the warm local stone, usually with interiors of conventional timber construction. Similarly in west Wiltshire and north Somerset water-powered wool mills appeared in considerable numbers. An exception to all the others is Stanley Mill at Stonehouse near Stroud (Illus 145, 146 and 147) [SO 814043], which is of cast iron and brick 'fire-proof' construction. Built in 1813 to draw its power from the River Frome, Stanley Mill provides a remarkable combination of the functional use of brick panels and stone pilasters on its outside with traceried iron arches supporting iron floor beams on iron columns. By the 1820s the iron-framed textile mill had become well established, although it was not until the 1860s or even later that the building of mills with timber beams and floors died out. One reason may have been the failure of a number of cast iron frame structures, such as the celebrated collapse of Lowerhouse Mill, Oldham, in 1844, and another the appreciation that, although iron itself was incombustible, if a fire did occur in an iron-framed building, the expansion of the members frequently resulted in the destruction of the shell of the building too.

It was to Lancashire that the cotton

146 Cast iron construction of Stanley Mill, Stonehouse (*Neil Cossons*)

147 Stanley Mill (*Neil Cossons*)

148 Tenement lace factory, Leopold Street, Long Eaton, Derbyshire [SK 488336]; dating from the late 1880s, the building is 530ft long and provided accommodation for numerous small lace-making concerns   (*Neil Cossons*)

industry migrated in the late eighteenth and early nineteenth centuries, and there the factory continued to evolve. Large numbers of these buildings still survive, offering the industrial archaeologist an opportunity to examine in detail their evolution. Initially water, for power, washing and bleaching, was the major locational factor, with the result that mills tended to be situated in remote valleys of the Pennines where such site advantages outweighed problems of communication. With the introduction of steam power, however, new factors influenced location and the cotton industry became concentrated in towns stretching from Stockport in Cheshire north to Preston. These new cotton towns grew up on the Lancashire plain, still enjoying the water necessary for various finishing and bleaching processes, but having easier access to Liverpool for raw materials, to Manchester for marketing the finished products, to coal and, by virtue of the concentration of large numbers of mills, to pools of skilled labour both for operating and maintaining the machinery.

An important example of this first phase of steam-powered mills was Orrell's Mill, Travis Street, Heaton Mersey, Stockport [SJ 867903], built in 1835 by William (later Sir William) Fairbairn (1789–1874), the celebrated Manchester engineer. The mill had six storeys and the main spinning rooms were 280ft long by 50ft wide. Cast iron columns and beams supported the floors. Despite being Listed, Orrell's Mill was demolished although the chimney still stands. A rapidly decreasing number of similar mills, usually of later date, can be found in most of the textile towns, elegantly simple in shape and design, with rectangular windows spaced and separated by almost their own width of brick wall.

From the 1860s onwards, and particularly after the widespread adoption of the American ring-spinning frame, cotton mills became much larger and were typically built of dark red brick with progressively increasing areas of glazing. The introduction of sprinkler systems for fire control necessitated high-level water tanks, which were at first simply placed on the roof of the mill, as at the 1851 Galgate silk mill at Ellel [SD 485557]. By the late 1870s, however, it was more common to enclose the tank within the structure of a tower that frequently bore the name of the mill in white tile lettering.

The gradual recovery of the Lancashire cotton industry after the devastating effects of the American Civil War led eventually to a new boom in building, which between about 1880 and 1920 brought the cotton mill to its ultimate state of development. Enormous brick-built spinning mills, often in shiny red Accrington brick with yellow brick detailing, great expanses of glass and highly ornamental towers, were built in large numbers, and they still dominate the skyline of most towns between Preston and Oldham. The demand created by large machinery for bigger and bigger spaces with fewer intermediate supports was satisfied by new constructional techniques employing initially fabricated wrought iron beams and later, as at Centenary Mill, Preston [SD 551297], built in 1895, rolled steel beams and concrete floors. Less load was carried by the external walls, which in many cases became almost entirely glass, the brickwork being reduced to little more than mullions between large glazed panels. All-concrete construction was slow to be adopted in Britain, although it rapidly reached an

149 Completed in 1907, Victoria Mill, Draycott, Derbyshire [SK 445333], was one of the largest lace tenement factories, 600ft long in fifty-eight bays (*Neil Cossons*)

150 Victoria Mill, Draycott, Derbyshire (*Neil Cossons*)

FACTORY POWER TRANSMISSION

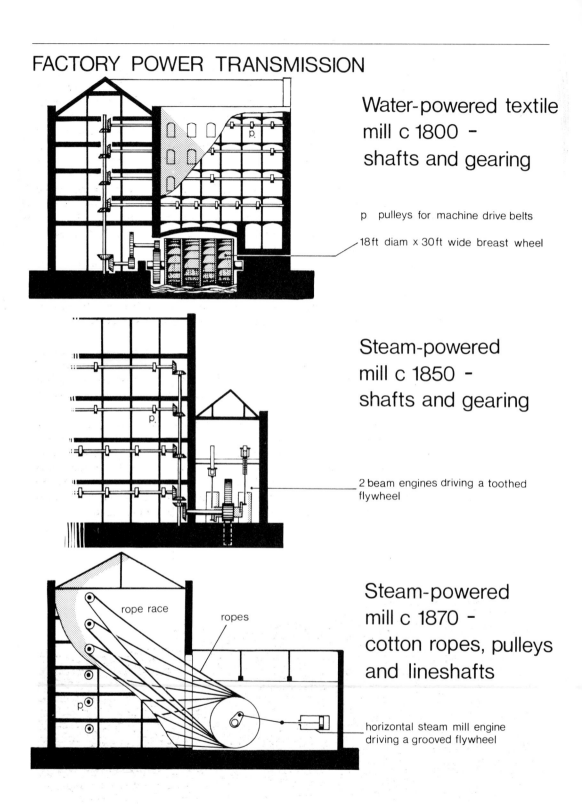

Water-powered textile
mill c 1800 -
shafts and gearing

p   pulleys for machine drive belts

18ft diam x 30ft wide breast wheel

Steam-powered
mill c 1850 -
shafts and gearing

2 beam engines driving a toothed
flywheel

Steam-powered
mill c 1870 -
cotton ropes, pulleys
and lineshafts

rope race

ropes

horizontal steam mill engine
driving a grooved flywheel

Illustration 151

advanced state of development abroad, notably in France. Concrete, however, was to bring the all-glass wall to the textile mill, one of the results of mushroom construction in which concrete pillars set well in from the skin of the building supported the floors on the cantilever principle. A good example is the Viyella factory designed by F. A. Broadhead on Castle Boulevard, Nottingham [SK 570394].

In parallel with the evolution of the mill's shape and structure came important changes in power transmission. The earliest water-powered mills had used timber millwork, transmitting the power by wooden shafts and gearing. In the latter part of the eighteenth century cast iron shafting and gears were introduced, to be superseded by lightweight wrought iron shafts revolving at higher speeds which were developed first by Fairbairn in the late 1820s. The greatest single advance came in the 1860s, when shaft drive was dispensed with altogether and ropes driven from the flywheel of the steam engine ran to each floor of the mill (Illus 151). The flywheel face was grooved to take as many as thirty cotton ropes, which ran up through the rope race to drive the line-shafts at each floor. Ropes were mechanically efficient, cheap to install and maintain, and if a breakage occurred, the whole mill did not have to suspend pro-

duction, as it did when a fault arose in a shaft-driven system. A specific type of engine evolved, too, in the steam mill engine, which became widespread in both Lancashire and Yorkshire. It was usually a horizontal compound with a variety of cylinder configurations (see Chapter 4 and Illus 45). A superb mill engine is preserved by the Northern Mill Engine Society at Dee Mill, Shaw, near Rochdale [SD 945093]. Nearby is that other typical feature of all large steam textile mills – the pool, or mill 'lodge', in which condenser water was cooled and stored.

Although the spinning side of the textile industry produced a large and very individual style of mill building, the weaving of yarns into fabric resulted in an equally distinctive if less spectacular type of structure. Typically weaving was carried on in a single-storey building, although in earlier mills looms occupied the ground floors of multi-storey spinning blocks. A good example of a weaving shed

152 The west block of the Tay Carpet Works, Lochee Road, Dundee [NO 398304], one of the largest textile mills in Britain, purpose-built in stages between 1851 and 1865 for jute spinning but later specialising in jute carpets. At the time of writing the building was being converted into student accommodation (*John R. Hume*)

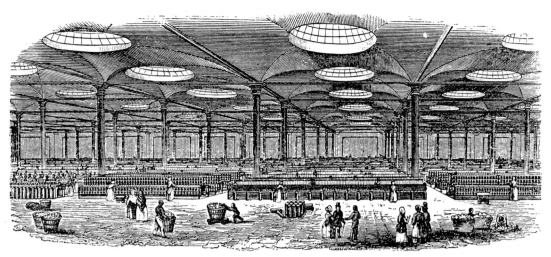

153   Interior of Marshall's one-storeyed flax mill at Leeds

stands in front of Cressbrook Mill, Derby-shire [SK 173726], its roof of ridge-and-furrow form, with glazed northlights on the steep-pitched faces and slates on the shallower sides. Wooden roof trusses with cast iron columns were almost universal for weaving sheds, the looms being arranged in lines between the rows of columns on which line-shafts were carried. North-east Lancashire in particular abounds in weaving sheds mainly built in the latter part of the nineteenth century, when weaving became a speciality of towns like Nelson and Colne, Burnley, Blackburn, Preston and Clitheroe. In many ways the weaving shed, with its large ground floor area and good all-over light-ing, formed the basis for the modern factory building to be seen on every inter-war trading estate.

On the east of the Pennines the early period of mill building, until, say, 1830, was generally similar to that on the west, although stone was almost universal as a building material. An early exception was Gott's Mill, Leeds [SE 291335], a large com-

154   Ackroyd's loom shed at Halifax – worsted goods

plex consisting of spinning mills and weavers' dwellings which was demolished in the 1960s.

Just as exceptional, although for completely different reasons, was another Leeds mill, which happily still exists: Marshall's flax mill [SE 295326], completed in June 1840, is based on the Egyptian temple of Karnak. Designed by Bonomi and David Roberts, the single-storey preparing and spinning mill stretches 132yd along Marshall Street, and is 72yd in depth. The interior room of the Temple Mill, as it became known, covers some 2 acres, and slender cast iron columns (which also act as drainpipes) support a ceiling 21ft high which has over 60 conical glass skylights 14ft in diameter rising above the roof. Along the façade stand squat columns flanking the windows and supporting a massive Egyptianesque entablature, and to the north, set back slightly from the street line, is the office block added in 1843. The original chimney, built rather after the style of Cleo-

patra's needle, cracked in 1852 and was replaced by a conventional one. John Marshall (1765–1846), who built the Temple Mill and was also involved in the Shrewsbury flax mill of 1797, established his linen industry in Leeds in the early 1800s. The peak of its prosperity was exemplified by his Egyptian adventure of the 1840s but later, under a second generation, the business declined, to end finally in 1886. Temple Mill is now used by a mail order firm.

Two great complexes in Bradford epitomise the West Riding's position in the textile industry in the second half of the nineteenth century, although, curiously

155 Titus Salt's great mills at Shipley, West Yorkshire [SE 140381]. Built in 1851 and the centrepiece of the model industrial settlement of Saltaire, it is now out of use, its future, like that of many Yorkshire textile mills, the subject of intense debate
(*Royal Commission on Historical Monuments, England*)

156 Albert Terrace, Saltaire, West Yorkshire
[SE 140381] (*Neil Cossons*)

enough, neither was concerned specifically with wool at the outset. Best known is Saltaire [SE 1438], the planned village surrounding mills (Illus 155), created by the model employer, social improver and philanthropist, Titus Salt (1803–76). Salt was born in Morley, near Bradford, and grew up in the worsted industry in partnership with his father at a time when the West Riding was beginning to outstrip the traditional centre of worsted manufacture in Norwich. His considerable business and inventive abilities enabled him to set up his own, and by 1836 he owned four mills. His success in spinning the fibres of the South American alpaca goat, previously regarded as unusable, led to a great increase in business at a time when a wide variety of differing warp and weft threads were being experimented with. By 1851 he had started a large new factory on the River Aire outside Bradford around which he also built the new settlement of Saltaire, with its neat rows of houses for employees. By the 1870s a church, hospital, baths and schools had been added to form the complete model village which survives, virtually unaltered, today, a stage in the progress from New Lanark to

Port Sunlight and Bournville.

The other major Bradford mill was built by Samuel C. Lister (1815–1906) at Manningham [SE 146348] and dates from 1873. Lister was an inventor and improver of processes, taking out more than 150 patents during his lifetime. Starting in the worsted industry, his major contributions included processes for combing wool and utilising waste silk, and it was on the strength of this latter technique that the great Manningham Mill complex developed. Velvet and plush were the main products which resulted from Lister's improvement of a Spanish loom for weaving pile cloth. The mill itself consists of two large six-storey blocks each capped by

157,158 Dunkirk Mill, Freshford, Avon [ST 785595]. The trade token of 1795 illustrates the original five-storey water-powered woollen mill. Closed in 1912, it stood for many years as a ruin before being cut down to three storeys and converted to residential use   (*Neil Cossons*)

159   Dunkirk Mill reduced to three storeys (*Neil Cossons*)

an ornamental and panelled parapet, and a series of lower buildings principally devoted to weaving. In the centre is the boiler house with a tall chimney resembling an Italian campanile.

The catastrophic decline in the last thirty years of the south Lancashire and west Yorkshire textile industry has left a magnificent but problematic legacy in the form of hundreds of mills, among the finest buildings of the Industrial Revolution, disused and unwanted. Some may be converted for other industrial uses, others for offices or residential accommodation, a few may become museums or craft centres. Both Saltaire and Manningham mills seek a new future and the same is true throughout the region, from Keighley to Stockport and Blackburn to Leeds. But new and original ideas are being applied and Pennine Heritage Limited, a charitable trust engaged on an ambitious programme to encourage the social and economic regeneration of the area, has taken the initiative, with Burnley Borough Council, to keep open Queen Street Mill, Harle Syke, Burnley [SD 868349], as a working steam-powered weaving mill. The Queen Street Manufacturing Company

was formed in 1894 as a co-operative with 4,000 shares, mostly held by local people. Shareholders were entitled to operate a number of looms in the mill and until its closure in 1982 this remained the method of working, many of the last workers being descendants of the original shareholders. In 1986 it re-opened, the 500hp steam engine providing power for a weaving shed of over 300 looms. Every effort is made to retain the atmosphere and organisation of a working mill using original machines and employing people with a tradition in the industry.

Other museums involving the re-use of industrial buildings include Armley Mill, Leeds [SE 276341], on the River Aire, the focal point of an industrial and social history trail from the centre of the city to Rodley, 6 miles upstream. At Armley the Leeds Industrial Museum covers most aspects of the area's industrial history including textiles, with spinning mules, a variety of power looms and fulling stocks.

Across the Pennines the Museum of the Lancashire Textile Industry, Holcombe Road, Helmshore [SD 777214] is housed in an early nineteenth-century stone-built mill, which was substantially rebuilt in 1859/60 following a disastrous fire. A part of the museum is Higher Mill, also open to the public, with an important collection of early textile machines and where the waterwheel and fulling stocks are regularly demonstrated. Quarry Bank Mill, Styal, Cheshire [SJ 834830], one of the finest remaining Georgian cotton mills, is also remarkable for the survival of the entire factory village including two chapels, a school, shop, houses for mill workers as well as the Apprentice House. In Dyfed the National Museum of Wales runs the Museum of the Woollen Industry in the former Cambrian Mills, one of the forty-three mills that made Dre-fach Felindre [SN 355385] an important woollen centre a century ago. Today the industry is almost extinct.

160   The teasel (*Dipsacus fullonum*)

CHAPTER 11

THE CHEMICAL INDUSTRIES

The chemical industries present the industrial archaeologist with even greater problems than the engineering machinery discussed in Chapter 7, and for generally similar reasons. Not only are the processes of the industry fairly complex but the structures surviving from its past are often difficult to identify in the field. The landscapes created by massive concentrations of chemical plant, in places like Widnes, for example, are among the most unattractive imaginable and, for this reason, derelict buildings and old waste tips of toxic materials are among the first to be removed in the interests of tidiness and public safety. An added difficulty results from the fact that the products of the chemical industry are rarely ends in themselves but are the raw materials for other manufacturing processes. The industry's evolution has therefore been governed by the demands of other industrial activities – of textile manufacturers for bleaches and dyes, of glassmakers for soda and of the fertiliser industry for sulphuric acid. To produce these chemicals, the industry demanded a wide variety of organic and inorganic raw materials, ranging from seaweed for alkalis and exotic foreign hardwoods for leather dyes to salt, copperas (derived from iron pyrites) and alum. Coal, besides providing the basis for town gas, was also an important raw material for many chemicals, although its main significance was as a fuel and as such an important factor in the location of chemical processes depending on heat. More recently oil has become the most important feedstock of the chemical industry, its use extending back a surprisingly long way. Scottish oil shales were once the most important home source, but the vast quantities now used for fuel and chemical

manufacturing purposes are nearly all imported or from the North Sea oilfields.

The varied nature of the chemical industry and its many products make systematic classification and examination difficult. Organic and inorganic raw materials were used, alkalis and acids were produced, and furnace techniques involving fusing and vitrification, evaporation resulting in crystallisation, and distillation were its most important processes. Two of the most industrially significant furnace processes of what is in essence part of the chemical industry, the manufacture of pottery and of glass, have already been considered in Chapter 9, so it is primarily with crystallisation and distillation that we are concerned in this chapter.

SALT

Common salt, sodium chloride, has long been and still is an important raw material for many chemical products, although for centuries before the Industrial Revolution its extraction, mainly by evaporation, was geared to its sale as an end product in its own right for direct human consumption and for the preservation of fish and meat. Although solar evaporation was used to a limited extent in medieval times, only at Lymington in Hampshire was the technique practised in relatively recent years: there for about sixteen weeks in the summer seawater was concentrated into a brine solution in evaporation ponds known as 'salterns' before being boiled in lead or brass pans to extract the crystalline salt. From September the brine obtained during the summer was evaporated, using Newcastle coal brought in by sea, an expensive process only made economic by

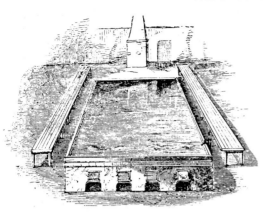

161 Evaporation pan

the saving resulting from solar evaporation and the large nearby market of the Royal Navy at Portsmouth, which needed salt for preserving beef and pork on board ship. The Lymington salt industry reached its peak of production in the mid-eighteenth century, when 50,000 tons a year were being produced, and finally closed in 1865. The low banks that surrounded the evaporation pools can still be seen on Keyhaven and Pennington marshes [SZ 315923]. Similar circular banks exist at Crosscanonby, near Maryport [NY 066401]. Saltworkers' cottages stood nearby until a few years ago.

The other main areas of salt extraction from seawater were the Firth of Forth, the Ayrshire coast around Saltcoats, and the estuary of the Tyne and the nearby coastal areas of Northumberland and Durham. The availability of cheap coal was a major locational factor, only the poorest quality slack, which was not worth the cost of transport far from the pithead, being used. It was often known as 'pancoal'. The process was carried out in heated pans made initially of lead but later of iron in which the water was evaporated until the salt crystallised, leaving behind a solution of calcium and magnesium salts known as 'bitterns'. In some areas, such as Lymington, the bitterns formed a profitable by-product in the form of Epsom salts, 4–5 tons being produced for every 100 tons of common salt. In Northumberland, Seaton Sluice [NZ 339769] was developed as a coal and salt port in the seventeenth century, and on the Firth of Forth east of Edinburgh the ancient salt centre of Prestonpans (its name derives from the process carried on there) continued seawater salt extraction down to 1959.

The discovery of rock salt in Cheshire about 1690 and on Teesside in 1863 provided the foundation for the modern British salt industry and the chemical processes based on it. Initially salt from natural brine wells had been evaporated in the Northwich and Middlewich areas of Cheshire, and near Droitwich in Worcestershire. The 'wich' place name ending is a strong, but not infallible, clue to the existence of a salt industry. The extensive mining in Cheshire – the great Marston Mine north of Northwich [SJ 6760] produced 110,000 tons in 1882 – gave way to brine pumping, in which water was circulated through boreholes sunk into the salt deposits and brought back to the surface as a solution from which the salt could be evaporated or, more recently, used in the chemical industry direct. Evidence of the extensive subsidence caused by salt working can be seen around Northwich in the form of extensive pools or 'flashes', and to the east of the town are brine wells [SJ 7471]. South of Middlewich the main Crewe to Manchester railway line suffers constantly from the sinking of the ground surface above salt workings. Some of the finest surviving structures of the salt

162 Salt pan

industry are in Winsford itself [SJ 599997]. They are the timber sheds used for drying salt, and their construction, which is entirely of timber as metal fittings would corrode in the salt-laden atmosphere, provides an interesting example of the timber-framed tradition of domestic building carried through into industrial structures.

To the north of Northwich at Winnington [SJ 6474] is the plant set up in 1873 by Ludwig Mond (1839–1909) and John Brunner (1842–1919) to produce synthetic soda by the Belgian Solvay process. This largely replaced the Leblanc process discussed below. Brunner, Mond & Co Ltd became one of the four largest chemical manufacturers in Britain, and in 1926 amalgamated with the other three – the United Alkali Co, the British Dyestuffs Corporation and Nobel Industries – to form Imperial Chemical Industries. Runcorn is the headquarters of the ICI Mond Division and is well placed for supply of its basic raw materials of salt, limestone and coking coal. In 1981 Cheshire Museums opened the Salt Museum at 162 London Road, Northwich [SJ 658732], and efforts are currently in hand to secure the preservation of the Lion Salt Works in Marston (Illus 163) [SJ 671755], whilst a few miles north-west, at Widnes, ICI have been instrumental in establishing a Chemical Industry Museum [SJ 514844]. The museum is based on a building of 1860 (Illus 163), erected for John Hutchinson, soda maker, and later used by Gossage & Son for soap making. Here Mond and Brunner worked together for ten years before moving to Winnington. There are also vestiges of the pyrites kiln on nearby Spike Island, the bases of acid absorption towers, an acid-condensing cistern and chlorine stills.

163 Lion Salt Works, near Northwich, Cheshire [SJ 671755], the only remaining site where brine is reduced to salt crystals by boiling in open pans   (*Cheshire Museums*)

164 Restoration of the Gossage building, Widnes [SJ 514844] for *Catalyst*, the chemical industry museum *(ICI Mond Division)*

SOAP

The growth of the wool and later cotton textile industries created new demands for soaps, bleaches, dyes and the mordants which fixed them. The two main types of soap used for cleaning fleeces and cloth were mixtures of fats or oils with mild alkalis, hard soap employing the alkali sodium carbonate (soda) and soft soap the alkali potassium carbonate (potash). These materials were boiled together for long periods to emulsify the ingredients, so a fuel, usually coal, was an additional requirement. From the thirteenth century onwards Bristol became an important soap-making centre based on the coincidence of local coal supplies and the great wool-producing areas of Goucestershire, Somerset and Wiltshire. So important was the industry that the medieval writer Richard of Devizes wrote: 'At Bristol there is no one who is not, or has not been, a soap maker.' Today the industry in Bristol is extinct, although its major industrial monument – the exotic brick-built factory of Christopher Thomas & Brothers, makers of Puritan soap, at Broad Plain in

the centre of the city [ST 597728] – dates only from the 1880s. The building, now converted to offices, is one of the small collection of surviving structures which represent that curiously Bristolian style of commercial architecture, sometimes known colloquially as 'Bristol Byzantine', of the 1870s and 1880s.

Before the soap industry could reach an industrial scale of production, the problem of its raw materials had to be solved. Soda and potash were obtainable from the ashes of wood and seaweed and both were also increasingly in demand from glassmakers. Salts of sodium being much more plentiful in nature than those of potassium, and the most abundant of all being sodium chloride, it was natural that the latter should be seen as a possible source of soda for the soap industry; and the French chemist Nicholas Leblanc (1742–1806) in 1791 succeeded in developing a workable process for converting common salt into soda. In the earliest Leblanc process the first stage was the treatment of common salt with sulphuric acid to form sodium sulphate (saltcake) with the liberation into the atmosphere of hydrochloric acid gas, and the second stage the heating of the saltcake with coal or coke and limestone or chalk to produce crude sodium carbonate (ball soda) in solution and calcium sulphide and coal ash as waste products. Waste heat from the furnaces was used to evaporate the soda solution, producing 'soda ash' or anhydrous sodium carbonate. The stages may be represented simply thus:

1 Sodium chloride + Sulphuric acid =
    $NaCl$ + H_2SO_4
  Sodium bisulphate + Hydrochloric acid
    $NaHSO_4$ + HCl
2 Sodium chloride + Sodium bisulphate
    $NaCl$ + $NaHSO_4$
  = Sodium sulphate + Hydrochloric acid
    Na_2SO_4 + HCl

The first reaction begins at ordinary temperatures, but requires heat. The end product, 'saltcake' is melted with limestone or chalk and coal or coke:

3 Sodium sulphate + Carbon =
$$\quad Na_2SO_4 \qquad + \quad 2C$$
$\quad$ Sodium sulphide + Carbon dioxide
$$\quad Na_2S \qquad + \qquad 2CO_2$$
4 Sodium sulphide + Calcium carbonate
$$\quad Na_2S \qquad + \qquad CaCO_3$$
= Sodium carbonate + Calcium sulphide
$$\quad Na_2CO_3 \qquad + \qquad CaS$$

From these later reactions some carbon monoxide is produced and of course coal ash.

The first works in England to operate the Leblanc process was at Walker, east of Newcastle-upon-Tyne, using salt from a brine spring struck in the Walker Colliery. Various previous soda-making processes had been tried at this works but in 1823 it had become solely a Leblanc soda factory. In the same year the second works in the country was established, by James Muspratt (1821–71) in Liverpool. On both Merseyside and Tyneside the industries thrived, and both areas became important for soap making. As Leblanc soda making grew, however, there was a rising tide of protest in Widnes, St Helens, Jarrow, South Shields and other places against the pollution resulting from the release of hydrochloric acid gas into the atmosphere. As much as 12½cwt of gas was produced

165   Boiling house

166   Soda crystallising house

from every ton of salt, and this flowed from the chimneys of the chemical works to defoliate the trees and poison livestock. The result of this agitation was the passing of the Alkali Works Act in 1863, which stipulated that at least 95 per cent of the hydrochloric acid gas had to be condensed. An alkali inspectorate was also set up to see that the law was obeyed. (This early involvement in clean air activity laid the foundation of the practical approac 1 to problems that still exists in Britain, where enforcement of the 'best practical means' of abatement is preferred to the setting of arbitrary emission levels.) The enormous chimneys used by the soda factories to dissipate the gases – one at St Rollox, Glasgow, was 420ft high – had to be replaced by condensers, most usually in the form of towers in which the gas passed upwards through beds of coke while water flowed down through them. The alkali manufacturers now had a new by-product, hydrochloric acid, with which to pollute rivers and streams instead of the atmosphere. Before long, however, all but the smallest works were using it for making bleach.

The soap industry of Merseyside, which developed in Widnes, Warrington and Liverpool, produced a wide range of products and eventually gave birth to a completely new industrial complex that was to become the home of one of the world's great soap combines. William Hesketh Lever (1851–1925) founded Port Sunlight [SJ 3484] on the Wirral or Cheshire side of the Mersey estuary in 1888, and developed there a factory and model village for his workpeople far in advance of anything previously built. Viscount Leverhulme, as he eventually became, was not a romantic idealist but a social realist as well as a successful businessman. He talked of the days when 'Workpeople will be able to live and be comfortable in semi-detached houses, with gardens back and front, in which they will be able to know more about the science of life than they can do in a back slum.' Port Sunlight was the realisation of this philosophy, the creation of an ideal community. Groups of 'Tudor' cottages with plenty of traditional half-timbering and moulded plasterwork were arranged in carefully contrived arcs around little greens and enclosed spaces at an average density of only eight dwellings per acre. In a way Port Sunlight did a disservice to the movement towards better workers' housing, for although it was important environmentally, it was not conceived with any thought of financial realism. The much more mundane Cadbury experiment at Bournville, near Birmingham [SP 0481], based on a return of 4 per cent on the investment in building in order to encourage local authorities to imitate it, had a greater influence on subsequent developments. The industrial archaeologist as a student of industrial landscapes should visit both. At Port Sunlight, in the Lady Lever Art Gallery, he will also find a fine portrait in oils of Thomas Telford.

BLEACHING AND DYEING

The demand for a chemical bleaching agent that was rapid in action was largely created by the cotton fabric side of the textile industry, which had grown beyond the stage where the natural action of sun, rain and wind on cloth spread out in bleachfields could cope with the enormous output. It was the bleaching action of chlorine, first recognised in 1785 by the French chemist C. L. Berthollet (1748–1822), which was eventually applied to fabrics. The manufacture of a chlorine-based bleach was first developed on a large scale by Charles Tennant (1768–1838), for which he set up the St Rollox chemical works in Glasgow in 1799. Previously sulphuric acid had been used to liberate chlorine from a mixture of common salt and manganese dioxide, but Tennant patented a solid compound of chlorine and lime known as chloride of lime or bleaching powder, which was less harmful to the people who made and used it than chlorine in aqueous solution. In 1800 Tennant was selling his bleaching powder at £140 per ton from his Glasgow factory. As the industry grew and techniques improved, the price dropped until in 1870 it had fallen to £8.50 per ton, presenting an enormous saving to cloth manufacturers. In the 1860s techniques for recovering chlorine from the waste hydro-chloric acid of Leblanc soda plants were developed, and this eventually became not only the main means of producing bleach but in many cases the primary source of income for the Leblanc works.

Cleaned and bleached cloth often had to be dyed, but although the soap and bleach industries were revolutionised in the early nineteenth century, development of 'fast' dyes came much later. The principal dye-wares used throughout Europe were much the same as they had been for centuries and included vegetable-based materials such as saffron, turmeric, woad and log-wood. A mill engaged in the logwood dye industry remained in use until 1964, and can still be seen at Keynsham in Avon [ST 656679]. Albert Mill, Keynsham, contains a logwood chipper and a set of stone edge-runners for crushing the wood chips, both powered by an external iron waterwheel of 18ft 6in diameter and 9ft width. The woods included fustics from Jamaica, South America, Greece and Turkey for yellow dyes; brazilwood for pinks and reds; ebony to give olive green for glove leathers; and New Zealand tanekaha to supply a golden brown colour.

In order to make the dye adhere to the fabric, mordants had to be used, and some of them significantly altered the character and colour of the dyes themselves. One of the earliest was copperas, which itself was used for ink and black dye. Copperas was obtained from the oxidation and hydro-lysis of iron pyrites (FeS_2), sometimes called 'fool's gold'. The process, carried out in large open pits initially at Queen-borough on the Isle of Sheppey and at Deptford, took up to five years, the copperas liquors ($FeSO_4 . 7H_2O$) being led away to cisterns as the slow atmospheric oxidation took place. In the eighteenth century numerous works taking advant-age of the pyrites found in locally mined coal grew up on Tyneside. Besides its use as a dye and mordant, copperas was also a source of 'oil of vitriol' or concentrated sulphuric acid, which resulted in a highly profitable by-product in the form of Venetian red, an iron oxide.

More important as a mordant was alum, a double sulphate of potassium and aluminium, which was produced first in England at Guisborough in Yorkshire in 1595. Alum shales outcrop extensively on the north Yorkshire coast and inland on the northern and eastern slopes of the Cleveland Hills. Huge quarries, as at Ravenscar [NZ 9701] and on the cliffs at Boulby [NZ 7519] and Kettleness [NZ 8415], were excavated during the nineteenth century to obtain the shales, which were subsequently calcined, usually in heaps on the floor of the quarry itself. The cal-cined shale was then put into stone leach-ing or lixiviation pits usually floored with large stone flags and the resulting liquor was evaporated in lead or iron pans over coal fires. Extensive remains of the alum extraction process have been excavated recently by the Teesside Industrial Archaeology Group on the edge of Boulby cliffs in Cleveland. Sandsend [NZ 862128], north of Whitby, has the scanty remains of a small wharf built for shipping out alum.

During the second half of the nine-teenth century the dye industry changed rapidly as the result of work begun by W. H. Perkin (1838–1907) in 1856 while studying under A. W. Hofmann (1818–92). Hofmann came to London from Giessen in Germany as the first superintendent of the Royal College of Chemistry, established in 1845. Hofmann and Perkin carried out pioneer work on coal-tar derivatives, and it was one of these, the first commercially successful synthetic dye, a mauve, that Perkin offered to Pullar's of Perth in 1856. The subsequent history of the synthetic dye industry during the latter part of the nineteenth century provides an example of a technological takeover even more startling in its proportions than the American rise to pre-eminence in machine tool design in the same period.

Germany had led the world in pure organic chemistry for more than twenty years before Perkin's original discovery, Hofmann being one of her leaders. By the 1870s Germany had overtaken British out-put of aniline dyes. Between 1886 and 1900 the 6 largest German firms took out 948 British patents, whereas the 6 largest British firms took out only 86. By 1900 Germany had 90 per cent of the world market. The prominence of the chemist in the German dye industry also provides a salutary indication of the appreciation of the need for high level research. In 1900 the 6 largest German firms employed some 18,000 workpeople, 1,360 commercial staff, 350 engineers and technologists and 500 chemists. At the same date there were less than 40 chemists, of generally lower quality, employed in the whole British dyestuffs industry. By the interwar years German chemical pre-eminence had widened into pharmaceuticals, synthetic perfumes and flavouring, saccharine, synthetic rubber and numerous other products.

Study of the Industrial Revolution is often preoccupied with technological innovation, growth and capture of world markets, especially when seen from the standpoint of Britain. The machine tool and chemical industries provide examples of how an advanced country with well established traditional techniques can fall back into a state of relative underdevelopment. The fact that Britain and the United States were forced into a position of having to catch up emphasised the importance of scientific and technical education and underlined the fact that the educational system necessary to provide scientists and science-based engineers needs to be set up a generation in advance.

SULPHURIC ACID

Sulphuric acid was one of the most important base chemicals of the 'chemical revolution' of the nineteenth century, being required in ever-increasing quantities. Indeed, its rate of consumption may be regarded as one of the measures of the commercial and industrial prosperity of a nation, so widely is it used. Both the Leblanc soda process and Tennant's bleach making depended on it, as did numerous subsequent developments. Knowledge of the acid dated back many centuries and descriptions of its distillation from green vitriol or ferrous sulphate ($FeSO_4 . 7H_2O$), itself derived from copperas, occur as early as 1570. Continuous manufacture in Britain probably began in Twickenham and Richmond in the 1730s and 1740s. A major advance came in 1746 when John Roebuck (1718–94) and Samuel Garbett (1717–1805) set up a sulphuric acid plant in Birmingham, probably to satisfy the increasing demand from local metal industries for the acid as a cleaner and stripper. In this and subsequent processes lead chambers were used (sulphuric acid does not attack lead) in which nitre or saltpetre (potassium nitrate, KNO_3) and pure sulphur were burned over a shallow depth of water on to which the fumes condensed. The process was repeated at inter-

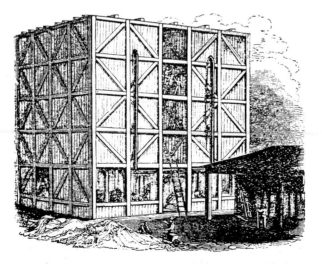

167   Sulphuric acid chambers

vals until the liquid had reached the required strength.

The availability of cheap sulphuric acid by the lead-chamber process was one of the great inventions of the Industrial Revolution, making available soda instead of the more expensive potash for the soap and glass industries, freeing greater supplies of potassium salts for agriculture and, after 1845, being used directly in the manufacture of phosphatic fertilisers (superphosphates), which became the principal outlet for sulphuric acid. In addition it was used for the manufacture of bleach and explosives. After 1830, when Chilean saltpetre (sodium nitrate, $NaNO_3$) replaced the potassium salt, sulphuric acid became cheaper still. By the 1870s the lead-chamber process had reached a state of great efficiency, with its main concentrations in the North East of England, Glasgow, Lancashire and London. Today the lead-chamber process is completely obsolete and remains of it are virtually non-existent, the high value of scrap lead encouraging rapid demolition. A direct contact process, eliminating the use of saltpetre, was propounded in the 1830s but not taken up commercially in Britain until 1914 although a British partnership had developed the first plant, in Alsace, in 1881. A major producing area is now Teesside, using local supplies of anhydrite (calcium sulphate, $CaSO_4$), mined at Billingham.

GUNPOWDER

Gunpowder manufacture is not truly a chemical industry process, as it involves the mixing of sulphur, saltpetre (potassium nitrate) and charcoal (carbon) without any reaction occurring between them. Of Chinese invention, its first European use – probably as the result of re-invention – was in Germany in the mid-thirteenth century and it quickly spread from there. Its use for blasting purposes in England probably dates from the 1620s, and in Cornish mines from 1689. More sophisticated and controllable explosives, including dynamite and gelignite, replaced it during the nineteenth century. The industry developed in several areas of

Britain and a number of sites still contain recognisable and comprehensible remains. In the Lake District at Blackbeck [SD 334859], near Bouth, lies the site of a mill operating from 1862 until 1928, which is now a caravan park. The approach lane was once a railway track from the Leven estuary. The office and weigh-house still survive at the site's entrance, and there are also some steam pipes from the original engine house, water power not being used here. The Low Wood works of 1799 stood near Haverthwaite beside the River Leven [SD 347837], but is now substantially overgrown. More extensive remains can be seen, however, at Elterwater [NY 328048], with two waterwheel pits, now occupied by turbines, a number of the original buildings, edge-runners and a small howitzer used for testing powders in the grounds of Elterwater Hall. The industry started in the Lake District in 1764, using saltpetre imported from India and later Chile and Germany, sulphur from Italy and Sicily and charcoal from local birch and alder trees, although juniper was used at Low Wood. The last mill closed in 1937.

There is another important gunpowder site, at Faversham in Kent [TR 009613], where the Chart Mills have been restored. For some 300 years before the closure of the works in 1934 Faversham was a major centre of the gunpowder industry. Much of the buildings and machinery was destroyed but in the Home Works, oldest of all and once the Royal Gunpowder Factory, some of the plant survived. Known as Chart Mills, they contain two pairs of gunpowder mills consisting of edge-runners, each pair worked in tandem off a single large waterwheel. After some thirty years of neglect, restoration by the Faversham Society is now well in hand. Another area of gunpowder manufacture was Devon, where there were three factories working in 1890. Remains of one of these can be seen on Dartmoor, where the buildings have been incorporated into Powder Mills Farm [ST 628769], which stands north of the B3212 Princetown to Moretonhampstead road. The walls of three wheelhouses and two tall chimneys can be seen on the moor behind the farm, while a small mortar once used for testing the powder stands by the farm entrance. Storage of gunpowder presented very special problems of security, and powder houses, usually small, substantially built brick or stone buildings, are a common feature of many mining and quarrying areas. The dangers arising from powder on board ships while they were in port were solved at Bristol by the construction of a powder house on the River Avon [ST 537765]. Here ships could discharge any gunpowder before entering the crowded quays and wharves of the city.

PAPER

As with gunpowder, the manufacture of paper hardly qualifies for inclusion among the chemical industries, although since the 1870s at least the pulp from which it is produced has been boiled with various acid and alkaline reagents to purify it. Up to the beginning of the nineteenth century all paper products were made by hand, using a vat and hand mould. The raw material from which the paper pulp was derived was essentially rag, but during the latter half of the nineteenth century this was progressively replaced by cellulose fibre from coniferous trees. A variety of additives were mixed with the pulp to improve the quality of the finished paper, and of these, china clay, used to make high-quality dense white papers, is the most important. In the original hand processes a fibrous suspension, highly diluted in water, is contained in the vat. The vat man dips the hand mould, a fine wire screen surrounded by a wooden frame (the deckle), into the vat and lifts out some pulp from which the water is allowed to drain. The deckle is then removed and the mould with the fibrous web of pulp lying on it is passed to the couch man. He transfers the web on to a woollen felt. Further webs on felts are stacked on it and the whole transferred to a screw press where excess water is removed by pressing. Finally the webs are removed from the felts and hung in a loft for drying in the atmosphere.

The limitations of this batch type of process are obvious, and the demand for paper, which had been increasing with the spread of printing, was eventually satisfied by the Fourdrinier machine and cylinder mould. Henry Fourdrinier (1766–1854) developed a machine in the early years of the nineteenth century in which the pulp was fed continuously on to a moving belt of gauze through which water was allowed to drain. Successive squeezing eliminated further water from the web until it was strong enough to support itself, when it passed to a series of steam-heated rolls that eliminated the remaining undesirable moisture. A modern papermaking machine is usually of this basic Fourdrinier type, often several hundred feet long. The proportion of the machine involved in removing water from the web either by drainage or steam represents over 90 per cent of this total length. The speed at which paper, and more particularly multi-layer boards, can be produced is determined by the rate at which the water can be removed from the webs. A development in this field during the early 1960s was the 'Inverform' machine in which water was removed by gravity from below and by vacuum box from above the webs. The prototype of this machine is preserved in Bristol City Museum. An important papermaking collection can be seen in the Greater Manchester Museum of Science & Industry, Liverpool Road, Castlefield, Manchester 3.

The distribution of eighteenth- and nineteenth-century paper mills in the period before the industry became focused on a relatively small number of large production units was based on three primary locational factors. A source of rags was a major requirement, so the proximity of a large urban centre was essential, and this centre also provided a market for the finished paper. The third requirement was large quantities of clear water. In the Bristol area alone the Bristol Industrial Archaeological Society has identified thirty-eight sites of extinct paper mills in addition to the seven where production still continues. Most of these were located on streams such as the Chew and Axe, flowing from the Mendips. At Bathford [ST 790671] a small mill specialises in the production of 'India' papers for bibles and dictionaries, made on a single 84in machine. A 1912 horizontal-tandem compound mill engine by Wood Brothers of Sowerby Bridge drove the machinery until 1966, when the mill was converted to electric power. The engine remains *in situ*. Wookey Hole Mill, near Wells [ST 532477], is probably the largest hand-made paper mill in the world, dating back to 1610 or even earlier. It produces mould-made account books, deckle edge notepaper and paper for banknotes. Of the abandoned mills in the area, numerous buildings survive, some converted to other purposes, but little equipment remains. At Slaughterford [ST 839738] a rag mill used for preparing the raw materials is now derelict but the iron waterwheel still survives.

RUBBER

The origins of the modern rubber industry are twofold, based on two quite distinct vegetable raw materials. One of these was gutta-percha, a tree gum from Malaya introduced in the 1840s for insulating purposes; it gained some importance in the manufacture of submarine telegraph cables and the first cables laid under the streets of London. Eventually the superior qualities of rubber made the harder and more brittle gutta-percha obsolete, but not before the irrepressible Victorian enthusiasm for anything new had resulted in household ornaments and even tableware being made of it. Several companies were formed, mainly in London, to process the gum, and the name of one, the S. W. Silver & Co Gutta Percha and Rubber Works, founded in 1852, is perpetuated in Silvertown [TQ 410800], between the Royal Victoria Dock and Woolwich Reach.

Rubber is made from the latex of a tree native to South America, its great attraction to European industrialists of the late eighteenth and early nineteenth centuries being its unique qualities of elasticity and impermeability. A patent was granted as early as 1820 to Thomas Hancock (1786–1865) for making rubber latex springs, and in 1823 Charles Macintosh (1766–1843), a Glasgow chemical manufacturer, patented a technique for dissolving rubber in coal-tar naptha, a by-product of the gas industry, and applying the solution to fabric. He set up a works in Manchester for making waterproof garments – the misspelt mackintosh. The problems of stickiness and perishability to which these early rubbers were prone was solved by the introduction of the 'vulcanisation' process, in which sulphur was mixed with the rubber. Developed in 1841 by Charles Goodyear (1800–66) in the United States, the process was offered to Macintosh in England, but Macintosh's partner Thomas Hancock worked out for himself how to vulcanise rubber and filed a British patent in 1844, beating Goodyear by days. Vulcanising resulted in a much more stable material and provided the foundation on which the rubber industry could expand, initially with products like rubberised fabrics and shoe soles and later on a bigger scale altogether as the result of the growth of the motor industry and the establishment of huge factories like Fort Dunlop on the outskirts of Birmingham

Much of the equipment used in the mixing of the constituents of rubber, which in the case of tyres includes powdered carbon, was until recently surprisingly primitive. Masticators, rather like enormous mangles, are used and an early example, from an Avon factory in Wiltshire, is preserved in Bristol Museum. Calendering, introduced in 1836 and another basic manufacturing process, consists of rolling rubber into the surface of fabric under great pressure between a series of horizontal rollers arranged one above another. A variety of criteria have affected the distribution of the rubber industry in Britain but an unusual locational factor was responsible for the establishment of the industry in the Bradford on Avon and Melksham area of north-west Wiltshire – the availability of empty wool textile mills. The industry still occupies some of these, although its modern expansion has been based on new purpose-built factories on larger sites.

OIL

During the twentieth century the chemical industry has had a new raw material in oil, which has provided the basis for a vast range of products, including detergents, organic solvents, epoxy resins, sulphur, sulphuric acid and numerous plastics. Most of this industry is based on imported or North Sea oil, but a few native sources are actively worked. In east Nottinghamshire around Eakring [SK 6762] and in north Leicestershire around Plungar [SK 7734] unmanned pumps may be seen lifting oil from wells. They are in effect beam engines – an electric motor driving one end, the other connected to the pump rods. Their characteristic movement has gained them the name 'nodding donkeys'. A more recent oilfield is at Wytch Farm in Dorset.

The other main source, now no longer worked, was oil shale, of which the largest concentration in Britain occurs in the Lothians of Scotland. Exploitation began in 1851 when James Young (1811–83) a brilliant scientist who had assisted Faraday and later managed Tennant's chemical factory in Manchester, started mining the shale, from which he refined paraffin and paraffin wax. The industry grew slowly until 1864 when Young's patent lapsed, and by 1870 ninety-seven firms had been founded of which nearly a third had already failed. American competition after 1900 precipitated a decline and the industry finally became extinct in 1963. Remains are numerous, the most obvious being the waste tips known as 'bings'. At Torbane, near Bathgate, West Lothian [NS 953668], stands the bing from Young's pioneer enterprise of 1851; this incidentally is where the geological name Torbanite, applied to the oil shales, originated. At Broxburn [NT 087728] in 1862 the discovery of large shale deposits resulted in a boost to the Scottish oil industry. This village and nearby Winchburgh to the north are products of the industry, which has left a spectacular landscape of bings to the east of the B8020 road running between the two. The refinery, founded in 1883, was south of Broxburn at Pumpherston. In north Somerset oil shales were worked early this century on the sea cliffs

east of Watchet at Kilve [ST 147439], where the remains of a distillation plant in the form of a brick tower still survive.

Perhaps the most spectacular source of oil in Britain, and one of the earliest to be commercially worked, can be seen in the so-called Tar Tunnel at Coalport, Shropshire [SJ 694025]. Excavated in 1787, probably to give access to coal, the tunnel struck considerable quantities of natural bitumen, which were exploited well into the nineteenth century. Today the tunnel is administered by the Ironbridge Gorge Museum Trust and is accessible to visitors, who may view the cavernous 'tar' wells leading off the brick-lined tunnel at intervals along its length.

The sector of the chemical industry using oil for its raw material is perhaps too modern a development to form a legitimate area of study for the industrial archaeologist. As has been pointed out elsewhere, however, it is not absolute date that provides a criterion by which the industrial archaeologist can work, and in industries where the rate of change is rapid much of undoubted historical and archaeological significance will be lost if it is not recorded. Again the point about the complexity of the process must be made, as this places additional responsibility on industries themselves to ensure that there is a rational and comprehensive approach to the preservation of archival material and the maintenance of a record of evolution. To the industrial archaeologist engaged in the examination of the physical remains of the chemical industries this chapter can only provide the most generalised of indications on the directions in which to look. Certainly the obvious remnants of the industry vastly understate its importance in the industrial development of Britain and even if the opportunities for conservation of significant plant and buildings are limited, and probably in many cases difficult to justify, the need for the retention and study of documentary material is paramount.

CHAPTER 12

PUBLIC UTILITIES

The continuing and rapid processes of industrialisation throughout the nineteenth century had profound effects upon the way of life of the population. Industrialisation brought with it large-scale urbanisation, destroying the old balance between town and country and creating within the newly bulging towns horrifying conditions of overcrowding, squalor and disease. Liverpool's population increased from 82,000 in 1807 to 202,000 in 1831, and this before the massive immigration from Ireland after 1845. Leeds, at the centre of the West Riding woollen industry, climbed from 53,000 to 123,000 in the same period. In Birmingham, Glasgow, Manchester and Sheffield the pattern was the same, while London continued to maintain its superiority in size over all other towns.

The techniques of town living had become well established before this explosive growth in the early nineteenth century, but the sudden increase in scale, coupled with overcrowding, completely swamped the simple processes of water supply from wells, and of sewage disposal through open gutters (or, in the more enlightened towns, by 'rakers' or night-soil men). The water closet, patented by Joseph Bramah (1748–1814) in 1778, could be little used because there were few proper sewers and often no regular water supply. Enormous pressures were put upon towns and their administrative systems, such as they were, but cholera epidemics, a prevailing *laisser faire* attitude to corporate initiative, a lack of adequate medical information and the total absence of any 'public service' technology all militated against reform and improvement. But reform did come, and a combination of private companies and,

increasingly, local authorities, gradually brought about the provision of water, gas and drains, transport, housing and other urban necessities. From the mid-1830s towns had powers to supply water, by the 1840s to provide gas and in the 1870s and 1880s to build tramways and supply electric light. The Public Health Act of 1875 was only one of a large number of legislative moves to ensure proper sanitation and maintenance of good general living conditions.

With these developments came a new breed of professionals. The British Association of Gas Engineers, formed in 1863 under the famous sanitary engineer Thomas Hawksley (1807–93), was followed ten years later by the Institution of Municipal Engineers. By the end of the century three more professional groups had been formed to cover sanitary engineering (1895), water supply (1896) and heating and ventilation (1897). Great works, privately and publicly financed, sprang up in and around the expanding urban areas and today provide some of the most tangible physical evidence of the improvement in the quality of town life during the second half of the nineteenth century.

WATER SUPPLY

A prime necessity of life and of many industries is water, and the need for larger and better supplies, of which those concerned with public health were the first to be aware, became generally recognised by the early nineteenth century. The major sources of supply are rivers and lakes, reservoirs constructed specially to store water and pervious water-bearing rocks underground. Pumping stations for lifting water from deep wells are most numerous in the Midlands and south-eastern England, although they also occur in other places where water is taken from rivers. Large dams and reservoirs are generally confined to mountainous country in Wales, Scotland and the Pennines and often provide water for cities such as Birmingham, Liverpool and Glasgow by long-distance aqueducts.

Some of the first large-scale water installations in Britain were built to serve London in the early years of the seventeenth century. Under the direction of one man, Hugh Myddelton (1560?–1631), and largely at his personal expense, the New River, some 40 miles long was built to bring spring water from Hertfordshire into the City. The New River Company was the first of London's great water supply companies and the aqueduct, much of which is still in use today, was formally opened on Michaelmas Day, 1613, when water was let into the Round Pond at Clerkenwell. Traces of the pond, together with remains of Smeaton's engine house of c1768, may be seen at the Metropolitan Water Board headquarters at New River Head, Rosebery Avenue, Islington [TQ 313828]. Of the conduit carrying the New River itself, a good section remains between Bullsmoor Lane, Waltham Cross and Greens Lane, N4 [TQ 318878]. A nineteenth-century straightening, by which the New River is carried in a siphon pipe across the Cuffley Brook, may be seen near Maidens Bridge, Forty Hill, Enfield [TQ 343987]. The old course is still traceable winding round Forty Hill. A further shortening, dating from 1859, runs between Myddleton Road [TQ 306916] and Hornsey High Street.

The New River Company, which took over the famous London Bridge Water Works, was soon to be followed by others, and by 1822 nine separate companies were serving the metropolis. This was reduced to eight in 1845, when the Southwark & Vauxhall company was formed by the amalgamation of two of them, and in 1902, after continued pressure from the London County Council, a single authority, the Metropolitan Water Board, was formed to take over them all.

The numerous companies set up in the early nineteenth century rarely had the capital to develop major sources of supply, especially where reservoirs or long aqueducts were required. Provision was generally intermittent, often with the water turned on for only an hour or two each day. This was very unsatisfactory where water was needed for street cleansing, fire-fighting, sewer-flushing and for public baths and wash-houses, the first of which had been opened in Liverpool in 1842. For these reasons most of the larger towns took over their private water companies, frequently following this with massive capital expenditure on reservoir or pumping schemes. Relatively few of the companies were large and efficient enough to resist these takeovers, although those serving Bristol, Portsmouth, south Staffordshire, and Sunderland and South Shields retained their independence.

In the early nineteenth century a number of Acts were passed authorising water undertakings to take water from rivers or to construct reservoirs without any restriction on the rate of abstraction, but generally speaking the rights of riparian owners using water to power mills and factories were protected by defining minimum amounts of compensation water. Dams were at first constructed of earth, a watertight core of puddled clay being faced on both sides by filling material; on the water side stone pitching covered the face to prevent erosion, while the outer face was covered in soil and then grassed. To prevent water from passing under the dam, the clay core was set in a trench dug down to a watertight foundation such as rock or shale. The early earth dams were mainly in the Pennines, built to serve cities like Sheffield and Manchester. The first large masonry dam, on the River Vyrnwy in Powys [SJ 018193] dates from 1881–92 and was built to serve Liverpool. It is 161ft high and 1,172ft long. Behind it on the lake side stands a remarkable turreted 'castle' containing the valve controls.

From the industrial archaeological point of view the most spectacular installations associated with water supply are the steam pumping engines built to lift water

168 Cast iron water tank of Perth waterworks
[NO 121232]   (*Neil Cossons*)

from wells or to pump it to high-level storage reservoirs. Engines were generally of the beam type, superbly finished and maintained, set in ornate and frequently quite exotic buildings, and surrounded by pools, trees and immaculately manicured formal gardens. Two such engines are preserved by the Bristol Waterworks Company at Blagdon in Avon [ST 503600], and at Papplewick in Nottinghamshire [SK 582522] two riotously ornamental rotative beam engines by James Watt & Co have come into the care of a preservation trust. Papplewick pumping station was erected in 1883–5 to pump water out of the Bunter sandstone for the growing needs of Nottingham, and represents the ultimate in elaborate construction and setting. In

Sunderland, Ryhope pumping station [NZ 404524] is also preserved, and in part of the adjacent boiler house a museum of water supply equipment has been established, again by a private preservation trust, in this case working in close liaison with Sunderland Museum. The four Cornish pumping engines at Kew Bridge Waterworks, Brentford (Illus 47 and 48) [TQ 188780], last worked in 1944; they are undoubtedly the finest single concentration of the breed in the world and are preserved by the Kew Bridge Engines Trust.

In the late nineteenth century and early twentieth vertical triple-expansion steam engines, similar in general layout to those used in ships, supplanted the beam type. A number were in use until recently including two 1,008hp Worthington Simpson engines installed at Kempton Park Waterworks in 1928 and believed to be the largest land-based triples in Britain. The same works has five further triples built by the Lilleshall Company of Shropshire in 1900, also out of use. At the opposite end of the scale a single triple, also by Lilleshall, can be seen by appointment at the Chelvey, Somerset, pumping station [ST 474679].

Reciprocating plunger or piston pumps were usual with most water pumping engines but towards the end of the nineteenth century centrifugal pumps, notably those made by Gwynne, were used increasingly. An extraordinary water pumping station, although now devoid of its original equipment, forms a noteworthy feature of Marshall Place, Perth (Illus 168) [NO 121232]. Designed in 1830 by Dr Adam Anderson, then rector of Perth Academy and later Professor of Natural Philosophy at St Andrews, it has a central rotunda with drum and dome flanked by rectangular north and south wings and an annexe to the west. The drum and dome forming the reservoir are of cast iron decorated with Ionic pilasters and supplied by the Dundee Foundry Company. This remarkable essay in the assimilation of classical forms to functional needs is not only ingenious but a surprisingly satisfactory piece of design. This Grade 'A' Listed building is now an art gallery. Numerous other humbler water towers can be found all over Britain, often in commanding positions and visible for many miles because of their need to be higher than the area they are supplying. Low-lying south Lancashire has a number of good examples, notably Victoria Tower on Greetby Hill, near Ormskirk [SD 423087], and a neighbour east of Tower Hill [SD 423085] to the south.

WASTE DISPOSAL

Disposal of town waste had become a major problem by the middle of the eighteenth century, and although London had since the 1660s, in theory at least, some sort of rubbish disposal organisation, most other cities had nothing at all. Rivers, streams or tidal estuaries and the sea provided the means of carrying away the unwanted detritus of urban humanity,

and in some parts of Britain this situation still applies. The Thames was London's *cloaca maxima*, which was supposed to take away on each tide the city's waste products. The realisation that diseases such as cholera and typhoid were water borne, and that all too often drinking water and waste water came into contact with each other, provided the great incentive to install sewers and sewage treatment plants. In two cholera epidemics in London in the middle of the nineteenth century nearly 20,000 people died, emphasising particularly the need for systematic methods not only of water supply and distribution but, more important, the disposal of waste water in underground pipes to areas away from the town, where it could be suitably treated.

In 1855 the Metropolitan Board of Works was created, with Sir Joseph Bazalgette (1819–91), its engineer, to provide a system of sewers to prevent 'all or any part of the sewage within the Metropolis from flowing into the Thames in or near the Metropolis'. Bazalgette's monumental undertaking provided the framework on which most of London's sewage disposal system still depends, and although much of it is below ground and not easily available for the industrial archaeologist to examine, some of the surviving surface remains exhibit a magnificence of conception and execution equal to the works of many a better known engineer. One of the main difficulties to be overcome in providing London with an efficient sewerage system was to carry the waste products away from the urban area itself, as most of the existing sewers flowed at right-angles to the Thames. Bazalgette's solution was to construct major sewers parallel with the river on each side of it – the Northern and Southern Outfalls – running to Barking in Essex and Crossness in Kent. Generally the gradient was sufficient for a gravity flow, but at intervals a pumping station was needed to achieve enough height to maintain an effective gradient. An example is at Greenwich High Road, Deptford [TQ 377772], where four beam pumping engines lifted low-level flow 18ft into the Southern Outfall. Only the Italianate pump house of 1864 remains.

The often extravagant lengths to which the water supply companies went with their pumping stations were exceeded only by the works built by those authorities responsible for the eventual disposal of the waste. The Metropolitan Board of Works perpetrated two such works which, in all their elaborate mid-Victorian improbability, are quite without parallel. One, the Abbey Mills sewage pumping station in West Ham [TQ 388832], was built between 1865 and 1868 and originally housed eight beam engines, which were removed in the 1930s. The Venetian-Gothic style building with its exotic interior cast iron work survives, however, a remarkable monument to the beginnings of the anti-pollution movement. Even more unlikely is the Southern Outfall pumping station in Thamesmead. Here the Crossness sewage treatment works [TQ 484811], also built in the mid-1860s, still remains complete, with four 125hp beam engines by James Watt & Co. Now out of use and iced over by hordes of invading pigeons, the incredible cast iron tracery of the central octagonal framework supporting the beam floor has taken on the appearance of a petrified cathedral (Illus 53). While efforts are being made to preserve Crossness pumping station, three other sewage pumping installations, already safe in the hands of local authorities, are accessible to visitors. In Shrewsbury the Coleham [SJ 496121] beam pumping engines are preserved and run from time to time on electric power; built in 1900 by W. R. Renshaw of Stoke-on-Trent they were in use until 1970 and then taken over by Shrewsbury Museums. In Leicester, Abbey Lane pumping station [SK 589066], again with beam pumps (built by Gimson in the exotic manner), is preserved as the focal point of the Leicestershire Museum of Technology. Eastney sewage pumping station [SZ 674993] is one of a number that clear sewage and surface water from low-lying Portsea Island, on which Portsmouth stands. Originally two Clayton beam engines, installed in 1868, provided the power, but they were scrapped and replaced by two large compound engines by James Watt & Co, installed in 1886–7. These in turn became redundant

in 1954, when four English Electric/Sulzer electric pumps took over the main load. The Watt engines and their engine house have been restored by Portsmouth Museums and opened to the public as the nucleus of an industrial museum. Also on the site are three T2 type 170bhp Crossley double-ended (opposed-cylinder) gas engines driving Tangye centrifugal pumps. Dating from 1904, these engines are still maintained for standby use and may eventually be preserved.

As an example, Portsmouth illustrates very graphically the improvement in living conditions and reduction in mortality that resulted from better public health, largely brought about by good drains and sewers. The Sewage and Drainage of Towns Act of 1845 marked the beginning of steady progress in a town which had a particularly acute drainage problem, especially on Portsea Island, where the highest and most densely populated area was only 12ft above the level of ordinary tides. Two large pumping stations were built to pump effluent from the sewers, at Eastney in the 1860s and Stamshaw in the 1880s. By the 1950s fifteen more pumping stations had been built to cope with Portsmouth's sewage and drainage. Over that same period the death rate dropped from an excessively high 25.37 per 1,000 in 1851 when the population was 72,000, to one of the lowest for large towns of 18.9 in 1891, when the population stood at 159,251; by 1955, with 238,700 people in Portsmouth, the death rate stood at 10.76, though many other factors had come into play by then.

Disposal of domestic rubbish had been achieved in some towns by using scavengers who dumped the waste material in specified areas away from housing. In many places, however, it was left to rot in the streets. Systematic collection became widespread in the second half of the nineteenth century, but it was not until the introduction of destructors that there was an alternative to dumping. Even today a large number of local authorities dump their rubbish. The idea of a destructor is a simple one, involving the burning of rubbish at high temperature to destroy all organic matter and reduce it in bulk. A minimum sustained temperature of about 1,250°F is needed to achieve complete combustion of all noxious contents of the waste, and most early destructors fell far short of this. Charles Jones of Ealing, who erected the first destructor near London in 1883, was also the first to grapple with the problem of fumes given off by incomplete combustion, and in 1885 designed what was known as 'Jones' Fume Cremator'. This did much to make destructors more acceptable to people living downwind of them, but it was not until forced draught, coke fuel and carefully designed combustion cells were developed in the 1890s that high temperature destruction of all organic material both eliminated the smell and reduced the waste to an innocuous clinker. Today destructors are widely used, and many of them, as examples of late Victorian public health engineering and architecture, could well bear more detailed examination by industrial archaeologists. So too could sewage treatment plants, once called sewage farms, of which numerous early examples are being modernised or replaced, with the destruction of what is frequently first-generation equipment. In towns, manhole covers frequently provide a clue to the type and design of the pipes beneath them and often bear the name or initials of the original authority responsible for construction. An almost completely extinct feature of sewage systems is the sewer gas lamp, built to burn fumes from the pipes below street level. An example of J. E. Webb's 'Patent Sewer Lamp' can be seen in Carting Lane, Strand, London WC2 [TQ 305806], and another, from Stourbridge, is preserved in the Blists Hill Open Air Museum, Iron bridge, Shropshire [SJ 695035].

GAS

The first practical demonstration of the combustible possibilities offered by a mixture of coal gas and air is generally attributed to William Murdock (1754–1839), principal engine erector in Cornwall for the firm of Boulton & Watt. In 1792, the year after he had taken out a patent for a preservative treatment for ships' bottoms that had led him into various distillation experiments, Murdock generated gas from coal and lighted a room in his house in Redruth. Although numerous others had experimented with gas given off by 'cooking' coal in an oven, Murdock's particular and important contribution, on which the beginnings of a practical gas industry were founded, was his systematic investigation of the comparative behaviour of different classes of coal under conditions of varying temperature and times of carbonisation. Although there was little immediate interest in Murdock's experiments, news of parallel work in France being carried out by Philippe Lebon (1767–1804), and the active support of the celebrated Manchester chemist William Henry (1774–1836), encouraged him further and he resumed his work in 1801. In the following year he illuminated the Soho foundry of Boulton & Watt to commemorate the Peace of Amiens, and before long the company was marketing commercially a gas-making plant using Murdock's horizontal retort in which to carbonise the coal. Heat from a furnace was applied to the retort through flues, and crude gas rose to be carried away to a vertical condenser, where a jet of water precipitated the tar and washed it into a tar pit. The system was used extensively for lighting factories, whose owners were eager to adopt something more effective than the traditional candles or whale oil lamps.

In 1812 the first company selling gas from a central generating station through mains to independent consumers was formally established. It was the Gas Light & Coke Company, which by 1815 had built more than 26 miles of underground mains in London. By then gas was being made in tapered horizontal retorts, charged and discharged by scoops, long-handled shovels and rakes and purified by passing it through water to which lime had been added. After purification, a somewhat imperfect process until the 1840s, gas was transmitted through iron street mains to houses, factories and many public buildings, where initially it was used exclusively for lighting. Early gas-lights can still be found with ceramic 'fish

HORIZONTAL GAS RETORTS
8 retort setting

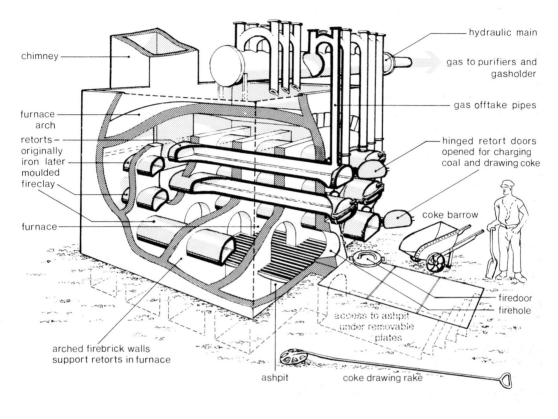

chimney

furnace arch

retorts – originally iron later moulded fireclay

furnace

arched firebrick walls support retorts in furnace

ashpit

coke drawing rake

hydraulic main

gas to purifiers and gasholder

gas offtake pipes

hinged retort doors opened for charging coal and drawing coke

coke barrow

firedoor
firehole

access to ashpit under removable plates

Illustration 169

tail' burners on which the gas burned as an open wall-flame. Not until the 1840s was air mixed with gas to achieve more efficient combustion; the most obvious and familiar example of this was introduced by the chemist R. W. Bunsen (1811–99) in his Heidelberg laboratory in 1855. In the 1860s gas became more widely used than merely for lighting with the introduction of the water geyser in 1865, the gas ring in 1867 and the gas fire with radiants in 1880. Gas cooking was not common until the 1870s, and gas for heating houses on anything like a large scale did not become established until the early 1900s. By then the traditional strong-

hold of gas – lighting in streets and buildings – was being threatened by electric-arc and incandescent filament lamps, which were introduced commercially in the mid-1880s. The invention in 1885 of the incandescent gas-mantle by the Austrian Carl Auer von Welsbach (1858–1929) enabled gas to hold its own and survive well into the mid-twentieth century, particularly in streets and railway stations, where lamps can still occasionally be found. To the industrial archaeologist gas-burning equipment offers an area of study worthy of energetic pursuit, as the rapid changeover from coal-produced gas to North Sea natural gas has

221

170 The retort house at the Westminster gasworks

resulted in the elimination of almost all early equipment.

Similarly the conversion to natural supplies of gas has almost completely eliminated the traditional gasworks, and there are now no carbonising plants in Britain. The basic processes of coal gas manufacture are still the same, comprising the destructive distillation of coal of low ash content in retorts which in most works today are vertical and mechanically charged. Gas from the retorts passes through various cleaning processes in which by-products such as coal tar and ammonia are recovered in 'washers' and 'scrubbers'. The gas is then pumped, using an 'exhauster', to a gasholder before being distributed to consumers at a controlled pressure. The approximate composition of piped coal gas is usually 55 per cent hydrogen, 30 per cent methane and 10 per cent carbon monoxide, with small quantities of other gases.

Although coal-gas manufacturing equipment is rapidly disappearing a few plants still survive, notably at Biggar in Lanarkshire (Illus 171) [NT 039377] preserved by the National Museums of Scotland, and Fakenham in Norfolk [TF 919293]. Gasholders, often misnamed 'gasometers', still have a storage role and are a familiar feature of many townscapes. The earliest gasholders were thought to present a danger from explosion, and gas companies were required to encase them in brick buildings (Illus 172). This curious idea, which in the event of a mishap would presumably have made every brick a projectile, was soon abandoned, and the cast iron and later riveted iron-plate cylindrical gasholder much as we know it today emerged to become one of the symbols – together with slag heaps and factory chimneys – of everything that was undesirable in the industrial landscape. At Fakenham in Norfolk a typical small town gasworks has been Scheduled as an Ancient Monument. The retort house dates from 1846 – although the retorts themselves are of 1907 and 1910 – and there is a small cast iron gasholder of 1888. What is probably the earliest surviving gasholder anywhere is at Fulham Gasworks, Sands End Lane [TQ 260768], dating from the 1830s. All these early gasholders consisted of cylindrical inverted 'bells' supported by gas pressure and sealed by water at the bottom. Later, several sections of cylinder were tele-

171 Biggar gasworks [NT 039377], Lanarkshire, an outstation of the National Museums of Scotland *(Neil Cossons)*

172 Gasholder houses of Warwick Gasworks [SP 278653] dating from 1822 and now offices *(Neil Cossons)*

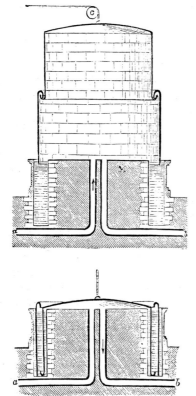

scoped one within another, a huge frame of cast-iron pillars and lattice girders acting as a support and guide. The No 3 gasholder at Fulham was a fine early example of ornate iron framing, and a later and very large example may be seen at Reading beside the River Kennet, near its junction with the Thames [SU 731738]. Later gasholders dispensed with the fixed guides on pillars and worked with spiral rails on the side of each telescoping section or 'lift'. A very fine set of seven late-nineteenth-century gasholders, now Listed, stand east of Bow Creek, Newham [TQ 385825], all that remains of the former Bromley-by-Bow gasworks. With the exception of preserved plant the gasholder is likely to be the only item associated with the manufacturing side of the coal-gas industry that will survive in use; a most typical feature of the nineteenth-century British industrial landscape.

ELECTRICITY

Today we take electricity so much for granted that it is difficult to imagine life without it. Not only is electrical energy fundamental to the standard of living of us all but it is also the major source of power for industry. Electric power has almost completely freed industry from the locational factors of the past, which tied it to streams and rivers for water power or to the coalfields when steam was the major prime mover. Though a few activities such as aluminium smelting, which consumes vast quantities of electricity, tend to be deliberately located near the point of generation or to generate for their own use, to almost every other industry, availability of an electricity supply is taken for granted. As with gas, the provision of usable electrical energy is a four-stage process comprising transport of fuel to the generating station, generation, transmission and consumption. Also like gas, the first electricity generating stations were mainly privately owned, of relatively small scale and located near their markets. The creation of a National Grid around 1930 by which all power stations were linked, the nationalisation of the electricity generating industry in 1948, and,

173 Telescopic gasometer, open and closed

174 Gasholder at Fakenham Gasworks, Norfolk [TF 919293], a typical small town gasworks, now preserved   (Neil Cossons)

above all, the enormous increase in scale of generating plant, has made it much more economical to locate power stations near the fuel source (usually coal) and transmit over long distances by overhead power line. Thus the power axis of the country has developed along the valley of the River Trent, with a string of large base-load stations close to the East Midlands coalfield. The location of nuclear power stations is governed by different factors, as the transport cost of fuel is negligible. Those so far commissioned in Britain are, in effect, market-located in that they are in coal-deficient areas. With the exception of Trawsfynnyd in North Wales, they are located on estuarine or coastal sites, for like traditional power stations they use steam turbines that need condenser coolant water. For reasons of safety, however, in the event of an accidental discharge of radioactive waste, nuclear power stations also tend to be sited in fairly remote areas.

Hydro-electric power, in which water turbines drive the generators, is not much used in Britain because there are few large rivers. There are, however, several small hydro-electric generating stations in Scotland and North Wales and three small ones in Devon, on the edge of Dartmoor (Illus 176). Also in North Wales are two pumped storage schemes which are used in effect to store energy. Electricity itself cannot be stored in large quantities and it is not efficient to keep much generating plant turning when not actually required for generating electricity. The most efficient power stations run day and night to meet the base load, other stations are then brought in as necessary to meet the peak demand. However, since it takes some hours to start a steam-driven generating set from cold, the grid control engineers have to predict what the demand is going to be several hours ahead. Hydro-electric generators can be started and stopped in a matter of seconds, so the overall demand can be met more efficiently if they are included in the national system. In a pumped storage

175 Hydro-electric power station, Powick, Hereford & Worcester [SO 835525]. Built in 1894 by Worcester Corporation, it was the first major low-head hydro-electric installation in Britain. The station closed in the late 1920s (*Neil Cossons*)

system the machinery is reversible, working either as turbine and generator or as pump and motor. At times of low demand, water is pumped uphill from a lower to a higher reservoir, using relatively cheap off-peak electricity. When demand is high, and especially if there is a rapid increase in demand, the water is allowed to flow back down through the machine, generating electricity again. The first pumped storage scheme in Wales, at Blaenau Ffestiniog, had a capacity of 300MW, and proved so useful that the Central Electricity Generating Board have since built a larger one at Dinorwig. This has a capacity of about 1800MW which can be available in ten seconds. The machinery at Dinorwig is contained in an enormous cavern excavated in a mountain, and little is visible outside except two lakes and some buildings at the entrance.

The electricity industry offers the industrial archaeologist some important

176 Hydro-electric generating station at Morwellham, Devon [SX 447698], built by the West Devon Electric Supply Company in 1934 and still in use *(Neil Cossons)*

remains at both the generating and consuming end of the energy chain, although for an industry which is so relatively new much in the way of equipment has already gone. The rapid rate of development of the technology of power generation, the changeover from direct to alternating current for consumers, and the postwar boom in efficient electrical appliances in the home has made almost any piece of electrical equipment more than thirty years old of historical interest.

The basis of all electrical power generated by mechanical means, as opposed to electrochemically in a battery, derives from the work of Michael Faraday (1791–1867), and was first demonstrated in 1831. On 17 October of that year he plunged a bar magnet into a coil of wire and generated, in his own words, 'a wave of electricity', and eleven days later he rotated a copper plate between the poles of a magnet and found that a current could be taken from the axis to the rim of the disc. Faraday's original experiment of holding the coil of wire stationary while varying the magnetic field forms in essence the basis of today's large power stations, although the bar magnet has been replaced by an electro-magnet and

the coils are so arranged that their windings are cut by the magnetic field as the magnet rotates. Thus the mechanical energy required to turn the magnets is converted into electrical energy in the windings.

By the mid-1830s E. M. Clarke of London, and others, were manufacturing hand-driven generators on a commercial basis, but the power produced was small and they were only laboratory machines. In the mid-1860s Charles Wheatstone (1802–75) and S. A. Varley in England and Werner Siemens (1816–92) in Germany, all working independently, developed 'self-excited' generators in which the field magnets were energised from the output of the machine. In Britain Werner's brother Charles William Siemens (1823–83) (born Carl Wilhelm Siemens, he changed his name when he became a naturalised British subject) helped develop practical generators and electric lighting, but the first really practical machines were made in 1870 by Z. T. Gramme (1826–1901), a Belgian engineer working in Paris. Gramme supplied the generators for the first public electric lighting in London, which used arc lights of French manufacture. R. E. B. Crompton (1845–1940) began his electrical career by importing equipment from Paris, but soon started manufacturing himself. His first generators were of a type designed by the Swiss engineer Emil Burgin, and Crompton made more than 400 of them. One was installed in the House of Commons. The first supply of electricity to the public was at Godalming, in the autumn of 1881, though only a few householders took the opportunity to have the new light in their homes. Several towns, including Taunton and Norwich, soon had a public electricity supply, though it did not become widespread until the 1890s.

Crompton was one of the pioneers in Britain of commercial electric lighting using arc lamps in which a continuous electrical discharge was induced between the tips of two carbon rods. Initially his self-contained lighting units, consisting of a portable steam engine driving a generator by belt and powering a number of lights, were used for agricultural shows and fêtes, but later they were installed in railway stations, the General Post Office in Glasgow where two arc lamps replaced 180 gas jets, and in 1882 at the Mansion House in London. Here a combination of arc lamps and incandescent bulbs, developed by Joseph (later Sir Joseph) Wilson Swan (1828–1914) in Newcastle-upon-Tyne, was used. The incandescent filament lamp consisted of an evacuated glass bulb in which a current-carrying filament glowed. Many people had tried to make such a light source, but were defeated by the three problems of finding a suitable filament material, sealing wires through the glass so that it did not crack when heated, and pumping out the air adequately. The advantage of the filament lamp was that its small size and simplicity in operation made it ideal for domestic use, whereas the arc lamp was far too bright, too bulky, and too complicated. Almost simultaneously Thomas Alva Edison in the United States invented a similar lamp, which he patented in Britain. Subsequently Edison and Swan amalgamated and formed the Edison & Swan United Electric Light Company later known as the Ediswan Company, registered in 1883 with a capital of £1m. The factory established by Ediswan at Ponders End, Enfield, in 1886 has recently been redeveloped and virtually all the original buildings have gone. Fortunately the site was surveyed in 1969 by Enfield Archaeological Society. Incandescent lamps rapidly became popular and in 1881 were used in the House of Commons, on the Inman liner *City of Richmond*, on a train from London to Brighton, and in the Savoy theatre, where the stage was lit by 824 lamps, with a further 370 elsewhere in the building.

All these early installations had their own generators, but in 1882 the Edison Company opened its Holborn Viaduct generating station, initially to provide current for street lighting but later extended to serve private consumers. In 1887 the London Electric Supply Corporation was founded to put into effect a huge scheme devised by S. Z. de Ferranti (1864–1930) who believed that the satisfactory development of electric power hinged on generation in quantity. The power station, at Deptford [TQ 375779], was designed by Ferranti himself and included two alternators designed for 5,000V and powered by 1,250hp steam engines, and four with 10,000V windings coupled to a single 10,000hp engine. The first current was transmitted from Deptford in 1889, although the station was not in regular use until 1891. Most of Ferranti's buildings remained at Deptford for many years, and another power station was built there, but that too has finished its working life and nothing now remains at the site.

Throughout the 1890s power stations, usually relatively small, were built in many British cities by the newly formed electric light companies or to provide light and also current for street trams. Frequently one power station served both functions. In Bristol the original Central Electric Lighting Station building of 1893 [ST 594728] still survives on Temple Back, but the Bristol Tramway Company's power station, built in the early 1900s across the road on Phillip Street, has been demolished. All these early power stations used reciprocating steam engines with either belt drive to the generators or in some cases direct-coupled crankshafts. The central-valve engine developed by P. W. Willans (1851–92) in the mid-1880s was the most widely used type, although by 1891 Bellis & Morcom of Birmingham were manufacturing smaller enclosed-crankcase high-speed verticals with forced lubrication that were ideal for generating work. Many of the latter can still be found, mainly dating from the 1920s and 1930s, generating electricity in hospitals. The problem with the reciprocating steam engine was the developing of sufficient speed to power a generator efficiently. The answer was the steam turbine, which was widely adopted soon after it had been invented by C. A. Parsons (1854–1931) in 1884. Today power stations use basically the same arrangement as that devised by Parsons, the steam turbine being direct-coupled to the alternator.

Initially most power stations distributed direct current on a two-wire system at 110V. This was later changed to a three-wire system at 220V offering 110V between each outer wire and the middle wire. As systems expanded, it was found necessary to raise the voltage to 440 and 220 respectively, with electric lights operating at the lower voltage and the larger electric motors connected across the 440V wires. As the number of consumers grew, the current flowing in the mains became heavier, the mains themselves became longer and loss of power through voltage drop reached serious proportions. The answer, originally proposed by Ferranti, was to transmit high-voltage alternating current with minimal losses and to break down the voltage to consumers' requirements at local sub-stations and transformers. This system is the basis of our modern electricity supply network based on a National Grid of 400,000 and 275,000V. The area electricity boards distribute within their areas at 132,000V and below, reducing to 33,000V for heavy industry, 11,000V for light industry and 415/240V for farms and domestic users. National Grid lines are almost invariably carried on pylons for cheapness, although occasionally, as in the Wye valley, they may be underground to preserve scenic amenities. At 11,000V power is generally carried on wooden poles in country areas or underground in towns.

The industrial archaeology of the electricity industry illustrates the irrelevance of absolute age when examining the historical significance of a site, a process or a piece of equipment. It is the degree of obsolescence which matters and, in an industry changing as rapidly as electricity generation and supply, obsolescence can occur very quickly. In 1948, when the generating industry was nationalised, some 300 power stations supplied a maximum load of about 10,000MW. Today more than four times that load is supplied by under 100 power stations, and the remaining stations of that era are obsolete. At one time old stations could be re-equipped with modern plant, but that has long since ceased to be possible. Many of the stations erected by the old private supply companies had distinctive architectural styles and detailing and, built in a period of general depression, represent some of the few large-scale examples of building and engineering design of their period. However, they too are rapidly disappearing. The most distinctive feature in the majority of modern power stations is the hyperbolic concrete cooling tower, which enables condenser coolant water to be returned to source, usually a river, at an acceptable temperature. The first concrete cooling towers in Britain were built at Lister Drive power station in Liverpool in the mid 1920s, but have since been demolished. They were minute by the standards of their majestic Trent valley successors.

The electricity supply industry now has its own museum, a group of galleries opened in 1986 at the Manchester Museum of Science & Industry. One of the major features there is a reconstruction of part of an early 1920s generating station including a complete turbine and generator of the period. The South Eastern Electricity Board and the Southern Electricity Board also have small museums of their own, at Tonbridge [TQ 588467] and Christchurch [SZ 157932] respectively. Numerous existing museums contain small electrical items such as early dynamos, motors, lighting and switchgear. Appropriately one of the largest collections is in the Newcastle-upon-Tyne Museum of Science & Engineering, where the work of C. A. Parsons, J. W. Swan and A. C. Reyrolle is well represented. Here, insulators, sections of cable, arc lamps and early incandescent bulbs abound. The most comprehensive range of material, however, is held by the Science Museum, South Kensington although most is not on display.

URBAN TRAMWAYS

The availability of electricity and of efficient electric motors encouraged a mode of transport that had been developing since the 1860s in a number of British towns. Initially horse-drawn, the street tram had been introduced from the United States to Birkenhead in 1860 by George Francis Train, who laid a 5ft 2in gauge line with flanged rails from Woodside Ferry to Birkenhead Park, then a fashionable residential area. Other lines followed, including a route in London from Notting Hill Gate to Marble Arch, but most had been removed by 1862, largely because of the damage the upstanding edge of the 'step rail' was causing to the tyres of horse-drawn carriages. However, grooved rails and flanged wheels were substituted in Birkenhead and on another line in the Potteries, and proved highly successful. By the late 1860s the horse-drawn tram was becoming accepted as an efficient means of moving people in town streets, where a pair of horses could haul a tramcar seating forty-six and having the low rolling resistance of the rail-borne vehicle, while the traditional bus with two horses was limited to about twenty-six seats. There is little material evidence surviving today of the early period of tramway development, although Hull Transport & Archaeology Museum has a single-deck horse car of the type used by Train which was built in 1867 and ran on Ryde pier in the Isle of Wight.

Legislation allowing the widespread growth of street tramways came with the Tramways Act of 1870, which, in terms of the development of efficient and coordinated systems, was something of a mixed blessing. Two clauses in particular penalised the new tram-operating companies. Not only did they have to lay and maintain their own tracks but they were also responsible for the road surface between the rails and for 1ft 6in on each side of them. In addition the local authority had the power to purchase the whole system after twenty-one years, a right which then recurred every seven years. This, not unnaturally, discouraged the tramway operators from installing expensive new capital equipment, for much expenditure would immediately make their takeover more attractive. The ultimate result of this bizarre state of affairs occurred in Bristol, where primitive open-top double-deck trams were still in use until the early 1940s, when they were replaced by buses. Bristol is still the only major British city without municipally owned transport.

Generally speaking, tramways were taken over by local authorities in the late nineteenth and early twentieth centuries, although by then it was often too late to develop any integrated inter-urban system on the American pattern because of gauge variations, though a surprisingly wide coverage was attained in Britain. By far the most popular was the standard 4ft 8½in used on railways although an ingenious variation found only in Glasgow, Huddersfield and Portsmouth involved a gauge of 4ft 7¾in. The reason for this was that conventional railway wagons could be run on the street tram tracks, thus giving them access to numerous industrial undertakings not normally enjoying a rail connection, but as the depth of flange on a railway wheel is greater than the depth of groove in a tram rail and the width of wheel tread substantially wider, the ¾in reduction in gauge allowed railway wagons to run on their wheel flanges along the flangeways of tram tracks. Elsewhere narrower gauges were used, 3ft 6in being universal in and around Birmingham and 4ft in the Potteries and north Staffordshire. One of Birmingham's narrow double-deck electric cars is preserved in the Birmingham Museum of Science & Industry, Newhall Street, Birmingham 3.

In 1879 mechanical power was permitted for trams under the Use of Mechanical Power on Tramways Act, but such severe restrictions were imposed for the protection of other road users, human and equine, that really imaginative developments were stultified at source. Despite the fact that 10mph was the maximum permitted speed, that all working parts had to be concealed from view and that machinery had to be practically silent, with no visible emission of smoke or steam, firms like Merryweather and Kitson produced reasonably successful steam engines for pulling trailer cars. A preserved example, from Portstewart in Northern Ireland, can be seen in Hull Transport & Archaeology Museum.

Electrification came in the 1880s in an experimental way and by the late 1890s had proved itself beyond all doubt as the best means of powering tramcars. At the start of large-scale electrification, in the late 1880s, there were some 800 route miles of tramway in Britain, and this had increased to 1,040 by 1900, the larger part still being horse- or steam-worked. Between 1900 and 1907 electric lines boomed and a total route mileage of 2,530 had been reached by the outbreak of World War I, the high point of the tramway era.

American practice considerably influenced the widespread development of electric tramways in Britain, although most of the initial experimental work had been carried out in Germany by engineers such as Werner von Siemens and Magnus Volk. Volk came to Britain in 1883 and built a 2ft 8½in gauge electric railway along the seafront at Brighton from the Aquarium [TQ 316038] to Black Rock. This odd little line, which still runs, represents the first use of electric traction in Britain. Street trams proper operated at about 600V DC, with current usually supplied to one (positive) wire and, after passing through traction motors and lighting, being returned to the power station through the (earthed) track rails. Trams had four wheels, with two axle-mounted motors, but later large eight-wheel bogie cars were introduced, notably in London, Glasgow and Liverpool. Current collection was usually by trolley poles, but Glasgow and Leeds and some Birmingham routes employed bow collectors, which obviated the need for complicated pointwork in the overhead wiring. In parts of London a conduit between the rails carried the current.

The period from about 1900 to the outbreak of World War I in 1914 was the golden age of the tram, the first form of urban transport accessible to the mass of the population. It was a harbinger of social change, continuing and developing the work begun by the suburban railway services in enabling people to move easily and cheaply between industrialised areas and their homes in more pleasant surroundings. Every major town had a tramway, and in Lancashire and Yorkshire particularly, end-on junctions of innumerable independent systems enabled the diligent traveller with an eye to economy rather than speed to make quite lengthy excursions. Thus the Pier Head in Liverpool could form the start of a tram journey into the upper Pennines beyond Rochdale by way of St Helens, Atherton, Bolton, Bury and Heywood. Seven miles over the top was Hebden Bridge, terminus of the West Riding network, running eastwards to beyond Leeds and Wakefield. Suburban housing estates developed along tram routes, and cities like Glasgow, Birmingham and Liverpool still reflect their one-time dependence on trams in the wide central reservations of their main road approaches, which once enabled trams to run completely separated from road traffic. It was the incompatibility of the tram with motor vehicles and its lack of flexibility when compared to the bus that led to its decline and eventual extinction. In addition the high cost of maintenance of track and overhead wires, and the very low operating costs of the diesel bus, which began rapidly to replace its petrol-driven predecessor in the late 1930s, made the tram in its traditional form largely redundant. A few cities, notably Sheffield and Leeds, began programmes of tramway modernisation, with ideas of developing high-speed reserved-track systems, but changes of management and of political complexion killed these schemes and 1963 saw the last of Britain's trams withdrawn from the streets of Glasgow. Only in Blackpool can a near equivalent still be found, with streamlined single-deck cars operating along the seafront.

An interim phase between the tram and the complete domination of public road transport by the diesel bus has also come to an end with the withdrawal of the last trolleybuses in Bradford, which, with Leeds, had been the scene of the first regular services in 1911. Of German origin the 'railless tram' had the attraction of manoeuvrability in restricted town centres, quietness, speed, and in later years remarkable acceleration. Numerous tram systems were abandoned in favour of trolleybuses in the 1920s and 1930s, and new routes were being built well into the 1950s in several cities. Again, however, some of the shortcomings of the tram applied to the electric bus, the cost of overhead wires and pointwork in particular leading to their abandonment in favour of high-capacity diesel buses, now often operated by one man only. Today no trolleybus systems are working in Britain, although vehicles are preserved, notably at Bournemouth and Bradford.

Trams have always enjoyed a large enthusiast following, and at Crich in Derbyshire [SK 345548] the Tramway Museum Society operates a thriving museum where over forty cars from places as far apart as Glasgow, Sheffield, Southampton, Johannesburg and Oporto are preserved, many of them in running condition. A regular service is operated on a ½ mile track. Trams also run regularly at the North of England Open Air Museum, Beamish [NZ 212549] and the Black Country Museum, Dudley [SO 948917]. Museums with collections of non-operational trams include the Glasgow Transport Museum and the London Transport Museum at Covent Garden.

The period from the 1870s to 1914 represented the great age of public transport, and the tram and cheap-excursion train gave millions of people a mobility completely unknown before. Although the tram has disappeared and relatively few people go to the seaside by cheap-day excursion, a surprising number of working reminders of this pre-automobile age still survive. In the Isle of Man, horse trams, introduced in 1876, still operate a summer service along the front at Douglas, providing a connection at the northern terminus with the Manx Electric Railway, a 3ft gauge rural tramway running to Ramsey. This itself connects with another electric line that connects Laxey to the summit of Snaefell. In north Wales a cable-operated 3ft 6in gauge tramway, opened in 1902, runs from Llandudno [SH 777827] to the 679ft summit of the Great Orme. Further south in Gwynedd the Fairbourne Railway [SH 615128], a 1ft 3in gauge steam-operated miniature line, occupies the trackbed of a horse tramway opened in 1916 to connect with ferries across the Mawddach estuary.

Evidence of urban tramways is rapidly disappearing, although a large number of bus depots are merely tram sheds with the tracks removed, covered up or, occasionally, left in situ. A fine example of the smaller tram shed, with a section of 3ft 6in gauge track in front of it, can be seen near Chester General railway station [SJ 413669], while on the forecourt of Ashby-de-la-

177 Ashby-de-la-Zouch station, Leicestershire, now offices, with the track of the Burton & Ashby Light Railway in the forecourt [SK 355163] *(Neil Cossons)*

Zouch station, Leicestershire (Illus 177) [SK 355163] is the terminus trackwork of one of Britain's few real inter-urban lines – the Burton & Ashby Light Railway, operated initially by the Midland Railway and abandoned by the LMS in 1926. In London the Kingsway Tramway Subway [TQ 305817], built for single-deck cars in 1905–8 and deepened to take double-deckers in 1930–31, has been partially converted into a two-lane underpass. A rare survivor in Liverpool is a section of horse-tram track in Queen Square [SJ 346906] whose unusual features are a centre flangeway with a section of tread on each side (instead of the normal side flangeway) and rail joints made at an angle to reduce noise and wear. In many towns where trams were used in narrow streets the overhead wires were supported from buildings rather than from poles, and the cast iron wall rosettes from which they hung can still be seen. They were particularly popular in Glasgow. In Liverpool a highly decorative rosette incorporating the city's emblem – 'the liver bird' – can still be seen here and there.

MISCELLANEOUS PUBLIC UTILITIES

Numerous other public utilities provide the industrial archaeologist with fragmentary evidence of their development, although generally such evidence is on display in a museum rather than still in use. The introduction of the penny post by Rowland Hill in 1840, the first efficient large-scale postal service in the world, led to the building of post offices in all towns and many villages, and to cast iron letterboxes appearing throughout the country. These have for long been objects of great affection, particularly the pillarboxes which appear in a variety of forms and bear several makers' names. The attractive 'Penfold' hexagonal boxes are relatively common, but less so are the dignified fluted pillarboxes found in Malvern, Worcestershire, and the magnificently crowned 'Liverpool specials' introduced in the 1860s to provide additional capacity for newspapers. A good example of the latter still stands on Edge Lane, Liverpool. Railway stations are a good source of early and unusual boxes.

The introduction of the successful electric telegraph in Britain, after many years of experiment, particularly in Germany, resulted from the collaboration of two complementary figures – the far-seeing William F. Cooke (1806–79) and the ingenious Charles Wheatstone (1802–75) – who installed a direct-reading system using five wires along the main line of the Great Western Railway between Paddington and West Drayton in 1839. Deflection of the needles on the telegraph instrument enabled any one of twenty letters to be indicated, but the high cost of laying five wires resulted in two-needle and even single-needle instruments being used on railways, where codes could be used. The best known of these telegraph codes, now the standard, was devised by the American Samuel F. B. Morse (1791–1872). The Science Museum has a fine collection of telegraphic equipment, including a remarkable two-needle instrument in the gothic style for use in the Palace of Westminster. The railways, which benefited directly from the introduction of the electric telegraph, became rapidly transformed in appearance, poles and wires following virtually every line. Indeed the railway was fundamental to the success of the telegraph system, as it could supply ready-made routes, with no problems of wayleaves for poles and wires along which a nation-wide all-purpose communications network could be built. Thus the social changes the railway had helped to create by increasing the mobility of people were furthered by a new demand for the sending of personal messages.

The electric telegraph, perhaps the least recognised but certainly one of the most important nineteenth-century innovations in communication, was not in fact the first form of telegraphic system to be used regularly in Britain. There was, of course, the sixteenth-century system of hilltop bonfires, which gave warning of the approach of the Spanish Armada; and in the 1790s a series of hilltop telegraph stations were built to connect the Admiralty in London first with Deal and later with Portsmouth, Yarmouth and Plymouth. Initially shutters were used to transmit messages, but semaphore arms later replaced them. Today a number of stations remain, such as that on Chatley Heath, Surrey [TQ 089585], built in 1823 to replace an earlier wooden structure. Elsewhere the name Telegraph Hill is a common reminder of the system, while the sign of 'The Telegraph' inn on Putney Heath [TQ 233737] illustrates clearly the earlier signalling equipment. The London to Portsmouth telegraph, the last in use, finally closed on 31 December 1847.

The electric telegraph was to a great extent superseded, at first over relatively short distances, by the telephone developed from German experimental beginnings by Alexander Graham Bell (1847–1922) in America and patented in Britain in 1876. The first telephone exchange was established by a private company in London in 1879 and others quickly followed. Inter-urban lines were established and a countrywide network gradually developed, most of it in the hands of the National Telephone Company. In 1912 the General Post Office acquired all private telephone systems, with the exception of one that still operates in and around Kingston-upon-Hull in

Yorkshire. The rapid rate of development of telephony, particularly since the introduction of subscriber trunk dialling in the 1950s, has resulted in most early exchange and transmission equipment disappearing, although numerous early handsets survive. Micro-wave transmitting, relay towers and multi-core cables have almost completely eliminated the poles and wires which were a feature, particularly of the Great North Road, in the inter-war period. The telephone kiosk, however, is still a link with the earlier days of the public telephone service, a distinguished piece of industrial design in cast iron by Sir Gilbert Scott (1880–1960), whose better known works include Liverpool Cathedral, Battersea power station and Waterloo Bridge.

The beginnings of modern fire-fighting by an organised fire brigade can be found in the first fire insurance companies set up in London shortly after the Great Fire of 1666. By the end of the eighteenth century almost every town and county had its own insurance company, some of which, as a result of their very direct pecuniary interest in reducing losses by fire, were beginning to operate their own fire-fighting forces. These companies issued plates to mark the properties insured with them, and many plates survive, illustrating the large number of companies. Fire engines, in the form of horse-drawn hand pumps, were used and numerous examples, mainly dating from the mid-nineteenth century, can be found in museums. An unusual small type of 'fire engine', developed by the Merryweather company, consisted of a manual pump with four carrying handles, which could be used in factories or country houses. An example can be seen in the Glasgow Museum of Transport. The replacement of manpower by steam was an obvious development, but initially this was only for powering the pumps. Throughout the second half of the nineteenth and well into the twentieth century the standard large fire engine, weighing up to 4 tons, was drawn by horses and had its pump powered by steam. Numerous examples of these engines, notably those built by Shand Mason and Merryweather, have been preserved in museums. Although self-propelled steam pumps had been tried, they were too heavy and cumbersome to be a success, and it was not until the early 1900s that the first petrol-driven fire engines began to supersede horse-drawn ones. For a short time petrol-engine-propelled fire engines with steam pumps were used, but before 1910 both road wheels and pumps were being powered by internal combustion engines. Of all the types of public service appliance, the fire engine has had greatest popular appeal, and large numbers are preserved in museums throughout Britain. They can be seen on display at Bristol, Glasgow, Leicester, Liverpool, the London Science Museum and Swindon, to name but a few. In Norwich the Norwich Union Insurance Group has a small museum relating to its work in fire insurance. Early fire stations, some with stables, bell turrets and smoke vents, can still be found, and deserve attention from the industrial archaeologist. The whole technology of built-in systems of the sprinkler type and automatic alarms is another area needing recording and documentation.

178 Cast iron stand pipe, Ticknall, Derbyshire (Neil Cossons)

CHAPTER 13

ROADS AND BRIDGES

ROADS

The development of the road system was intimately tied up with the growth of settlements, and early roads were simply paths from one village to another. They took the easiest, usually the driest, route, avoiding steep hills, dense woodland or land under crops. With the exception of Roman roads and new motor roads built mainly in the last thirty years, almost all the roads along which we travel today have their origin as primitive paths in a period when long-distance overland travel, let alone the wheeled vehicle, was virtually unknown.

A road, theoretically, is not a strip of land, but a right of passage and, during the Middle Ages, the keeping open of a way passable for travellers on horseback and for trains of packhorses was accomplished with varying degrees of success under manorial jurisdiction. As trade increased with the widening of the known world at the end of the fifteenth and the beginning of the sixteenth centuries, it became difficult for the roads to cope with the increasing traffic especially where this increase coincided with the breakdown of the manorial courts. A tenant who had recently secured his freedom from the agricultural and other servile duties imposed by customary law could hardly be expected to agree willingly to an increase in the amount of labour and time he spent on the highways of the manor.

This common law liability on the inhabitants of each parish to keep their roads in good repair was reinforced in 1555 by an Act of Parliament 'for the mending of highways'. Under the Act each parish had to appoint annually a surveyor of highways, or waywarden, who was given power to call out the available labour of the village or town to work on the roads for four days per year. With various amendments, such as increasing the period of statute labour to six days and the granting of powers to levy rates up to 6d in the pound, the 1555 Act remained the basis of highway administration for nearly 300 years.

In some parishes this system worked fairly well. Where the roads of a parish were used by the inhabitants only, they received some attention in turn, although perhaps not every year. When John Smith was waywarden he would naturally devote most time and labour to the roads he used, and perhaps neglect those used by Thomas Brown. But Thomas Brown would probably be surveyor before long, so things would even themselves out. In some parishes, however, a trunk route between two large towns might follow a parish road, and excessive wear and tear would result. In others a main road might cut across the corner of a parish, and although it would be used by long-distance travellers, its maintenance would still be the responsibility of the parishioners. In these situations the system of parish road maintenance fell into disrepute. On a porous, well drained subsoil heavily used but little cared for roads might stand the strain, but where the soil was of clay the road inevitably became, in the words of the time, 'deep and foundrous'. Stones might be laid on the surface but would soon sink into a sea of mud, to be followed by the wheels that rolled them in. Horses died, bogged down to their shoulders in mud. Roads were in places 60–100yd wide where travellers had attempted to skirt a treacherous area. As many as ten horses or oxen might be required to move a load of 1–1½ tons over heavy ground and in winter, haulage of heavy loads stopped altogether. In the early eighteenth century Daniel Defoe noted that it took 2–3 years to move a large tree trunk from the neighbourhood of Lewes to Chatham dockyard. A few miles would be achieved each summer, with as many as twenty-two oxen pulling the tree on a vehicle known as a tug, but by September the roads would be so soft that the journey would have to be abandoned until the following June.

It was these circumstances, repeated in greater or lesser degree all over the country, that led to the first turnpike Acts, under which tolls could be levied to repair the roads. The principle of making travellers pay a contribution towards the upkeep of the roads and bridges they used had been established as early as the twelfth century, some 400 years before the birth of the turnpike system. Grants of 'pavage' were made for the upkeep of roads and streets, and of 'pontage' for the construction and repair of bridges, usually by the king, to lords of manors or heads of religious houses, enabling them to collect tolls in specified areas. In 1279 Edward I granted pontage for three years to the 'bailiffs and good men' of Huntingdon, empowering them to collect tolls for the upkeep of the bridge. The great bridge at Swarkeston in Derbyshire, a fine surviving example of a medieval bridge [SK 369285], was the object of similar grants in the reigns of Edward II and Edward III. These grants may be called the forerunners of the turnpike Acts of later days, but they did not form the genesis of the system.

The first turnpike road resulted from an Act passed in 1663 empowering the justices of Hertfordshire, Huntingdonshire and Cambridgeshire to erect a gate in each county and levy tolls on the Great North Road. No further turnpike Act was passed until 1695–6 when Acts for the London to Harwich road and a section of road between Attleborough and Wymondham near Norwich were placed on the statute book. Increasing numbers of Acts followed in succeeding years (Illus 179), but 1706–7 established a precedent that became standard for all future turnpike roads. Instead of the local justices being empowered to become the road authority, a body, consisting usually of local gentry, was set up to act as turnpike trustees. In all cases where a road was turnpiked the initiative was local. Parliament did not decide that certain stretches of highway were more in need of extra care than others, but local people, interested in certain parts of the roads, formed themselves into committees, subscribed the legal expenses, petitioned Parliament, and having obtained their Acts, became the trustees.

The key to the functioning of a turnpike trust was its power to raise tolls. At first toll lists were simple, but they gradually became more and more complicated as differential charges were introduced and various restrictions and allowances were made for wheel width, wheel construction, weight of lading, and number of draught beasts. On a few points there was general agreement between one trust and another. No tolls were levied on foot travellers, and tolls charged by the Acts were maxima, which could be lowered, but not raised, at the discretion of the trustees. The charges for horses, without vehicles, whether led, driven or ridden, varied between $\frac{1}{2}$d and 2d each. Cattle were generally charged 10d per score, and sheep and pigs 5d. The greatest variation occurred in the schedules of charges for vehicles, some forty separately identifiable goods and passenger vehicles appearing in the toll lists of the various Acts. In 1753 an Act prohibited the use of wagons with wheels less than 9in wide, unless drawn by oxen or less than five horses, and two years later another Act allowed three years' exemption from tolls for wagons with 9in wheels. In 1765 preferential treatment was given to wagons with the fore wheels on shorter axles than the rear wheels, on the grounds that a greater width of road would be effectively rolled, and in 1774 wagons with 16in wheels or rollers were given complete freedom from tolls for five years.

The period 1750–80 saw the greatest geographical expansion of turnpiking, although mileage continued to increase but at a slower rate down to the late 1830s.

TURNPIKE ROADS IN 1715

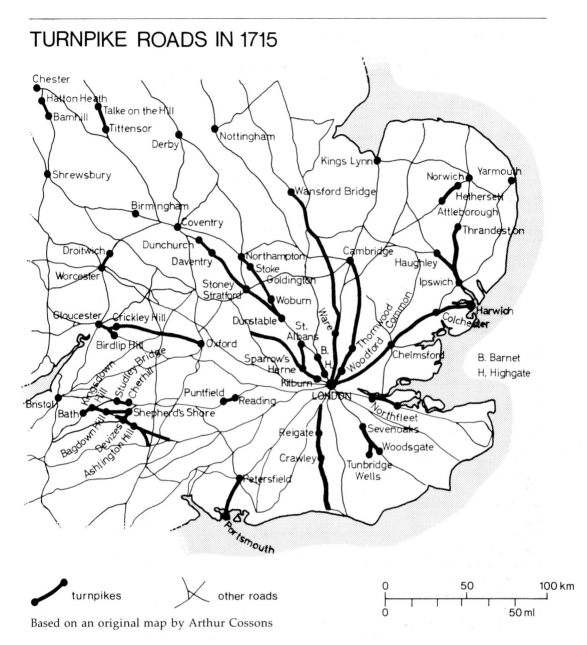

Chester
Hatton Heath
Talke on the Hill
Barnhill
Tittensor
Derby
Nottingham
Shrewsbury
Kings Lynn
Norwich Yarmouth
Wansford Bridge
Hethersett
Birmingham
Attleborough
Coventry
Thrandeston
Droitwich
Dunchurch
Cambridge
Haughley
Daventry
Northampton
Worcester
Stoke
Ipswich
Stoney
Goldington
Stratford
Woburn
Harwich
Gloucester Crickley Hill
Dunstable
Colchester
Birdlip Hill
Oxford
St. Albans
Studley Bridge
Cherhill
Thornwood Common
B.
Chelmsford
B. Barnet
Kingsdown Hill
Puntfield
Sparrow's
H.
Woodford
H. Highgate
Bristol
Reading
Bath
Shepherd's Shore
Harne
Kilburn
LONDON
Northfleet
Devizes
Bagdown Hill
Reigate
Sevenoaks
Ashlington Hill
Woodsgate
Crawley
Tunbridge
Wells
Petersfield
Ware
Woodford
Portsmouth

turnpikes   other roads

0   50   100 km
0   50 ml

Based on an original map by Arthur Cossons

Illustration 179

At this peak period most main roads, especially in England, were under the care of nearly 4,000 trusts whose responsibility covered some 22,000 miles of road out of an estimated total of 105,000 miles. Turnpikes were most numerous in heavily populated industrial areas, counties such as Suffolk and Essex having only some 10 per cent of their roads under trust maintenance. All other roads were still, of course, the responsibility of the parishes, and were generally in a poor state. It was not until 1835, after nearly 300 years, that the statute labour basis of maintenance was replaced by a rating system, with parishes formed into districts each covered by a district surveyor.

Throughout the eighteenth century highway legislation had been based on the supposition that it was impossible to keep roads in good repair without restrictions on the types of vehicle using them. Hence the idea prevailed that carts and wagons could be so constructed that they repaired rather than damaged the roads, with consequent agitation for broad rollers rather than wheels. At the root of all this was a fundamental lack of knowledge of any systematic or scientific approach to the construction or maintenance of the roads themselves. Credit for the introduction of new roadmaking techniques which, as the timings of the mail coaches indicated, revolutionised road travel, must go to three men – 'Blind Jack' Metcalf, John Loudon Macadam, and Thomas Telford. John Metcalf (1717–1810) was born at Knaresborough, Yorkshire. He had been musician, jobmaster, fish dealer, recruiting agent, hosiery merchant, horsedealer, and possibly trader in smuggled tea before he took up roadmaking, with a contract to build some 3 miles of the Boroughbridge to Harrogate road, turnpiked in 1765. Blind from the age of six, Metcalf had an uncanny ability to assess the lie of the land and determine the most favourable route across it, gaining a picture by extensive walking or riding. When he retired in 1792, he had improved some 180 miles of road for a score or so of trusts in the West Riding of Yorkshire, south Lancashire and north Derbyshire. Metcalf was the first of the great road engineers to appreciate the need for a well drained, firm foundation. A smooth convex surface of stone and gravel was laid over bundles of ling or heather set on a foundation of prepared subsoil. Ditches on either side of the road, which was elevated between them, ensured the surface would be free-draining. This was a great advance in roadbuilding technique over contemporary practice, and although the amount of road he improved was relatively small, Metcalf's contribution was of fundamental significance.

Macadam (1756–1836) and Telford (1757–1834) were almost exact contemporaries whose chief work dates from a little later than that of 'Blind Jack'. Macadam's name is associated with the system of road surfacing using broken stone instead of gravel rather than the variations of his method that bear his name today. His plan was as follows: 'Now the principle of roadmaking I think the most valuable, is to put broken stone upon a road, which shall unite by its own angles, so as to form a solid hard surface.' This material, no stone of which was to exceed 6oz in weight, was to be laid to a depth of about 10in and be well consolidated. He did not care particularly what lay underneath, arguing that a subsoil base drained by side ditches and protected from rain penetration by a sound surface would support any weight. Great care had to be exercised in breaking stone for Macadam's roads. He insisted that surveyors trained in his system should be equipped with a pair of scales and a 6oz weight, or a 2in metal ring through which the stones had to pass. A 6in layer of these angular stones was laid as evenly as possible, followed by a further 6in some weeks later when the first had consolidated under traffic. A surface 18ft wide cost in the region of £88 per mile.

The relative cheapness of the Macadam system led to its adoption by the majority of turnpike trusts. By the late nineteenth century 'water-bound macadam' road was almost universal throughout Britain, and the name of its inventor had become part of the English language. Macadam himself became surveyor of the Bristol Trust in 1816, and by 1819 the 180 miles of road of this largest turnpike trust in the country were already well known for their admirable state of repair. The fact that, once improved, a macadamised road demanded much less maintenance than other roads attracted many trusts. Macadam was appointed Surveyor-General of the Metropolitan Roads in 1827, and he and numerous members of his family advised dozens of trusts up and down the country in succeeding years.

Thomas Telford was one of the great civil engineers of his generation, a famous bridge and canal builder but mainly memorable perhaps as an improver of roads. The son of a shepherd and trained originally as a stonemason, Telford was appointed Surveyor of Public Works for Shropshire in 1787. Besides undertaking a

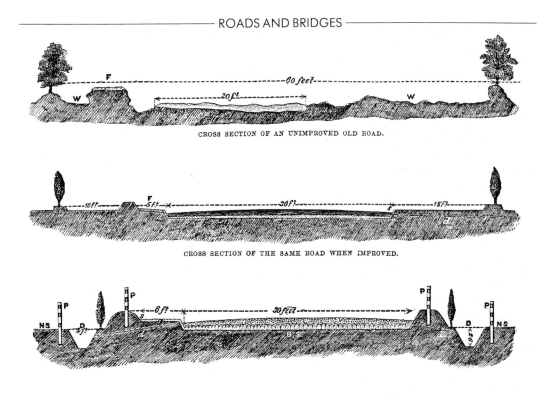

CROSS SECTION OF AN UNIMPROVED OLD ROAD.

CROSS SECTION OF THE SAME ROAD WHEN IMPROVED.

180   Cross sections through roads

prodigious programme of bridge building, he gained wide experience of road work both in Shropshire and, later, in the Highlands of Scotland, where he built or improved many hundreds of miles of road as part of a scheme to bring life back to that depressed and depopulated region. Telford's system of road construction was similar to that developed in France in the 1770s by Pierre Trésaguet (1716–94). It consisted of laying a solid course of large stones on the prepared and level bed of the road 'in the form of a close neat pavement'. Over this was laid a 6in spread of hard broken stones, each as nearly cubical as possible, and on top of this again a 2in top layer of gravel. Great care had to be taken in laying the stone foundation and in applying the top surface of gravel, with its precisely specified 1 in 60 fall from the crown to the sides of the road. The cost of Telford's roads was relatively high because of the heavy foundation, and as a result they did not find as much favour as Macadam's 'elastic' system.

Nevertheless in 1815, when the Holyhead Road Commission was set up, Telford was called on to survey the route and engineer a new and efficient road out of the chaotic situation administered by no less than twenty-three separate turnpike trusts. South of Shrewsbury the major improvements consisted largely of easing gradients and building short bypasses to avoid narrow sections in villages. In Wales, however, a much more radical approach was needed, and the road as it stands today is a remarkable tribute to Telford's engineering skill. West of Betws-y-Coed the existing route wound north along the Conwy valley and then west beside the coast to Bangor. Even today the section of this old road through the Sychnant Pass [SH 750770] between Conwy and Penmaenmawr is formidable; to the early mail coaches it was often impossible. Telford surveyed a new route westward from Betws-y-Coed that included a winding ascent up the valley of the Llugwy to Capel Curig, a spectacular feat of road engineering rendered almost

181 Tollhouse on the old Holyhead road, near Cluddley, Shropshire [SJ 618106]   *(Neil Cossons)*

ordinary by the section which follows – from Llyn Ogwen through the Nant Ffrancon Pass. Here, without involving a gradient steeper than 1 in 22, Telford carefully edged his alignment up the steep side of the glacial valley towards its head. This is the real civil engineering that distinguished Telford from most contemporary road improvers, who did little more than remodel the surface of the existing alignment.

It is worthwhile reviewing the impact of turnpiking, its decline, and the remains of the turnpike era the industrial archaeologist can find on the ground today. Despite the obvious benefits, the new restrictions of gates on the 'King's Highway' were not without opposition and riots occurred in a number of places. Around Bristol in the 1730s and 1740s colliers from south Gloucestershire and farmers from north Somerset destroyed gates and burned tollhouses. In South Wales, too, farmers resisted turnpiking with force as late as the 1840s. This was the period of the 'Rebecca Riots', when gangs of small farmers, whose hardships resulting from economic depression were aggravated by the tolls, roamed Pembrokeshire and Carmarthenshire destroying the tollgates. The mob was usually led by a man in woman's clothes, named after Isaac's wife 'Rebecca' from *Genesis*, who receives the promise that her seed should possess the 'gate' of those who hate her. These local difficulties were usually short-lived, however, and the increasing number of travellers and carriers had, by

the 1820s when Macadam's and Telford's improvements had become widespread, every reason to bless the new roads and their superior surfaces. For the first time for nearly 2,000 years the speed of long-distance land transport in Britain was limited by the capacity of the horse rather than the condition of the road. In 1784 the introduction of tightly scheduled mail coaches permitted the traveller to reach Birmingham from London in 12hr and Exeter in 17¼hr. By 1834 English coaches drove at an *average* speed of 9–10mph, only the severest winter weather causing dislocation of their services.

Generally speaking, it was not until well into the railway era that the turnpike trusts began to suffer financial difficulties, and at first some of them actually benefited from traffic attracted by the new lines. By the late 1840s, however, some trusts were appealing to the local justices for rates to be levied for the upkeep of roads, and in 1851 insolvent trusts were allowed to apply to the Secretary of State for provisional orders to reduce interest and extinguish arrears. Throughout the 1860s, 1870s and 1880s, the turnpike system was abolished as the various Acts expired. Most of these Acts were for specified periods, usually twenty-one years, and then subject to renewal. After 1831 this renewal became automatic under the terms of the Annual Continuance Acts, which extended for one year all Acts due to expire. An increasing number of trusts asked for their Acts to be excluded from the annual continuance process and in 1895 the last turnpike Act expired. The system had taken 232 years to grow, flourish briefly, and expire, and with its expiry came something of a decline in the standard of rural roads.

Visible evidence of turnpiking is still surprisingly common throughout much of Britain. Nothing much survives of the toll roads themselves, although occasionally road works may reveal an early nineteenth-century surface buried in the foundations of its modern counterpart. Similarly, and for obvious reasons, the gates have disappeared. There are, however, many hundreds of tollhouses and milestones and, here and there, signposts also. Most tollhouses date from the early nineteenth century, and frequently have a form which makes them instantly recognisable (Illus 181, 182 and 183). The half-hexagonal end with windows giving a view in each direction down the road, the hipped roof often with a prominent overhang to the eaves, and the area of wall above the central window where the tollboard would originally have hung, are all typical features. Few tollhouses still have their boards. Notable examples which do are to be found at Steanor Bottom Bar, Todmorden in Lancashire [SD 945198] at the junction of Calderbrook Road and Roch-

dale Road; Dundee Road, Perth [NO 124227] and on the Holyhead Road at Llanfair PG, Anglesey [SH 532715]. The latter, a Telford tollhouse, has the veranda that typified a number of his other tollhouses and appeared less frequently elsewhere, as at Ashton Gate, Bristol [ST 573717]. A slate tollboard from a demolished tollhouse is mounted beside the A6(T) at Shardlow, Derbyshire [SK 442303]; nearby are the abutments of Cavendish Bridge built across the Trent in 1758 and swept away by floods in 1947.

The erection of milestones was a statutory responsibility of the turnpike trusts,

182 Blue Vein Tollhouse near Box, Wiltshire [ST 831673], in 1935 *(Arthur Cossons)*

183 Blue Vein Tollhouse. Tollhouses are still fairly numerous, but particularly susceptible to unsympathetic modernisation or demolition for road improvement. In 1935 the tollhouse (right) was still substantially as built; by 1985 Tollhouse Cottage as it is now called has been enlarged but the essential character of the original building is still intact *(Neil Cossons)*

although as early as 1698 parishes had been required to put signposts at cross-roads. Few of these latter survive but long runs of milestones can still be seen, often beautifully maintained by the county highway authorities. Many trusts had distinctive patterns. Telford designed his own milestone for the Holyhead road – a chamfered tapering stone with a cast iron plate. Others were made entirely of cast iron and frequently had a 'V' plan to make for ease of reading. A fine example by I. & F. Thornewill of Burton-on-Trent, dated 1828, is on show at the Staffordshire County Museum, Shugborough [SJ 991224], one of a series on the A50(T) between Uttoxeter and Newcastle-under-Lyme, of which many survive *in situ*. Numerous examples of the similar iron posts erected by the Bristol trust can be seen along the A38(T) between Bristol and Bridgwater. A distinctive cylindrical type (Illus 184) again in cast iron, occurs frequently in

Derbyshire, the roads from Leek to Buxton and Ashbourne each having a substantially complete series. Signposts are less common, but a notable example is the stone obelisk at Craven Arms, Shropshire [SO 433827]. Although these early signs are reasonably safe from destruction, more recent examples, erected in the present century, are now becoming extremely rare and will almost certainly disappear with metrication and the adoption of international symbols. Even rarer survivals of the turnpike era, however, are the vehicle weighing machines introduced after an Act of 1741 put a levy of extra tolls on carts and wagons laden beyond certain specified limits. One at Woodbridge in Suffolk [TM 272491], operated on the steelyard principle, may owe something to the work of John Wyatt (1700–66), a prominent designer of weighing machines. The Woodbridge machine (Illus 187), mounted on the end wall of 'Ye Olde Bell and Steel-

184,185,186 Examples of cast iron mileposts

yard', is suspended by a hook from a large pulley-block which is itself suspended from another block housed under a small roof. A small wooden platform is attached to the massive cantilever bracket that carries the steelyard, to enable the weigh-man to adjust the lead weight or poise and so effect a balance. The yard is some 20ft long but the load and fulcrum centres are only 2⅝in apart.

Although the introduction of motor vehicles brought about a new revolution in road construction, various attempts to improve on macadamisation were made in the nineteenth century. Tar was applied as early as 1845 in Nottingham and in the 1870s in Sheffield and Liverpool. Asphalt, a naturally occurring bitumen from Limmer in Hanover and later from Lake Asphalt in Trinidad, was also used, initially for paving and subsequently for road surfaces. Tar spraying of macadam roads was widely adopted as a way of combat-

187 Wagon weighing machine based on the steelyard principle, Woodbridge, Suffolk [TM 272491]
(*Royal Commission on Historical Monuments, England*)

ing the dust caused by the suction effect of rubber-tyred vehicles. Road surfaces in towns were generally made of granite sets after the 1830s, and huge quarries in Scotland, North Wales and Charnwood Forest, Leicestershire, were opened to supply the stone. Laid initially on sand and after about 1870 on concrete, these sets are still common, particularly in side streets. Wood blocks, with their advantage of quietness, were used in many towns from the 1840s down to the 1920s, but have now almost completely disappeared. Special tracks for carts and wagons were frequently installed in dock areas. These consisted of large, well fitted blocks of granite laid railway-fashion in two lines to match the distance between the vehicle wheels, and separated by a band of ordinary sets. In 1825 they were laid in Commercial Road, London; a length in Exchange Street East, Liverpool, where the stones are known as 'wheelers', can still be seen.

Despite the massive modernisation of roads in recent years, they still provide a fruitful source of interest for the industrial archaeologist. Cast iron kerbs and gullies, bollards and street signs survive in profusion, as in High Street, Dorking [TQ 166495], and more recent signs, often vitreous-enamelled, erected by the Automobile Association, Royal Automobile Club, Cyclists' Touring Club and the various petrol companies can still be seen though in rapidly declining numbers.

BRIDGES

From the industrial archaeologist's point of view bridge building, so intimately connected with the turnpike road movement, is a profitable area of study. In the mid-eighteenth century bridges were still the exceptional way of crossing large rivers, and many of those that did exist were of medieval origins and too narrow for horse-drawn vehicles. Fords and ferries predominated, and a large river like the Yorkshire Ouse, although having some twenty ferries, had only one bridge. Indeed it was not until 1888 that there was a general statutory obligation for public authorities to build bridges. A few bridges were maintained before 1750 by county quarter sessions or hundreds, but most were repaired by ancient and often inadequate endowments. The General Highway Act of 1773 allowed magistrates to make indictments in respect of bridges, which meant that counties were ultimately held responsible for upkeep. In Scotland the state-aided Commission for the Highland Roads, established in 1803 and with Thomas Telford as engineer, built some 1,200 in 25 years. With the rapid increase in traffic brought about by turnpiking, and the demand for shorter routes, a period of major bridge construction began in the latter years of the eighteenth century.

All bridges are based on one or more of three fundamental structural forms: the beam, of which the slab of rock or fallen tree trunk are the simplest forms; the arch, in which the deck is supported by a structure of wedge-shaped arch stones or voussoirs; and suspension, in which the deck is hung by suspenders from a continuous cable. In eighteenth-century Britain all important bridges were of the arch type, constructed on the empirical evidence available from earlier bridge builders and from buildings such as the great medieval cathedrals. At this period the first theories of arches were developed, notably in France where the Corps des Ingénieurs des Ponts et Chaussées under the guidance of Jean Rodolphe Perronet (1708–94) was applying scientific techniques to constructional problems. But Britain lagged behind badly; in the 1730s, for example, it had proved impossible to find a British engineer to build Westminster Bridge and the work was given to Charles Labelye (1705–62) a Swiss engineer who had been educated in France. (His bridge lasted a little over a century before being replaced by the present structure.) Robert Mylne (1734–1811) carried out much of the pioneer work in England on arch-bridge design, his first major work, Blackfriars Bridge, London, being completed in 1769. (It was replaced by the present wrought iron structure in 1869.) In this bridge Mylne incorporated elliptical arches, an innovation in Britain; inverted arches in the piers between the springings of the two adjacent arches bearing on them; and the multiple or crocket wedge support for the timber bridge centres, which enabled the centring to be lowered gradually and any weakness in the arch itself to be detected at an early stage.

John Rennie (1761–1821) is much better known, but may be regarded as a successor to Mylne in the field of bridge building. Born at Phantassie, near East Linton, some 20 miles from Edinburgh, Rennie grew up in contact with the crafts of millwrighting, blacksmithing, stonemasonry and carpentry and learnt much about them from one of his father's tenants, Andrew Meikle (1719–1811), the celebrated mechanical engineer and windmill improver. After an education at Edinburgh University, which brought him into contact with leading scientific minds, Rennie established himself as an engineer working on canals, docks, steam engines,

land drainage schemes, roads and mills, as well as some notable bridges. His most famous masonry bridges were Waterloo Bridge, London, completed in 1817 and now replaced by a reinforced-concrete beam structure; and London Bridge, completed in 1831 as successor to the famous medieval bridge and now removed to Havasu City, Arizona. The foundations of both these bridges were on piles built within cofferdams. Rennie's Waterloo and London Bridges, and his other Thames bridge, at Southwark, have all now been replaced, but Kelso Bridge over the River Tweed, his first major structure, still stands at the southern approach to the town [NT 727336]. It has five elliptical arches, each of 72ft span, and was virtually a small-scale prototype for Waterloo Bridge. Rennie's bridge-building abilities, like those of Telford a few years later, stood him in good stead for his work on canals in which, besides innumerable humble occupation crossings, mostly built to a standard design, he was responsible for a number of aqueducts, including the spectacular structure across the River Lune at Lancaster [SD 484639]. These will be considered in Chapter 14. His standard bridges may be seen in profusion along the Lancaster Canal and the Kennet & Avon Canal. Most have walls curved on plan, so acting as arches springing from the buttress piers at each end; and in addition the walls are battered, making the whole bridge immensely strong.

Before turning to iron bridges, in which Rennie had been involved at Southwark, a number of other surviving masonry structures are worth noting. In Chester, Gros-

188 Dunkeld Bridge, Perthshire [NO 027424], built across the River Tay to the designs of Thomas Telford between 1805 and 1809 has five large river arches and two small land arches; it is 685ft long   (*Neil Cossons*)

venor Bridge across the Dee [SJ 403656], designed by Thomas Harrison (1744–1829) and opened in 1832, has the widest masonry span in Britain – 200ft, with a rise of 40ft. The complete arch has, in fact, a span of 230ft, as it extends into the abutments to carry the thrust more effectively down to piling foundations. Harrison also designed the elegant Skerton Bridge in Lancaster [SD 479623]. Telford's masonry bridges never reached the standards of structural elegance of his graceful cast iron bridges. His first major work, Montford Bridge [SJ 433153] of 1792, carrying the Holyhead road over the Severn west of Shrewsbury, is very much in the eighteenth-century classical tradition, but his next, Tongueland Bridge [NX 692533] across the Dee near Kirkcudbright, with its single 112ft span, is of considerable technical interest. Here Telford first introduced hollow spandrels to lighten the load on the foundations, but, instead of piercing with tunnels as Smeaton and Edwards had done, he replaced the normal rubble fill with a series of parallel walls within the spandrels themselves. Pierced spandrel bridges may be seen at Pontypridd, Glamorgan [ST 074904], built in 1755 by William Edwards (1719–89), and Coldstream, Berwickshire [NT 848402], designed by John Smeaton (1724–92) and completed in 1763. In the latter example the tunnels are covered at the ends with ornamental discs. Returning to Telford and his masonry bridges, Dean Bridge, Edinburgh [NT 243740], over the Waters of Leith, completed in 1832, is perhaps his finest surviving stone structure, while Over Bridge, Gloucester [SO 816196], is interesting for its ingenuity. The splaying of the 150ft span arch, in which the two faces of the bridge are in effect chamfered to form 'cow's horn voussoirs', is based on Perronet's Pont de Neuilly over the Seine.

The completion in 1779 of the first metal bridge structure in the world, the Iron Bridge (Illus 189) over the River Severn near Coalbrookdale in Shropshire [SJ

189 The Iron Bridge [SJ 673034], the first major civil engineering work in the world to use iron structurally. Cast at the nearby Coalbrookdale Works in 1779, it is now the focal point of the Ironbridge Gorge Museum. The tollhouse on the south bridge approach is a museum and information centre *(Neil Cossons)*

673034], marked the beginning of the end of stone as the major bridge-building material. The Iron Bridge derives all its structural principles from its stone predecessors and is, in effect, a natural successor to the works of Edwards and Smeaton, who pioneered the reduction in self-weight of bridge structures. Like stone bridges, it has a compression arch, but close examination of the methods of construction reveals that techniques more appropriate to timber fabrication have been used in its assembly. The various components were designed to pass through one another and mortice or dovetail together, and are secured by wedges. No bolts or rivets were used. The bridge has a span of 100ft and the rise is 45ft. There are five main ribs of 12in by 6½in section and 70ft long, virtually hinged at the springing and at the crown. They were cast in open sand moulds at the Coalbrookdale works of Abraham Darby.

190 Craigellachie Bridge across the Spey at Aberlour, Banffshire [NJ 285452], designed by Thomas Telford. The single 150ft span has four ribs, largely original, but the spandrel frames have been renewed in steel (*Neil Cossons*)

Credit for the design of what is perhaps the most important monument of the Industrial Revolution in Britain is usually accorded to Thomas Farnolls Pritchard (*d*1777), a Shrewsbury architect, who certainly prepared drawings for a 120ft flat-arched iron bridge as early as October 1775. In association with the ironmasters John Wilkinson (1728–1808) and Abraham Darby III (1750–91), Pritchard discussed schemes for a bridge, but his death in 1777 left the project entirely in Darby's hands. Who was responsible for the design of the 1779 bridge as constructed remains, therefore, something of a mystery.

There is no doubt, however, that the Iron Bridge proved to be an inspiration to other civil engineers. Thomas Telford used iron for the bridge at Buildwas, a few miles upstream from Coalbrookdale. The previous masonry bridge had been swept away by a flood in 1795 and Telford replaced it with a single iron span of 130ft weighing 173 tons, in contrast to the 378 tons of the first 1779 iron bridge. Buildwas Bridge [SJ 645044] survived until 1906, when it was replaced by the present steel structure.

Numerous designs for iron bridges were tried between 1795 and 1820. In 1796 a 236ft iron span was completed across the River Wear at Sunderland to the designs of Rowland Burdon, a local MP, who in the previous year had patented a system of construction involving separate openwork cast iron voussoirs held together with wrought iron straps instead of the ribs being cast complete, as at Ironbridge or Buildwas. The idea was not a complete success and two subsequent bridges built at Staines, 1802, and Yarm, 1805, collapsed soon after completion. Sunderland Bridge survived for half a century before requiring substantial modification and eventual replacement. Two bridges incorporating Burdon's patent still survive – at Spanish Town, Jamaica, 1801, and Newport Pagnell, Buckinghamshire, where Tickford Bridge [SP 877437] across the River Ouzel, completed in 1810, still carries the heavy traffic of the A50.

Open-frame voussoirs fell into disrepute as a result of these and other collapses, and Coalport Bridge of 1818 [SJ

191 Cast iron plaque, Craigellachie Bridge:
'CAST AT PLAS KYNASTON RUABON DENBIGHSHIRE
1814' *(Neil Cossons)*

702021] is an example of the return to ribs cast in complete sections. There are few eighteenth-century survivors of this type of construction, but those that do exist usually have characteristic features suggesting that the founders had some influence in the design. Thus the spans at Cound, Shropshire [SJ 556053], dated 1797 and presumably supplied to Telford, those at Bath over the Kennet & Avon Canal [ST 758654], one of two supplied to Rennie, and the bridge at Tewkesbury [SO 893330], of unknown date, all have a diminishing circle motif in the spandrel of the arches.

By 1815 really large iron bridges were being built, notably by Telford and Rennie. At Betws-y-Coed [SH 799558] Telford's graceful arch provides a splendid example of the ironfounders' art. The outside ribs carry the legend, in finely proportioned openwork lettering, THIS ARCH WAS CONSTRUCTED IN THE SAME YEAR THE BATTLE OF WATERLOO WAS FOUGHT, across the full width of the arch. In the

spandrels are enormous heraldic flowers – roses, thistles, shamrocks and leeks – a degree of decoration seldom seen in Telford's work. The arch was cast by William Hazledine at Plas Kynaston and erected by William Stuttle. Both their names are cast into the base of the balustrading. The Waterloo Bridge is surprisingly little known, perhaps because a good view of the arch involves scrambling down the river bank almost to water level. The effort is well worthwhile, however, and an examination of the underside of the arch reveals the sympathetic way in which it has been strengthened and widened without destroying its original character. In Scotland Telford's magnificently sited bridge at Craigellachie [NJ 285452], with its ornamental castellated towers and 152ft arch of trussed iron ribs (Illus 190 and 191), has also been carefully renovated in recent years, using new components and epoxy resin adhesives. Similar large, although less spectacular, Telford bridges are Holt Fleet Bridge, Ombersley, Hereford & Worcester [SO 824634]; Mythe Bridge, Tewkesbury [SO 889337]; and Galton Bridge, Smethwick [SP 015893]. Unfortunately John Rennie's masterpiece in cast iron, the 240ft span Southwark Bridge over the Thames, built between 1814 and 1819, no longer survives. It was replaced by the present steel-arched bridge in 1922.

The need for spans larger than were feasible even with cast iron bridges became a real one by the 1820s, when the new roads and greatly increased traffic created a demand for shorter and more direct routes. The suspension bridge satisfied this need, and wrought iron, becoming readily available as a result of Henry Cort's pioneer work in the 1780s on the development of the puddling process, meant that for the first time material existed from which suitable chains could be made. A number of suspension bridges were built in south Scotland. The greatest, with a span of 300ft, was completed in 1820 by Captain Samuel (later Sir Samuel) Brown, RN (1776–1852), and crossed the Tweed at Kelso. (It has since been demolished.) Brown had introduced the chain cable to the Royal Navy and in 1817 took out a patent for wrought iron links which he incorporated in the Union Chain Bridge across the Tweed at Loan End near Berwick [NT 933511] (Illus 192). Completed in 1820, this earliest surviving suspension bridge has a span of 361ft and is hung from twelve wrought iron chains from Benjamin Hall's Pontypridd ironworks in South Wales. Major repairs have been undertaken on two occasions, the first in 1871–2 by the Berwick and Norham and Islandshire Turnpike Trustees and the second in 1902–3 by the Tweed Bridge Trustees who now care for the bridge. A steel cable has been added on each side above the chains to help them support the platform.

In 1819 the Act was passed for building Menai Bridge [SH 556714] to carry the Holyhead road from Anglesey to the mainland of Wales. Its designer, Thomas Telford, initially favoured a cast iron arch construction similar to a scheme put forward in 1801 by Rennie, but Admiralty insistence on unobstructed navigation through the strait resulted in his adopting the suspension principle, and on a scale far exceeding anything previously built. Work began on the piers in 1819 and on the manufacture of the iron chains in 1821. The links, each a little over 9ft long, were wrought at Upton Forge [SJ 560113] in Shropshire, sent to Hazledine's Coleham works in Shrewsbury for testing on a specially designed tensile machine and forwarded thence by canal to Chester and sea to Menai.

Telford, acutely conscious of the step he was taking into the unknown, tested each link of the sixteen suspension chains 100 per cent in excess of the calculated working load and then tested each complete chain in tension before final erection. The stones of the towers are dowelled together with iron pegs and the chains which they support run back 60ft into tunnels blasted in the rock. The main span is of 579ft, with a headroom of 100ft to satisfy Admiralty navigation requirements. Each of the main piers is 153ft high and is approached by a masonry viaduct of three arches on the Caernarfon side and four on the Anglesey side of the Strait. Completed in 1826, like its smaller neighbour at Conwy

[SH 786777] on the Chester road, Menai Bridge formed the last link in the road from Holyhead to London. Despite Telford's care in design and construction, various components have had to be replaced. In 1839 the unstiffened timber deck was wrecked in a storm; a heavier timber deck lasted until 1893, when Sir Benjamin Baker reconstructed it in steel; and this in turn was replaced in 1940, when the tolls were also abolished and the chains replaced in high-tensile steel.

The success of Menai encouraged others to build suspension bridges. William Tierney Clark (1783–1852) designed the old Hammersmith Bridge, built in 1827 and replaced sixty years later, and a beautiful 271ft span suspension bridge at Marlow [SU 852862], completed in 1832 and still standing. So is Clark's major work, the 666ft span suspension bridge at Budapest. Victoria Bridge, Bath [ST 741650], across the River Avon, completed in 1836 to the designs of J. Dredge, is of unusual construction, as the suspension rods from the catenary chains are inclined towards the piers instead of being vertical, a device intended to increase structural stiffness. Undoubtedly the most spectacular of the great nineteenth-century suspension bridges, however, is the epic Clifton Bridge [ST 564731], designed by I. K. Brunel in the late 1820s and finally completed in modified form in 1864. The first moves to bridge the Avon gorge at Clifton date from 1753, when William Vick, a Bristol wine merchant, bequeathed £1,000 to the Society of Merchant Venturers with the instruction that it should be allowed to accumulate to £10,000 when, it was hoped, a bridge could be built. By 1829 the amount had increased to £8,000, and a competition was held to seek a suitable design. Numerous schemes were submitted, including an improbable gothic structure by Telford, who was one of the judges, and several by Brunel. A modified Brunel design was finally selected, work began in June 1831, the foundation stone was laid in 1836 and in 1840, when the piers were substantially complete, money ran out. The chains were sold in 1853 to the South Devon Railway for use on Brunel's other major bridge, the Royal

192   Union Chain Bridge [NT 933511], Loan End, Northumberland   *(Royal Commission on Historical Monuments, England)*

Albert Bridge over the Tamar at Saltash [SX 435587]. In 1859, when Brunel died, Clifton Bridge was no further advanced, but the prosperity of the 1860s coupled with sorrow at the loss of a great engineer, at the relatively early age of 53, revived interest in the scheme. A new company was formed by some of the principal members of the Institution of Civil Engineers and, utilising the chains from the recently demolished Hungerford suspension bridge across the Thames, also designed by Brunel, they opened Clifton in December 1864. With little modification it stands today, linking Gloucestershire and Somerset 245ft above the Avon. The span is 702ft 3in and the total weight of ironwork 1,500 tons. Incidentally, the piers of Brunel's Hungerford Bridge still help to support the rail and foot bridge between Waterloo and Charing Cross [TQ 305803].

The beam type of bridge had little application on roads in the nineteenth century, although it was extensively used on railways. Recently, however, beam bridges in steel and prestressed concrete have appeared in profusion on motorways and other modern roadworks. The early development of reinforced concrete was pursued largely in France by engineers such as François Coignet (1814–88) and his son Edmond (1850–1915), and François Hennebique (1842–1921). The structural use of concrete poured *in situ* was adopted only slowly in England and no major bridge in the new material appeared until after World War I. A very early example in mass concrete still survives across the River Axe at Seaton in Devon [SY 252899]. It was completed in 1877 and has a central span of 50ft. On a much larger scale the reinforced concrete Royal Tweed Bridge at Berwick [NT 995528], opened in 1928, exemplifies the ponderous designs of the inter-war years before prestressing brought to concrete the elegance and daring worthy of the great nineteenth-century pioneers.

Before leaving road bridges altogether, a curious and somewhat bizarre answer to the problems of spanning large rivers and at the same time maintaining headroom for navigation is worthy of brief mention.

193   Traffic coming ashore from the gondola, Middlesbrough transporter bridge

(Neil Cossons)

The transporter bridge, in effect an aerial ferry, had a brief period of popularity at the end of the nineteenth century and beginning of the twentieth as a solution to the problem in flat country or urban areas of low-level approach roads making a fixed bridge unpractical. By supporting a girder at high level between two towers, vehicles could be carried across the gap on a platform suspended by cables from a trolley running on rails above. The idea was originally proposed by a British engineer in the 1870s, but was first put into practice by the Frenchman F. Arnodin in 1893 at Portugalete, near Bilbao, in Spain. Four transporter bridges were built in Britain and three of these are still extant. The largest, in fact the largest in the world, crossed the Mersey between Widnes and Runcorn. It was of the suspension type with a span of 1,000ft and was in use from 1905 until 1961, when the present high-level steel-arch structure replaced it.

In 1906 a smaller transporter bridge, also of suspension type, was completed across the Usk at Newport [ST 318863]. Of 645ft span, it was in regular use until corrosion of the steel cables necessitated closure. It is hoped to restore the bridge and return it to operation. The Middlesbrough transporter bridge (Illus 192, 193) [NZ 500213] is of a completely different form of construction, as its overhead deck is cantilevered, the outer ends being anchored with massive vertical cables. Opened in 1911, it has a span of 570ft and accommodation for 600 passengers and up to 10 vehicles on the electrically propelled carriage. Much less known than these two is the privately owned transporter bridge across the River Mersey at Warrington [SJ 597877], connecting the two halves of the extensive soap and chemical works of Messrs Joseph Crosfield & Son Ltd. Compared with Newport and Middlesbrough, it is small, with a semi-cantilevered span of only 187ft. Built in 1916, and out of regular use since 1964, it was the last of the total of sixteen transporter bridges in the world to be constructed.

194 South entrance to the Blackwall Tunnel, Greenwich [TQ 391795], built in 1897 (*Neil Cossons*)

CHAPTER 14

RIVERS AND CANALS

From the end of the Roman occupation until the mid-eighteenth century rivers were the main arteries of communication in Britain. They formed natural highways and were of paramount importance in influencing the settlement of people, the location of towns and the development of trade and commerce. Although susceptible to drought and flooding, rivers offered much greater reliability than roads, particularly where these crossed clay country. The Romans not only supplemented their comprehensive road system by river transport but sought to improve the latter with embankments. In the case of the Trent and the Witham they even cut a canal – the Fossdyke (Torksey Lock, SK 837781 to Brayford Pool, Lincoln, SK 970713) – in order to establish direct communication between them. A thousand years elapsed before any further improvements were carried out, although legislative procedures established rights of navigation over many rivers. There were numerous obstructions, however, shallows in dry weather, fishgarths for catching fish, and the dams and weirs of millowners being the major difficulties. In the sixteenth century eight Acts were passed dealing with rivers and the improvement of navigation, including one in 1571 to bring the River Lee to the north of London by making an artificial cut. By 1750, on the eve of the great era of canal building, Britain had 1,000 odd miles of navigable river, some of which, such as the Aire & Calder from 1699, had only been rendered navigable by the construction of cuts and pound locks. The early river engineers, such as Andrew Yarranton (1619–84?), had accumulated considerable experience of the problems of establishing navigations and their work, together with that of the fen drainers, provided the essential technological foundation for the canal engineers of later years.

A prominent feature of many improved rivers was the flashlock, which had its origins in the Middle Ages, often as a compromise between navigation and milling interests. Where water was impounded for a mill, a device was needed to pass boats through the weirs; and in between mills also, weirs were often necessary to maintain adequate depths of water for navigation. If a section of the weir was made removable, usually by the insertion of a gate, boats could pass through. These flashlocks, when opened, resulted in a powerful flush of water running downstream and boats simply 'shooting the rapids'. Those going upstream had to wait until the main force of water had subsided, when they were winched through the lock against the flow. The lock would then be closed and the water level allowed to build up for the next vessel. In a dry summer this might take several days and could, in extreme conditions, prevent navigation altogether. In many cases these flashlocks were replaced by pound locks, similar to those found on canals today, for flashlocks were highly dangerous and wasteful of time and water. A variation of the flashlock, usually known as a staunch, operated on a similar principle but was normally kept open to the river flow. Staunches were installed where flashlocks or pound locks were not always desirable, particularly on rivers with numerous mills, as impounded water would tend to back up the tailraces of waterwheels and reduce their efficiency. Also, if a river was crossed by a ford, as for example at Tempsford on the

Great Ouse [TL 161542], it was essential that the river level was not increased at the crossing point. The method of operation of staunches was even more tedious than that of the flashlocks, a man usually preceding the boat to close the gates and allow sufficient water to build up.

Most flashlocks and staunches took the form of vertically hinged gates; these were rarely single but generally a pair of mitre gates like those on any canal lock. The angle between them was commonly 90 degrees, in contrast to the 120 or 130 degrees of canal and more modern river locks. In East Anglia guillotine staunches were sometimes used and then the gate was raised vertically like a sash window and the boats passed underneath. A third and very simple type consisted of planks let into vertical slots in masonry walls, and was similar to the stop-planks commonly used on canals to isolate sections for repair. Perhaps the oldest form, however, was the beam and paddle weir, in which a beam was swung horizontally over a wooden cill across the bed of the lock. When closed, vertical boards or 'rimers' were put between beam and cill, and against these were set square planks with handles to hold back the water.

Most of the remaining flashlocks are decayed and ruinous, but a fine and nearly complete beam and paddle type can be seen on a small tributary of the Thames just below Eynsham Lock [SP 446089], Oxfordshire. Although traffic on this ½ mile navigation to Eynsham Wharf ceased in 1925, the beam still survives, bolted to the stop-post and supporting a foot-bridge. A substantially complete staunch on the Great Ouse survives at Castle Mills [TL 094509], with brickwork, c1840, intact and the decrepit remains of gates. Its purpose was to deepen the shallows below Castle Mills Lock, 300yd above. Tuddenham Mill Stream, a tributary of the Lark, which in turn flows into the Great Ouse, also has a well preserved gate staunch [TL 732729], with mitre gates, each with a single paddle (or sluice). There is a guillotine staunch, complete except for the spoked wheel used to lift the gate, at Bottisham Lode [TL 516651], which probably dates from the 1820s and was in use until

navigation on this obscure tributary of the Cam ceased about 1900.

Like the navigable rivers, canals were chiefly used to move heavy bulky goods for which roads were unsuitable. Britain was slow to begin building canals, but, once started, quick to extend a network over much of England, with separate systems in Wales and Scotland (Illus 197, 199). By 1850 the 1,000 miles of river navigation that had existed in 1750 had been expanded to a total of 4,250 miles as a result of canal building. The first canals were dug to connect or supplement existing river navigations or to link otherwise isolated agricultural or industrial communities with navigable water. The Exeter Canal, completed in 1566, was the first 'deadwater navigation' in the British Isles. It was followed in England by the Sankey Brook Navigation from the St Helens coalfield in south Lancashire to the River Mersey. Financed by Liverpool merchants, salt refiners and the town corporation, it was substantially complete by 1757 and can undoubtedly claim the distinction of being England's first canal. Its economic success was immediate and high dividends were paid. Soon after came the Bridgewater Canal, built by John Gilbert and James Brindley (1716–72) to connect the Duke of Bridgewater's collieries at Worsley with Manchester. On its completion in 1761, the price of coal in Manchester dropped by half. The canal revolution had begun.

James Brindley, the 'father of English canals', was born in Derbyshire and began work as an apprentice wheelwright and millwright at Sutton near Macclesfield. By 1742, at the age of twenty-six, he had his own business in Leek, where Brindley Mill [SJ 977570] survives as a memorial to his early career. His considerable abilities became well known in Staffordshire and brought him for the first time into contact with a canal scheme, to connect the Trent and Mersey rivers, for which he was asked to carry out a survey. The Trent and Mersey project was to remain a dream for some years, but it was his work in connection with it that brought Brindley to the notice of the Duke of Bridgewater and gained him his first definite commission for a canal. The 'Bridgewater', and the masonry aqueduct which Brindley designed to take his canal over the River Irwell, fired the imagination of the age. The three great arches carried the canal 38ft above the level of the river, enabling flats (sailing barges) to pass beneath. Completed in July 1761, it became a local wonder – 'Vessels o'er vessels, water under water, *Bridgewater* triumphs – art has conquered nature.' It survived until 1893, when construction of the Manchester Ship Canal, which was built largely on the site of the Mersey & Irwell Navigation, necessitated its demolition. The abutments, however, can still be seen [SJ 767977], and give an indication of the massive construction. The replacement is a still more remarkable structure, a unique swinging aqueduct designed by Sir E. Leader Williams, engineer of the Ship Canal. A pivoted steel tank 235ft long, 18ft wide and 6ft deep provides a crossing for the Bridgewater 26ft above the Manchester Ship Canal. When passage of the ship canal is required, the tank is swung by hydraulic power on its central pier, the total weight of the span and its load of water being 1,450 tons. The first barge passed over Barton swing aqueduct on 21 August 1893, and Brindley's pioneer structure was then demolished.

At the west end of the Bridgewater Canal, Worsley Mine was an integral part of the project, and the line of the canal was continued into the vertical rock face at Worsley Delph [SD 748005] to form the basis of an underground network of waterways on which the coal was brought out. Underground channels known as soughs were in use before 1750 for draining coal workings north of Worsley, and it seems probable that these were adapted to give direct access by boat between the coal-faces and the main line canal. James Brindley was closely involved with the underground scheme in its early years, as was John Gilbert, the duke's superintendent engineer, agent and surveyor, who was probably responsible for extending it in the years down to his death in 1795. The network grew steadily until about 1840, when some 46 miles of underground waterways extended under Walkden and Farnworth. To tap deeper seams, separate systems were also dug at levels below the main line and connected to it by shafts; the deepest was 83ft below the level of the entrance tunnels. Further north a higher level system was connected to the main level by a 150yd underground inclined plane on which the boats were worked on wheeled cradles running on rails. At the Delph can be seen the two entrances to this system, cut about 30ft apart in the rock face. Note also the hand-crane with a wooden gib used for inserting the stop-

195 Barton swing aqueduct, Eccles, across the Manchester Ship Canal [SJ 767976] (*Neil Cossons*)

planks [SD 747004] and the drydocks on the Bridgewater Canal. Examples of the long narrow boats, nicknamed 'starvationers', which were used in the tunnels can be seen in the Boat Museum, Dockyard Road, Ellesmere Port [SJ 405775].

Following the success of the Bridgewater the number of canals multiplied rapidly before 1773 and after 1787, the movement reaching a crescendo in the 'mania' of 1789–93. Three main types were developed – wide canals for some main lines, particularly those associated with rivers; narrow canals, with 7ft locks, for hilly inland routes that frequently suffered from poor water supplies; and tub-boat canals, where gradients were particularly steep. Wide canals were built mainly in Lancashire and Yorkshire, in the East Midlands, and in the south wherever connection with tidal water was important. The gauge was usually about 14ft. The pattern of the narrow waterways was set by the Staffordshire & Worcestershire, largely engineered by Thomas Dadford, Senior, one of Brindley's assistants, and Trent & Mersey canals, completed in 1772 and 1777 respectively. The need to economise on constructional costs where large numbers of locks and tunnels were needed resulted in major concentrations of narrow canals round Birmingham and also in South Wales. Tub-boat canals were built in Shropshire and the South West. Within these groups there were numerous minor variations, but, generally speaking, a *narrow boat* 70ft by 7ft could travel anywhere south of the Rivers Trent and Mersey, except on the tub-boat canals, and a *barge* 58ft by 13ft 6in anywhere north of that line. Larger barges worked on the river navigations.

The lack of uniformity in canal size and the total absence of planning prevented the canal network from ever being an integrated system. The geography of Britain meant heavily locked waterways, with consequent problems of water supply for summit levels; and many areas, notably much of Scotland, the far north of England and the south-west peninsula, were quite unsuited to artificial waterways. The web of canals was densest in the industrial Midlands where Birmingham, first en-

tered by canal in 1772, became a focus of waterways. The estuaries of the Thames, Severn, Humber and Mersey were soon connected, the Pennines traversed, and London linked with the Midlands and North. In the south of England more than 430 miles of canal were dug, but with one or two exceptions few navigations paid dividends higher than 5 per cent. Of little industrial importance, the largely agricultural south did not have the traffic potential to make profits. By contrast such waterways as the Aire & Calder network, the Loughborough Navigation in Leicestershire and the Trent & Mersey Canal carried huge quantities of raw materials and manufactured goods. In 1824 the last two were paying dividends of 197 per cent and 75 per cent respectively. In South Wales too a series of short and generally unconnected canals provided for the thriving coal and iron trade of the valleys, stimulating the growth of coastal centres such as Cardiff and Newport, and supplying coking coal and iron ore to great ironworks complexes such as those at Merthyr Tydfil. The terrain in much of South Wales, and parts of the North East around the valleys of the Tyne and Wear, was totally unsuited to canal construction, however, and in these areas parallel development of horse tramroads began, to feed canals or rivers.

As already mentioned, the early canals were built as cheaply as possible. A typical 'Brindley' canal, such as the Staffordshire & Worcestershire, follows the contours with hardly an embankment or cutting of any size upon it. The extra length resulting from their winding courses mattered little when boatmen's wages were low and effective competition non-existent. The threat of road and railway competition led to an increase in the efficiency and enterprise of waterways and to efforts at improvement. Harecastle Tunnel [SJ 837542 to 849517] on the Trent & Mersey canal was doubled in 1827, the new tunnel (16ft high and 14ft wide) taking only 3 years to build in contrast to the 11 years taken for the original bore (12ft high by 9ft 3in wide) of the 1770s. Engineering techniques had improved. In other cases routes were shortened, a not-

196 Ellesmere Port [SJ 405775] now the home of the Boat Museum (*Neil Cossons*)

able example of the straightening of a contour canal being the Oxford, which was reduced from 91 to 77½ miles between 1829 and 1834. New canals themselves were made as straight as possible, even at the expense of considerable civil engineering work to maintain the level. Thus Telford's Birmingham & Liverpool Junction (now the Shropshire Union main line), completed in 1835, has long stretches of embankment and cutting, including the 2 mile long Tyrley Cutting [SJ 693315], the deepest in the country.

The obstacles facing canal engineers were overcome in a variety of ways. Locks were the normal method of climbing hills, tunnels and cuttings for going through them and aqueducts for crossing rivers or valleys. The river improvers with their flashlocks and staunches anticipated the common pound lock used on most canals in England. A century after its first known use in continental Europe, in 1373, the pound lock was in use on river navigations in Britain. It consisted of lifting or swinging gates enclosing a 'pound' of water of sufficient length to accommodate a boat. On the River Wey, made navigable from the Thames to Guildford, Surrey, under an Act of 1651, pound locks with turf sides, now reinforced, have survived in substantially original form, as at Paper-

court [TQ 034568] and Walsham Gates [TQ 050578]. Sheffield Lock on the Kennet Navigation, Berkshire [SU 649706], is also turf-sided.

On canals the lock evolved with a brick or masonry pound, generally rectangular in plan and of the minimum dimensions capable of handling the largest type of craft using the canal. Thus the smallest amount of water was consumed. In the Midlands a typical 'narrow' lock has a chamber 7ft wide and about 76ft long designed for boats of 6ft 10in beam and up to 72ft in length. The extra length of the chamber allows for the inward-opening bottom gates. The mode of operation is simple. A boat working down requires a full lock to enter. When the boat is in the chamber and the gates are closed, sluices, usually known in this context as paddles, at the lower end or tail of the lock are opened and as soon as the levels inside and outside are the same, the gates can be opened and the boat passes through. In locking up the procedure is followed in reverse.

Lock gates are generally of timber, oak being most commonly used, although on the Montgomeryshire and Ellesmere

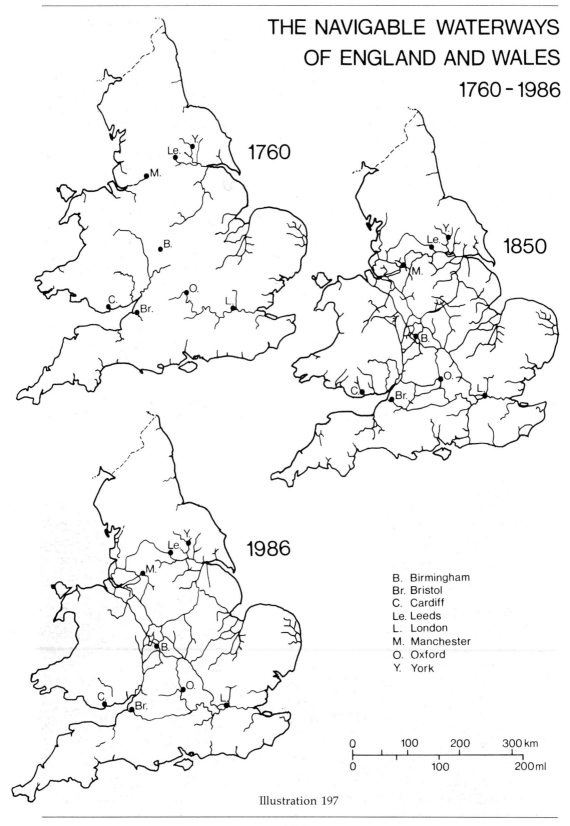

THE NAVIGABLE WATERWAYS
OF ENGLAND AND WALES
1760 - 1986

1760

1850

1986

B. Birmingham
Br. Bristol
C. Cardiff
Le. Leeds
L. London
M. Manchester
O. Oxford
Y. York

| 0 | 100 | 200 | 300 km |
| 0 | | 100 | 200 ml |

Illustration 197

canals cast iron gates were used in the early nineteenth century. A pair from the former canal can be seen at the Waterways Museum, Stoke Bruerne, Northamptonshire [SP 743500]. The gates at the tail of the lock are the heavier because they extend the full depth of the lock, whereas those at the upper end or head need only be the depth of the upper pound of the canal. Double gates are generally used on river navigations and barge canals, but in narrow locks single top gates and double bottom gates are commonly found. Both upper and lower gates bed against a cill at the bottom of the chamber, the upper cill being exposed when the lock is empty. Cills are often made of timber, although concrete has been increasingly used in recent years. Gates have a vertical timber at the hinge end known as the heel post which fits into a hollow quoin in the masonry wall of the lock. Only a light iron strap is needed to maintain the gate in place as water pressure holds the heel post tightly into the quoin when the gate is closed. The outer end of the gate also has a vertical post called a breast or mitre post, which fits a rebate in the opposite wall of

the lock or, in the case of double gates, the equivalent post of the partner gate. A gate is operated by a balance beam, which, as the name suggests, provides the counterweight to the gate itself. Traditionally this beam was of timber but in many modern replacement gates rolled steel joists with concrete balance weights have been used. The guillotine gate is not common on British canals, but examples can be found on the old Shropshire Canal section of the Shropshire Union north of Hadley [SJ 672133] and at King's Norton stop-lock at the junction of the Stratford-upon-Avon Canal with the Worcester & Birmingham [SP 053795]. Modern guillotine gates can be seen on the Rivers Nene and Great Ouse, where their use more easily enables flood water to run through the lock.

Locks are filled and emptied by sluices, generally known as paddles but also called slackers in the Fens and cloughs in the North of England. Gate paddles fitted on the lock gates themselves are found at head and tail of most river navigation

198 Gailey Lock on the Staffordshire & Worcestershire Canal [SJ 920104]   (*Neil Cossons*)

THE NAVIGABLE WATERWAYS OF SCOTLAND

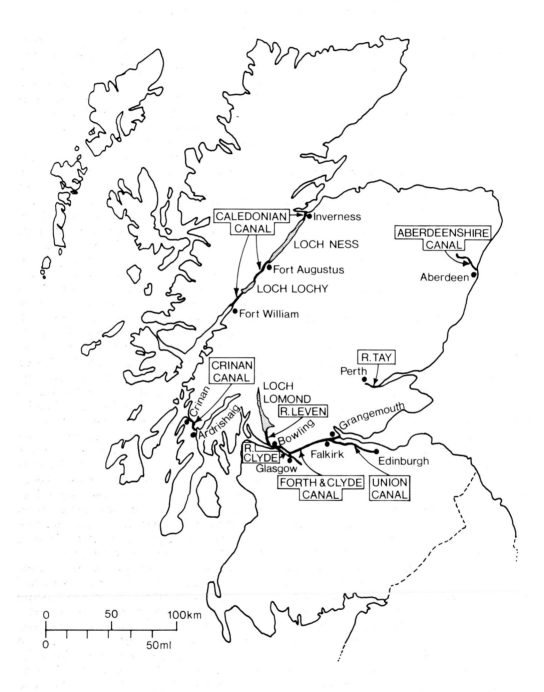

Illustration 199

locks, and on the tail gates and occasionally head gates of canal locks. Ground paddles are mounted in the wall of the lock and admit water through culverts; they are generally used in combination with gate paddles at the head of a lock. Ground paddles used for drawing off water from a lock are rare features but can be seen on some of the wide locks on the stretch of the Grand Union between Napton and Birmingham. The paddle itself usually consists of a slab of elm that slides vertically in a frame across the sluice aperture. A wide variety of mechanisms for lifting or drawing paddles can be found, the most common being the rack and pinion arrangement incorporating a pawl to hold the paddle in the drawn position. Worm-and-nut gearing is used on the ground paddles of the Leeds & Liverpool Canal, and on the same navigation pivoted gate paddles can be found, a very rare feature. On the River Wey at Worsfold Gates, near Send, Surrey [TQ 016557], some paddles still operate in their most primitive form; they are lifted by hand and held in position by pegs through holes in the handles. Nearby are the Navigation's workshops, which are still in use. Nowadays, of course, many locks are mechanised, as on the Caledonian and Aire & Calder Canals and the rivers Trent and Thames.

Groups or 'flights' of locks are commonly found on canals where great differences in level occur in a relatively short distance. The largest flight in Britain is at Tardebigge on the Worcester & Birmingham Canal, where thirty narrow locks raise the canal 217ft in about 2 miles. The summit lock at Tardebigge is, in fact, the deepest narrow lock in the country, with a fall of 14ft; this is exceptional and the average is 6–8ft. A flight almost equal to Tardebigge can be seen at Devizes, where the Kennet & Avon Canal climbs out of the Vale of Pewsey through twenty-nine wide locks. This flight is far more spectacular, however, as the locks are very close together and most of them in a straight line. At Combe Hay [ST 748604] on the Somersetshire Coal Canal one can see most of the locks of a flight of twenty-two completed in 1805 after the failure of a novel boat lift. The canal was closed in the 1890s, and later part of its bed was utilised for the Limpley Stoke to Hallatrow branch of the Great Western Railway, opened in 1910.

A variation on the simple flight of locks is the staircase, where the top gate of one lock forms the bottom gate of the one above. A notable example is to be seen at Foxton [SP 692895] where the Leicester line of the Grand Union Canal descends by means of two staircases, each of five locks. To economise in the use of water – always important to the canal operator – sideponds were frequently built in association with staircases of locks, and these are used at Foxton. The side-pond consists of a chamber beside the locks at a level halfway between the upper and lower pounds and communicating with the pounds by culverts controlled by ground paddles (side-pond paddles). When a boat enters the full pound and the gates are closed, the side-pond paddle is opened first, until the levels equate and slightly less than half the water is in the side-pond. The side-pond paddle is then closed and the remainder of the water in the lock released into the lower pound in the normal way. The saving occurs when a boat locking up enters the empty lock, which can then be almost half-filled with water from the side-pond. Thus only the remaining half has to be drawn from the upper pond. A well known staircase of wide locks is Bingley 'Five Rise' [SE 108400] on the Leeds & Liverpool Canal. Here there are no sideponds and water passes direct from chamber to chamber. The largest staircase in Britain, of eight locks, is at Banavie [NN 114770] on the Caledonian Canal.

A curious and unique flight of three locks is to be seen at the Bratch [SO 867938] on the Staffordshire & Worcestershire Canal, where at first sight the locks appear to be arranged in a staircase. However, each lock has its own gates, the top gate of one lock being only a few feet from the lower gates of the lock above. Further south at Botterham [SO 860914] on the same canal is a double lock or rise of normal type with a common gate between the two chambers, while to the north lies Compton top lock [SO 884989], said to be the first lock built by Brindley. It is interesting to speculate as to whether Brindley, or perhaps Thomas Dadford, devised the principle of the staircase immediately after building the Bratch locks or whether he was already aware of continental examples, such as the staircase at Béziers on the Canal du Midi in France. Other locks of interest include the sectional cast iron lock chambers at Beeston [SJ 554599] in Cheshire, devised by Telford to overcome the problems of soft sand, and Northgate Locks, Chester [SJ 403666], which are partly cut in solid rock. On the Staffordshire & Worcestershire Canal circular weirs instead of the normal straight cill type are used for the culverts that convey surplus water from the head to the tail of some of the locks.

Besides problems of water supply, long flights of locks imposed considerable delays to traffic, particularly where this was heavy. Thus from as early as the 1780s canal engineers sought means of replacing locks with other mechanisms such as inclined planes, lifts and a variety of patent balance-lock and caisson devices. In Britain no inclined planes remain in use, but their overgrown alignments, often almost completely obscured by trees and undergrowth, can still be found here and there. There were twenty or so in south-west England alone, notably on the Bude Canal and the Torrington Canal in north Devon. On both these, canal tub boats were used which had wheels permanently fitted to them so that they could be hauled up and down the inclines on rails. Perhaps the most spectacular and well-preserved canal incline, also used by tub boats, is at Coalport in Shropshire [SJ 695028]. Here the Hay Inclined Plane bridges the vertical fall of 207ft between the upper line of the canal and the basin at the foot of the Severn Gorge with its short link downstream to Coalport where goods were transhipped from the tub boats into sailing barges – Severn trows – on the river.

The incline installed at Foxton, Leicestershire [SP 692895] in 1900 was part of a grand scheme to enable 14ft barges to work through from the Thames to the Trent, but because another incline at Watford was never built only narrow boats ever used it. The incline was of the counterbalanced type, with movable tanks or caissons on wheels into which the boats were floated. A steam engine at the top provided power but trouble was experienced with subsidence of the rails and the volume of traffic did not justify the expense of keeping a boiler in steam with staff in attendance. The incline had ceased to be used regularly by 1910 and the machinery was sold for scrap in 1928. Today the original locks are in active use, and the unfortunate incline, having returned to nature, has had much of the undergrowth cleared by volunteers in recent years.

The only canal lift still in use in Britain is that at Anderton [SJ 647753], near Northwich. It allows boats to pass between the Trent & Mersey Canal and the River Weaver Navigation some 50ft below. A proposal for a lift had been put forward as early as 1865 by E. Leader Williams, engineer to the Weaver Navigation, with the idea of facilitating the interchange of traffic between the two waterways, but not until 1872 were the necessary Acts passed and Emmerson & Co given the lift contract. The design was by Edwin Clark of Clark, Standfield & Clark, consulting engineers of Westminster. As completed in 1875, the Anderton lift had two wrought iron caissons 75ft × 15½ft × 5ft rising and falling a distance of 50ft 4in within a substantial tubular iron framework. Each caisson could take two narrow boats or one barge and weighed 240 tons with its water. The caissons were supported on 3ft diameter hydraulic rams, the two rams being connected by a 5in pipe. Removing 6in of water, weighing some 15 tons, from the lower caisson made the heavier upper caisson descend, and water passed through the transfer pipe to the other ram caused the second caisson to rise. The final lift of 4ft was achieved by closing the transfer pipe and connecting the upper press to a steam-powered hydraulic pump and accumulator. Although a press burst in 1882, the Anderton design was a good one and formed the basis for other lifts in France and Belgium. In 1903 electricity replaced steam power for the hydraulic pumps and in 1908 further substantial modifications dispensed with hydraulic operation altogether in order to simplify working and increase capacity. As rebuilt, the lift's caissons are counterbalanced by cast iron weights and can be operated independently. Power is provided by an electric motor driving through gears. In 1913 the lift transferred a record 226,000 tons of traffic, more than would have been possible before reconstruction. Today, after extensive renovation, it is still in regular use, mainly by pleasure boats, and a 'voyage' in it is a fascinating if slightly unnerving experience. One may make an excellent trip, from Weston docks, Runcorn [SJ 503830], up through the large 220ft × 41½ft locks of the Weaver to Anderton and up the lift, and then along the Trent & Mersey Canal through three tortuously narrow tunnels to the delightful little canal hamlet of Preston Brook. Here, at the junction of the Trent & Mersey and Bridgewater Canals [SJ 568806] are canal cottages, a large warehouse now used as a club, and a small roofed drydock.

On many canals there was no alternative to a tunnel when it came to cutting through hilly country. Canal tunnels are usually, although by no means always, on the summit level, crossing the watershed between one side of the navigation and the other. The first were on the Trent & Mersey Canal at Preston Brook (1,239yd) [SJ 570799], Saltersford (424yd) [SJ 624753], Barnton (572yd) [SJ 630749], and Harecastle. The latter, with its 2,880yd bore, carried the summit level under Harecastle Hill, the watershed between the valley of the Trent and the Cheshire plain. The original tunnel at Harecastle, like others on the canal, had a very small bore – only 9ft 3in wide and 12ft high [SJ 837542]. Boats had to be legged through, the 'leggers' lying on narrow boards sprung out from either side of the boat and walking on the sides of the tunnel to push it through. In 1827 a new tunnel, parallel with the old, was completed to designs of Thomas Telford. It was of large section and had a towpath, but this has now been demolished. For some ninety years both tunnels were worked on a one-way system, but eventu-

ally in 1918 colliery subsidence necessitated the closure of the older bore.

Of even smaller section than the old Harecastle tunnel is Standedge tunnel [SE 006079 to 040120] on the Huddersfield Narrow Canal, which in places is only 8ft 6in high and 7ft 6in wide. Standedge, completed in 1811, is the longest canal tunnel in Britain (5,698yd) and on the highest summit above sea level. The 4½ mile level through the Pennines between Diggle and Marsden is 645ft above Ordnance datum. Although the canal was abandoned in 1944, the tunnel is still navigable. A through passage in a properly organised party is an eerie experience, as the bore opens out at intervals into caverns blasted in the rock where boats can pass. A faint glimmer of light penetrates occasionally through the ventilation shafts, and the rumble of trains in the neighbouring railway tunnel sounds through the interconnecting galleries used by the engineers of half a century later to gain access to their workings. Several of the larger canal tunnels are now impassable, although in most cases their portals and ventilation shaft tops can still be traced. The 3,817yd Sapperton Tunnel in Gloucestershire, on the summit level of the Thames & Severn Canal beneath the Cotswolds, is waterless and in part collapsed. For some years before its closure in 1911 the canal had water supply problems, owing largely to the dry and porous limestone country through which it passed. The east portal [SO 965006] of Sapperton is one of the few canal tunnel entrances to have any architectural pretensions, with two niches (but no statues) flanked by finely cut pilasters. The west portal [SO 944034] by contrast is very simple.

The 3,795yd Lappal Tunnel between Halesowen and Selly Oak on the Birmingham Canal has, like Harecastle, suffered from mining subsidence and collapsed. So too has Norwood Tunnel, 2,895yd, on the Chesterfield Canal, and Butterley Tunnel, 3,063yd, on the Cromford Canal. The longest tunnel still in regular use on a through navigation in Britain was Blisworth [SP 729529 to 739503], 3,056yd, on the Grand Union Canal in Northamptonshire until the restoration of Parkhead locks put the 3,172yd Dudley Tunnel on a pleasure craft route. Blisworth Tunnel caused its builders a great deal of trouble, the result of geological complications and faulty brickmaking. Work stopped in 1796, and it was not until 1802 that a new start was made with another tunnel on a slightly different line to designs by William Jessop (1745–1814). This was eventually completed in March 1805, nearly five years after the rest of the canal had opened. Before the tunnel was finished, a double-track horse tramroad ran over the hill from Blisworth Wharf to what is now the foot of Stoke Bruerne locks. Time in the Blisworth area will be well spent in a visit to the Canal Museum at Stoke Bruerne [SP 743500], where there are a number of open-air exhibits, including a boat-weighing machine, plus a unique collection housed in an old grain warehouse covering the rich history of 200 years of canals and their people.

Of all the engineering works of the great canal builders, aqueducts have fired the imagination and excited the greatest wonder. Designed to bridge valleys that could not easily be negotiated by flights of locks, they were objects of incredulity at the time they were built. Many have survived the railway age, which had its own proliferation of great viaducts, with their splendour undiminished. Brindley's pioneer Barton Aqueduct – 'the castle in the air', Smeaton is alleged to have called it – has already been mentioned. In fact it was the highest and visually most spectacular of Brindley's numerous aqueducts, most of which are squat brick or masonry structures providing little more than multiple culverts for the rivers underneath. The Dove Aqueduct [SK 269269] on the Trent & Mersey Canal near Burton-on-Trent is a typical example. With approaches it is 1¼ miles long and has twenty-three low arches. Others carry the Staffordshire & Worcestershire Canal over the Trent at Great Haywood [SJ 994229] and the Sow at Milford [SJ 973215].

William Edwards' precedent of pierced spandrels, which appeared in his graceful Pontypridd Bridge of 1755, was used by Benjamin Outram, engineer to the Peak Forest Canal, when he built Marple Aque-

200 Dundas Aqueduct near Limpley Stoke, Wiltshire [ST 784625]   (Neil Cossons)

duct [SJ 956900] across the River Goyt. Designed to reduce the structure's self-weight, the holes also visually lighten and enhance the appearance of the aqueduct. For real elegance and panache, however, the masonry aqueducts of John Rennie (1761–1821) are unsurpassed. Of classical proportions and detailing, his Dundas Aqueduct (Illus 200), a single-arch span carrying the Kennet & Avon Canal over the River Avon near Monkton Combe [ST 784625] in Wiltshire blends into the steep wooded valley and completes the landscape in a very English way. The warm limestone provides a perfect medium for an architectural treatment of the structure appropriate to nearby Bath. Three miles to the south the canal recrosses the river at Avoncliff [ST 805600], but here neither the design nor the present condition of the structure are as good. The stonework is covered with mysterious masons' marks; the sag in the centre of the river span is thought to have occurred soon after the aqueduct was completed in 1805. A larger and more severe example of Rennie's work is the Lune Aqueduct, Lancaster [SD 484639], which has five arches, each of 70ft span, carrying the Lancaster Canal 51ft above the surface of the river. Built in a hard grey sandstone, its top decorated with a handsome Doric cornice and balustrade, it too blends into the harsher north Lancashire landscape, a fine combination of functional simplicity and elegance in design. The architect, Alexander Stevens (1730–96), possibly collaborated with Rennie on its detailing.

The supreme heights of engineering accomplishment resulted from the use of cast iron in the building of aqueducts, although, unlike the first iron bridge, the earliest examples had an experimental lack of confidence. Possibly the first use of the material was in a small aqueduct in Derby, now demolished, but here it formed only a part of the whole. One month after the opening of the Derby structure, in March 1796, the crossing of the river at Longdon-on-Tern in Shropshire was completed [SJ 617156] with an aqueduct in which cast iron had real structural significance, not only in the construction of the trough itself but also in the supporting legs and partly cantilevered towpath. Thomas Telford, who made the claim, 'I believe this to be the first aqueduct for the purposes of a navigable canal which has ever been composed of this metal' has for long been credited with its design and construction but there can be little doubt that William Reynolds (1758–1803) the ironmaster of Ketley, had an important role, probably suggested the idea, certainly made the castings and may well have designed them too. Telford put it up. Longdon-on-Tern Aqueduct is a modest structure, with two full spans, one across the river, and two half spans springing from the brick and masonry abutments. The cast iron sections are arranged in a similar manner to the voussoirs of a masonry arch and bolted together through flanges. The towpath is attached to the outside of the trough, which is thus of the minimum cross-section necessary for a boat to pass. This presented a problem in that great effort was needed to pull a boat through as it was difficult for water to flow between the sides and bottom of the boat and the trough itself. Longdon undoubtedly provided valuable experience for the later construction of Pont Cysyllte Aqueduct [SJ 271420] and this particular design feature was not repeated there; at Pont Cysyllte the towpath projects inwards over a wide trough, leaving plenty of space for the water to pass.

201 Claverton pumping station, Avon [ST 791644], designed by John Rennie to lift water from the River Avon into the Kennet & Avon Canal; the beam pumps were driven by a 17ft 6in diameter waterwheel   (*Neil Cossons*)

It was the Ellesmere Canal, an ambitious project intended originally to link the waterways of the Severn, Dee and Mersey that was to pose some of the greatest challenges to the canal engineer in Britain. The promoters chose William Jessop, a man who less than two years later the Grand Junction Canal Company also engaged as 'from his experience and abilities looked upon as the first engineer of the kingdom'. Jessop was undoubtedly experienced and certainly a man capable of tackling the difficult task of carrying the canal across the valleys of the rivers Ceiriog and Dee as part of a project to tap the coal and iron district around Ruabon and the Irenant quarries near Valle Crucis, Llangollen. In 1793 Jessop, then nearly 49, took on the 36 year old Thomas Telford as 'General Agent, Surveyor, Engineer, Architect and Overlooker of the Works', a part-time appointment for a man who, as already seen in Chapter 13, was also to become a great civil engineer of bridges and roads, but at that time was unacquainted with canal construction. This is not the place to measure the respective roles of Jessop and Telford in building the two greatest aqueducts in Britain; what is clear however is that Jessop's contribution has been greatly underestimated and in terms of conception and design was almost

202   Pont Cysyllte Aqueduct, Clwyd [SJ 271420] (*Neil Cossons*)

certainly greater.

The aqueduct across the Ceiriog at Chirk [SJ 287372] has always been somewhat overshadowed by the proximity of its great neighbour, but on any other canal it would be regarded as an outstanding work. It has ten arches, each of 40ft span, carrying the canal 70ft above the river. Although the structure of the piers and arches is of stone and appears conventional in every respect, the trough itself consists of cast iron plates, flanged and bolted together, which effectively tie in the side walls of the aqueduct. It was appreciated that a puddle-clay lined trough of the type used by Brindley, together with the massive masonry necessary to contain the pressure of water, would impose impossible weights on the foundations of the piers; hence the use of cast iron. The foundation stone of Chirk Aqueduct was laid on 17 June 1796 and it was completed in 1801.

The canal runs north from the aqueduct through the 459yd Chirk Tunnel (one of the first to have a towpath) towards the much larger valley of the Dee. Here, at Pont Cysyllte [SJ 271420], across the Vale of Llangollen, the canal is carried more than 120ft above the river on an aqueduct which has remained one of the great engineering achievements of all time. Compared with the alternative, of locks down each side of the valley, an aqueduct seems the obvious solution; it is the scale

and sheer engineering elegance of that solution, however, which gives Pont Cysyllte a justified place amongst the industrial archaeological sights of Britain.

At Pont Cysyllte, as we have said, a trough construction entirely of cast iron was adopted, and the side sections, as at Longdon, are wedge shaped to form an arch-like structure. Unlike Longdon, however, the trough is supported underneath by cross-braced cast iron ribs (Illus 202), four beneath each span. The trough width is 11ft 10in and the deck of the towpath, 4ft 8in wide, is supported over the water surface on iron pillars. Cast iron railings protect its outer edge, but on the opposite side the water level is only a few inches below the unprotected edge of the trough wall. Nineteen spans, each of 53ft, make a total length of 1,007ft between the approach embankments, the south one of which, with its height of 97ft at the tip, was the greatest earthwork in Britain at the time of its construction. The piers supporting the trough are of some interest in that, to reduce weight, they are of hollow construction from a height of 70ft upwards, with external walls only 2ft thick. Internal cross walls, used also in the hollow spandrels of Chirk Aqueduct and most of Telford's road bridges, provide the necessary structural stiffening. Today the Pont Cysyllte Aqueduct has much the same appearance as it did on its opening day in November 1805 and, although neglected and in ill-repair for many years, it is now Scheduled as an Ancient Monument by the Department of the Environment and kept in a sound condition befitting perhaps the greatest single engineering epic of the canal age.

As the network of canals spread and the internal trade of the nation developed, a whole new transport industry supporting merchants, boatmen, suppliers of provisions, warehousemen, lock-keepers and lengthmen grew up also. This industry made its impact on the landscape in the form of new buildings ranging from tiny and uncompromisingly simple canal-side cottages to new townships with handsome mansions and warehouses. Few canal buildings exhibit any conscious architectural expression, and many of the

203   Narrow boats at Hawkesbury, Warwickshire [SP 362846], at the junction of the Coventry and Oxford Canals   (*Neil Cossons*)

smaller ones are a straightforward and economical translation of contemporary domestic traditions to new circumstances. Exceptions are inevitable and one only has to look at the Regency-style bridge-men's houses on the Gloucester & Berkeley Canal, the barrel-roofed Stratford-upon-Avon Canal cottages or the round-tower canal houses of the Thames & Severn to appreciate that here and there some architectural thought was involved. These are the exceptions, however, and the general rule, as exemplified by hundreds of little known and unpretentious structures, is in great contrast to the railway buildings of the following century.

At various places on the canal network junctions and transhipment points resulted in concentrations of canal-side buildings which in some cases have developed into independent communities. Some of these new towns of the canal era, small in comparison with the developments which were to occur in the age of the railways, still survive substantially intact and are among the earliest specialised industrial urban groupings in Britain. Perhaps the best known, and certainly the most highly developed of these communities, is Stourport-on-Severn [SO 810710], built at the end of the eighteenth century as a trading and transhipment centre where the Staffordshire & Worcestershire Canal locks down to the River Severn. It became, in effect, an inland port between the Midlands and the sea, where goods

204 Shardlow, Derbyshire [SK 444304], the inland port on the Trent & Mersey Canal near its junction with the River Trent (*Neil Cossons*)

could be transferred from canal narrow boats to river-going barges and sailing trows that voyaged down to Bristol and the South Wales ports. Here in Worcestershire Brindley 'caused a town to be erected, made a port and dockyards, built a new elegant bridge, established markets and made it the wonder not only of this county but of the nation at large.' Although the bridge was replaced by a larger cast iron span during the nineteenth century, the centre of Stourport has changed little. It just survived the neglect following the decline of canals and is now reviving as a leisure boating centre. A fine brick warehouse with clock tower, stately merchants' houses and humble cottages all reflect the unselfconscious inspiration of the early Industrial Revolution. At Shardlow [SK 444304], near the junction of the Trent & Mersey Canal and the River Trent, stands another such point of interchange, built purely for commercial purposes but exhibiting through the architecture of its warehouses a functional beauty deriving from the simple use of traditional building materials. Today

Shardlow is devoted to leisure boating and there is a canal museum. Warehouses of a more spectacular scale may be seen at Ellesmere Port [SJ 405775], another junction, between the Wirral line of Jessop and Telford's Ellesmere & Chester Canal and the River Mersey. Dating originally from 1795, Ellesmere Port continued to grow until the 1850s, suffered a temporary relapse, and thrived again after the com-

205,206,207,208 Completing the circle: Telford's great warehouse at Ellesmere Port [SJ 405775] in 1969, and two days after its destruction by fire in 1970. The site today is part of the Boat Museum. A number of redevelopment schemes have been considered including a proposal, now shelved, to 'recreate' the warehouses for residential and commercial use   *(Neil Cossons, The Boat Museum Trust)*

pletion of the Manchester Ship Canal in the 1890s, although its prosperity then no longer came from inland canal traffic. Unfortunately Telford's great general warehouse, one of the finest structures on Britain's waterways, has now gone, destroyed by fire in 1970, (Illus 205–208) but other impressive buildings still survive and the general arrangement and layout of the port and its facilities now form the home of the Boat Museum, a major inland waterway museum complex housing the largest collection of boats in Europe. Boat restoration takes place in the museum and there are comprehensive displays on canal history, the development of Ellesmere Port and the use of working horses on the canals. The four steam engines which powered the hydraulic power system are on view and in steam from time to time.

Today much of the canal network, the larger part of which is no longer used at all for commercial purposes, is undergoing a

transformation. Groups of enthusiasts working in cooperation with the British Waterways Board are energetically putting many of the more scenic routes back into commission for leisure purposes. The Stratford-upon-Avon Canal, the Peak Forest, Ashton and Caldon are all open again and work is proceeding on the Kennet & Avon where restoration of the twenty-nine locks at Devizes is the major outstanding task. Moreover, the amenity value of waterways is also being recognised by local authorities, and enterprising conservation schemes have been carried out in the Little Venice area of Paddington; at Farmer's Bridge, Birmingham, the junction of the Birmingham Canal Navigation main line and the Birmingham & Fazeley Canal; and at the nearby Gas Street basin. Tree planting, landscaping and the rehabilitation of derelict canal-side cottages all contribute to the success of schemes which amply demonstrate that the canal in an urban area does not have to be an eyesore.

Although the future of the narrow canal must lie in amenity use, there are a number of commercial waterways actively in operation and employing up-to-date cargo handling methods. Centred on the Humber are the Aire & Calder Navigation, giving access for 700 ton barges to Leeds and Wakefield, the South Yorkshire giving 700 ton access to Mexborough and 400 ton to Rotherham, and the Trent Navigation to Nottingham. The Weaver Navigation can take sizeable ships, as can the Gloucester & Sharpness Canal, a link in the navigation of the Severn up to Stourport. The South East has the Thames and the River Lee. Current freight waterway development is upon river navigations, such as the Yorkshire Ouse to Selby and the lower Trent to Gainsborough and this is likely to be the pattern in the future. Meanwhile the fate of the Manchester Ship Canal hangs in the balance. Opened in 1894 to provide Manchester with a navigable link to the Mersey, it has been a victim of containerisation with the retreat in 1977 to Ellesmere Port of Manchester Liners to be followed by other companies. With hardly any traffic Salford is contemplating developing the docks for tourism.

On the majority of inland navigations the commercial traffic that brought them into existence in the late eighteenth and early nineteenth centuries has gone for ever and only the archaeological remains reflect the buoyant enthusiasm, panache and grinding labour of the canal promoters, their engineers and navvies. Fortunately, for many who use canals for leisure boating the archaeology provides much of the attraction, be it engineering, architecture or merely a sense of the picturesque. It remains to be seen whether the canal system can stand up to the pressures of over-use which clearly present problems in some areas and the, fortunately few, examples of insensitive restoration in which preservation groups with more enthusiasm than technical skill or aesthetic sense fall far short of the qualities that their engineer and navvy forebears of two centuries ago applied with such unconscious ease. As in so many areas of industrial archaeological conservation, the reconciliation of re-use – and the opportunity of a viable future – with the integrity of the monument is a major issue.

209   Restoration of a lock on the Kennet & Avon Canal   (Neil Cossons)

CHAPTER 15

RAILWAYS

The railway captured the imagination of the people as did no other form of industrial technology. In Britain, the country of origin of the steam locomotive, and elsewhere too, the opening of a new railway line was almost always an occasion for festivities and rejoicing. A century or more later the demise of steam on British Railways in the late 1960s evoked a wave of nostalgia quite without precedent. Today more than 1,100 steam railway locomotives are preserved in Britain in museums, on privately owned branch lines, or merely on short stretches of track where they can be put into steam for a few hours at a weekend. The railway was the first form of transport with which the mass of the populace had any contact, and as such it has been regarded as rightfully subject to both public criticism and affection. Criticism of railways and their methods of operation has always been a fashionable sport, while affection, of almost equally long standing, has centred largely around the mystique of the steam locomotive. Much of the enormous bibliography which railways have generated is also devoted to steam power, so in this chapter the civil engineering works, the 'real estate' of the railways, will be considered primarily.

The idea of using rails for vehicular traffic dates back much further than the steam locomotive, and this early period, which might be called the 'prehistory' of railways, can be a fruitful area of study for the industrial archaeologist. The profusion of field remains and frequent wealth of documentary and cartographic information has enabled a remarkably complete picture to be built up of the role of the railway before the coming of steam power. Specifically archaeological evidence has made a major contribution. The first use of rails in Britain was probably in the late sixteenth century in Shropshire, Nottinghamshire and Northumberland. In these areas lines were built for moving coal relatively short distances to rivers or the coast, where boats could load it. The rails were made of wood, as at first were the wheels that ran on them. Not until the second quarter of the eighteenth century were iron wheels employed and wooden rails faced with iron plates to reduce wear.

The first known use of iron rails was in 1767. Cast at Coalbrookdale in Shropshire, they were thereafter used extensively on local lines in and around coal workings and also in South Wales. They were 'edge rails', designed for use with flanged wheels, and were probably laid on timber cross sleepers. In the 1780s iron rails of an 'L' section – with the flange cast on the rail instead of on the wheel – were introduced and quickly became popular. In South Wales, for example, some 300 route miles of this 'plateway' were in use in the early years of the nineteenth century, and in Shropshire, the birthplace of the iron edge rail, the L section plates became almost universal. The new rails were supposedly stronger than the edge rails, but it is doubtful if the other claimed benefit – that the vehicles could be used off the rails in colliery yards – was found to be particularly useful.

A note on terminology is relevant here, as a variety of sometimes conflicting nomenclature has been applied to these early pre-locomotive railways. All were technically railways, in that the vehicles ran on rails, although the term 'railroad' was more widely used before 1830 and was later adopted as standard in North America. In the North of England particularly, where edge rails were favoured, 'waggonway' was used, and this persisted until relatively recently. Elsewhere, however, 'tramroad', 'dramroad' and 'tramway' were after 1790 applied specifically to lines employing L section rails. The origin of these terms is uncertain, but they possibly derive from the old German or Scandinavian words for a beam of wood, a 'traam', which might have been the rail. Certainly 'trammy' and 'tram' were applied to the vehicles themselves in the sixteenth century. There is no evidence to support the theory that 'tramroad' had any connection with the name of Benjamin Outram, one of the chief protagonists of the cast-iron rail. Later in the nineteenth century, of course, the word tramway was revived in a different context, to describe the new passenger-carrying street tramways, first horse-drawn and later electrically propelled. Yet another word specifically applied to the early railways using L section iron rails was 'plateway', from which the modern term 'platelayer' originates.

Three distinct forms of pre-locomotive railway developed before 1830 and all were in operation side by side at the outbreak of the steam-powered railway revolution. The first type, as we have seen, comprised lines built and usually owned by coal owners to connect their collieries with existing river or sea transport. Successors to these, operated by British Coal in County Durham, include the Bowes Railway, with lines radiating south-westwards from Jarrow Staithes [NZ 353650] towards Pontop. A section of the Bowes Railway is preserved and operated by the Tyne & Wear Industrial Monuments Trust. The second type of tramway was built as an adjunct to a canal and was usually owned by the canal company. Tramways were less restricted by topography than canals, and from the 1780s onwards were built in large numbers as feeders to canal branches. The third variety came into being on 26 July 1803 when the Surrey Iron Railway was opened as a double-track public tramway from the Thames at Wandsworth to Croydon, 9 miles away. This line, which was seen as a possible first stage in a route from London to

210 The Causey Arch of 1727 across the Houghwelburn Ravine at Tanfield, County Durham [NZ 201559]   (E. H. Jeynes)

Portsmouth, heralded the era of public lines promoted as common carriers by separate railway companies.

Of the colliery-owned and operated lines, numerous remains survive, particularly in the North East. One of these remains, at Tanfield in County Durham, is the Causey Arch, built in 1727 and generally accepted as the oldest existing railway bridge (Illus 210) [NZ 201559]. It is a spectacular masonry structure about 60ft high, its span of 103ft the fifth largest of any masonry railway bridge in Britain. Near Whitfield, also south of the Tyne, early eighteenth-century tramway earthworks are to be seen at High Spen [NZ 137596].

One of the earliest surviving railway buildings is a weigh-house of 1799 at Brampton Sands, Cumbria [NY 550600], on the alignment of the Brampton Railway, an extension of the Parker Fell waggonway opened about 1775. Near Kirkhouse, cuttings and embankments are easily traceable [NY 567599], while the earthworks of the Parker waggonway, south of Whitehaven harbour, can be seen at Monkwray Brow [NX 969167]. This line, owned by Sir James Lowther, was opened in 1738.

The 6 mile Middleton Colliery Railway in Leeds, dating from 1758, was built under Parliamentary Acts and is thus claimed to be the first officially authorised railway. Not a great deal can be seen of the original alignment, but the incline, known as the 'Old Run', can still be traced and stone sleepers are visible on Hunslet Moor where they have been re-used as platform edging. A section of the railway is operated with steam locomotives by the Middleton Railway Trust.

Lines feeding canals are well represented archaeologically and, unlike the colliery lines which are mainly in the north, they are concentrated primarily in midland and southern England where the canal network was densest. One of the earliest examples ran from the Froghall basin terminus of the Caldon Canal in Staffordshire [SK 028476] to limestone quarries at Cauldon Lowe. The canal itself, a branch from the Trent & Mersey, at Etruria passes through the Churnet valley and some of the finest scenery in north Staffordshire. It has been restored by the Caldon Canal Society. Remains of the tramway, built originally in 1777, and realigned in 1783 and again in 1802 (by John Rennie), are numerous. At Woodcock there is a ruined bridge and at Whiston a complete bridge, an embankment and the remains of one of three self-acting in-

clined planes [SK 029476].

In Derbyshire extensive remains can be seen of the Peak Forest tramway engineered by Benjamin Outram and opened in 1796 from Bugsworth (now politely renamed Buxworth) basin [SK 020822] to Chapel-en-le-Frith and limestone quarries at Doveholes. The 85yd tunnel at Chapel Milton [SK 058817] must be the earliest railway tunnel in the world. Much of the alignment can be traced, including long lines of stone sleeper blocks. A wagon is preserved in the National Railway Museum, York.

Another well preserved line extended from Willesley on the Ashby-de-la-Zouch Canal in Leicestershire to limestone quarries at Ticknall and Cloud Hill in Derbyshire. The best sites are in Ticknall itself, where a bridge crosses the main street (Illus 211) [SK 356240] and a 138yd cut-and-cover tunnel has been put in to preserve the amenities of the approach to Calke Abbey [SK 355238]. On the Somersetshire Coal Canal sparse remains can be seen of an inclined plane tramway that was laid as a temporary link at Combe Hay [ST 748604] while a flight of twenty-two locks was being built. The alignment of a similar type of tramway, later used as a bridle

211 Bridge across the A514 in Ticknall, Derbyshire [SK 356240], completed in 1802 to carry the Ashby & Ticknall Tramway to local limestone quarries   (*Neil Cossons*)

path, links the two ends of Blisworth Tunnel [SP 729529 to 739503]. It was used between 1800 and 1805 to connect the two ends of the canal while the tunnel itself was under construction. A permanent inclined plane for the transhipment of goods from canal boats to wagons connected the terminus of the Tavistock Canal above Morwellham with quays on the River Tamar 247ft below [SX 447698]. It was opened in 1817. The remains of slate sleepers are preserved in the Morwellham Quay Open Air Museum.

Of the lines built to link sections of canal, the longest was the Cromford & High Peak Railway in Derbyshire, opened in 1831 to join the Cromford Canal with the Peak Forest Canal near Whaley Bridge. Tapping the limestone resources of the Peak, it spanned 34 miles of central Derbyshire, reaching at its summit a height of 1,266ft above sea level. Inclines connected the central sections with the termini. Much of the line, which was using steam locomotives as early as 1834, remained in use as a railway rather than a tramway until 1967. Miles of its trackbed can be walked, including the two great inclines – Middleton and Sheep Pasture. At Middleton Top [SK 275552] the steam winding engine is preserved.

The biggest mileage of canal-owned tramways was in South Wales, where almost all the companies had extensive feeder networks. The Monmouthshire Canal, for example, owned 14 route miles of railway, comprising nine separate lines. A particular advantage many of these coal-carrying lines enjoyed was that the down gradient favoured the loaded trains. There is a bridge at Blaenavon in Prince Street, and a milepost at Abersychan. Also in Gwent, although not on canal-owned lines, are the 2,050ft Pwll-Ddu Tunnel, opened in 1815 partly through old mine workings [SO 248114], and a fine bridge carrying an incline on the Redbrook branch of the Monmouth Railway, opened in 1812 [SO 537103].

It was inevitable that the success of the tramway as an aid to canal and river transport should result in its use as a common carrier in its own right for providing cross-country links. The Surrey

Iron Railway of 1803 was the first and others followed quickly. By the 1820s several of these horsedrawn public railways were being authorised each year, mainly for freight haulage, although as early as 1807 the Oystermouth Railway running along the coast between Swansea and the Mumbles was carrying fare-paying passengers. It is important to appreciate that the railway proved its value, and perhaps even its superiority over the canal, before the introduction of steam power, and that by the mid 1820s inter-city routes were being proposed. Lines such as the Sirhowy (1802), the Severn & Wye (1809), the Mansfield & Pinxton (1817) and the Stratford & Moreton (1821) were all conceived as horse railways, and as such were highly successful. Some of their major civil engineering works remain, such as the bridge across the River Avon at Stratford [SP 205548] now used as a footbridge. Some re-erected track of the Surrey Iron Railway can be seen on its original alignment at Purley Rotary Field [TQ 316622] and some more, though not on the old route, at the Joliffe Arms [TQ 290543] and outside Wallington branch library [TQ 288638]. In Ayrshire there are notable tramway bridge remains at Gatehead [NS 383369], where the Kilmarnock & Troon Railway crossed the River Irvine, and the remains of an early skew bridge on the Doura branch of the Ardrossan & Johnstone Railway [NS 338423].

It took just twenty-five years for the locomotive to prove itself the most suitable means of applying the power of steam to railways. Richard Trevithick (1771–1833) built what is generally considered to be the first steam railway locomotive at the Coalbrookdale Ironworks in Shropshire in 1802, and two years later operated a similar machine successfully on the Penydarren Railway in South Wales [ST 083969]. For a quarter of a century the locomotive developed spasmodically, in competition with the use of stationary steam engines to haul trains with cables, until in 1829 the railway engineer George Stephenson, in an effort to decide which form of power to apply to the Liverpool & Manchester Railway, then in an advanced stage of construction, proved beyond all doubt that the steam engine should move with the train. The Rainhill trials of 1829, won by Stephenson's own *Rocket*, were the turning point in the fortunes of the locomotive and the effective beginning of the railway revolution.

A number of 'pre-Rainhill' locomotives are preserved, and they demonstrate clearly the evolution of design. Trevithick was a pioneer of high-pressure steam in stationary engines – that is engines operating at a pressure of 20–25lb per sq in – and it was this use of high pressure that provided the key to the successful development of the locomotive. The great size of the low-pressure beam engine, and more particularly its enormous condensing apparatus, prevented its use as a mobile power source. Trevithick's own locomotive, which has not survived, employed a horizontal cylinder of small bore and long stroke rather like his stationary engines. Similarly other early locomotives were adaptations of available high-pressure designs. *Wylam Dilly* in the Royal Scottish Museum, Edinburgh, and *Puffing Billy* in the Science Museum, London, both dating from 1812–13, are in effect grasshopper engines on wheels, whereas the Hetton Colliery locomotive of 1822, preserved by the National Railway Museum, and the Killingworth locomotive in the Newcastle Museum of Science & Engineering have the more direct form of drive of the Maudslay table engine. By the late 1820s locomotives were being built with pistons connected directly to their wheels through piston and connecting rods. *Sans Pareil* and *Rocket*, both contenders at Rainhill and now in the Science Museum, London, are of this type. More important at this date, however, was the way in which the boiler was developing, with numerous tubes between firebox and smokebox giving it a good steaming rate. It was primarily the superiority of its boiler that gave *Rocket* the edge over its competitors at Rainhill. Within five years Stephenson engines such as *Northumbrian* and *Planet* had established the general form of the locomotive, which was to survive virtually unaltered until the demise of steam power on British Rail in the 1960s.

The success of the steam locomotive was very much a personal triumph for George Stephenson (1781–1848) and his son Robert (1803–1859). In 1825 the elder Stephenson had engineered the first public railway on which steam locomotion was used, although initially only on a small scale, between Stockton and Darlington. Five years later he built the Liverpool & Manchester, the first railway to carry passengers and the first to be completely steam-worked from the beginning. Both were built to the now standard gauge of 4ft 8½in. The origins of this gauge are obscure but it seems likely to have evolved from the tramways of the North East, a natural derivation from the width between pairs of horse-drawn cart wheels. The Stephensons were unrivalled as railway engineers in the early 1830s, and it was their appreciation that one day all local lines would be joined together in a nationwide network that led to the adoption of the 4ft 8½in gauge throughout most of the country. Only one major line, the Great Western, brainchild of the brilliant engineer Isambard Kingdom Brunel, did not adopt standard gauge.

Lines such as the Stockton & Darlington and the Liverpool & Manchester, and other contemporaries like the Canterbury & Whitstable and the Leicester & Swannington, had been built to satisfy specific local requirements for the haulage of goods, but in the event the traffic pattern was quite different; passenger receipts were more than double freight takings on the L & MR right down to the mid-1840s, and the national consciousness suddenly became aware that big profits were there for the taking. By 1836 nearly 2,000 route miles of railway had been authorised, including most of what were to become the major trunk routes focused on London. The first of these was Stephenson's superbly engineered London & Birmingham, to be quickly followed by routes from the capital to Southampton, Brighton and Bristol, by an extension of the L & BR northwards into Lancashire, and by a collection of small lines which eventually linked London and York, the North East and Scotland. Three of these – the Midland Counties, the Birmingham & Derby Junc-

THE RAILWAY NETWORK IN BRITAIN
1840-1986

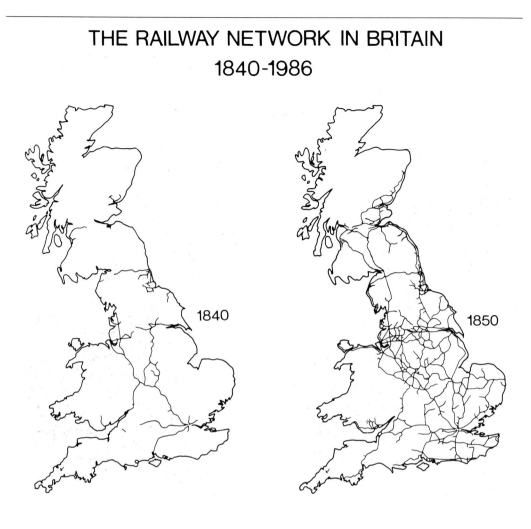

1840

1850

Illustration 212

tion and the North Midland – amalgamated in 1844 to form the Midland Railway, one of the largest companies not to have a London terminus, a fact which was significantly to alter the skyline of the Euston Road a quarter of a century later.

The 'railway revolution' born out of the success of lines like the Liverpool & Manchester and London & Birmingham got going in earnest in the 1840s. It was one of the most remarkable phenomena of the whole period of Britain's industrialisation. The landscape changes the railway brought about were more widespread and more fundamental than those created by any other industry, and this is reflected today in the profusion of remains. The direct effects could be seen in terms of embankments and cuttings, viaducts and tunnels, on the one hand, and by new towns such as Crewe and Swindon, which were creations of the railway companies themselves, on the other. Less direct but just as obvious was the increase in general economic activity brought about by the improvement in transport, a trend that had begun with canals and accelerated rapidly with the coming of railways. Railways performed the same basic economic function as canals, shifting bulk goods at low cost. In addition, however, they offered the equivalent, on a larger scale, of

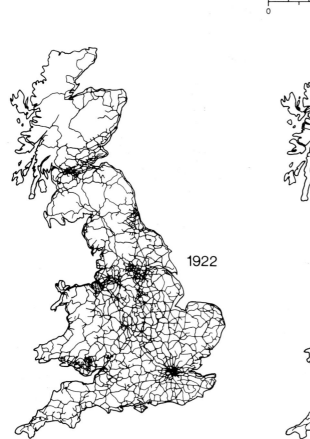

1922

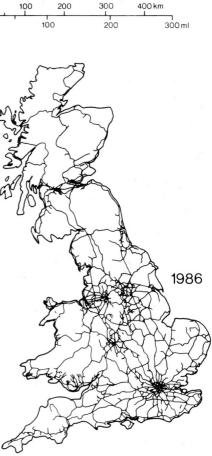

1986

the best eighteenth-century post roads, which provided rapid communication for people, mail and specialised freight.

The enormous impact the railway had on the economy and the scale of its development are worth studying. To the success of the second-generation steam railways – early main lines like the London & Birmingham of 1838 and the Great Western of 1841 – may be directly attributed the enormous boom in railway building which reached a peak in 1848, when 1,253 miles were opened. The peak years for sanctioning construction were 1845 (2,816 miles), 1846 (4,540 miles) and 1847 (1,295 miles). Many lines promoted in

these frantic years of the mid-1840s were never built, so that by 1851, when a total of 12,698 miles had been authorised, only a little over half (6,803 miles) had been completed. This in itself was a formidable figure. During the years 1846–8 railway investment was absorbing 5–7 per cent of the national income, about half the total capital investment and equivalent to about two-thirds of the value of all exports. It entailed a wage bill of £16 million for a construction force of 250,000, and by 1850 there were 60,000 employees running the new railways. The significance of railway building in the national economy was such that during the late

1840s and the 1850s the railway industry itself could be regarded as a major factor in determining the cyclic movements of the economy. Iron, coal and brick prices moved in parallel with the timing of railway contracts; indeed the demands of the railways were almost solely responsible for the enormous growth in iron rolling mills during the 1850s and 1860s. By 1850 railway locomotives were burning 1 million tons of coal a year, and, although this was only some 2 per cent of national production, the railway-stimulated industries all consumed their share too. Railway development led directly to increased urban growth, while the railway industry itself became one of the greatest breeding grounds of the new technocrats who were to be the mainstay of Victorian industrial might. The effect on other transport systems was cataclysmic. By the 1850s the long-distance road coach had been virtually eliminated and most canals rendered unprofitable. There was a real deterioration in road conditions in many parts of Britain as the turnpike trusts were wound up and road maintenance became again the responsibility of a reluctant parish.

With the completion of the Great Northern main line between King's Cross and York in 1852, nearly all the major routes of the modern railway system in England had been developed. All the major industrial areas, cities and ports were linked by a network which, although its individual components belonged to dozens of separate companies, could be regarded as a national railway system. There was still much filling in of the gaps to be undertaken, however, and both Wales and Scotland, with the exception of the industrial lowlands, were virtually without railway lines. By 1914, its approximate peak, the total network of the United Kingdom was 23,000 miles. The £1,300 million invested in the system had created the most expensive, extravagant, wasteful and at the same time spectacular symbol of Victorian success.

213 Camden Roundhouse, London [TQ 282843], converted to a theatre in 1967
(*Royal Commission on Historical Monuments, England*)

British railways were very costly to build, and at an average of £40,000 per mile were three or four times as expensive as American and most continental systems. They became an engineer's paradise, with lavish standards of finish to major bridges and viaducts, tunnel portals and stations. There were real reasons, however, for the heroic quality of much railway engineering and architecture, particularly in the late 1830s and early 1840s. Firstly, engineers such as the Stephensons and Brunel, while consciously designing for the future, had to allow for the limited locomotive tractive effort and relatively underdeveloped mechanical knowledge of their day. So they built lines with easy gradients – the London & Birmingham had a ruling gradient of 1 in 330 – and therefore committed themselves to building heavy earthworks. Secondly, there was the problem of making the railway a socially acceptable means of travel, and this was solved by magnificent termini, architecturally acceptable in a city environment, line-side stations of a vernacular or domestic style often beautifully attuned to their geographical and social surroundings, and major engineering structures handled with a panache and yet sympathy for landscape unequalled to this day. Euston or Temple Meads had the same function as the airline terminals of today, being designed not merely to book the passenger on to a train but to inflate his ego, enhance the prestigiousness of the railway experience, and reassure him that it was not dangerous after all.

Both the Stockton & Darlington and the Liverpool & Manchester railways were built before this attitude had become fashionable – they were after all built primarily as goods lines. On the S & DR stone sleeper blocks can still be seen on disused inclines at Brusselton [NZ 215256] and Etherley and there are the earthworks of abandoned stretches of the line at Low Etherley [NZ 170289] and North Leaze. A fine stone three-arch bridge by Ignatius Bonomi crosses the River Skerne at Darlington North Road [NZ 289157]; this is perhaps the first bridge of the steam age, and although it has been widened, the south face is original. Another bridge, of cast and wrought iron, crossed the River Gaunless near West Auckland but it was removed in 1901 and can now be seen in the York Railway Museum – one of the first pieces of conscious industrial archaeological preservation. Here too is an S & DR chaldron wagon, very like the thousands that worked the colliery lines of the North East until relatively recently; examples can also be seen at the North of England Open Air Museum, Beamish. Two locomotives from the line – *Locomotion* of 1825 and *Derwent* of the late 1830s – are preserved at Darlington Railway Museum, North Road Station [NZ 289157].

The masonry arch in a variety of shapes and sizes was by far the commonest type of railway bridge structure until the 1860s and 1870s, when fabricated girders began to appear. The Liverpool & Manchester has two fine masonry viaducts by George Stephenson in the nine-arch Sankey Viaduct near Warrington [SJ 569947] carrying tracks 70ft above the valley floor, and a smaller one of four arches at Newton-le-Willows [SJ 591954]. On the same railway the skew arch bridge carrying the main Liverpool to Warrington road over the line at Rainhill [SJ 491914] has been widened, but the basic structure of the arch with its intricate compound curves is still intact beneath the present deck. Little remains of early station buildings, although the original L & MR eastern terminus at Liverpool Road, Manchester [SJ 830978] still has some of the original offices and reception areas. Line-side buildings were domestic in style, influenced if anything by contemporary road and canal architecture. The cottage situated in Bridge Road, St Johns, Stockton-on-Tees [NZ 447184], on the S & DR, and claimed to be the first railway booking office, is preserved as a museum. There is a building with more obvious lineage at Ratby [SK 518053] on the Leicester & Swannington Railway, opened in 1832; with its half-hexagonal end and panel for a non-existent tollboard, it is a perfect replica of a contemporary tollhouse and is now, since the demolition of the gem at Glenfield, the only one of its kind on the line and a curious example of the transfer of style from one transport system to another.

The remains of the first inter-city main lines, like the London & Birmingham and Great Western, are surprisingly common, and as spectacular today as when J. C. Bourne recorded them in his dramatic series of lithographs of the early 1840s. At Tring, Hertfordshire [SP 940137] the great cutting is 2½ miles long and 60ft deep, and at Roade another bites 70ft deep into the Northamptonshire hills [SP 750525]. The greatest work on the L & BR, however, is Kilsby Tunnel [SP 565715 to 578697]; nearly 1½ miles long it is marked on the surface by the brick towers of its ventilating shafts, the largest of which are 60ft in diameter. All these works reflect George Stephenson's insistence on gentle gradients; had the line been built twenty years later, Kilsby Tunnel could have been avoided altogether.

Stations on the L & BR have not fared so well. The destruction of the Euston arch, Philip Hardwick's magnificent gateway to the world's first main line railway, was a major loss. It is perhaps some consolation that Euston's demise was a major contributory factor towards creating an informed and articulate lobby prepared to argue the case for preservation. Indeed the industrial archaeologist of the future may well look back on the loss of Euston as the first great sacrificial price that had to be paid before other monuments of Britain's industrial heritage could be spared. North of Euston, however, at Camden, stands a very tangible memorial to the early days of the L & BR – the roundhouse locomotive shed [TQ 282843] designed by George Stephenson and built in 1847 at the head of the mile-long incline up from the terminus itself (Illus 213). Initially the trains were cable-hauled out of Euston, locomotives taking over at Camden for the journey north. Hardwick's other terminus building, at Curzon Street, Birmingham [SP 080871], with its Ionic columned façade and office block substantially intact, maintains a dignity and presence truly monumental in character. It has recently been restored.

Another early main line built in the grand manner, and of which considerable evidence survives today, was the Great Western connecting Bristol with the Metropolis. Conceived in Bristol and engineered by Isambard Kingdom Brunel, only 30 years old when the railway's Act was passed in 1836, the Great Western was part of a splendid vision, the child of a brief spell when Bristol recalled its former glories and saw itself again as the Gateway to the West. Brunel alone among the engineers of his period rethought the railway from basic principles and argued that in engineering terms a much wider gauge – he adopted 7ft – would provide a better ride, permit higher speeds, give greater carrying capacity and allow much more latitude for future development than 4ft 8½in. There can be no doubt that he was right, in engineering terms, but unfortunately there were other factors to be considered. Goods and passengers had to be changed wherever the standard and broad gauge met, and there was no possibility of through-running trains or rolling stock. By the end of the nineteenth century, when Britain had the second densest rail network in the world (after Belgium), the Great Western had to capitulate and change to the standard gauge, an operation which was completed in 1892.

The journey west from Paddington is a triumphant succession of major civil engineering works culminating in the minute (by modern standards) but still surprisingly complete terminus at Temple Meads, Bristol. The first Paddington station has gone, replaced by the magnificent multiple-aisle transepted train shed of 1854, designed by Matthew Digby Wyatt. The transepts give the whole roof structure a remarkably complex appearance, but they did once fulfil a useful purpose, providing clearance for carriage traversers, now extinct mechanisms for moving individual vehicles laterally from one track to another.

The first major work westwards from Paddington is Hanwell Viaduct [TS 150840] spanning the valley of the Brent in eight yellow brick arches and demonstrating in a restrained way Brunel's predilection for the Egyptian style, to be seen also in his Clifton suspension bridge at Bristol. The arms of Lord Wharncliffe were placed on the south face in honour of one of the

214 The west portal of Box Tunnel, Wiltshire [ST 829689], on the Great Western main line (*Neil Cossons*)

staunchest supporters of the Great Western Bill in Parliament. At Maidenhead comes the first crossing of the Thames [SU 901810], on two 128ft semi-elliptical arches, their rise of only 24ft 6in making them the flattest brick arches constructed at that date. Westwards again the line passes through the great cutting at Sonning [SU 759743], originally planned as a tunnel some 2 miles long, before reaching Reading and the route up the Thames valley towards Didcot. In following the Thames the line departs from the traditional route to the west, taken by the Bath Road and the Kennet & Avon Canal, to pursue a more northerly course across north Wiltshire to a summit west of Wootton Bassett. The descent into the valley of the Avon through the 2 mile tunnel at Box is the climax of the line. Box Tunnel, with its gradient of 1 in 100, was to be for Brunel what Kilsby had been for the Stephensons – the civil engineering *tour de force* of the line, the one major work on the successful completion of which the railway depended. In addition

to the engineering problems of this greatest railway tunnel so far attempted (it killed over 100 men during construction) almost every conceivable bad omen was called down upon it, with predictions of wholesale death and disaster for any who ventured inside. But the tunnel was completed, nine months behind schedule, in the summer of 1841. At its western end [ST 829689] Brunel, always susceptible to a setting in which to make a grand gesture, created a portal that epitomises the early railway age and the man (Illus 214). Its dignified architectural style and enormous proportions sit perfectly in the cutting east of the Bath Road, which the railway here rejoins. Only Brunel could stage-manage this supreme advertisement for the new Great Western Railway at the entrance to that 'monstrous and extraordinary, most dangerous and impracticable tunnel at Box'. West of Box the line continues its descent towards Bath, which it enters through a beautifully finished cutting along the edge of Sydney Gardens and a great viaduct of seventy-three arches on which stands the station, now much altered. Between Bath and Bristol are five more tunnels (there were originally seven but two were opened out in 1894), a twenty-eight arch viaduct at Twerton and four large bridges now all substantially modified. In Bristol itself is the grand finale, the terminus at Temple Meads, the most complete early railway terminus in the world, with its 72ft span timber-roofed train shed and Tudor-style office block fronting on to Temple Gate. After years of neglect both have now been restored.

An aspect of any major railway project, for which no real precedents in other forms of transport existed, was the provision of repair and maintenance facilities for locomotives and rolling stock. On the London & Birmingham a works was established approximately halfway along the line at Wolverton, and on the Great Western a similar 'green field' situation was chosen by Brunel about a mile north of the market town of Swindon in north Wiltshire. On Brunel's Great Western over 70 of the total of 118 route miles had a ruling gradient of less than 1:1,000, on 40 more this was increased to 1:750 and only in the western section, between Wootton Bassett and Bath, were steep gradients encountered at all, the 3 miles including Box Tunnel involving the sharpest section

at 1:100. The choice of Swindon as a suitable place to set up a locomotive works thus stemmed not only from its approximate mid-point position. It was a place where locomotives suitable for the heavy gradients of the western section could be changed and also, as an added advantage, a point where the projected branch to Gloucester and Cheltenham could meet the main line.

Swindon was the first of the major railway towns, for Wolverton was eventually to be eclipsed by Crewe. Despite Swindon's enormous industrial diversification in the last twenty-five years or so, it retains something of the flavour of the Great Western about it. Neat terraces of workers' houses faced in the local stone were built by the railway company around the entrance to the works on the south side of the line, and these, together with the institute and church, formed a new

215 Wrought iron bow-string girder bridge completed in 1849 and designed by I. K. Brunel to carry the Windsor branch of the Great Western Railway across the Thames [SU 961773] (*Neil Cossons*)

town second only perhaps to Saltaire near Bradford as an example of planned urban development. One of these railway-built buildings, possibly designed by Brunel himself, houses the Great Western Railway Museum, which contains a small but comprehensive collection of locomotives, including the replica broad-gauge *North Star*, and innumerable small items which add up to form the complex organism that was a railway. The Great Western name is still kept alive by numerous preservation societies, and its locomotives and stock are run at Didcot by the Great Western Society, on the Dart Valley Railway in Devon and on the Severn Valley Railway, centred on Bridgnorth, Shropshire.

Curiously, some of the most widespread pieces of archaeological evidence of the early days of the Great Western are sections of broad-gauge rail designed by Brunel and made redundant by standardisation of gauge. Brunel designed his broad-gauge track with a continuous longitudinal timber sleeper beneath each rail to give good but resilient support, and these longitudinals were tied every 15ft and the ties initially piled into the trackbed. On the timbers were laid rolled-wrought-iron rails of 'top hat' section fixed down by bolts through the base flange or 'brim' of the hat. It seems probable that Brunel devised this particular section to give maximum strength for a minimum amount of iron, and also possibly to arrive at a section that could be rolled satisfactorily without suffering the lamination experienced on other types of rolled iron rail at this period. With the eventual adoption of standard 'I' section bullhead rails, first in iron and later steel, the 'bridge rail', as Brunel's rail was called, became redundant; but it was reused for fencing stakes and as such can be found all over the old Great Western system, as far west as Cornwall and Pembrokeshire and north-west in Cheshire on the line to Birkenhead Woodside. A similar rolled section can be seen in the roof girders of the Swindon railway works drawing office. Another type of rail, used on the Great Western and by some standard-gauge companies and devised by W. H. Barlow, aimed at dispensing with the

216 Even small branch lines had superbly designed and engineered viaducts like this one near Riddings, Cumbria, built in 1864 to carry the Langholm branch of the Border Union Railway across Liddel Water and into Scotland [NY 411756] (*John R. Hume*)

longitudinal timber baulk altogether, the rail being laid directly into the ballast. Of an expanded 'top-hat' section with a base width of 12in, it was not a great success, but sections of the rail can still be found quite frequently in the form of gate-posts to goods and coal yards, mainly on old Great Western lines.

Although few other railways were to be built throughout to the standards of the Great Western, dozens of major engineering structures and thousands of minor ones dotted the immense network of lines which grew up throughout the remainder of Victoria's reign. Some 25,000 bridges were added by the railways to the British landscape between 1830 and 1860 alone. The majority still survive, many in substantially original condition and most still in use. A number of bridge types have already been mentioned and the point made that in the early period of railway building brick or masonry-arch structures were by far the most numerous. The largest masonry span in Britain is the 181ft Ballochmyle Viaduct [NS 508254], built in 1848 on the Glasgow & South Western Railway between Kilmarnock and Dumfries to the designs of the Scottish engineer John Miller. Almost as spectacular is the seven-arch Victoria Bridge across the River Wear in Sunderland [NZ 396575], com-

pleted in 1838 by the Durham Junction Railway, with a largest span of 161ft.

Most major brick and stone-arch bridges on British railways have multiple arches with spans ranging from 25 to 50ft. A fine early example with unusually large spans of 60ft is the twenty-arch Dutton Viaduct [SJ 583764] built by George Stephenson and Joseph Locke to carry the Grand Junction Railway linking Birmingham with Manchester and Liverpool across the valley of the River Weaver in Cheshire. By far the longest arch structure, however, was built as late as the 1880s, when the

217 As built in 1848, Chirk Viaduct, Clwyd [SJ 286373] had laminated timber approach arches; these had been replaced by stone before 1860, the change in detailing identifying the different dates of construction   (*Neil Cossons*)

218 Chirk Viaduct with stone approach arches   (*Neil Cossons*)

219 Harringworth Viaduct with its eighty-two brick arches carries the Midland line from Kettering via Melton Mowbray to Nottingham across the valley of the River Welland [SP 914975] (*Neil Cossons*)

Midland Railway put in its alternative route to the Soar valley line running from Kettering via Oakham and Melton Mowbray to Nottingham through the rich Jurassic iron-ore fields of east Leicestershire. Harringworth Viaduct (Illus 219) [SP 914975] across the Welland Valley, Rutland's only major industrial monument, is some 3,500ft long and has 82 brick arches.

By the end of the nineteenth century almost all bridges were being built in wrought iron or steel, but concrete was just sufficiently developed and accepted as a building material to be used in some of the last viaducts constructed on British lines. There is an example at Glenfinnan [NM 910813] on the Mallaig extension of the West Highland Railway, opened in 1898,

which has twenty-one arches each of 50ft span and is built on a curve of 12 chains radius. The concrete is not reinforced but simply poured into timber form-work, the curve being achieved by tapering the piers so that simple semi-cylindrical arches could be used. To allow for any possible differential settlement of the piers, a sliding joint consisting of two steel plates is incorporated in the crown of each arch, but no noticeable movement has occurred since the bridge was built. At Calstock in Cornwall (Illus 220) [SX 434687] the railway viaduct across the Tamar is built of concrete blocks cast on site.

Of the variety of metal bridges built to carry railways, the earliest large-span types were beam structures made in the form of tubular or plate girders. The Britannia tubular bridge [SH 542710] built by the Chester & Holyhead Railway across the Menai Strait was the most important of these, not merely as a railway structure but as a landmark in the evolution of civil engineering. It marked the first use of the beam principle for a long span bridge, and its design and construction was the culmination of the model experiments carried out by William Fairbairn (1789–1874) and their translation into usable theoretical terms by Eaton Hodgkinson (1789–1861). Robert Stephenson, engineer to the Chester & Holyhead, approached Fairbairn, a shipbuilder and engineer of Millwall, London, as early as April 1845 regarding the desirable shape of the tubular deck of a wrought iron suspension bridge he was proposing. By December of 1845 Fairbairn, in consultation with Hodgkinson, who was later appointed Professor of Mechanical Principles of Engineering at University College, London, had evolved a rectangular-section beam design, cellular at the top and bottom to resist any possible collapse through compression or failure through tension. Fairbairn advocated the use of the tubes as simple beam structures, suggesting that chains would be unnecessary. A one-sixth scale model of one of the tubes was tested to destruction before the eventual design was arrived at and construc-

tion of the Menai Bridge and its smaller neighbour at Conwy [SH 787776] could begin. Conwy was built first as the tubes were smaller and only had to be raised some 18ft. It proved a useful trial run for the larger-scale and much more hazardous operation at Menai. Both bridges consisted of a pair of parallel tubes, each containing a single track. At Menai, Stephenson was able to avoid heavy underwater engineering by siting the central pier on the Britannia rock in the middle of the strait. By early 1846 the working drawings for the piers were well advanced, at a period when Stephenson was still considering the use of chains. The piers, were, in fact, built considerably higher than the level of the tubes and the holes through their tops for the chains that were never used are a feature of the bridge today. As at Conwy, the tubes were built

220 Calstock Viaduct, Cornwall, across the River Tamar [SX 433687]. Opened in 1907, it is built of concrete blocks made on the Devon side of the river by the contractor J. C. Lang of Liskeard. It is 1,000ft long and 117ft above the river   (*Neil Cossons*)

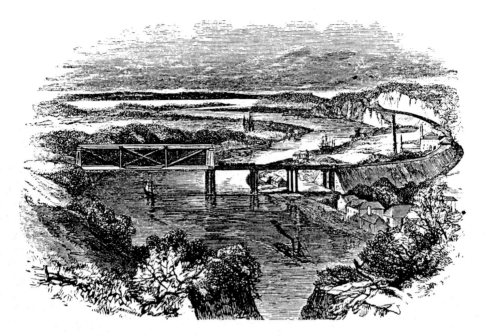

221 Bridge over the Wye

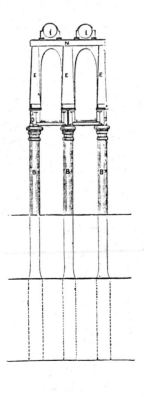

222 Tower for tubular bridge

on shore and floated into position, hydraulic rams being used to elevate them. When all were raised, they were riveted end to end to form a pair of continuous beams, 1,511ft long, Stephenson himself driving the last rivet on 5 March 1850, so completing the world's longest span bridge at that time and also, at £600,000, the most costly. The bridge carried main line traffic to and from Holyhead until July 1970, when a fire in wooden staging inside the tubes resulted in their distortion beyond all hope of repair. Today a steel-arch structure sits, far from happily, between the piers, and the most important single monument of wrought iron bridge building and early structural theory in the world is gone. Conwy still survives, however, and, although strengthened with intermediate piers near each end, illustrates the constructional technique, but it has neither the dimensions nor the grandeur of the great Menai Bridge.

223 Brunel's Royal Albert Bridge, Saltash, spanning the Tamar between Devon and Cornwall [SX 587435]   (Neil Cossons)

224 Meldon Viaduct, Devon, built by the London & South Western Railway in 1874 [SX 565924] (*Neil Cossons*)

225 The interlaced piers of Meldon Viaduct (*Neil Cossons*)

Slightly later in the 1850s wrought iron was used for an ingenious railway bridge designed by I. K. Brunel to carry the line of the South Wales Railway over the Wye at Chepstow (Illus 221, 222) [ST 539941]. The two parallel main spans, of 300ft, consisted of plate girders supported by chains from piers at each end, but instead of carrying the chains back to an anchor point on the ground, Brunel held the piers apart by wrought iron tubes 8ft in diameter. The tubes could not support themselves over this distance, so they were in turn supported from the bridge deck by wrought iron 'A' frames. Brunel's Chepstow Bridge was replaced by the present lattice steel structure in 1962, but the much more sophisticated design which derived from it still carries the old

Great Western main line across the Tamar from Devon into Cornwall.

The River Tamar represented the most formidable obstacle to the westward progress of the Cornwall Railway from Plymouth and, as at Menai, the exacting Admiralty stipulations about clearance for shipping had to be met to the letter. Brunel was faced at Saltash with the problem of bridging 1,000ft of tidal water at a height of 100ft. The design eventually decided upon owed something to Chepstow, but here the tubes were elliptical in section, arched in profile and self-supporting. Besides withstanding the inward pull of the suspension chains, they shared with the chains the load of the bridge deck. Each of the spans is of 445ft, the composite truss, consisting of tube, catenary chains, suspender rods and deck, being 70ft deep at its centre and containing 1,600 tons of wrought iron.

The problem of the central pier was solved by using a 37ft diameter cylinder or caisson – the 'Great Cylinder', weighing about 300 tons – which was lowered vertically through the water and mud to rest on the bed rock of the estuary floor.

The whole end of the cylinder was sealed off by the use of an airtight bulkhead, and in this pressurised space the foundations of the masonry pier were built. This was the first example of the use of a pressurised caisson for underwater work. Saltash Bridge (Illus 223) [SX 435587] was opened to traffic by Prince Albert on 2 May 1859 but by then Brunel, who had gone abroad for his health before the second span had been raised, was within a few months of death. He returned to cross his bridge on a couch placed on a flat truck. Four months later he died and the inscriptions on the piers of Saltash Bridge, 'I. K. BRUNEL – ENGINEER – 1859', were placed there in his memory by the grateful directors of the Cornwall Railway.

By the 1860s wrought iron bridges were becoming numerous. In the main they utilised fabricated plate 'I' section girders

226 Bennerley Viaduct, built in 1879, carried the Great Northern Railway's Derbyshire Extension across the valley of the Erewash [SK 475440]; efforts are being made to preserve it as a footpath and cycle track (*Neil Cossons*)

for small spans and lattice girders over greater distances. A fine example of a large wrought iron girder bridge is to be seen at Runcorn [SJ 509835], where the L & NWR main line to Liverpool crosses the Mersey (and the later Manchester Ship Canal) on three 305ft spans. The bridge was completed in 1863. At Charing Cross a nine-span wrought iron lattice girder bridge designed by Sir John Hawkshaw was opened in the following year on the site of Brunel's Hungerford suspension foot-bridge, which had been acquired by the South Eastern Railway and demolished. In later years Charing Cross Bridge was widened to carry three further tracks. Wrought iron, sometimes in combination with cast iron, was also used for a series of remarkable and elegant lattice girder via-ducts that crossed steep valleys at high level. The first of them, built at Crumlin, Monmouthshire, in 1857, had ten 150ft spans in the form of lattice beams known as Warren triangular girders after Captain James Warren, who, with W. T. Manzoni, patented the system in 1848. The essence of the design is that no members in the girders are subjected to bending stresses, only to simple tension and compression. The piers were made of cast iron columns braced laterally and diagonally with wrought iron rods, giving the whole via-duct a delicate and ethereal quality which belied its strength. Crumlin Viaduct has been dismantled, as have two of basically similar design built in 1859 at Belah, Westmorland, and Deepdale, County Durham. But two remain, the spectacu-larly sited Meldon Viaduct in Devon (Illus 224 and 225) [SX 565924], built by the London & South Western Railway and completed in 1874 and Bennerley Viaduct on the Nottinghamshire and Derbyshire border (Illus 226) [SK 475440] opened in 1879 by the Great Northern Railway to carry its Derbyshire Extension across the valley of the River Erewash. These alone represent the lattice girder and pier type of construc-tion.

The final and in some respects greatest period of railway bridge building came very late in the evolution of the network and was part of a move to shorten existing and often circuitous routes. The last barriers to direct railway communication were the great estuaries of the Tay, the Forth and the Severn, estuaries which were not to be tackled by the roadbuilders until nearly a century later. The first major railway bridge of this type was completed across the Tay in 1878, and in the follow-ing year, as a result of design and con-struction faults, was swept away in a gale with the loss of seventy-five lives. It was a wrought iron lattice girder structure like its successor which stands today, the last of the great wrought iron bridges and, with a total length of 10,711ft, the longest railway bridge in Britain. The present bridge was designed by W. H. Barlow and opened on 20 June 1887. Beside it can still be seen the stumps of the piers of Bouch's narrow and spindly creation. The second Tay Bridge was the first civil engineering work in Britain in which an effort was made to calculate and allow for lateral wind pressure. It was designed to resist 56lb per sq ft, giving a generous margin of safety and resulting in a rather solid and ungraceful structure. The next estuary to be tackled was the Severn, which was crossed in two places. The first crossing was completed in 1879 near Sharpness with a wrought iron bowstring girder bridge, 4,161ft long and carrying a single track. It was hardly a trunk route bridge, however, being designed mainly to give access to the Forest of Dean coalfield, and after being struck and badly damaged by a barge in 1960, it was subsequently demol-ished. The main crossing of the Severn came much lower down the estuary in the form of Britain's longest tunnel, opened in the 1880s.

The bridging of the Firth of Forth was the grand finale for the nineteenth-century bridge builders. It was the largest cantilever bridge in the world when opened in March 1890, and the first large civil engineering structure to be built in mild steel instead of the traditional wrought iron. The scheme to bridge the Forth started in earnest in 1873 when the Forth Bridge Company, a consortium of the North British, Midland, and Great Northern railways, was formed. Thomas Bouch, designer of the first Tay Bridge was appointed engineer and work had already started on an enormous suspension bridge when the Tay disaster occurred. Work on the Forth Bridge came to a standstill, the suspension bridge scheme was dropped and two new engineers, Benjamin Baker and John Fowler, were appointed in place of Bouch. In 1882 the contract was let for a cantilever bridge based on three towers made of 12ft diameter steel tubes rising 361ft above high water. From each tower the lattice-braced cantilevers stretch out towards those of the next tower, the connection being made by two suspended lattice girder spans. Approach spans at each end are of conventional lattice girders on tapered granite piers. The central tower stands on the little island of Inch Garvie but the other two have concrete bases built in caissons; wrought iron caissons 70ft in diameter were in fact sunk into the clay bed of the firth under each of the four tubes of the towers. The Forth Bridge has a total length of 8,296ft.

In addition to the main types there were a number of minor types of railway bridge in Great Britain. Some were quite numerous but have now gone, like Brunel's timber viaducts in Devon and Cornwall, of which only the masonry piers can be seen here and there. Wooden viaducts still run across the Mawddach estuary south of Barmouth [SH 624150] and further north on the same line at Penrhyndeudraeth [SH 619384]. Cast iron, too was used as a bridge-building material surprisingly late in the railway age. At Ironbridge, Shropshire, the Albert Edward Bridge of 1863 is still in use [SJ 661038]; it was designed by John Fowler, later of Forth Bridge fame, and cast by the nearby Coalbrookdale Company. In Derby an even later cast iron arch, of 1878, crosses Friargate [SK 347364]. Built by the Great Northern Railway, it was cast in the Derby foundry of Andrew Handyside, and exhibits *par excellence* the decorative possibilities of cast iron; the parapet panels and spandrels are full of floral ornament and also display the town's coat of arms, all cast in relief.

The large numbers of viaducts on British railways reflects the need for well graded, direct routes across undulating country, the same factors that resulted in so many tunnels. In towns, too, viaducts and tunnels are numerous, the obvious answers to high land costs. Paradoxically, tunnels in particular are nowhere near as common on lines in the mountainous areas of Wales and Scotland, where the economic incentive for a direct route was usually low and the topography so severe that circuitous valley-located routes involving minimum engineering works and therefore minimum expenditure were the norm. It must be remembered too that many of the lines in Wales and Scotland were built late in the railway era after the first flush of extravagance had died away. Thus there is only one tunnel in Wales over 2 miles long, at Blaenau Ffestiniog [SH 687505 to 697469], and there are none at all in Scotland. Britain's major railway tunnels are therefore concentrated in the Pennines and lowland England, cutting through what in many places appear to be insignificant hills. Kilsby Tunnel through the Northamptonshire uplands has already been mentioned as an example of a shallow-depth bore made necessary by Stephenson's stringent gradient requirements. Another early Stephenson tunnel, the first railway tunnel in the world over a mile in length, is at Glenfield in Leicestershire [SK 545065 to 561061] on the Leicester & Swannington Railway, opened in 1832. Its narrow single-track bore is now closed. Quite unavoidable, however, was the tunnel under the Pennines at Woodhead [SK 114999 to SE 156023] between Manchester and Sheffield, completed in 1845 after a seven year saga of death and disease in the workings and the shanty navvy encampments on Pikenaze Moor above. Built initially for a single track, it was later duplicated, and then in the 1950s replaced altogether by a modern double-track tunnel put in to accommodate the 1,500V DC electrification scheme initiated by the London & North Eastern Railway. The stark portals can be seen, however, and one of the bores is now doing useful work carrying a power line that would otherwise have necessitated unsightly pylons across the moors.

To the industrial archaeologist the most obvious evidence of tunnels is their portals and, on the longer bores, their

227 The memorial in the churchyard of All Saints Parish Church, Otley, West Yorkshire [SE 202455], to the men who died in the construction of the Bramhope Tunnel   (*Neil Cossons*)

ventilating shafts. Unlike the canal builders the railway engineers used tunnels as an excuse for architectural extravagance, of which numerous examples can still be seen. The south portal of Primrose Hill Tunnel [TQ 276843] on the London & Birmingham 1½ miles out of Euston is Italianate in style, while at Shugborough in Staffordshire [SJ 982216 to 988216] one end of the tunnel is castellated and the other Egyptianesque. In the latter case the cosmetic architectural treatment, like that of the adjacent bridges, was required by the Earl of Lichfield, owner of the estate through which the line passed. Two other 'fortified' portals are to be found at Red Hill [SK 496308] on the Midland main line between Leicester and Derby and at Grosmont [NZ 829051] on the abandoned alignment of Stephenson's Whitby & Pickering Railway. At Bramhope, West Yorkshire, the 2 mile tunnel on the Harrogate line has an ornate castellated north portal [SE 256437] which is reproduced on a

smaller scale at nearby Otley churchyard (Illus 227) [SE 202455] as a memorial to the men killed during its construction.

Britain's longest railway tunnel came late in the railway era and, like the longest bridges, spanned an estuary. From the 1850s the mouth of the Severn had been an obstacle to rail traffic between South Wales and London, which had to travel via Gloucester. In 1863 the first attempt at a shorter route was completed with the opening of the Bristol & South Wales Union Railway to New Passage [ST 544864] and a ferry connection to Portskewett and the South Wales Railway. Little remains of this venture today other than the stone landward section of the original timber pier and the flourishing New Passage Hotel. At Blackrock on the Monmouthshire side [ST 514881] two bridges and an overgrown cutting are all that remain of the connection with the main line. A tunnel as the final answer to crossing the Severn by rail was devised as early as the 1860s, taken up by the Great Western Railway in 1872, and eventually completed in 1886 at a cost of more than £1½ million. The Severn Tunnel when completed represented the ultimate in the engineers' fight against adversity. A natural freshwater stream, the Great Spring, was broken into and the workings were flooded by the river, delaying operations for about three years. The Great Spring has had to be pumped ever since, initially by steam engines and now by electricity. At Sudbrook [ST 508874] the huge 29ft shaft through which most of the Great Spring water is pumped can still be seen, but the six superb 70in Cornish beam pumps have been scrapped.

The design of passenger railway stations presented engineers and architects with considerable problems, for they were working in a field where no precedents existed. The logistics of handling large numbers of people arriving and departing simultaneously represented something completely new, and demanded a particular type of building combining all the basic functions in a logical and well articulated way. Thus the *layout* of stations is peculiar to the nature of railways themselves and represents a response to a specific challenge. In architectural terms, however, the designers of railway stations exhibited less originality, and, although the great roofs of termini were undoubtedly allied closely to the function of the station, the treatment of façades, of booking-office blocks and of railway hotels was frequently pedestrian and derivative in the extreme. On the other hand the railway companies were responsible for some very good architecture both in large city stations and simpler rural surroundings. Railway architecture has become a study in itself and railway buildings, which often reflected the relative wealth and desire for prestige of their owners, illustrate in microcosm many of the essentials of Victorian architectural thought. As we have seen, the first railways required little in the way of buildings, but as early as 1830 the termini of the Liverpool & Manchester Railway, of which the Manchester one still survives, had the essentials of booking office, waiting rooms and a sheltered platform for the passengers. By the late 1830s the U-shaped terminus station that was to become the standard had evolved, with arrival and departure platforms linked by a cross platform containing the entrances, waiting rooms and offices. An early example, now demolished, was Nine Elms, designed by Sir William Tite. Brunel's Temple Meads, Bristol, is another, which happily still exists.

Most early termini had one arrival and one departure platform, often separated by a number of tracks on which empty rolling stock could be stored. As traffic increased, the area of sidings in the centre was reduced and further platforms added. This happened at King's Cross [TQ 303830], the London terminus of the Great Northern Railway, which was designed by Lewis Cubitt and opened in 1852. King's Cross is a classic terminus, its simple brick façade penetrated by the arches of the double train shed behind expressing so perfectly its 'arrival' and 'departure' functions. Cubitt's claim that the station would fulfil itself architecturally through 'the largeness of some of its features, its fitness for its purpose, and its characteristic expression of that purpose' is admirably demonstrated.

Much more typical in London and other major provincial termini has been the combination of the hotel with the station offices in the transverse section of the U, resulting in the train shed being completely obscured. Nowhere is the duality of function and treatment better demonstrated than at St Pancras [TQ 302829], the terminus built by the Midland Railway when it finally gained access to the capital in the late 1860s. Both components of the station are larger than life; the iron and glass train shed by W. H. Barlow and the Butterley Company is enormous, its span of 240ft then being the largest in the world, and in front Sir Gilbert Scott's romantic red-brick Victorian Gothic hotel is, in its architect's words 'possibly too good for its purpose'! St Pancras is still, happily, an operating station dominating the Euston Road, the ultimate expression of Victorian confidence and the might of the railway.

Other London termini incorporating hotels are Paddington (where Philip Hardwick's building of 1854 is architecturally interesting as an early example of French Renaissance and Baroque influence in England), Charing Cross, Cannon Street, Liverpool Street and Marylebone. The last named, where the hotel now provides the headquarters for the British Railways Board, shows a marked disparity in size between the huge hotel block and the miniature station behind it. Marylebone, the terminus of the last main line into London, was built in the late 1890s by the Manchester, Sheffield & Lincolnshire Railway, which, to celebrate its new-found status, changed its name to the Great Central Railway in 1897. Today Marylebone only handles suburban traffic, the main line to the north through Rugby, Leicester and Nottingham having gone after little more than sixty years of life.

Through stations presented peculiar problems of design, particularly when, as was often the case, the town lay on one side of the railway. It was considered undesirable for passengers to have to cross the lines, so there was sometimes just one long single platform for both up and down trains. At Reading and Slough

228 Shrewsbury, a station in the Tudor style [SJ 494129], undergoing restoration; increasingly British Rail is valuing its outstanding architectural assets   (*Neil Cossons*)

229 St Enoch underground station, Glasgow, built as the headquarters of the Glasgow District Subway Company in 1895 and now a travel centre [NS 599650]   (*John R. Hume*)

Brunel built stations of this type, with up and down station buildings both on the south side of the line, and at Derby Francis Thompson did much the same along the street side of an immense 1,050ft long platform [SK 363355]. Although there were clearly some advantages in this type of layout for the passengers, the operating difficulties were considerable, since trains had to cross each other's paths on entering and leaving the station. Only one survives today in operational form, at Cambridge [TL 462573], the GWR stations having been rebuilt, and those at Derby, Chester General, Huddersfield and Newcastle having been given extra platforms. Thompson's Chester station of 1848 [SJ 413669] still retains its great façade – over 1,000ft of vaguely Venetian symmetry in stone-faced brick punctuated by little towers. The awning was added later.

Almost every conceivable architectural style can be found somewhere in British railway stations. Initially classicism was favoured, as at Euston and Birmingham Curzon Street [SP 080871], and it later spread

to Huddersfield [SE 144169], Monkwearmouth, Sunderland [NZ 396577] and, finest of all, Newcastle Central [NZ 245638]. Huddersfield, by J. P. Pritchett, is an example of a station planned to be balanced by the same architect's designs in other adjacent buildings, in this case the George Hotel and Lion Arcade in St George's Square. Similarly at Stoke-on-Trent [SJ 879456] R. A. Stent matched the second Stoke station with the neo-Jacobean North Stafford Hotel on the opposite side of the square, while in Ashby-de-la-Zouch, Leicestershire (Illus 177) [SK 355163], the frontage of the beautiful little Grecian station of 1849 (now converted to offices) was part of a grand plan to develop a spa town. Perhaps the last purely classical station façade is that of Bath Green Park (Illus 8, 9, 10 and 11) [ST 745647], built in the early 1870s as the terminus of the Midland's branch from Mangotsfield and the Somerset & Dorset Railway.

The Tudor style appears in Bristol Temple Meads and Shrewsbury (Illus 228) [SJ 494129] but is exemplified in its purest form in the Carlisle Citadel station of 1847, designed by Sir William Tite and described as Britain's 'finest piece of railway architecture in the sixteenth century collegiate style'. 'Jacobean' stations are mainly small, as at Maldon, Essex [TL 853077], and Stone, Staffordshire [SJ 896346], although an unusually large railway building in this style is the old General Office of the Bristol & Exeter Railway beside the approach to Temple Meads station in Bristol [ST 596724], completed in 1854 to the designs of S. C. Fripp. The Italian idiom was used by Tite in the late 1830s on the London & Southampton Railway and the original Southampton terminus [SU 426112] survives as a nightclub. Campaniles in the same vein appeared in the pumping stations installed by Brunel on his 'atmospheric' railway along the south Devon coast, but only Starcross [SX 977819], dating from 1846, is in anything like complete condition.

From an architectural point of view the stations of cities and large towns must be considered in the context of the other public buildings, with which they often compare well. It is in small towns and villages, however, that railway architecture really comes into its own, and where stations and often other railway buildings most frequently reflect the characteristics of individual companies. Their variety is enormous, but careful observation of the works of a particular railway will soon reveal similarities of style and frequent use of standardised components. Indeed one of the major contributions made by the larger British railway companies was in the development of prefabricated buildings based on a range of standardised components. Thus throughout the territory of the Midland Railway, for example, from St Pancras to Carlisle and Lincoln to Avonmouth, one may find signal boxes, station waiting rooms, level crossing gates, platform lamps and awnings fitting into one style. The typical Midland signal box (Illus 230) was of unit construction, comprising standard timber posts, beams and panels that could be built in any number of bays, depending on the number of signal and point levers in the frame. Waiting rooms, too, were of standard design and, although usually built of brick, included standard components such as doors, barge-boards and cast iron window frames. It is in this field of what might be called 'vernacular railway architecture' that much interest lies,

230, 231 Typical Midland Railway signal box at Bardon, Leicestershire [SK 443126] and cast-iron awnings at Loughborough [SK 544205] (*Neil Cossons*)

and where, as the result of the great reduction in the number of passenger stations over the last ten years, considerable recording and preservation effort is needed. Fortunately railways have received the attentions of innumerable enthusiastic devotees anxious to record every detail of a particular system, and although their efforts have concentrated mainly on locomotives and rolling stock, other aspects of railway operations are receiving increasing attention.

The whole field of operational railway preservation is in itself a remarkable phenomenon, which has resulted in a number of lines being kept running after official closure and others being revived and brought back into use, sometimes after many years of complete dereliction. The first line in the country to be saved by enthusiast interests was the Talyllyn Railway, which in 1951 had been brought to the point of closure by declining slate traffic and road competition. Built in 1865 to serve slate quarries at Bryn Eglwys, it was opened for goods in the same year and for passengers in 1866. Today the 2ft 3in gauge line, covering the 6¾ miles from Wharf Station, Tywyn [SH 586005], to Abergynolwyn [SH 671064], carries over 130,000 passengers each season. Also at Tywyn is a narrow-gauge railway museum. Other operating narrow-gauge railways in Wales include the Festiniog,

232 Ribblehead Viaduct, North Yorkshire, on the Midland line from Settle to Carlisle [SD 760794]; high maintenance costs threaten its continued use *(Neil Cossons)*

running from Porthmadog [SH 571384] to Dduallt; the Welshpool & Llanfair Light Railway, based at Llanfair Caerinion, Powys [SJ 106068]; and the Vale of Rheidol, British Rail's only steam-operated line, which runs from Aberystwyth [SN 585815] to Devil's Bridge [SN 738769]. Also in Wales and unique in Britain is the Snowdon Mountain Railway, a 2ft 7½in gauge rack line that climbs from Llanberis [SH 583597] to a height of 3,493ft. It was opened in 1896 and operates with 0-4-2T inclined boiler locomotives of Swiss manufacture.

Standard-gauge preservation schemes are widespread throughout the country and vary enormously in their aims and methods of operation. Most are concerned primarily with running steam locomotives and, although ostensibly 'preservation societies', few go further than preserving locomotives and stock in original condition. Some, such as the Keighley & Worth Valley, based at Haworth [SE 035373] in West Yorkshire, and the Bluebell Railway centred on Sheffield Park station [TQ 404237] in Sussex, include locomotives and rolling stock painted in non-original liveries, whilst others like the Dart Valley Railway at Buckfastleigh [SX 746663], Devon, and the Severn Valley at Bridgnorth [SO 715926], Shropshire, maintain locomotives and rolling stock in the colours of their old owners. It is perhaps a little regrettable that, despite all this wealth of interest in railway preservation, as yet no line has been retained as a living example of how it used to be operated, with appropriate locomotives, stock, signal and telegraph equipment and so on.

CHAPTER 16

PORTS AND SHIPPING

The Industrial Revolution in Britain needed good internal transport systems, but equally important was the provision of facilities for import and export. The 'workshop of the world' was dependent on trade, and by the middle of the nineteenth century over 40 per cent of the entire world output of traded manufactured goods were produced in Britain, through whose ports passed over a quarter of total international trade. Over 90 per cent of British exports were composed of manufactured goods, which comprised only 7 per cent of imports. At no other time has one country so dominated the world economy. First canals and then railways gave manufacturers access to the coast, where sophisticated ports developed to handle goods in and out. Capital at least equal to that absorbed by canals was invested in the construction of these ports, although it was spread over a longer period. In recent years decline in the fortunes of many traditional ports as the result of changes in patterns of trade and the impact of containerisation and roll-on roll-off technology has left huge expanses of dockland empty and derelict. This in turn has stimulated a new form of urban renewal which, all over the country, has placed new values upon these otherwise unwanted areas.

In 1700 British trade was concentrated very heavily on London, which handled over 80 per cent of the nation's imports, 70 per cent of her exports and no less than 86 per cent of her re-exports. Defoe remarked that London 'sucked the vitals of trade in this island to itself'. In 1700 also London opened its first 'wet dock' at Rotherhithe. Previously London, like all other ports, had been entirely tidal, with ships either tying up at wharves and lying on the bottom over low tide or mooring in the river and being loaded and unloaded by lighter. The Rotherhithe wet dock consisted of a basin with entrance locks, through which ships could pass into an area of water at constant level. There cargoes could be transferred safely and quickly between ship and shore. In Bristol, Britain's second port after London, ships made their way laboriously up the River Avon to the wharves of the city, where they lay on the bottom over low water. Bristol's exceptional tidal range, which is 42ft at Portishead near the mouth of the river, meant that a ship in port would be grounded twice a day, and vessels trading regularly with the city had to have specially strengthened hulls.

It could take as long as four months to turn a ship round in Bristol, and many had their backs broken while they were there. In 1712 a wet dock was completed lower down the Avon at Sea Mills [ST 550760] and, although long disused, substantial evidence of it can still be seen in the form of a masonry wall and entrance lock. Sea Mills never became a real competitor to Bristol, being too far away from the commercial centre, and eventually it was used only by whaling ships, whose unwholesome cargoes were not welcome in the city.

The new trading activity of the eighteenth century, much of it transoceanic, led to rapid growth in other west coast ports. This growth was most dramatic in Liverpool. Defoe in 1720 thought its expansion 'one of the wonders of Britain . . . what it may grow to in time I know not'. At the end of the sixteenth century there had been fewer than 200 houses there and the Dee estuary, with Chester at its head, took prominence over the Mersey. By 1700 Liverpool's population was between 5,000 and 7,000, but it had reached 10,000 by 1720 and 30,000 by 1750 – and canals had not yet connected the town with the heart of industrial England. Bristol also doubled its population in the first half of the eighteenth century, reaching 90,000 by 1750, but then growth slackened as the port lost ground first to Liverpool and then Glasgow. Liverpool's first wet dock was completed in 1715 and a further six were added in the succeeding century.

In Glasgow improvements in the Clyde were made by John Golborne between 1773 and 1781 and by the Clyde Trust after 1809; and on the east coast Hull, with its Baltic trade and close waterway connections with the West Riding, had formed a dock company by 1774 and opened three interconnected docks by 1829. Completely new ports were also created, often for specific purposes, such as coal shipment. Seaham [NZ 435495] was the creation of the Marquess of Londonderry, who had coal interests in County Durham. On the west coast Maryport [NY 030365] in Cumberland developed for similar reasons. Other new ports were canal-inspired, like Grangemouth [NS 925825], opened in 1777, at the eastern end of the Forth & Clyde Canal, or Goole [SE 745230], opened in 1826 at the Humber end of the Aire & Calder Navigation.

Between 1753 and 1830 some 370 acres of wet docks were provided in England alone. Harbour commissioners or trustees were formed at numerous places round the coast to put port finance on a firmer basis and carry out improvements in response to the growth of trade. They engaged outstanding civil engineers to advise them, including such illustrious names as John Smeaton (1724–92) and John Rennie (1761–1821). Rennie alone was involved in over seventy harbour schemes. Not surprisingly the struggle with the sea to provide safe harbourage for ships led to many technological innovations including steam dredging, hollow walls and the diving bell. Although the cost of improvements was enormous, most of them enjoyed a much longer life than other works of the period, particularly the canals, which were soon to be ruined by railways. Their long-term use-

fulness, coupled frequently with very high standards of workmanship and materials, has meant that numerous port installations have survived to the present. As yet relatively little work has been done on the industrial archaeology of ports, which, with today's rapid rate of change in cargo handling and increase in vessel sizes, are likely to undergo radical alterations in the next few years. The closure of Bristol's city docks in favour of concentrating traffic at Avonmouth and, in Liverpool, the shut down of all docks south of the Pier Head are examples.

As a port complex now almost completely extinct but offering much of interest to the industrial archaeologist, the estuary of the Lune in Lancashire is worthy of examination. Before the late seventeenth century the port of Lancaster confined itself mainly to coastal trade, but shortly after 1700 the opportunity was taken of widening its scope to include the West Indies. Warehouses were built in large numbers along St George's Quay (Illus 233) [SD 474623], and several of mid-eighteenth-century date still survive, their gable walls complete with wooden beam cranes or 'lucams', which were used for hoisting goods to upper floors. Some merchants built dwelling houses, of which several remain, but the most notable reflection of Lancaster's importance as a port in the eighteenth century is the fine Custom House, erected in 1764 to the design of Richard Gillow. A number of streets running back from the quay area to Cable Street were laid out around 1800, with names like Antigua Street, Barbados Street and Jamaica Street, but these have long gone, swept away by the railway in 1849.

Also in the early eighteenth century Sunderland Point [SD 426560], which lies between the Lune estuary and Morecambe Bay, was promoted as an outport for Lancaster by Robert Lawson, a prominent local merchant. Here ships too big to make the difficult passage up to Lancaster itself could moor; a jetty was built and moderate prosperity enjoyed for a few years. The village is little changed today, with its two terraces of houses accessible from Overton by a causeway submerged by the tide

233 The Custom House, Lancaster [SD 474623], now a maritime museum   (*Neil Cossons*)

twice daily. According to legend the first bale of cotton to reach Lancashire was landed at Sunderland Point, to begin the industry for which the county was to become most famous. Across the river from Sunderland Point was Glasson [SD 445562], a safer anchorage, which soon took over as the unloading point for cargoes that were then shipped by lighter to Lancaster. In 1751 the port commissioners placed a chain and mooring stone there, and in 1791 a wet dock large enough to accommodate twenty-five merchant ships was completed. In 1826 Glasson Dock was linked with the Lancaster Canal, which necessitated the construction of a large inner basin. In 1834 a patent slip was laid down, in 1836 a gridiron or frame on which ships could be repaired at low

water was put in, and in 1838 a graving dock was opened. Today Glasson is the home only of pleasure craft and the odd surviving Morecambe Bay prawn boats or 'nobbies', the graving dock filling with rubbish, and the fine five-storey warehouse demolished for car parking. Yet the place has an air of former glory, and, like Lancaster itself, exudes the atmosphere of a once important port.

There is little remaining today in Bristol docks of eighteenth-century date with the possible exception of one or two small warehouses at the south end of Broad Quay. The whole harbour, which was tidal until the early nineteenth century, was completely remodelled by William Jessop who installed an entrance basin – Cumberland Basin [ST 570723] – with lock gates, and in effect created a huge wet dock occupying the whole of the bed of the River Avon and its tributary the Frome for over a mile upstream. River water was diverted down a new specially excavated channel, the New Cut. These enormous works were completed in 1809 and for a time enabled Bristol to compete with the up-and-coming Liverpool. As the size of ships increased, however, problems of access along the tortuous Avon arose, and Jessop's entrance locks were soon found to be too small. I. K. Brunel, who had recently brought the Great Western Railway into the city, was called in by the Bristol Dock Company to carry out improvements, which he completed in 1848. A new south entrance lock [ST 567723], whose chamber can still be seen, was built for Cumberland Basin, and improvements made to the dredging system by the use of a steam-powered cable-hauled scraper. The engine of this boat is on display in Bristol Maritime Heritage Centre [ST 579723], and in the nearby Bristol Industrial Museum a gallery is devoted to the history of the port. By the 1860s problems of increased shipping sizes arose again and the Port of Bristol Authority, the then municipal owners of the docks, undertook to build a new and larger north entrance lock, which is in use today.

Bristol city docks are now hardly used but contain a wealth of material of relevance to the industrial archaeologist. The newer docks built after 1877 at the confluence of the Avon with the Bristol Channel – Avonmouth, the smaller Portishead, and in recent years Royal Portbury – have for a century been the focal points of Bristol's port activities. At the entrance to Cumberland Basin in the shadow of a modern road swingbridge is a gridiron, installed in 1884 for the repair of small vessels, while over the entrance lock and Brunel's now redundant lock of the 1840s are two wrought iron girder swing bridges [ST 567723]. The first of these, dating from 1848, was installed by Brunel and is thought to be the earliest wrought iron girder bridge in existence, if not the first

ever constructed. The second bridge, built over the new entrance lock in the 1870s, is almost identical.

Like many ports in the nineteenth century Bristol used, and to a small extent still uses, hydraulic power to drive the numerous ancillary installations like lock gates, capstans and cranes. The hydraulic press, consisting of a small hand pump and reservoir connected to a hydraulic cylinder and ram, had been patented in 1795 by Joseph Bramah and was soon to be widely adopted for engineering work and, as modified by Matthew Murray (1765–1826) of Leeds, for baling cloth. In 1812 Bramah proposed the installation of hydraulic power mains on a municipal basis, with a central generating station and users paying by meter for the power they used. Although this far-sighted idea was not adopted for a further sixty-five years, it was in essence the basis for numerous dock installations. Both Bramah and Murray developed hydraulic cranes but it was the work of William (later Sir William) George Armstrong (1810–1900), whose first hydraulic crane was erected in Newcastle in 1846, that made hydraulic power widely acceptable both in docks and elsewhere. Armstrong devised the weight-loaded hydraulic accumulator to provide sufficient head, air vessels to balance the fluctuations between supply and demand and smooth out pump pulsations, and the hydraulic jigger (consisting of a jack with pulley sheaves mounted at each end) by means of which the effective stroke could be multiplied and excessively long jack cylinders obviated.

The first public hydraulic supply was installed in Hull in 1877, to be followed in London by the installations of the Wharves & Warehouses Steam Power & Hydraulic Pressure Company, which in 1883 operated some 7 miles of mains on both sides of the Thames. In the following year this company was absorbed into the London Hydraulic Power Company, which by the 1930s supplied over 8,000 separate hydraulic machines through 184 miles of mains. The large public hydraulic-power companies have closed, in Hull because of war damage, and in Liverpool as recently as 1970 as the result of a dwindling consumer demand. The Glasgow and Manchester systems have also closed down. (An electrically powered hydraulic generator pump is on display, working in the local history gallery of the Merseyside Museum, William Brown Street, Liverpool 3.)

By the standards of these installations, that at Bristol is small, supplying power only for the port authority's own use. The generating station is near the Cumberland Basin at the Underfall Yard [ST 572722], where there are three electrically driven pumps by Fullerton, Hodgart & Barclay of Paisley. A brick accumulator tower near the generating station is no longer used, but outside is a modern steel tower where the weight can be seen falling and rising intermittently as water is taken from the mains and then replenished. The system is used regularly for the older swing bridges of Cumberland Basin and the lock gates. Prince's Street Bridge [ST 586723], although not now hydraulically powered, also has a small booster accumulator tower.

Numerous examples of hydraulically operated machinery can still be seen in most ports of any size, the accumulator tower usually being the most obvious clue to their existence. Of these, the campanile-style tower standing between the entrance locks at Grimsby [TA 281113], Humberside, must be the most spectacular. Dating from the early 1850s, it is 313ft high and was built by the Manchester, Sheffield & Lincolnshire Railway to provide a head for the hydraulic mains of the port and support a freshwater tank for ships. It is not an accumulator tower in the true sense of the term, but an artificial head of water for the hydraulic mains, consisting of a 33,000 gallon tank into which water was pumped by a steam engine. The enormous cost of providing a tower like that at Grimsby was instrumental in the development of the accumulator proper, in which a large weight is raised on a piston to create the same sort of pressure. The Grimsby tower now serves only as a television relay station and for supplying water to wash down the fish pontoon. Other towers may be seen in Liverpool docks and at Glasgow.

Here and there bridges are still powered by hydraulics, including the famous swing bridge across the Tyne at Newcastle [NZ 253637] built by Armstrong in 1876, and the Barton Aqueduct on the Manchester Ship Canal (Illus 195) [SJ 767976]. The best known of all, Tower Bridge, London [TQ 337802], an engineering masterpiece and architectural absurdity to the designs of Sir Horace Jones, architect to the City of London, and Sir John Wolfe-Barry, was opened in 1894 and operated hydraulically until 1977 when electric power took over. Most of the hydraulic equipment is still *in situ* and the bridge is open to the public. East of Tower Bridge Road on the south side of the river are the distinctive chimney and accumulator tower of the hydraulic power station which provided the water under pressure. In Rotherhithe the hydraulic machinery which operated the bridge carrying Redriffe Road over the passage between Greenland Dock and Russia Dock [TQ 362793] has been preserved. In addition, three nineteenth-century hydraulically operated swing bridges may still be seen in London's dockland, carrying Preston Road over the Blackwall Entrance to the West India Docks in Tower Hamlets [TQ 383802] (1894), Connaught Road over the passage between Royal Victoria and Royal Albert Docks [TQ 416806] (1879) and Woolwich Manor Way across the passage connecting the Royal Albert with the basin at Gallions [TQ 437806] (1879), both in Newham.

The growth of trade through British ports in the early years of the nineteenth century necessitated a completely new approach to the provision of port installations, particularly warehousing. Traditionally quayside warehouses had been relatively small, of up to four storeys, and with timber floors supported on timber beams presenting problems of load capacity and fire risk. The warehouses in Lancaster, already mentioned, typify what might be called the 'pre-industrial' warehouse building. Other examples may be seen in ports as far apart as King's Lynn, Norfolk; Boston, Lincolnshire; Bideford and Exeter in Devon where appropriately some warehouse buildings form part of the Exeter Maritime Museum [SX 921921].

One of the King's Lynn buildings, incidentally, on Nelson Street overlooking Mill Fleet, provides a fine example of a new use for an old industrial building, for here the granaries have been sensitively converted into offices. In Portsoy, Banffshire [NJ 589665] a group of miscellaneous harbour buildings have been converted into council houses.

Bristol also has a number of early warehouses of traditional construction, alongside others which represent the transition to a larger scale of port building that developed mainly in London and Liverpool. One of these transitional warehouses was J. & R. Bush's tea bond on Prince Street [ST 586725], overlooking the traditional heart of the city's harbour at the junction of the Avon and Frome. Dating from the 1830s, it is a five-storey structure and originally had timber floors supported by cast iron columns. Bush's warehouse is now a gallery, restaurant and office. The boldly featured stone exterior, with its prominent string courses and arch-headed windows, heralded a more exotic style of Bristol warehouse that developed after 1850, but in terms of constructional technique nothing more advanced was built in the port until the great tobacco bonds of the early 1900s. The city docks continued to be provided with relatively small warehouses, appropriate to the size of ships trading there, of which a few classic examples survive. Two warehouse façades, also converted to new uses, beside Bathurst Basin [ST 587722] exhibit in a restrained way the polychrome brickwork and ogee arches which typified large numbers of buildings in the Victoria Street area in the third quarter of the nineteenth century, a style which has since become known, with some architectural inexactitude, as 'Bristol Byzantine'. The prize example of the style is on Welsh Back [ST 588726], built in 1869 to the designs of two local architects, Archibald Ponton and W. V. Gough. It epitomises Bristol Byzantine at its most exotic and yet, despite its unusual outside appearance, the internal structure is of conventional timber joists and floorboards. The building is now a club.

London's early wet docks, like that at Rotherhithe, had no warehousing of their own – indeed the Rotherhithe Dock had a double row of poplar trees round the basin as a protection against wind. Similarly Brunswick Dock, Blackwall, opened in 1790, was chiefly intended for the safe accommodation of the East India Company's ships, and the only building of note was the masting house. Not until the opening of the West India Docks in 1802 was a system of warehousing provided, solving at once two major problems – the difficulty of unloading ships in tidal water and, by the provision of a Customs wall, the pilfering of cargoes, which had been causing merchants grave concern.

The origins of large-scale port warehousing may still be seen, in a somewhat diminished state, in St Katharine Dock, London. The purpose of the dock was to provide both an unloading place for ships and quayside warehousing as close as possible to the commercial heart of London. The St Katharine Dock Company Act was passed in 1825 for an enclosed wet dock system immediately to the east of the Tower of London [TQ 339805]. Thomas Telford was chief engineer, with Philip Hardwick (1792–1870) as architect. The two major criteria which Telford and Hardwick had to apply in developing the 23 acre site were the need to obtain as much quayside length as possible for unloading purposes and the provision of the maximum amount of warehouse storage space. Room had also to be made for several vessels docking together as, unlike today, arrival times were very dependent on the weather. The final design consisted of two irregularly shaped docks each linked to a smaller entrance basin, although here the originally intended second entrance lock was never built. In having all its warehouses built up to the water's edge, St Katharine Dock was unique. Normal practice was to have an open quay, transit sheds and a road between the water and the warehouses. The idea at St Katharine's, however, was to save double handling by taking goods straight from the ship's hold to the appropriate floor of

234 Albert Dock, Liverpool [SJ 342898] before rehabilitation *(Neil Cossons)*

the warehouse by means of overhead cranes.

The result was a magnificent range of six-storey warehouses, cube-like, compact and functional, with a ground floor arcade of giant cast iron Doric columns and full-height round-headed blank arches embracing the windows above. Most were designed by Thomas Telford but the block on the west side facing the Tower Bridge approach was by Hardwick. Architecturally their importance lay in the combination of utilitarian function and a classical discipline of design, and they represented an important stage in the development of buildings adapted specifically to the large-scale requirements of the nineteenth century. The constructional technique of the initial buildings was in fact fairly conventional, with timber floors, but those added in the late 1850s had an iron frame and stone slab floors. After suffering extensive bomb damage in 1940, after which several of the buildings were demolished, St Katharine Dock was eventually closed in October 1968 and since then has become the centre of a waterfront redevelopment which itself, sadly, resulted in the loss of several of the finest remaining warehouses.

Although London had always retained its lead as Britain's major port, the eighteenth and nineteenth centuries saw Liverpool take Bristol's place as the second most important, with Hull, Glasgow and at the end of the period, Manchester, all overtaking her also. Liverpool's small cluster of wet docks near what is now the Pier Head formed the basis for the remarkable linear development of docks, eventually exceeding 7 miles in length and which is illustrated in Illus 236. The evolution of this dock estate during the nineteenth century was influenced by a number of factors, including the need for more dock and warehouse space as traffic increased, the building of larger vessels, the coming of steamships, and the need for greater security, which led to the separation of the dock area from the city. In much of this development the central figure was Jesse Hartley, who was dock engineer from 1824 until his death in 1860 and whose indelible stamp still character-

ises much of Liverpool's dockland. This linear development and need for greater security was emphasised by the great wall that Hartley built on the landward side of the dock estate and alongside which the present Dock Road runs. Entrances were protected by huge sliding gates and towers that have all the appearance of miniature fortifications. Only Stanley Dock [SJ 337921], opened in 1848, lies outside the wall, but this was because it formed the link between the main dock system and the Leeds & Liverpool Canal. By the time of Hartley's death the line of docks stretched from Canada Dock on the northern edge of Liverpool to Brunswick Dock in the south, the latter the first dock to be built by Hartley himself.

Undoubtedly Hartley's masterpiece is Albert Dock [SJ 342898], close to the traditional heart of the port and immediately south of the Pier Head. Albert Dock (Illus 234 and 235) is the logical extension of the principle established in St Katharine Dock, London, in the late 1820s, but here the rectangle of open water is surrounded by an almost complete wall of warehousing coming right up to the edge of the quay, although still retaining the arcade with cast iron columns at ground floor level. The columns are modelled on Greek Doric prototypes and are hollow drums 12ft 6in in circumference and 15ft high. Encased with walls of brick, the five floors of the warehouses are supported on iron columns, the spaces between them spanned by cast iron beams of inverted-Y section tied laterally with wrought iron tension rods. From these beams spring the brick arches of the floors, the whole method of construction evolving directly from the pioneer work of Strutt and Bage in Derbyshire and Shrewsbury at the end of the eighteenth century. At Albert Dock, however, even the roof trusses are of iron, and the roof itself is made of wrought iron plates. Tucked into the north-east corner is the Dock Traffic Office, dating, like the warehouses, from the mid-1840s but in this case designed by Philip Hardwick, who had collaborated with Telford at St Katharine Dock and meanwhile built a triumphal arch at Euston. Hardwick's design for Euston seems to have influenced him in Liverpool, and the Tuscan portico of the Dock Traffic Office, entirely constructed in cast iron, symbolises *par excellence* Victorian commercial achievement and self-confidence.

Albert Dock, however, is not the only site of industrial archaeological significance in the Port of Liverpool. Whole areas of the city are rich in dockland archaeology. Within the estate are swing bridges, including cast iron examples designed by Hartley at Albert, Salthouse and Wapping Docks, and a curious timber footbridge across the entrance to Canning Dock [SJ 342899], supposedly by John Rennie. Similarly the warehouses and transit sheds, particularly those of the Hartley era, are almost universally of a monumental scale and impeccable standard of construction. By contrast much of the private warehousing inland from the Dock Road is mean and penny-pinching. Despite the Liverpool Warehouse Act of 1843, which introduced reduced premiums for brick and iron structures, many were still built with timber floors up to the latter part of the nineteenth century. Other worthwhile sites include Hartley's Victoria Tower [SJ 333921], completed in 1848 at the entrance to Salisbury Dock, and the remnant of the Floating Landing Stage [SJ 337904] at the Pier Head by G. Fosbery Lyster and Sir William Cubitt (1876). Victoria Tower, built of the same grey granite as his other dock works, is unmistakably Hartley, the stone blocks carefully dressed and fitted together like a jigsaw puzzle. It carries an unusual six-faced clock and bell to ring out warnings. The Landing Stage, on the other hand, is much more utilitarian. Built on iron pontoons and originally nearly ½ mile long, it was the place from which Liverpool's transatlantic liners departed – Cunard and White Star until they moved to Southampton, Canadian Pacific more recently. Now it is only used regularly by the Mersey ferries.

Unlike London, Liverpool had no other major function during the nineteenth century and first part of the twentieth than being a port, so the down-town part of the city, more so than any other in Britain, reflects a deep involvement with ships and commerce even today. Marine insurance offices, shipping company offices,

235 Albert Dock houses the Merseyside Maritime Museum, a northern outpost of the Tate Gallery, shops, offices and flats *(Merseyside Maritime Museum)*

THE LIVERPOOL DOCK SYSTEM
1760-1986

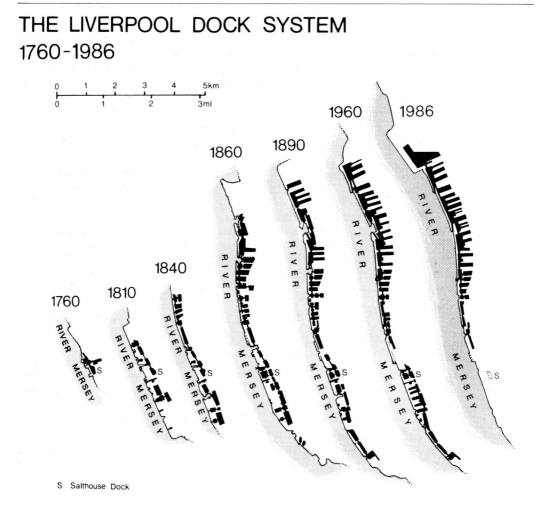

Illustration 236

dockside pubs, warehouses and merchants' houses are all still there, some still thriving but others in the final stages of decay. The Sailors' Home in Canning Place [SJ 345900], dating originally from the 1840s, came into this last category. Externally a fair representation of Hardwick Hall, its cast iron inside closely resembled an American penitentiary. It was demolished in the early 1970s before public attitudes had caught up with its qualities. In a healthier state is the Albany [SJ 340906] on Old Hall Street, dating from 1858 and one of the finest of the Victorian office blocks that grew up immediately inland from the

waterfront. It is built round a courtyard that is spanned by a delicate cast iron bridge reached by a spiral staircase. The yard provides light to the inner offices, as do skylights above galleries at each side of the building.

The industrial archaeologist in dockland has unrivalled opportunities for the discovery of obscure and obsolete equipment in addition to the more obvious large-scale installations. Winches and hand cranes frequently bear makers' names cast into them, as do iron mooring bollards. Cranes alone are worthy of detailed examination, as almost any which are not electrically powered may be regarded as obsolete. Harwich [TM 262325] has what is probably the oldest crane in Britain, dated 1666; it consists of a fixed wooden house containing a treadmill and a swinging jib mounted on heavy framing at one end and turning through 180 degrees. It has been moved from its original site in the old harbour area. Steam cranes were introduced about the same time as Armstrong was experimenting with hydraulic power, but few of either type now survive. A heavy lift steam crane with riveted wrought iron plate jib dating from the 1870s [ST 584722] can be seen in Bristol, and there is a smaller example in Dover [TR 319410]. Electric cranes, introduced in the 1890s, are now almost universal, although the earlier types, like the one at Southampton dated 1893, are becoming increasingly scarce.

To enable ships to navigate coastal waters safely, lighthouses have been provided from ancient times, but it was not until the eighteenth century that there was any systematic approach to the design of either the tower or the light it carried. John Smeaton (1724–92), who built the third Eddystone Lighthouse 14 miles from Plymouth in 1759, was one of the first to examine the civil engineering problems, and his dovetailing of the core stones of the tower became a standard technique. Smeaton's light continued in use at the Eddystone until 1882, when it was decided to build a new tower on a different part of the reef because the foundation rock was becoming undermined. Smeaton's lighthouse was then re-erected on Plymouth Hoe [SX 478538], where it may still be visited. In 1836 Parliament transferred all English lighthouses to the care of Trinity House, while in Scotland the Commissioners for Northern Lighthouses, established in 1786, were responsible for a number of notable lights.

In recent years the urban waterfront – what until the mid-1970s was seen as an unprepossessing and intractable liability – has become the focus of a remarkable change of attitude. Indeed, the move towards heritage-led rehabilitation has its most remarkable manifestations in the revival of Britain's derelict docklands. Thus Albert Dock which J. A. Picton in 1875 described as 'a hideous pile of naked brickwork' in his *Memorials of Liverpool* is now valued, not as one of the supreme archaeological monuments to the rise of the first industrial nation, but for its

237 Gloucester docks [SO 825185], heart of a waterfront development which will include the National Waterways Museum (*Neil Cossons*)

potential in catalysing commercial redevelopment. In London, Swansea, Hull, Exeter and Bristol the same trend can be seen.

The Floating Harbour in Bristol, neglected for years and an eyesore in the heart of the city, is now central to a new strategy of urban revival based upon several vital ingredients – wholesome water, maintained at a constant level, accessible and suitable for recreational use; historic buildings that lend themselves to new residential, retailing, office or cultural purposes, and the presence of one or more preserved ships. Bristol has all these attributes. Conversion of Bush's warehouse, an early nineteenth-century tea bond, to house the Arnolfini Gallery, restaurants and offices, and the return to the city and subsequent restoration of Brunel's iron ship *Great Britain*, set in train the se-

quence of events which has led to almost every re-usable historic building becoming a desirable property. Transit sheds and warehouses now house shops, restaurants, museums and galleries and the water is home to historic ships, boating and water sport. Some of what has resulted in the name of conservation is little more than façadism – the retention of an old frontage or shell behind or within which a completely new building has been constructed; Bush's warehouse is an example of this. Elsewhere the structure has been retained. The most recent phase of this revivalist trend is to redevelop the open spaces adjacent to the waterfront in a flavour compatible with what is already there, post-modern housing reflecting various waterfront and warehouse clichés. On a larger scale this is what the St Katharine Dock now offers.

With the setting up of dockland development corporations, notably in London and Liverpool, additional stimulus was given to the adaptive re-use process, to the

238 Dunoon Pier, Argyll [NS 176764], restored to the condition in which it was rebuilt by the Town Commissioners in 1896   (*John R. Hume*)

extent that in London's docklands in particular, on both the north and south sides of the Thames, almost every eligible waterfront property downstream of Tower Bridge has now been converted, mainly for residential purposes. Improved access provided by the Docklands Light Railway and the extension of the Jubilee Line can only encourage further development in the long term but how far historic buildings will have any relevance remains to be seen. They may not provide a sufficient return on investment; replicas or pastiche will undoubtedly prove to be cheaper and more convenient.

On Merseyside, without the strong economic stimulus provided by the proximity of the City, the revival of Liverpool's waterfront is rather more laborious but again the heritage formula, emanating in the main from Albert Dock and its maritime museum, is generating re-use. Handled with skill the distinctive qualities of these dockland areas can be enhanced, but the pressure to make them all

239,240,241 Clevedon Pier, Avon [ST 402719], built in 1868 by Hamilton's Windsor Ironworks, Liverpool, partly collapsed in 1970 during strength testing; now under restoration, the pavilions have been rebuilt on their original wrought iron frames

(Bath Evening Chronicle, Neil Cossons)

the same is strong, a seductive ambience indistinguishable in flavour from Baltimore or Vancouver.

SHIPBUILDING

During the first century or more of industrialisation in Britain the nation's trade was handled by sailing ships that changed relatively little in design or size. Shipbuilding was an industry steeped in tradition and slow to respond to new requirements. It was no accident that Captain James Cook (1728–79) circumnavigated the world in what was basically a Whitby collier. This was the best type of vessel available to the British Admiralty, so it was used for the job. Towards the end of the eighteenth century came a gradual move to improve ship design led by the French, although later the North Americans took the lead in merchant shipbuilding. Despite conservatism of design and constructional techniques the British merchant fleet grew enormously during the eighteenth century, the total tonnage rising from 323,000 tons in 1700 to reach the 1 million ton mark by 1788.

There were, however, improvements to individual parts of ships and to the techniques of constructing them. In the 1780s copper sheathing of wooden hulls to prevent attack by the Teredo ship worm was introduced, while in the early 1800s Sir Marc Isambard Brunel, father of I. K. Brunel, designed mass-production machine tools for the manufacture of pulley blocks (see p 134) for the Royal Navy.

Although the first steam paddle boat to run commercially, the *Comet* designed by Henry Bell (1767–1830), had indicated the potential of the new form of power as early as 1812 on the Clyde, it was some years before steam navigation had any real impact. In April 1838 the 703 ton *Sirius* made the first transatlantic crossing mainly by using its steam engine, beating by a few days the paddle steamer *Great Western*. Designed by I. K. Brunel, the *Great Western* was the first ship built specifically for the transatlantic trade. She was 236ft long and weighed 4,000 tons, but the hull was of traditional timber construction although heavily strengthened with iron knees and bolts. Not until the hulls of ships were built completely of iron could the potential of the steam engine be fully realised.

The first iron vessel had been launched into the River Severn at Preens Eddy below Ironbridge as early as 1787. Designed and built by the local ironmaster John Wilkinson (1728–1808), it was no more than a barge, probably of similar general appearance and constructional technique to the mid-nineteenth-century iron tub boat preserved on the Shropshire Canal in the Blists Hill Open Air Museum [SJ 694034]. The demand of the steam engine prompted active investigation of the possibilities of iron hulls and this, coupled with the success of Brunel's *Great Western* in 1838, encouraged both her owners and designer to think on a completely new and unprecedented scale when planning their next ship. That ship was the *Great Britain*, the first screw-propelled all-iron merchant ship to enter Atlantic service. Designed by Brunel, she was the largest ship afloat when Prince Albert launched her in Bristol on 19 July 1843. Unlike most vessels however *Great Britain* was not built on a slipway but in a drydock that had been specially constructed to accommodate her enormous bulk, anticipating a technology that has only recently become commonplace. That dock still exists, holding once more the ship to which it gave birth [ST 578724]. After a varied but successful career involving a number of alterations to engines and rig, *Great Britain*'s active life ended in 1886 when she was abandoned as a hulk in the Falkland Islands. Then, a century and a quarter after her launching, she was returned to Bristol showing signs of age but not of any major deterioration, a remarkable testimony to the skill and workmanship of her builders. *Great Britain* is now well on the way to complete restoration and, together with the nearby Maritime Heritage Centre, is open to the public.

Although the *Great Britain* in her dock is perhaps the most spectacular combination of maritime and shipbuilding archaeology to be found anywhere, there are numerous other remains of significance to the industrial archaeologist. Unfortunately ship-building tends to produce few lasting remains other than the ships themselves, and the adoption of prefabrication and welding techniques in an industry that since the 1920s has been in an almost perpetual state of flux and reorganisation has meant that there is often little of significance left to see.

There is ample evidence of the ships themselves however. Best known is per-haps the *Cutty Sark* preserved at Green-wich [TQ 383778], an important ship not only for her record-breaking runs in the tea and wool trades but for her composite con-struction – iron frames with wooden hull planking, to which the copper anti-fouling sheathing could be fastened without fear of electrolytic action. HMS *Gannet* of 1878, now at Chatham is also of composite build. The research ship *Discovery*, built in Dundee in 1901, has returned there for long-term preservation; further down the coast at Anstruther, Fife [NT 565037], the Scottish Fisheries Museum has a collection of fishing boats. The North Carr lightship, built in 1933 and taken out of commission in 1975, is also open to visitors there. Important collections of ship models may be seen in museums in Glasgow, New-castle-upon-Tyne Museum of Science & Technology (the *Turbinia* is still on display at the old science museum site) [NZ 246657], Merseyside Maritime Museum (where the pilot vessel *Edmund Gardner* is preserved), Bristol Industrial Museum, the Science Museum, London, and the National Mari-time Museum, Greenwich. Naval ship-building has perhaps left more to posterity than the merchant ship side of the industry. In addition to HMS *Victory* and the *Mary Rose* at Portsmouth, HMS *Warrior*, the first British iron warship, of 1861, is now being preserved there, after an extensive pro-gramme of restoration at West Hartlepool. Built at the Thames Ironworks, Blackwall, as an armoured frigate, she had a peaceful career, to leave active naval service in 1929 and became an oil-pipeline jetty at Pem-broke Dock. The remains of Penn's works at Payne's Wharf, Borthwick Street Dept-ford [TQ 372781], where her engines were installed, can still be seen. Almost exactly opposite, across the Thames in Millwall

[TQ 374783], is the site of the Napier Yard, next to the buildings of the former Millwall Ironworks, where Brunel's third ship, the *Great Eastern*, was launched in 1858. The timber slipway, constructed for the sideways launch can be seen at low tide. Elsewhere on the Thames, HMS *Belfast* is preserved in the Pool of London and the ketch, *Kathleen and May*, rests in St Mary Overy Dock. But generally, ship preserva-tion is suffering from a lack of good berths with sufficient funding and numbers of visitors. A major national initiative is needed.

The Naval dockyards, too, are rich in important structures relating to both the building of ships and their subse-quent operation. The four dockyards at Portsmouth, Chatham, Sheerness and Plymouth (Devonport) all contain an assortment of buildings of all periods from the seventeenth century onwards, includ-ing stores, docks, workshops, barracks, foundries, ropewalks, dwellings and chapels. Particularly important are the No 53 Boat Store at Chatham [TQ 765700], built in 1813 for building and repairing men-of-war; the cast and wrought iron framed boathouse of 1858 at Sheerness [TQ 910753]; and the cast iron framed fire station at Portsmouth [SU 630005]. The Sheerness boathouse is one of the earliest known multi-storey iron-frame buildings, and was designed by Colonel G. T. Greene, Director of Engineering and Architectural Works at the Admiralty from 1850 to 1864. Being a frame building, the whole struc-ture is supported by its frame, and the external walls are non-loadbearing panels of standardised form. Beams supporting the floors are fabricated from wrought iron plate and angle riveted together to form H girders, the earliest known large building in Britain where this form of construction occurs. Since 1960 the Navy has stopped using Sheerness Dockyard, but at Ports-mouth most of the important structures are either accessible as part of the Naval Heritage Project, or by special permission. At Chatham the Historic Dockyard Trust is actively engaged on a major pro-gramme of rehabilitation. A visitor centre provides an introduction to tours of the yard.

CHAPTER 17

CONCLUSION

In this review of the major industries an attempt has been made to link processes and the stages of their evolution with the surviving visual evidence. This has not always been possible, however, with the result that imbalances occur which in no way reflect the relative importance of various industrial activities. Thus the chemical industry, of enormous and generally unrecognised importance throughout the Industrial Revolution, has received less than its due because the physical remains, or at any rate the significant and comprehensible ones, have virtually disappeared. The present state of industrial archaeological knowledge, together with the variability of individual enthusiasms, contributes to this problem; canals and railways are more inspiring than lead-chamber sulphuric acid plants, even supposing any were still to exist. With the increasing amount of disciplined and well organised work within the field of industrial archaeological recording, however, these imbalances are being redressed, particularly as local societies build up comprehensive surveys of the whole range of sites within their own areas.

Numerous industries have hardly been mentioned at all, but this does not mean to say that they have no archaeological significance. Food processing, clothing, and boot and shoe making are some of the areas which have been neglected but, in the case of the latter, a detailed analysis of the industry in and around Northampton will reveal through surviving buildings the transition from a domestic to a factory-based industry in the mid-nineteenth century. This change occurred to some extent as a result of the introduction of American-made sewing machines, initi-

ally for closing the uppers but later for sole and welt sewing. Examples can be seen in Northampton Museum. In the 'domestic' system the uppers were cut and stitched together (closed) at a central premises and then sent out to hand-sewers working usually in sheds at the bottom of their gardens. These 'shops' can still be seen in many Northamptonshire towns and villages. By the end of the nineteenth century the processes had all been gathered together into factories, with the cutting of the leather (clicking) and closing on the top floor where there was most light and the machines were not heavy, lasting and attaching on the floor below and at the bottom the leather stores and heavy cutting presses. This simple functionalism, with the work flowing down through the building, still exists in some Northampton factories.

Thus the physical evidence of buildings and to a lesser extent machines survives to illustrate the stages in the transition from a cottage industry to that ultimate in mid-nineteenth-century shoe factories, the Manfield Building. To find out *why* shoes are made in Northampton requires evidence of a completely different type. Only a detailed analysis of documentary sources and a thorough appreciation of a range of geographical factors will build up the picture of coinciding elements – of cattle for leather, perhaps of oak trees providing bark for tanning, of agrarian unrest and unemployment associated

242 Battersea Power Station [TQ 290775]. Only the shell of this famous London landmark still stands, awaiting a new use *(Royal Commission on Historical Monuments, England)*

243 Interior of Barracks Mill showing the classic cast iron column and beam construction pioneered at the end of the eighteenth century; important early industrial buildings are still being revealed as the result of regional surveys (*Royal Commission on Historical Monuments, England*)

with enclosure – creating the conditions for the growth of the industry. Northamptonshire tended at first to specialise in cheaper shoes, as the top end of the market was largely the province of London-based shoemakers located near their discerning customers. Northamptonshire shoemakers prospered on army contracts, initially for Cromwell's New Model Army, eventually gaining a virtual monopoly of all service footwear. All this, but particularly the relationship of the physical evidence to other sources, is the concern of the industrial archaeologist.

Besides the evidence of its own specific technology, the brewing industry affords the industrial archaeologist an opportunity to examine functionalism in building design and construction at its purest. In addition, the appreciation of the role which many of the spectacular structural elements, particularly of maltings, play in both urban and rural landscapes is a refined aesthetic experience in its own right. Malting as an essential part of the brewing process has been carried on both at the brewery itself or in separate establishments. The process consists of encouraging barley to germinate and thereby change its starch content into sugar, at which stage the process is arrested in drying kilns. Before the development of large-scale breweries, malting was a local and small-scale activity carried out in almost every town. Even so, some had marked concentrations of small malthouses. Marshfield in Gloucestershire, for example, had dozens, and the characteristic perforated tiles from the drying floors are commonplace there.

The development of large-scale maltings, often separate from the breweries themselves, in the second half of the nineteenth century resulted in some of the most visually stimulating and dynamic examples of functional building to emerge during the Industrial Revolution. East Anglia and the Home Counties, areas not noted for their high degree of industrialisation, are rich in these sophisticated and often beautiful buildings. The main part of the structure usually has three or more floors for the germination process, often with floor to ceiling heights of only 6ft or even less, with small rectangular windows, louvred to serve as vents. Very typically there are tie irons passing through the building whose presence is evident on the exterior in the form of tie plates – huge crosses or discs of cast iron regularly spaced along the façades. Attached are the kilns with their tall pyramidal roofs and cowls. The architectural personality of these structures derives from the common ingredients of functional elements often combined with great size, so that they make their presence felt in the landscape in a very positive way. Often, because of their rural situation, it is difficult to associate them with an industrial process at all; they are more an extension of the agricultural tradition of building.

Their extensive floor areas and attractive proportions have led to some highly successful conversions of disused maltings to new purposes. Best known are the Snape, Suffolk, maltings now a hall for the Aldeburgh Music Festival [TM 392575]. The oasthouse in which hops are dried, also for brewing, is another distinctive structure common in Kent but also to be found in Hereford & Worcester. Cylindrical kilns with their characteristic windvane cowls are, generally speaking, older than the rectangular type; both are in demand for conversion to dwellings. This functional simplicity extends, too, to some of the older whisky distilleries in Scotland, of which the main concentration is in Strath Spey. The malting process is basically the same and the characteristic cowled pyramidal roofs can still be seen here and there.

In contrast, the early remains of the motor manufacturing industry are much less visible. Little research has been carried out on them, still less has been published, and many of the buildings themselves – particularly those dating from the earliest pre-production line period – have few obvious characteristics to distinguish them. Recent investigation however has revealed that the stages in the transition from trestle to track assembly can still be traced through the surviving buildings. Of the equipment virtually nothing is known to survive. Illus 244, showing finished car chassis awaiting their bodies drawn up outside the Standard Works in Coventry [SP 312788] in 1907, illustrates the nondescript nature of the buildings required for trestle assembly. The north-light roof construction is typical of small engineering shops of the period with a direct relationship between size of buildings and output of vehicles. Over the same period that many of the techniques of individual construction have become virtually extinct – Morgan still perpetuates the system – the name Standard, like so many others, has disappeared too. Introduced as a low-priced model the name emphasised the interchangeability of its parts, a notable advantage at the time. Half a century later that was taken for granted, but in an increasingly competitive market a name which could be interpreted as meaning ordinary had become a liability.

These industries are important not only for the intrinsic characteristics of their own processes but for their role in creating the personality of an area. The industrial archaeologist in studying landscapes is involved in the analysis of their personalities, which depends not only on collecting and collating detailed field evidence

244 Standard motor car works, Coventry, 1907 [SP 312788]; simple, non-specialised buildings housed the motor industry in the years before assembly-line production techniques were introduced   (*Larkin Brothers*)

245,246 A century separates Dunkirk Mill at Nailsworth in Gloucestershire [SO 845005] dating from the early years of the nineteenth century, from Ring Mill and Mavis Mill, Coppull, Lancashire [SD 563147]. The nature of Britain's historic industrial landscapes will undergo profound change before the end of the century; detailed study and sensitive policies towards rehabilitation are essential.
(*Neil Cossons, Royal Commission on Historical Monuments, England*)

and relating it to documentary sources but also on a subtler aesthetic appreciation of the components of that landscape in terms of building materials, of the size and shape of windows, the pitch of roofs, the depths of mouldings and string courses, the design of rainwater goods, the types of paving and road surfacing. Here the work of the industrial archaeologist is wedded immutably to the field evidence, and only by exhaustive and detailed examination of large numbers of structures can the components that make up the personality of an area be isolated and identified. Industrial landscapes, even of the late nineteenth century, possess as much visual variety, structural and architectural individuality as do their rural predecessors, in which the regional variations of the vernacular tradition have long been

accepted. The industrial archaeologist in extracting from the surviving buildings and other features of the landscape the specific characteristics that create its personality is carrying out a vital archaeological function, and providing what may be the only basis for defining rational conservation policies. He can only analyse those characteristics after recording in painstaking detail large numbers of individual structures and comparing the results. Students of vernacular architecture have long used a system of recording which enables a basic tabulation of constructional details, materials, etc, to be made. The technique is as valid for industrial buildings, particularly housing, and the results of analysis contribute in the same way not only to our understanding of the social and economic context, but also of the intangible visual characteristics of an area.

Over the twenty-five years or so in which industrial archaeology has grown up a number of distinct trends have become obvious. The two main areas of activity, recording and preservation, have their own adherents working separately and in many cases almost independently of each other. The typical regional industrial archaeology society tends to be engaged in the processes of recording and

publication, sometimes in Listed Building matters, but rarely taking on the task of preserving a site or building itself. This is the area of interest of preservation and museum trusts, sometimes working in association with local authorities, and engaged mainly on the preservation of sites for archaeological or historical reasons, opening them to the public from whom they derive the large part of their revenue income. In addition, there are building preservation trusts, some of which specialise in industrial buildings, but whose primary objective is their adaptation to new, economically viable, and broadly sympathetic uses.

On the recording front the achievements of the major societies have been considerable and although coverage is inevitably patchy the data accumulated, particularly since the mid 1970s, is impressive. At a national level the work carried out by the Royal Commission on the Ancient & Historical Monuments of Scotland over nearly twenty years is now being reflected in England and Wales. The English Commission has also carried out a number of thematic studies and is now responsible for the Industrial Monuments Survey. The Commissions hold substantial photographic archives, under the auspices of the respective National Monuments Records, in England and Scotland.

The need for a sound and developing academic base for industrial archaeology has in part been met by the establishment of the Ironbridge Institute, a teaching and research centre based at Coalbrookdale in Shropshire, and run jointly by the Ironbridge Gorge Museum Trust and the University of Birmingham. The Institute runs postgraduate diploma and masters courses in industrial archaeology and heritage management, an ambitious programme of short courses, and sustains an active research and consultancy service. There is an admirable research library – the best of its kind anywhere – together with the outstanding resources of the Elton Collection of illustrations and books on the history of industry and transport.

In the North East the Tyne & Wear Industrial Monuments Trust, set up in 1975 for the promotion, protection and permanent preservation of the region's industrial heritage, has a similar wide-ranging brief. It is constituted as a broadly based enabling agency to carry out preservation and recording work, secure public access and management agreements, produce publications and collaborate with other like-minded organisations. The Trust's projects include the Bowes Railway [NZ 285587], Fulwell Windmill [NZ 392595] and

Corbridge Pottery [NY 992652].

The role of the Historic Buildings & Monuments Commission for England (English Heritage), and its Scottish and Welsh equivalents, in relation to industrial archaeology still needs to be determined. It is already clear that Listed Building and Ancient Monument issues in this field are becoming steadily more numerous. At a tactical level the two main problems facing English Heritage are the pressure to adapt industrial buildings to new uses, often in a manner that substantially destroys their integrity and value, and the question of the protection in perpetuity of industrial monuments of outstanding national significance, for which the process of Guardianship was originally designed. In the former case there has been a tacit acceptance that adaptive re-use is a technique peculiarly suited to industrial buildings, partly deriving from the fact that they are perceived to have less value than those of earlier periods, partly because it is believed that this is the only means of retaining them. Sometimes this may be so, but the indiscriminate application of the adaptive re-use process irrespective of the value or importance of the building concerned points to the need for a radical review of the procedure for giving consent to change. The problem is exacerbated by generally low levels of expertise and the relative inexperience of local authority planning departments where officials with responsibility for conservation are often fairly junior and have little or no specialist training.

When it comes to the long term protection of sites, monuments and buildings of undoubted national importance, and for which adaptation to some new use would be a wholly inappropriate procedure, then the issues become more fundamental requiring a longer term strategic initiative. Had the importance of industrial sites and monuments been widely recognised in the 1930s, or even as recently as the 1960s, then the accepted procedure – of taking them into the Guardianship of the state – would have been applied. As it is Guardianship is now used only on a very restricted basis, the result of a need to contain costs and avoid new commitments rather than any policy-based decision aimed at estab-

lishing a balanced portfolio of properties. The virtual embargo on taking new sites into the care of the nation has derived from the rather dubious policy of what we have we hold, what we do not have we cannot afford. Recently however the announcement by English Heritage that it proposes to transfer the care of a number of its Guardianship sites to other agencies suggests the beginning of a change of heart in which resources will be applied in relationship to need, by a strategic policy, rather than historical precedent.

The two key issues are therefore the cultural acceptability of industrial sites and monuments and the processes by which they might be protected. That the most significant remains of the Industrial Revolution are in need of care and attention is beyond dispute. That it is only in the last twenty or so years that the advancing threshold of public taste and attitude has led to a recognition of the importance of the industrial heritage does not mean that it is any less important; on the contrary, extraordinary cultural value and vulnerability to ill-informed treatment makes the need for formal protection a high priority. Clearly, the nature of industrial sites, monuments and buildings makes Guardianship a peculiarly expensive and possibly inappropriate mechanism for securing their future, but the need is in no way diminished. What we must ensure is the establishment of a strategy for the Industrial Revolution that gives the quality of care traditionally afforded by Guardianship without the inordinate burdens that would entail. Much of the industrial heritage is held in the voluntary sector. Financial support for existing agencies tied to carefully worked out management agreements would provide good value for money and take advantage of what is already well-established and successful. A 'National Trust for Industrial Archaeology' might, similarly, provide at a national level an efficient and effective means of making limited resources go further but, more importantly, provide an organisation dedicated to the single objective of guaranteeing the future of those key monuments of the Industrial Revolution as an essential part of the national estate.

APPENDICES

GAZETTEER OF SITES

Many of the sites listed in this gazetteer are mentioned in the text and a page reference is given with each entry where this is the case. The gazetteer is arranged by county for England and Wales but in the case of Scotland where the administrative areas are now regions and districts, the old county names have been retained within each region to provide a more precise location. Grid references are presented in the standard form with the grid letters followed by a six-figure reference. In some cases, where an area rather than a specific point is referred to, a four-figure reference is provided indicating the kilometre square within which the site comes.

Most of the sites described in the text and listed in the gazetteer are on private property and, although the majority can be viewed from public areas, access to them is by courtesy of the owners. It must be remembered that in many cases owners are unaware of the significance of their buildings or plant. Visitors are advised to make prior arrangement and on no account to regard access as automatically forthcoming. Although some firms welcome individual visitors and even parties, others do not, and often for reasons of safety cannot permit entry to their sites. Remember too that in, for example, derelict mining areas where public access is not restricted there may be hidden shafts or workings. Keep a sharp lookout for these and never enter derelict mines or surface workings, where rocks may fall, without guidance from a local expert who has permission and knows the site well.

SCOTLAND

BORDERS

Berwickshire	Grid ref	Page
Chirnside, bridge and paper mill	NT 853561	
Coldingham, railway bridge	NT 853627	
Coldstream, brewery	NT 843396	
Coldstream, bridge	NT 848402	245
Duns, farm chimney and engine house, Chalkielaw	NT 803542	
Eyemouth, harbour	NT 947642	
Eyemouth, bridge	NT 943647	
Hutton, Union Suspension Bridge	NT 933510	249, 250

Peeblesshire

	Grid ref	Page
Innerleithen, St Ronan's Mill	NT 335379	
Innerleithen, Ballantyne's Mill, Walkerburn	NT 360371	

Roxburghshire

	Grid ref	Page
Eckford, suspension bridge, Kalemouth	NT 709274	
Hawick, hosiery works	NT 498147 & NT 504143	
Hawick, Wilton Mills	NT 502152	
Kelso, bridge and tollhouse	NT 727336	245
Kelso, suspension bridge	NT 735338	
Melrose, railway station	NT 547339	
Melrose, suspension bridge	NT 545346	
Roxburgh, viaduct	NT 702304	

Selkirkshire

	Grid ref	Page
Galashiels, Buckholm Mill	NT 481373	
Galashiels, Lindean Mill	NT 482313	
Galashiels, Netherdale Mill	NT 494360	
Selkirk, Philiphaugh Mill	NT 457282	49
Selkirk, Philiphaugh sawmill	NT 450278	49
Selkirk, Yarrow Mill	NT 470292	
Yarrow, Ashiestiel Bridge	NT 439351	

CENTRAL	Grid ref	Page

Clackmannanshire

Alloa, glassworks	NS 881923	172
Alloa, corn mills	NS 889928	
Alloa, Kilncraigs mills	NS 888927	
Alloa, waggonway bridges	NS 884927 &	
	NS 886929	
Alva, Strude Mill	NS 887975	

Stirlingshire

Edinburgh & Glasgow Union Canal including the Avon	NS 967758–	
Aqueduct (NS 967758)	NS 865794	
Falkirk, firebrick works, High Bonnybridge	NS 839796	
Falkirk, ironworks	NS 889811	
Forth & Clyde Canal	NS 785785–	
	NS 973825	
Grangemouth, docks	NS 9282	300
Larbert, Carron Ironworks	NS 880824	115
St Ninians, Cambusbarron limekilns	NS 770930	
St Ninians, Hayford mills	NS 776928	

Bo'ness, West Lothian (p328), and Dunblane, Kilmadock and Kincardine in Perthshire (p331), are for administrative purposes in Central Region

DUMFRIES & GALLOWAY

Dumfriesshire

Annan, Annan Bridge	NY 191666	
Annan, Annandale Distillery	NY 194683	
Annan, boiler works, Newbie	NY 183652	
Hoddam, windmill and horse gin, Shortrigg	NY 162744	
Sanquhar, Wanlockhead lead workings and Museum of		
the Scottish Lead Mining Industry	NS 873125	52, 152

Kirkcudbrightshire

Gatehouse-of-Fleet, cotton mills	NX 599564 &	
	NX 603564	
Gatehouse-of-Fleet, tollhouse	NX 602566	
Kirkbean, Southerness lighthouse	NX 977543	
Kirkcudbright, harbour	NX 684512	
Kirkcudbright, Tongueland Bridge	NX 692533	245
New Abbey, Monksmill watermill	NX 962663	

Wigtownshire

Penninghame, Bridge of Cree and tollhouse,		
Newton Stewart	NX 412657	
Portpatrick, harbour	NW 998542	

FIFE	Grid ref	Page

Fife

Anstruther, harbour and Scottish Fisheries Museum	NO 5603	313
Burntisland, railway station	NT 233857	
Crail, harbour	NO 612073	
Dunfermline, linen mills	NT 097867 &	
	NT 090878	
Falkland, Bonthrone maltings	NO 268071	
Inverkeithing, Halbeath railway bridge	NT 132832	
Kirkcaldy, Bennochy linen mill	NT 273913	
Kirkcaldy, Dysart Colliery	NT 310939	
Kirkcaldy, ropery	NT 278900	
Tayport, steam sawmill	NO 461277	
Thornton, beam engine house	NT 292973	

GRAMPIAN

Aberdeenshire

Aberdeen, Bridge of Don	NJ 946093
Aberdeen, Girdleness lighthouse	NJ 962053
Aberdeen, harbour	NJ 9506
Aberdeen, Wellington Suspension Bridge	NJ 943049
Birse, Potarch Bridge	NO 608973
Chapel of Garioch, iron bridge, Inveramsay	NJ 741246
Crathie, suspension bridge	NO 267943
Crathie, wrought-iron bridge	NO 262941
Echt, tollhouse	NJ 728097
Ellon, windmill, Hilton	NJ 942342
Fraserburgh, Kinnaird Head lighthouse	NJ 999677
Huntly, watermill	NJ 532392
Inverurie, paper mills	NJ 782192
Logie Buchan, Tipperty tile works	NJ 970268
Meldrum, watermill, Foresterhill	NJ 828293
Methlick, Tangland iron bridge	NJ 888361
Peterhead, Buchan Ness lighthouse	NK 137423
Skene, beam engine, Garlogie	NJ 782055

Banffshire

Aberlour, Craigellachie Bridge	NJ 285452	248
Aberlour, iron railway bridge	NJ 225412	
Banff, Bridge of Banff	NJ 696638	
Banff, harbour	NJ 689648	
Boyndie, brick and tile works	NJ 661658	
Fordyce, Mill of Durn	NJ 583638	
Fordyce, Portsoy harbour and warehouses	NJ 589665	304
Fordyce, tollhouse, Durn	NJ 591648	
Fordyce, windmill, Sandend	NJ 560658	
Keith, Isla Bank mills	NJ 428514	
Keith, Strathisla Distillery	NJ 429511	

Banffshire cont	Grid ref	Page
Mortlach, Glenfiddich Distillery	NJ 324410	
Rathven, Buckie boatyard	NJ 424658	
Rothiemay, cast-iron bridge	NJ 548481	

Moray

Elgin, Longmorn-Glenlivet Distillery	NJ 234583	
Elgin, Newmill woollen mill	NJ 225631	
Inverallan, railway bridge, Castle Grant	NJ 032302	
Knockando, Cardow Distillery	NJ 191431	
Rothes, Glen Grant Distillery	NJ 276495	
Urquhart, Old Spey Bridge and tollhouse, Fochabers	NJ 340594	

Nairnshire

Ardlach, Ferness Bridge	NJ 960463	
Nairn, railway station	NH 882559	

HIGHLAND

Caithness

Canisbay, Duncansby Head lighthouse	ND 407734	
Dunnet, Dunnet Head lighthouse	ND 203768	
Halkirk, Georgemas Junction station	ND 154593	
Latheron, harbour, Portomin	ND 165293	
Thurso, Forss Mill	ND 037687	
Watten, Achingale Bridge	ND 243543	
Watten, Achingale Mill	ND 241534	
Wick, Thrumster station	ND 337452	

Inverness-shire

Ardnamurchan, Glenfinnan railway viaduct	NM 910813	286
Caledonian Canal, including entrance locks at Corpach (NN 096776) and Clachnaharry, (NH 644467), 'Neptune's Staircase' at Banavie (NN 114770) and aqueducts at Glen Loy (NN 149818), Mount Alexander (NN 122777) and Torcastle (NN 132792)	NN 096776– NH 644467	261
Croy & Dalcross, Culloden Moor viaduct	NH 763450	
Duirinish, Skye, Glendale watermill	NG 168498	
Duthil & Rothiemurchus, Boat of Garten Station and Railway	NH 943189	
Harris, whaling station, Bunaveneadar	NB 131038	
Inverness, three suspension bridges	NH 661436& NH 664439& NH 664446	

	Grid ref	Page

Ross & Cromarty

Cromarty, brewery	NH 791673	
Cromarty, lighthouse	NH 787678	
Fodderty, Conon Bridge tollhouse	NH 540557	
Glenshiel, Shiel Bridge	NG 934189	
Kincardine, Gledfield Mill, Ardgay	NH 583903	
Rosskeen, Dalmore Distillery and steam engines	NH 666687	

Sutherland

Farr, Strathy limekilns	NC 852657	158

LOTHIAN

East Lothian

Dunbar, harbour	NT 680793	
Prestonkirk, Preston watermill, East Linton	NT 595779	48, 57
Prestonpans, Prestongrange pumping engine	NT 374737	69, 98
Prestonpans, salt works	NT 385746	
Tyninghame, sawmill	NT 611790	

Midlothian

Cranston, Lothian Bridge	NT 391646	
Edinburgh & Glasgow Union Canal including	NT 246728–	
Slateford Aqueduct (NT 220727)	NT 206702	
Edinburgh, Dean Bridge	NT 243740	246
Edinburgh, Haymarket station	NT 240731	
Edinburgh, Leith harbour and warehouses	NT 2777	
Lasswade, Polton paper mill	NT 291650	
Musselburgh, Esk net mills	NT 339723	
Newtongrange, Lady Victoria Colliery and		
steam winding engine	NT 333636	98

West Lothian

Addiewell, oil shale bings	NT 005628	
Bo'ness, harbour, railway and Open Air Museum	NT 000819	
Dalmeny, Forth railway bridge	NT 1379	292
Edinburgh & Glasgow Union Canal including the	NT 105706–	
Almond Aqueduct (NT 105706)	NS 967758	
Linlithgow, Wairdlaw limekilns	NS 996730	
Winchburgh, industrial village	NT 0874	214

ORKNEY	Grid ref	Page
Orkney		
Birsay, Boardhouse mills	HY 253274	
Dounby, Click Mill	HY 325228	45
Evie & Rendall, Helicliff Mill	HY 388241	
Hoy, lighthouses	HY 268061 &	
	HY 247066	
North Ronaldsay, lighthouses	HY 784560	
Stenness, Tormiston Mill	HY 319125	
SHETLAND		
Shetland		
Dunrossness, Norse mills, Southvoe	HU 401145	45
Dunrossness, Norse mills, Troswick	HU 406172–	
	HU 407171	
Dunrossness, Sumburgh Head lighthouse	HU 407079	
Sandness & Walls, Norse mills, Huxter	HU 173572	
STRATHCLYDE		
Argyll		
Ardnamurchan, lighthouse	NM 416675	
Campbeltown, horse gin	NR 685148	
Crinan Canal	NR 853853–	
	NR 788943	
Dunoon, pier	NS 176764	310
Glenorchy & Inishail, Bonawe Ironworks	NN 009318	113
Inveraray, Aray Bridge	NN 098091	
Inveraray, Craleckan Ironworks	NN 027001	110
Islay, Rinns of Islay lighthouse	NR 163514	
Kilmore & Kilbride, Connel Bridge	NM 911343	
Lismore & Appin, Ballachulish slate quarries	NN 085583	
Lismore & Appin, Kinlochleven aluminium works	NN 190617	
Tiree, harbour	NL 9839	
Ayrshire		
Ardrossan, beam engine house, Saltcoats	NS 257414	
Auchinleck, Highhouse Colliery	NS 549217	
Ayr, harbour and lighthouses	NS 3322	
Cumnock, Bank railway viaduct	NS 574205	
Dalmellington, ironworks	NS 442083	128
Kilbirnie, Stoneyholm Mill	NS 317545	
Kilmarnock, bonded warehouses	NS 428381	
Kilmarnock, Caledonia Works	NS 424382	
Kilmarnock, Vulcan Foundry	NS 424383	
Kilmaurs, railway viaduct, Gatehead	NS 383369	274
Mauchline, Ballochmyle Viaduct	NS 508254	285
Sorn, Catrine village	NS 5225	

	Grid ref	Page

Bute

Bute, salt pan, Ascog	NS 107633	
Little Cumbrae, lighthouses	NS 138514 & NS 153514	
Rothesay, cotton mill and watercourses	NS 086643	
Rothesay, pier	NS 089648	

Dunbartonshire

Bonhill, Argyll Motor Factory, Alexandria	NS 390807	
Dumbarton, Denny ship-testing tank	NS 402748	
Dumbarton, engine of PS *Leven*	NS 395753	

Forth & Clyde Canal, including an aqueduct at
    Kirkintilloch (NS 657739) and stables at Shirva
    (NS 691753)
	NS 785785–
	NS 650733 &
	NS 513700–
	NS 449734	

Kirkintilloch, Lion Foundry	NS 655740	

Lanarkshire

Forth & Clyde Canal	NS 650735– NS 594700	
Biggar, gasworks	NT 039377	222
Cardowan, colliery winding engines	NS 665683	
Crawford, Leadhills mining village	NS 8815	
Dalserf, Avonbank bleach works, Millheugh	NS 725508	
Glasgow, Broomyard cotton works	NS 606642	
Glasgow, cotton mills, Carstairs Street	NS 611628	
Glasgow, Eagle Pottery, Boden Street	NS 614638	
Glasgow, Fairfield Shipward, Govan Road	NS 548660	
Glasgow, Partick sewage pumping station	NS 564664	
Glasgow, St Enoch underground station, St Enoch Square	NS 599650	296
Glasgow, Templeton's carpet factory, Templeton Street	NS 603641	
Hamilton, Avon Bridge and tollhouse	NS 735547	
Lanark, Cartland Bridge	NS 869444	
New Lanark, model industrial village	NS 8842	181
Shotts, ironworks	NS 879598	

Renfrewshire

Abbey, Cartside Mill, Milliken Park	NS 415625	
Gourock, Wemyss Bay station and pier	NS 193685	
Greenock, Shaws watermill	NS 272753	
Greenock, Shaws waterworks	NS 2672– NS 267748	
Greenock, Victoria Harbour and steamboat quay	NS 287759 & NS 283763	
Kilbarchan, handloom weavers' cottages	NS 401632	
Paisley, Ferguslie mills, Maxwellton Road	NS 467634	
Paisley, Vulcan Works, Renfrew Road	NS 486644	

Renfrewshire cont	**Grid ref**	**Page**
Port Glasgow, Gourock ropeworks	NS 326745	
Renfrew, Clyde Navigation Trust depot	NS 511681	
Renfrew, engine of PS *Clyde*	NS 554659	
Renfrew, Inchinnan bridges	NS 492679	

TAYSIDE

Angus

Arbroath, harbour	NO 643405	
Arbroath, signal tower, Ladyloan	NO 641404	
Arbroath, water tower, Keptie Hill	NO 637408	
Barry, Carnoustie station	NO 567344	
Brechin, Den Burn mill	NO 602599	
Dundee, Camperdown mills	NO 383317	18
Dundee, Dens jute works	NO 408309	
Dundee, harbour and RRS *Discovery*	NO 410303	
Dundee, Tay jute works, Lochee Road	NO 398304	197
Dundee, Tay railway bridge	NO 395263–	292
	NO 392293	
Kirkden, Friockheim railway viaduct	NO 588496	
Logie Pert, North Water Bridge and tollhouse, Marykirk	NO 686650	
Montrose, Chapel Works	NO 717577	
Newtyle, old station	NO 300413	

Kincardineshire

Kinneff & Catterline, Todhead lighthouse	NO 869770	
Stonehaven, harbour	NO 878853	
Strachan, wooden bridge	NO 674922	

Kinross-shire

Kinross, horse gin house, Middle Balado	NO 093026	

Perthshire

Auchterarder, Glenruthven mills	NN 955129	
Dunblane, Springbank woollen mills	NN 778017	
Dunkeld, bridge and tollhouse	NO 027424	245
Edradour, distillery	NN 959579	
Errol, Inchcoonans tile works	NO 238233	
Kilmadock, Deanston cotton mills and village	NN 715017	
Kincardine, Blairdrummond sawmill	NS 720986	
Kinclaven, Stanley cotton mills	NO 114328	
Perth, Smeaton's bridge	NO 121239	
Perth, waterworks	NO 121232	218

ENGLAND

Avon	Grid ref	Page
Bath, Green Park station	ST 745647	296
Bath, Victoria Bridge	ST 741650	249
Bath, canal bridges	ST 758654	248
Bitton, mine ventilating furnace	ST 690710	100
Blagdon, pumping station	ST 503600	217
Bristol, Underfall Yard	ST 572722	81, 137, 140, 303
Bristol, Bush's warehouse (Arnolfini Gallery)	ST 586725	304
Bristol, Clifton suspension bridge	ST 564731	249
Bristol, Fairbairn crane	ST 584722	309
Bristol, SS Great Britain	ST 578724	312
Bristol, Temple Meads station	ST 596724	283, 296, 297
Bristol, Welsh Back warehouse	ST 588726	304
Claverton, canal pumping station	ST 791644	55, 147, 265
Clevedon, pier	ST 402719	311
Combe Hay, canal locks	ST 748604	261
Freshford, Dunkirk Mill	ST 785595	201
Henbury, Stratford watermill	ST 562784	
Kelston, brass mills	ST 695680	145
Keynsham, Albert Mill	ST 656679	209
Keynsham, brass mills	ST 657688	145
Priston, watermill	ST 695615	56
Saltford, brass mills	ST 687671	145

Bedfordshire

Cardington, airship hangars	TL 082468	
Stevington, Stevington windmill	SP 992527	
Stewartby, brickworks and model village	TL 0142	157

Berkshire

Maidenhead, railway bridge	SU 901810	282
Windsor, railway bridge	SU 961773	283

Buckinghamshire

Bletchley, Denbigh Hall railway bridge	SP 853353	
Brill, windmill	SP 653142	
Ivinghoe, Ford End watermill	SP 941166	
Lacey Green, windmill	SP 819009	39
Marlow, suspension bridge	SU 852862	249

Buckinghamshire cont	Grid ref	Page
Newport Pagnell, Tickford Bridge	SP 877437	247
Old Wolverton, Wolverton Aqueduct	SP 801418	
Pitstone, windmill	SP 945157	38
Quainton, windmill	SP 746203	
Wolverton, railway viaduct and town	SP 815422	283

Cambridgeshire

Bourn, windmill	TL 312580	38
Burwell, windmill	TL 590665	40
Cambridge, station	TL 462573	296
Cambridge, Cheddars Lane pumping station	TL 465593	
Great Chishill, windmill	TL 413388	42
Great Gransden, windmill	TL 277557	
Lode, watermill	TL 520625	
Old Fletton, brickworks	TL 1997 & TL 186966	158
Over, windmill	TL 381689	
Stretham, pumping engine	TL 517730	68
Waterbeach, Bottisham Lode staunch	TL 516651	254
West Wratting, windmill	TL 604510	40, 41
Wicken Fen, windmill	TL 562706	44

Cheshire

Anderton, boat lift	SJ 647753	262
Beeston, cast-iron lock	SJ 554599	262
Bunbury, watermill	SJ 573581	
Burtonwood, Sankey Viaduct	SJ 569947	280
Chester, General station	SJ 413669	231, 296
Chester, Grosvenor Bridge	SJ 403656	245
Chester, Northgate locks	SJ 403666	262
Chester, shot tower	SJ 415666	153
Congleton, iron aqueduct	SJ 866622	
Crewe, railway works and settlement	SJ 605555	
Dutton, viaduct	SJ 583764	285
Ellesmere Port, canal basins and warehouses and Boat Museum	SJ 405775	256, 268
Macclesfield, Arighi Bianchi iron-fronted store	SJ 920737	
Macclesfield, Chester Road mills	SJ 909737	189
Macclesfield, Frost's Mill	SJ 918737	189
Macclesfield, silk weavers' workshops	SJ 914733	
Marston, Lion Salt Works	SJ 671755	205
Nantwich, iron canal aqueduct	SJ 643526	
Nether Alderley, Alderley Old Mill	SJ 844763	57
Preston Brook, canal hamlet	SJ 568806	263
Runcorn, railway bridge	SJ 509835	292
Runcorn, Waterloo Bridge	SJ 508828	
Styal, Quarry Bank Mill and village, and Textile Museum	SJ 835829	50, 189
Warrington, transporter bridge	SJ 597877	252
Widnes, Gossage Building and Catalyst: Museum of the Chemical Industry	SJ 514844	205

Cleveland	Grid ref	Page
Boulby, alum shale quarries	NZ 7519	209
Guisborough, Tocketts Mill	NZ 627182	
Middlesbrough, transporter bridge	NZ 500213	252
Skelton, Skelton Park iron mine	NZ 644180	
Stockton-on-Tees, ticket office	NZ 447184	280

Cornwall		
Botallack, Botallack tin mine	SW 364333	145, 153
Botallack, Levant copper mine	SW 375341	69, 148
Calstock, Calstock Viaduct	SX 433687	286
Camborne, Dolcoath mine	SW 661405	
Camborne, East Pool engines	SW 674416 & SW 679419	69, 148
Camborne, South Crofty mine	SW 669409	141, 148
Camborne, Trevithick's cottage	SW 636389	148
Carthew, Wheal Martyn china clay works and China Clay Museum	SX 004555	52, 162
Cotehele, quay and warehouse	SX 423681	
Delabole, Old Delabole slate quarry	SX 075840	
Hatton Quay, limekilns	SX 413656	
Hayle, Harvey's Foundry	SW 558372	69, 79
Launcells, Hobbacott Incline	SS 244049	
Madron, Ding Dong mine	SW 435344	
Parkandillack, clay works and engine	SW 945568	162
Redruth, Tolgus tin streaming works	SW 690438	57, 149
Saltash, Royal Albert Bridge	SX 435587	249, 291

Cumbria		
Backbarrow, Backbarrow furnace	SD 356846	
Barrowdale, Honister slate quarry	NY 210143	
Beetham, Heron watermill	SK 497799	
Blawith, Nibthwaite blast furnace	SD 295883	
Boot, Esdale watermill	NY 176013	
Broughton-in-Furness, Duddon blast furnace	SD 197884	113
Carlisle, Shaddon Mill	NY 395557	
Clifton, Wetheriggs Pottery	NY 555263	168
Elterwater, Elterwater gunpowder mill	NY 328048	211
Finsthwaite, Stott Park bobbin mill	SD 373882	
Kendal, Laithes snuff mill	SD 513903	
Nenthead, smelt mill	NY 784433	
Riddings, viaduct	NY 411756	284
Satterthwaite, Stony Hazel finery forge	SD 336907	
Ulverston, Newland blast furnace	SD 299798	113
Whitehaven, Barracks Mill	NX 974177	314
Whitehaven, candlestick chimney and Wellington Terrace	NX 968182	
Workington, Jane Pit engine house	NX 995277	96

Derbyshire	Grid ref	Page
Belper, North Mill	SK 345481	193
Buxworth, canal basin and tramways	SK 020822	273
Calver, Calver Mill	SK 245744	190
Church Gresley, Green's pottery	SK 305187	168
Cressbrook, Cressbrook Mill	SK 173726	189
Crich, Tramway Museum	SK 345548	231
Cromford, Arkwright's mills	SK 298569	187
Cromford, High Peak Junction	SK 314559	
Cromford, industrial housing	SK 295567	
Cromford, Leawood pumping station	SK 315557	
Dale, Cat and Fiddle windmill	SK 438398	36
Derby, Cotchett's silk mill	SK 356364	185
Derby, Friargate railway bridge	SK 347364	293
Draycott, Victoria Mill	SK 445333	195
Heage, Morley Park blast furnaces	SK 380492	114
Heage, windmill	SK 367507	
Long Eaton, Leopold Street lace factories	SK 488336	194
Matlock Bath, Masson Mill	SK 294573	187
Rowsley, Caudwell's Mill	SK 256657	
Shardlow, inland port	SK 444304	268
Sheldon, Magpie mine	SK 173682	149
Swarkeston, bridge	SK 369285	236
Ticknall, tramway bridge	SK 356240	273
Wirksworth, Middleton Top winding engine	SK 275552	274

Devon

	Grid ref	Page
Dartmouth, Newcomen engine	SX 879515	60
Exeter, iron footbridge	SX 924927	
Exeter, quay warehouses	SX 921921	303
Haytor Vale, Haytor quarries and tramway	SX 759775	
Mary Tavy, Wheal Friendship arsenic calciner	SX 508796	
Morwellham, harbour	SX 447698	274
Morwellham, hydro-electric generating station	SX 447698	226
Okehampton, Meldon Viaduct	SX 565924	292
Plymouth, old Eddystone Lighthouse	SX 478538	309
Princetown, Powder Mills Farm	ST 628769	211
Seaton, concrete road bridge	SY 252899	250
Starcross, atmospheric railway engine house	SX 977819	297
Sticklepath, Finch Brothers' foundry	SX 639940	57, 124
Tiverton, industrial housing	SS 958120	
Uffculme, Fox Brothers' textile mill, now Coldharbour Mill Museum	ST 062122	22

Dorset

	Grid ref	Page
Holwell, oldest pillar box *in situ* in Britain at Barnes Cross	ST 694117	
Sturminster Newton, Sturminster Mill	ST 782135	
Sturminster Newton, White Mill	ST 958006	
Swanage, water tower	SZ 032780	
Weymouth, Sutton Poyntz turbine pump	SY 706839	

Durham	Grid ref	Page
Beamish, vertical colliery winding engine re-erected in the North of England Open Air Museum	NZ 212549	81, 96
Burropfield, Lintzford paper mill	NZ 151571	
Darlington, Coniscliffe Road pumping station	NZ 254139	
Darlington, North Road railway station	NZ 289157	280
East Hedleyhope, coke ovens	NZ 166406	
Hamsterley, Derwentcote cementation furnace	NZ 131565	126
Seaham, Seaham Harbour	NZ 435495	105, 300
Shildon, Brusselton Incline, sleeper blocks and bridge	NZ 211256	280
Shildon, Timothy Hackworth's house	NZ 233258	
Tanfield, Causey Arch	NZ 201559	272
Weardale, Killhope lead mill	NY 827429	50, 150

Essex

	Grid ref	Page
Aythorpe Roding, windmill	TL 590152	
Bocking, windmill	TL 755253	
Coggeshall, Abbey Mill	TL 852222	
Colchester, Bourne Mill	TM 006238	
Great Bardfield, Gibraltar windmill	TL 681308	39
Halstead, Townford Mill	TL 813304	
Harwich, navigation light towers	TM 253308	
Harwich, treadmill crane	TM 262325	309
Kelvedon, Easterford watermill	TL 867192	
Langford, steam pumping engine	TL 834088	
Maldon, saltworks	TL 854072	
Mistley, maltings	TM 117320	
Mountnessing, windmill	TQ 631980	
Stock, windmill	TQ 698989	
Thaxted, tower windmill	TL 610309	
Upminster, windmill	TQ 556867	

Gloucestershire

	Grid ref	Page
Bibury, Arlington watermill	SP 114068	
Caincross, Ebley woollen mill	SO 829046	
Cam, woollen mill	ST 754999	
Clearwell, Clearwell Caves iron mines	SO 587083	
Coates, Sapperton canal tunnel, east portal	SO 965006	263
Coleford, Whitecliffe blast furnace	SO 568103	
Frampton-on-Severn, canal bridgekeeper's lodge	SO 746085	
Gloucester, docks	SO 825185	309
Gloucester, Over Bridge	SO 816196	246
Nailsworth, Dunkirk Mill	SO 845005	318
Nailsworth, Egypt watermill	ST 849999	
Newland, Redbrook Incline bridge	SO 537103	
Stonehouse, Stanley Mill	SO 814043	193
Tewkesbury, Mythe Bridge	SO 889337	248
Woodchester, Frogmarsh wool store	SO 841018	

Hampshire	Grid ref	Page
Binstead, West Court hop kilns	SU 765412	
Bursledon, windmill	SU 482108	
Fareham, Funtley iron mill	SU 550082	119
Lymington, salterns	SZ 328940 &	
	SZ 315923	204
Portsmouth, Eastney pumping station	SZ 674993	68, 219
Portsmouth, naval dockyard and block making		
machinery	SU 630005	134, 313
Totton, Eling tide mill	SU 365125	52
Twyford, water pumping station	SU 493249	
Whitchurch, silk mill	SU 463479	189

Hereford & Worcester

Arley, Victoria Bridge	SO 767792	
Astley, Yarranton's furnace	SO 805668	
Belbroughton, Nash's scythe works	SO 919772	
Blakedown, Churchill forge	SO 883795	
Hereford, Broomy Hill pumping station	SO 496394	
Holt Fleet, cast iron bridge	SO 824634	248
Kidderminster, Brinton's carpet mills	SO 831764	
Mortimer's Cross, watermill	SO 426637	
Newnham Bridge, watermill	SO 644688	
Powick, hydro-electric power station	SO 835525	225
Redditch, Forge needle mill	SP 046686	57
Stoke Heath, Danzey Green windmill in the Avoncroft		
Museum of Buildings	SO 953683	37
Stourport, canal basins	SO 810710	267
Tardebigge, canal locks and engine house	SO 988689–	261
	SO 956672	
Worcester, porcelain works and Dyson Perrins Museum	SO 852544	168

Hertfordshire

Berkhamsted, horse wheel	SP 994123	
Cheshunt, Turnford pumping station	TL 364049	
Hatfield, Mill Green watermill	TL 240097	
Hertford, fulling stocks, Horn's Mill	TL 321117	
Ware, maltings	TL 360140	

Humberside

Barton-upon-Humber, Ferriby Sluice	SE 974211	
Brigg, Wrawby windmill	TA 035087	
Flamborough, old lighthouse	TA 250708	
Grimsby, hydraulic tower	TA 281113	303
Hessle, Whiting Mill	TA 022254	
Horkstow, suspension bridge	SE 973190	
Hull, Humber Dock	TA 098181	

Humberside cont	**Grid ref**	**Page**
Hull, reinforced concrete factory	TA 096295	
Hull, Springhead pumping station	TA 042295	
New Holland, Manchester Square model village	TA 083237	
Skidby, windmill	TA 021333	
Stamford Bridge, watermill	SE 713556	

Isle of Man

Castletown, harbour and Nautical Museum	SC 266675	
Douglas, Clinch's brewery, North Quay	SC 381754	
Douglas, harbour	SC 384753	
Foxdale, mine engine houses	SC 263780 &	
	SC 253778	
Laxey, *Lady Isabella* waterwheel	SC 432851	51, 56, 149

Isle of Wight

Bembridge, windmill	SZ 640875	39, 42
Calbourne watermill	SZ 414869	
Carisbrooke, Carisbrooke Castle donkey wheel	SZ 487877	
Newtown, salterns	SZ 418911	
Yafford, watermill	SZ 446822	

Kent

Chatham, dockyard, sawmills and ropery	TQ 7669	313
Chillenden, windmill	TR 268543	38, 41
Cranbrook, Union windmill	TQ 779359	39, 41
Dover, Fairbairn jib crane	TR 319410	309
Dover, Shakespeare Cliff railway tunnel	TR 296394–	
	TR 308399	
Faversham, Chart gunpowder mills	TR 009613	211
Herne, windmill	TR 184665	39
Higham, Strood Tunnel	TQ 738711	
Maidstone, Hayle paper mill	TQ 756538	
Margate, Draper's windmill	TR 363700	
Meopham, windmill	TR 639653	
Mersham, Swanton watermill	TR 038388	
Sandwich, White Mill	TR 322586	
Sheerness, boat store	TQ 910753	125, 313
Sissinghurst, oast houses	TQ 807384	
Sittingbourne, Dolphin barge yard	TQ 910643	
Wittersham, Stocks windmill	TQ 913273	

Lancashire

Burnley, Queen Street Mill, Harle Syke	SD 868349	82, 202
Clitheroe, Low Moor industrial community	SD 730418	
Coppull, Ring Mill and Mavis Mill	SD 563147	318
Ellel, Galgate silk mill	SD 485557	194
Garstang, Wyre Aqueduct	SD 491448	
Haslingden, Higher Mill, Helmshore	SD 777214	179

Greater London cont

	Grid ref	Page
Deptford, Penn's works, Borthwick Street	TQ 372781	313
Deptford, power station, Deptford Green	TQ 375779	228
Fulham, gasworks, Sands End Lane	TQ 260768	222
Fulham, pottery, New King's Road	TQ 244761	168
Greenwich, Blackwall road tunnel entrance	TQ 391795	252
Greenwich, *Cutty Sark*	TQ 383778	313
Hanwell, Wharncliffe Viaduct	TQ 150804	281
Hounslow, Kempton Park waterworks	TQ 110709	82
King's Cross, station	TQ 303830	295
Morden, Morden Hall Park snuff mills	TQ 262686	
Newham, gasholders, Bow Creek	TQ 385825	224
Newham, hydraulic bridges	TQ 416806 &	
	TQ 437806	303
Paddington, station	TQ 266813	281
Regent's Park, Macclesfield Bridge	TQ 275834	
Rotherhithe, hydraulic bridge	TQ 362793	303
St Katharine Docks	TQ 339805	304
St Pancras, station	TQ 302829	295
Thames Tunnel	TQ 352800	159
Thamesmead, Crossness pumping station, Belvedere Road	TQ 484811	219
Tottenham, pumping station, Markfield Road	TQ 344888	
Tower Bridge	TQ 337802	303
Tower Hamlets, hydraulic bridge	TQ 383802	303
Wallington, Surrey Iron Railway, Public Library, Shotfield	TQ 288638	272, 274
Wandsworth, Ram Brewery	TQ 256747	67
Whitechapel, bell foundry	TQ 339815	
Wimbledon, Common windmill	TQ 320725	

Greater Manchester

Bolton, Atlas Mills and Steam Museum	SD 701101	82
Eccles, Barton Aqueduct	SJ 767977	255, 264, 303
Manchester, Castlefield Basin	SJ 831975	
Manchester, Central station	SJ 827977	25
Manchester, Liverpool Road station and Greater Manchester Museum of Science & Industry	SJ 830978	280
Marple, aqueduct	ST 956900	264
Oldham, cotton mills	SD 927027	
Radcliffe, waterwheel pump	SD 767066	
Reddish, Houldsworth Mill	SJ 892933	
Shaw, Dee Mill engine	SD 945093	82, 197
Stockport, Mersey railway viaduct	SJ 890906–	
	SJ 893901	
Tyldesley, Astley Green Colliery winding engines	SD 705999	96, 97
Westhoughton, incline, embankment and crossing house	SD 674061	
Worsley, canal basin	SD 748005	255

Merseyside	Grid ref	Page
Birkenhead, Bidston windmill	SJ 287894	45
Birkenhead, Port Sunlight model village	SJ 3484	208
Liverpool, Albert Dock, dock traffic office and Merseyside Maritime Museum	SJ 342898	306
Liverpool, Oriel Chambers, Water Street	SJ 341904	
Liverpool, Royal Liver Building	SJ 338904	
Liverpool, Stanley Dock	SJ 337921	306
Liverpool, Victoria Tower, Salisbury Dock	SJ 333921	307
Newton-le-Willows, Huskisson Memorial, Parkside	SJ 606955	
Rainhill, railway station	SJ 491914	280
St Helens, Ravenhead glass works	SJ 5094	172

Norfolk		
Billingford, windmill	TM 167786	
Denver, windmill	TF 605013	
Fakenham, gasworks	TF 919293	222
Fritton, St Olaves wind pump	TM 457997	
Halvergate, Stracey Arms drainage mill	TG 442090	
Horsey, Horsey Mere wind pump	TG 453223	43, 44
Little Cressingham, wind and watermill	TF 869002	
Norwich, Jarrold's Works, Cowgate	TG 235093	
Reedham, Berney Arms drainage mill	TG 465051	44
Snettisham, windmill	TG 682335	
West Newton, Appleton steam pumping station	TF 707273	

Northamptonshire		
Blisworth, canal tunnel	SP 729529– SP 739503	263, 274
Braunston, canal basin and bridge	SP 540659	
Harlestone, watermill	SP 707646	
Kettering, railway station	SP 864780	
Kilsby, railway tunnel	SP 565715– SP 578697	281
Northampton, Manfield Building, Campbell Square	SP 755609	314
Roade, railway cutting	SP 750525	281
Towcester, Stoke Bruerne canal locks, warehouse and museum	SP 743500	259. 264

Northumberland		
Allendale, lead smelt mill and flues	NY 8153	
Blyth, coal staithes	NZ 3280	105
Broomhaugh, horse wheel house	NZ 014616	
Corbridge, pottery	NY 992652	168, 320
Cornhill on Tweed, Heatherslaw watermill	NT 933384	
Haydon Bridge, horse wheel house	NY 892680	
Kielder, railway viaduct	NY 632924	
Loan End, Union Suspension Bridge	NT 933510	249, 250
Otterburn, tweed mill	NY 888928	
Seaton, Seaton Sluice	NZ 339769	204

Nottinghamshire

	Grid ref	Page
Awsworth, Bennerley Viaduct	SK 471437– SK 476441	292
Beeston, Anglo Scotian Mills	SK 525373	
Bestwood, colliery winding engine	SK 557478	
Calverton, framework knitters' cottages	SK 621491	
Mansfield, textile mill	SK 548617	
North Leverton, windmill	SK 776820	
Nottingham, canal warehouses, Canal Street, and waterways museum	SK 573393	
Nottingham, lace market, Stoney Street	SK 576397	
Papplewick, steam pumping station	SK 582522	68, 217
Ruddington, framework knitter's shop	SK 572329	184
Stapleford, lacemakers' cottages	SK 506379	185
Strelley, bell pits	SK 505417	
Sutton Bonnington, frameshops	SK 503256	184

Oxfordshire

Abingdon, cast iron bridge	SU 495970	
Chipping Norton, Bliss tweed mill	SP 293268	
Didcot, goods shed and Great Western Railway Society	SU 525906	
Eynsham, flash lock	SP 446089	254
Garford, Venn watermill	SU 430949	
Henley, Nettlebed brick kiln	SU 703868	156
Hook Norton, brewery	SP 349332	
Mapledurham, watermill	SU 669768	
Wheatley, windmill	SP 589052	39
Woodstock, Combe sawmill	SP 418150	

Shropshire

Charlcotte, blast furnace	SO 638861	113
Chirk, aqueduct and viaduct	SJ 287372	159, 266
Cluddley, tollhouse	SJ 618106	240
Coalbrookdale, Great Warehouse and Museum of Iron	SJ 667046	
Coalbrookdale, Old Furnace	SJ 667047	
Coalport, Coalport Bridge	SJ 702021	247
Coalport, Hay Inclined Plane	SJ 695028	262
Coalport, tar tunnel	SJ 694025	214
Craven Arms, milepost	SO 433827	242
Eyton upon the Weald Moors, Wappenshall canal junction	SJ 664146	
Hadley, guillotine locks	SJ 672133	259
Ironbridge, Albert Edward Bridge	SJ 661038	293
Ironbridge, Bedlam furnaces	SJ 677034	48, 116
Ironbridge, the Iron Bridge	SJ 673034	246
Ironbridge, Severn warehouse and wharf	SJ 667036	
Jackfield, Craven Dunnill tile works	SJ 686029	23, 157
Longdon-upon-Tern, iron aqueduct	SJ 617156	265
Market Drayton, Tyrley canal cutting	SJ 693315	257
Minsterley, Snailbeach lead mines	SJ 375022	149

Shropshire cont	**Grid ref**	**Page**
Montford, Montford Bridge	ST 433153	245
Pant, incline and brake drum	SJ 273218– SJ 274218	158
Pennerley, Tankerville Mine	SO 355995	149
Shrewsbury, Bage's flax mill	SJ 500140	190, 192
Shrewsbury, Coleham sewage pumping station	SJ 496121	219
Shrewsbury, Howard Street warehouse	SJ 495130	
Shrewsbury railway station	SJ 494129	296

Somerset

Bridgwater, brick and tile works	ST 301376	157
Bridgwater, docks	ST 197276	
Bridgwater, railway traversing bridge	ST 300374	
Chapel Allerton, Ashton windmill	ST 414504	38, 44
Charterhouse, lead works	ST 504557	152
Clapton, watermill	ST 414064	
Coleford, canal aqueduct	ST 684487	
East Harptree, Smitham chimney	ST 555546	152
High Ham, Stembridge windmill	ST 433305	38
Kilve, oil shale retort	ST 147439	214
Priddy, St Cuthbert's Lead Works	ST 545505	151
Shipham, calamine mining site	ST 445574	144
Street, Clark's shoe factory and model village	ST 483368	
Westonzoyland, pumping station	ST 340328	
Wookey Hole, paper mill	ST 532477	213

Staffordshire

Burton on Trent, Clay Mills sewage pumping station	SK 263258	
Burton on Trent, maltings	SK 235230	
Cheddleton, flint mill	SJ 974525	57, 165
Eccleshall, Millmeece pumping station	SJ 830339	
Froghall, basin terminus	SK 028476	273
Gailey, canal wharf and lock	SJ 920104	259
Hanley, Etruscan bone and flint mill	SJ 872478	165
Harecastle, canal tunnel	SJ 837542– SJ 849517	256, 263
Leek, Brindley's Mill	SJ 977570	254
Longton, Gladstone Pottery and Museum	SJ 912434	166
Tunstall, Chatterley Whitfield Colliery	SJ 885534	95, 102

Suffolk

Bardwell, windmill	TL 941738	
Brent Eleigh, cast iron bridge	TL 934482	
Framsden, windmill	TM 192597	
Fritton, Priory windmill	TM 458998	
Glemsford, silk mill	TL 825465	
Herringfleet, windmill	TM 466976	
Holton, windmill	TM 402776	38, 42
Ixworth, Pakenham windmill	TL 931694	

Suffolk cont	**Grid ref**	**Page**
Leiston, Garrett's Long Shop	TM 444625	
Mildenhall, staunch	TL 708743	
Pakenham, watermill	TL 937695	
Saxtead, Saxtead Green windmill	TM 254644	42
Snape, maltings	TM 392575	317
Woodbridge, Buttrum's windmill	TM 264493	
Woodbridge, tide mill	TM 275487	51
Woodbridge, wagon weighing machine	TM 272491	242

Surrey

Betchworth, limekilns	TQ 208514	160
Cobham, telegraph tower, Chatley Heath	TQ 089585	233
Godalming, Catteshall papermill	SU 982444	53
Guildford, semaphore house	TQ 002492	
Guildford, Shalford watermill	TQ 002477	
Outwood, windmill	TQ 327456	41
Purley, Surrey Iron Railway track, Rotary Field	TQ 316622	274
Send, Worsfold Gates turf-sided lock	TQ 016557	261

East Sussex

Brighton, Volk's electric railway	TQ 316038–	230
	TQ 335033	
Hastings, net-drying shops	TQ 827094	
Hove, Goldstone pumping station, and British Engineerium	TQ 286066	19
Lewes, Ashcombe tollhouse	TQ 389093	
Ninfield, Ashburnham iron furnace	TQ 685170	
Nutley, windmill	TQ 451291	
Polegate, windmill	TQ 581041	40
Robertsbridge, Hodson's Mill	TQ 736242	
Upper Dicker, Michelham Priory watermill	TQ 557093	
Wadhurst, cast iron tombstones	TQ 641318	

West Sussex

Amberley, Chalk Pits Museum	TQ 028118	23
Balcombe, Ouse railway viaduct	TQ 323278	
Clayton, Jack and Jill windmills	TQ 304134	
Clayton, North Portal, Clayton Tunnel	TQ 299141	
Henfield, Wood's watermill	TQ 217317	
Hurstpierpoint, Cobbs watermill	TQ 274189	
Singleton, Weald & Downland Museum	SU 875129	111
Washington, limekilns	TQ 119123	

Tyne & Wear

Elemore, vertical colliery winding engine	NZ 356457	96
Fulwell, windmill	NZ 392595	320
Marsden, limekilns	NZ 404644	
Monkwearmouth, railway station	NZ 396577	296

Tyne & Wear cont

	Grid ref	Page
Newburn, Lemington glass cone	NZ 184646	171
Newcastle, Armstrong swing bridge	NZ 253637	303
Newcastle, High Level Bridge	NZ 251637	
Rowlands Gill, Whinfield coke ovens	NZ 152581	
Ryhope, pumping station	NZ 404524	68, 217
Springwell, Bowes Railway	NZ 285587	319
Sunderland, Victoria railway bridge	NZ 396575	285
Wallsend, Willington Viaduct	NZ 316666	
Washington, colliery winding engine	NZ 303575	

Warwickshire

Bearley, Edstone Aqueduct	SP 162609	
Harbury, Chesterton windmill	SP 348594	
Hawkesbury, canal junction	SP 362846	267
Rugby, canal aqueducts and roving bridge	SP 503771	
Stratford on Avon, tramway viaduct	SP 205548	274
Warwick, canal aqueducts	SP 301654	
Warwick, gasholder buildings, Saltisford	SP 278653	223
Wooten Wawen, iron aqueduct	SP 159630	

West Midlands

Birmingham, Curzon Street station	SP 080871	281, 296
Birmingham, Gas Street Basin	SP 062866	
Birmingham, gun barrel proof house, Banbury Street	SP 078866	
Birmingham, Sarehole Mill	SP 099818	
Coventry, Cash's model factory	SP 335806	187
Coventry, Standard motor-car works	SP 312788	317
Cradley, chain-making works, Station Street	SO 959867	125
Dudley, canal tunnels	SO 945917	
Dudley, Newcomen engine reconstruction and Black Country Museum	SO 948917	58, 198
Dudley, wharf crane, Bumblehole Yard	SO 953883	
Smethwick, Chance's glassworks	SP 007897	
Smethwick, Galton Bridge	SP 015893	248
Stourbridge, glass cone, Wordsley	SO 894865	172

Wiltshire

Box, Blue Vein tollhouse	ST 831673	241
Box, railway tunnel	ST 857695– ST 829689	282
Bradford-on-Avon, Abbey Mill	ST 826609	22
Chippenham, railway viaduct	ST 912731	
Corsham, stone mines	ST 877685	
Devizes, Caen Hill Locks	SU 976614– SU 995615	261
Great Bedwyn, Crofton pumping station	SU 262623	79
Limpley Stoke, Dundas Aqueduct	ST 784625	264
Swindon, railway housing	SU 155850	283
Swindon, railway works	SU 140850	283

West Yorkshire cont	**Grid ref**	**Page**
Marsden, Standedge canal tunnel	SE 006079–	
	SE 040120	263
Otley, Bramhope Tunnel memorial	SE 202455	294
Shipley, Saltaire mills and model village	SE 140381	200
Slaithwaite, Clough House Mill and steam engine	SE 068144	
Stanley, Stanley Ferry Aqueduct	SE 355231	

WALES

Clwyd
(the old counties of Denbighshire and Flint)

Bersham, blast furnaces	SJ 308492	
Bersham, industrial trail and museum	SJ 272518–	
	SJ 315492	
Brymbo, ironworks and furnace	SJ 2953	
Chirk, aqueduct and viaduct	SJ 287372	266, 285
Dyserth, Cwm iron mines	SJ 072777	
Froncysyllte, Pont Cysyllte Aqueduct	SJ 271420	265, 266
Halkyn, lead mines	SJ 203707	
Holywell, textile mills	SJ 131714	
Llansantffraid, Felin Ysaf watermill	SH 803749	
Mold, Afonwen paper mills	SJ 131714	
Rossett, watermill	SJ 364572	56
Ruabon, Wynnstay Colliery engine house	SJ 294433	97
Whitford, Mostyn Quay	SJ 158810	

Dyfed	Grid ref	Page
(the old counties of Cardiganshire, Carmarthenshire and Pembrokeshire)		
Ambleston, Wallis woollen mill	SN 014256	
Carew, French tidemill	SN 042038	52
Cydweli, tinplate works	SN 421079	147
Dolaucothi, gold mines	SN 670410	153
Dre-fach Felindre, textile mill and Museum of the Woollen Industry	SN 355385	202
Frongoch, lead mine	SN 723745	
Kilgetty, ironworks and Grove Colliery	SN 142073	
Llandybie, limekilns	SN 613165	
Llandyssul, Maesllyn Mill	SN 368447	
Narberth, Blackpool watermill, Canaston Bridge	SN 061144	
Newcastle Emlyn, Felin Geri watermill	SN 300423	
Ponterwyd, Llywernog silver/lead mines and museum	SN 735808	153
Porthgain, harbour	SM 815327	
Solva, watermill	SM 806259	

Mid-Glamorgan

	Grid ref	Page
Aberdare, cast iron tramway bridge, Robertstown	SN 997037	
Abereynon, Penydarren Tramroad	ST 083977– ST 080981	274
Blaencanaid, blast furnace	SO 035042	
Hengoed, Maesycwmmer Viaduct	ST 155949	
Hengoed, Ystrad Mill, Ystrad Mynach	ST 145929	
Merthyr Tydfil, cast iron bridge	SO 038072	
Merthyr Tydfil, Cyfarthfa Works and blast furnaces	SO 038070	
Merthyr Tydfil, Dowlais Works	SO 072078	
Merthyr Tydfil, Ynysfach Works	SO 045057	
Mountain Ash, waddle fan, Abergorki Colliery	ST 050990	101
Pontypridd, single-arch stone bridge	ST 074904	245
Pontypridd, Ty Mawr Colliery winding engine, Hopkinstown	ST 054909	
Trehafod, Lewis Merthyr Colliery	ST 036910	22, 99, 102

South Glamorgan

	Grid ref	Page
Aberthaw, cement and lime works	ST 083662	
Barry, docks	ST 1267	
Cardiff, Bute East Dock	ST 192757	
Cardiff, Bute East Dock warehouse	ST 191759	
Cardiff, Bute Street, shipping offices	ST 191746	
Cardiff, Mountstewart Square, shipping offices	ST 189746	
Penarth, docks	ST 1772	
Porthkerry, viaduct	ST 083668	
St Fagan's, Esgair Moel woollen mill and other industrial buildings in the Welsh Folk Museum	ST 118772	181
Treforest, tinplate works	ST 087880	
Whitchurch, Melingriffith water pump and Glamorganshire Canal	ST 142801	147

West Glamorgan	Grid ref	Page
Aberdulais, ironworks and Neath Canal	SS 775994	147
Crynant, Cefn Coed Coal and Steam Centre	SN 784033	
Landore, Siemens' Laboratory	SS 662957	
Landore, viaducts	SS 6695	
Neath, blast furnaces, Banwen Pyrddin	SN 868104	
Neath, Neath Abbey Ironworks	SS 738977	
Swansea, docks, Maritime and Industrial Museum	SS 657925	

Gwent
(the old county of Monmouthshire)

	Grid ref	Page
Abersychan, Cwmbyrgwm water balance	SO 251033	94
Blaenavon, Big Pit Colliery	SO 239088	102
Blaenavon, ironworks and water-balance tower	SO 250094	94
Butetown, industrial housing	SO 104092	
Chepstow, cast iron road bridge	ST 536944	
Cwmavon, Forge Row, industrial housing	SO 270064	
Llanelly, charcoal blast furnace	SO 232138	
Llanfoist, canal and wharf	SO 285130	
Newport, docks	ST 3187	
Newport, transporter bridge	ST 318863	252
Pontypool, Old Glyn Pit	ST 265999	96
Tredegar, Sirhowy Ironworks	SO 143102	
Tredegar, Trefil Viaduct	SO 130107– SO 134107	

Gwynedd
(the old counties of Anglesey, Caernarfonshire and Merioneth)

	Grid ref	Page
Amlwch, harbour	SH 449934	144
Bethesda, Penrhyn slate quarries	SH 6265	155
Betwys-y-Coed, Waterloo Bridge	SH 799558	248
Blaenau Ffestiniog, Gloddfa Ganol slate quarries	SH 698470	156
Blaenau Ffestiniog, Llechwedd slate caverns	SH 708471	156
Bontddu, gold mines	SH 6619	
Conwy, suspension bridge and tubular bridge	SH 786777	287
Dolbenmaen, Cwm Ystradllyn slate mill	SH 550434	
Garn Dolbenmaen, Brynkir woollen mill	SH 527424	
Gwynfynydd, gold mines	SH 735275 & SH 737282	153
Harlech, Llanfair slate mines	SH 596298	156
Llanberis, Dinorwic slate quarries and Welsh Slate Museum	SH 586603	155
Llandudno, Great Orme Railway	SH 777827	231
Llanfair PG, tollhouse	SH 532715	241
Llansantffraid, Felin Isaf watermill	SH 804747	
Menai, suspension bridge	SH 556714	249
Parys Mountain copper mines	SH 4490	144
Porthmadog, harbour and Maritime Museum	SH 570384	
Sychnant Pass	SH 750770	239
Tywyn, Talyllyn Railway	SH 586005– SH 671064	298

Powys

(the old counties of Breconshire, Montgomeryshire and Radnorshire)

	Grid ref	Page
Abercrave, blast furnaces	SN 811125	
Brecon, head of Brecon & Abergavenny Canal	SO 046283	
Church Stoke, Bacheldre watermill	SO 243929	
Clydach, ironworks	SO 232128	
Elan Valley, reservoirs and dams	SN 9263	
Hirwaun, blast furnaces	SN 957057	
Llandidloes, Bryntail lead mine	SN 913869	
Llangynog, lead mines	SJ 046274 &	
	SJ 051256	
Montgomeryshire Canal, including Vyrnwy Aqueduct	SO 139930–	
(SJ 253196) and Carreghofa Locks	SJ 226075	216
Newtown, weavers' cottages and textile museum	SO 107919	
Welshpool & Llanfair Light Railway	SJ 175064–	
	SJ 106068	298
Ystradgynlais, Ynyscedwyn ironworks	SN 782094	

MUSEUMS OF INDUSTRY

The following are the principal museums holding industrial, technological and transport collections. They are listed alphabetically by place.

ABERDEEN, Aberdeenshire
  Aberdeen Maritime Museum,
  Provost Ross's House, Shiprow, Aberdeen
  Tel: 0224 585788

ACTON SCOTT, Shropshire
  Acton Scott Historic Working Farm,
  Wenlock Lodge, Acton Scott,
  Church Stretton, Shropshire SY6 6QN
  Tel: 06946 306/307

AMBERLEY, W Sussex
  Amberley Chalk Pits Museum,
  Houghton Bridge, Amberley,
  Arundel, W Sussex BN18 9LT
  Tel: 0798 831370

APPLEDORE, Devon
  North Devon Maritime Museum,
  Odun House, Odun Road,
  Appledore, Devon EX39 1PT
  Tel: 0237 474852

AYSGARTH, N Yorks
  The Yorkshire Museum of Carriages &
  Horse Drawn Vehicles,
  Yore Mill, by Aysgarth Falls, Aysgarth,
  N Yorkshire.
  Correspondence to Frenchgate Head, Richmond,
  N Yorks DL10 7AU
  Tel: 0748 823275

BARLASTON, Staffs
  Wedgwood Museum,
  Josiah Wedgwood & Sons Ltd,
  Barlaston, Stoke-on-Trent, Staffordshire ST12 9ES
  Tel: 0782 204141

BATH, Avon
  Bath Postal Museum,
  8 Broad Street, Bath BA1 5LJ
  Tel: 0225 460333
  Bath Industrial Heritage Centre,
  Camden Works,
  Julian Road, Bath, Avon BA1 2RH
  Tel: 0225 318348

BATLEY, W Yorks
  Yorkshire Fire Museum,
  Bradford Road, Batley, W Yorks
  Tel: 0274 736006

BEAMISH, Co Durham
  Beamish, North of England Open Air Museum,
  Beamish, nr Stanley, Co Durham DH9 0RG
  Tel: 0207 231811

BEAULIEU, Hants
  National Motor Museum,
  John Montagu Building, Beaulieu,
  Brockenhurst, Hants SO42 7ZN
  Tel: 0590 612345

BELFAST, N Ireland
  Ulster Folk & Transport Museum,
  Witham Street, Belfast BT4 1HP
  Tel: 0232 451519 [See also, Holywood]

BERSHAM, Clwyd
  Bersham Industrial Heritage Centre,
  Bersham, nr Wrexham LL14 4HT
  Tel: 0978 261529

BIGGAR, Lanarks
  Biggar Gasworks Museum,
  Biggar, Lanarkshire.
  Correspondence to Department of Science,
  Technology & Working Life,
  The National Museums of Scotland,
  Chambers Street, Edinburgh EH1 1JF
  Tel: 031-225 7534
  Gladstone Court,
  Biggar, Lanarkshire ML12 6DT
  Tel: 0899 21050

BIRMINGHAM, W Midlands
  Birmingham Museum of Science & Industry,
  Newhall Street, Birmingham B3 1RZ
  Tel: 021-236 1022
  Birmingham Railway Museum,
  670 Warwick Road, Tyseley, Birmingham B11 2HL
  Tel: 021-707 4696
  Sarehole Mill,
  Colebank Road, Hall Green, Birmingham B13 0BD
  Tel: 021-777 6612
  Correspondence to Birmingham Museum &
  Art Gallery, Chamberlain Square,
  Birmingham B3 3DH
  Tel: 021-235 4202

BLACKBURN, Lancs
Lewis Museum of Textile Machinery,
Exchange Street, Blackburn, Lancs
Tel: 0254 667130
Correspondence to Blackburn Museum & Art
Gallery, Museum Street, Blackburn, Lancs BB1 7AJ

BLAENAU FFESTINIOG, Gwynedd
Llechwedd Slate Caverns,
Blaenau Ffestiniog LL41 3NB
Tel: 0766 830306

BLAENAFON, Gwent
Big Pit Mining Museum,
Big Pit, Blaenafon, Gwent NP4 9XP
Tel: 0495 790311

BOLTON, Greater Manchester
Hall i'th' Wood Museum,
Green Way, off Crompton Way, Bolton BL1 8UA
Tel: 0204 51159
Tonge Moor Textile Museum,
Tonge Moor Road, Bolton, Lancs BL2 2LE
Tel: 0204 21394
Correspondence to Bolton Museum & Art Gallery,
Le Mans Crescent, Bolton BL1 1SA
Tel: 0204 22311, ext 379
Steam Museum,
The Engine-House, Atlas No 3 Mill,
Chorley Old Road, Bolton BL1 4LB
Tel: 02572 65003 (Honorary Secretary – home)

BO'NESS, West Lothian
Bo'ness Heritage Trust,
Bo'ness Station, Bo'ness
Tel: 0506 825855

BOURNEMOUTH, Dorset
Bournemouth Transport & Rural Museum,
Correspondence to Russell-Cotes Art Gallery
& Museum, East Cliff, Bournemouth BH1 3AA
Tel: 0202 21009

BRADFORD, W Yorks
Bradford Industrial Museum,
Moorside Road, Eccleshill, Bradford BD2 3HP
Tel: 0274 631756
National Museum of Photography, Film & Television,
Pictureville, Bradford BD1 1NQ
Tel: 0274 727488
West Yorkshire Transport Museum,
Ludlam Street Depot, Mill Lane,
off Manchester Road, Bradford BD5 0HG
Tel: 0274 736006

BRISTOL, Avon
Bristol Industrial Museum,
Prince's Wharf, Prince Street, Bristol BS1 4RN
Tel: 0272 251470
Harvey's Wine Museum,
12 Denmark Street, Bristol BS1 5DQ
Tel: 0272 277661
SS *Great Britain*,
Great Western Dock, Gas Ferry Road,
Bristol BS1 6TY
Tel: 0272 260680

BRIXHAM, Devon
British Fisheries Museum,
The Old Market House, The Quay,
Brixham, Devon
Tel: 0845 2861

BROMSGROVE, Hereford & Worcs
Avoncroft Museum of Buildings,
Stoke Heath, Bromsgrove B60 4JR
Tel: 0527 31363

BROOK, Kent
Wye College Agricultural Museum,
Brook, Ashford, Kent.
Correspondence to
Hon Curator, Wye College
Agricultural Museum, Wye,
Ashford, Kent TN25 5AH
Tel: 0233 812401

BUCKIE, Moray
Buckie Maritime Museum & Peter Anson Gallery,
Town House West, Cluny Place,
Buckie, Moray AB5 1HB
Tel: 0542 32121
Correspondence to
Falconer Museum,
Tolbooth Street, Forres, Moray IV36 0PH
Tel: 0309 73701

BUCKLER'S HARD, Hants
Buckler's Hard Maritime Museum &
Village Display,
Buckler's Hard, Hants SO42 7XB
Tel: 0590 616203

BURNLEY, Lancs
Weavers' Triangle Visitor Centre,
85 Manchester Road, Burnley, Lancs BB11 1JZ
Tel: 0282 53007 – evenings
Museum of Local Crafts & Industries,
Towneley Hall, Burnley, BB11 3RQ
Tel: 0282 24213

BURTON UPON TRENT, Staffs
Bass Museum of Brewing History &
Shirehorse Stables,
Horninglow Street, Burton on Trent, Staffs DE14 3PP
Tel: 0283 511000

BURY, Greater Manchester
Bury Transport Museum,
Castlecroft Road, off Bolton Street, Bury, Lancs
Tel: 061-764 7790

CAERNARFON, Gwynedd
Seiont II Maritime Museum,
Victoria Dock, Caernarfon, Gwynedd
Tel: 0248 712528

CAMBRIDGE, Cambs
Whipple Museum of the History of Science,
Free School Lane, Cambridge CB2 3RH
Tel: 0223 334540

CARDIFF, S Glam
Welsh Folk Museum,
St Fagans, Cardiff CF5 6XB
Tel: 0222 569441
Welsh Industrial & Maritime Museum,
Bute Street, Cardiff CF1 6AN
Tel: 0222 481919

CASTLETOWN, Isle of Man
The Nautical Museum,
Castletown, Isle of Man
Correspondence to
Manx Museum & National Trust,
Douglas, Isle of Man
Tel: 0624 675522

CHALFONT ST GILES, Bucks
Chiltern Open Air Museum,
Newland Park, Gorelands Lane,
Chalfont St Giles, Bucks HP8 4AD
Tel: 02407 71117

CHATHAM, Kent
Chatham Historic Dockyard Trust,
The Historic Dockyard, Chatham ME4 4TE
Tel; 0634 812551

CHEDDLETON, Staffs
Cheddleton Flint Mill,
Leek Road, Cheddleton, nr Leek, Staffordshire
Correspondence to
Burton House, Tittensor,
Stoke-on-Trent ST12 9HH
Tel: 078 139 2561

COALVILLE, Leics
Snibston Discovery Park,
Ashby Road, Coalville, Leicestershire LE6 2LN
Tel: 0530 510851

COGGES, Oxon
Cogges Farm Museum,
Cogges, Witney, Oxon
Tel: 0993 774699

CORNHILL ON TWEED, Northumberland
Heatherslaw Mill,
Ford Forge, Cornhill on Tweed TD12 4TJ
Tel: 089 082 338

CORRIS, Powys
Corris Railway Museum,
Station Yard, Corris, Machynlleth,
Powys SY20 9SH
Tel: 0654 761624

CORSHAM, Wilts
The Underground Quarry Centre,
Park Lane, Corsham, Wilts SN13 0QR
Tel: 0249 716288
Correspondence to 1 High Street, Seend,
Melksham SN12 6NR

COVENTRY, W Midlands
Museum of British Road Transport,
St Agnes Lane, Hales Street, Coventry CV1 1PN
Tel: 0203 832425

COWES, Isle of Wight
Cowes Maritime Museum,
Beckford Road, Cowes,
Isle of Wight PO31 7SG
Tel: 0983 293341

CREGNEASH, Isle of Man
Cregneash Village Folk Museum,
Cregneash, Isle of Man
Correspondence to
Manx Museum & National Trust,
Douglas, Isle of Man
Tel: 0624 75522

CRICH, Derbys
National Tramway Museum,
Crich, Matlock DE4 5DP
Tel: 0773 852565

DARLINGTON, Co Durham
Darlington Railway Centre and Museum,
North Road Station, Station Road, Darlington,
Co Durham DL3 6ST
Tel: 0325 460532

DARTMOUTH, Devon
Newcomen Engine House & Dartmouth Museum,
The Butterwalk, Dartmouth, Devon TQ6 9PZ
Tel: 0803 832281

DERBY, Derbys
Derby Industrial Museum,
The Silk Mill, off Full Street, Derby DE1 3AR
Tel: 0332 255308
Royal Crown Derby Museum,
Royal Crown Derby Porcelain Co Ltd,
194 Osmaston Road, Derby DE3 2UN
Tel: 0332 47051

DEVIZES, Wilts
Canal Centre,
The Wharf, Devizes, Wilts SN10 1EB
Tel: 0380 721279

DISS, Norfolk
Bressingham Steam Museum,
Bressingham, Diss, Norfolk IP22 2AB
Tel: 0379–88 386

DONCASTER, S Yorks
Museum of South Yorkshire Life,
Cusworth Hall, Doncaster DN5 7TU
Tel: 0302 782342

DOUNE, Perthshire
Doune Motor Museum,
Carse of Cambus, Doune, Perthshire FK16 6HD
Tel: 0786–841 203

DOVER, Kent
Crabble Corn Mill,
Lower Road, River, Dover, Kent CT17 0UY
Tel: 0304 823292
Dover Transport Museum,
Connaught Pumping Station,
Connaught Road, Dover
Tel: 0304 204612
The Grand Shaft,
Snargate Street
Correspondence to Dover Museum, Ladywell,
Dover CT16 1DQ
Tel: 0304 201066

DRE-FACH FELINDRE, Dyfed
Museum of the Welsh Woollen Industry,
Dre-fach Felindre, Llandysul, Dyfed SA44 5UP
Tel: 0559 370929

DUDLEY, W Midlands
The Black Country Museum,
Tipton Road, Dudley,
West Midlands DY1 4SQ
Tel: 021-557 9643

DUNDEE
Dundee Heritage Trust
(Custodian of RRS *Discovery*),
Maritime House, 26 East Dock Street,
Dundee DD1 9HY
Tel: 0382 25282

DUXFORD, Cambs
Duxford Airfield (Imperial War Museum),
Duxford, Cambridge CB2 4QR
Tel: 0223 833963

EAST CARLTON, Northants
East Carlton Steel Heritage Centre,
East Carlton Park, East Carlton,
nr Market Harborough, Leics LE16 8YD
Tel: 0536 770977

EAST LINTON, East Lothian
Preston Mill,
East Linton, East Lothian
Tel: 0620-860 426

EDINBURGH
National Museum of Scotland,
Chambers Street, Edinburgh EH1 1JF
Tel: 031-225 7534

ELLESMERE PORT, Ches
The Boat Museum,
Dockyard Road, Ellesmere Port,
Cheshire L65 4EF
Tel: 051-355 5017

EXETER, Devon
Exeter Maritime Museum,
The Haven,
Exeter EX2 8DT
Tel: 0392 58075

FALMOUTH, Cornwall
Falmouth Maritime Museum,
Bell's Court, off Market Street, Falmouth,
Cornwall; Steam tug *St Denys*,
Custom House Quay, Falmouth
Correspondence to Hon Secretary,
Higher Penpol House,
Mawnan Smith, nr Falmouth, Cornwall
Tel: 0326 250507

GATESHEAD, Tyne & Wear
Bowes Railway Centre,
Springwell Village, Gateshead,
Tyne & Wear NE9 7QJ
Tel: 091-416 1847

GLASGOW
Art Gallery & Museum,
Kelvingrove, Glasgow G3 8AG
Tel: 041-357 3929
Museum of Transport,
Kelvin Hall, Bunhouse Road, Glasgow G3 8PZ
Tel: 041-357 3929

GLASTONBURY, Somerset
Somerset Rural Life Museum,
Abbey Farm, Chilkwell Street, Glastonbury,
Somerset BA6 8DB
Tel: 0458 31197

GLOUCESTER, Glos
National Waterways Museum,
Llanthony Warehouse, The Docks,
Gloucester GL1 2EH
Tel: 0452 307009
The Robert Opie Collection Museum of Packaging
and Advertising,
Albert Warehouse, The Docks,
Gloucester GL1 2EH
Tel: 0452 302309

GOLCAR, W Yorks
Colne Valley Museum,
Cliffe Ash, Golcar,
Huddersfield HD7 4PY
Tel: 0484 659762

GREAT YARMOUTH, Norfolk
Maritime Museum for East Anglia,
Marine Parade, Great Yarmouth, Norfolk NR30 2EN
Tel: 0493 842267

GRESSENHALL, Norfolk
Norfolk Rural Life Museum,
Beech House, Gressenhall, Dereham,
Norfolk NR20 4DR
Tel: 0362 860563

HALIFAX, W Yorks
Calderdale Industrial Museum,
The Piece Hall, Halifax
Tel: 0422 358087
Folk Museum of West Yorkshire,
Shibden Hall, Halifax HX3 6XG
Tel: 0422 352246

HARTLEPOOL, Cleveland
Hartlepool Maritime Museum,
Northgate, Hartlepool TS24 0LT
Tel: 0429 272814

HELMSHORE, Lancs
Helmshore Textile Museums,
Holcombe Road, Helmshore,
Rossendale BB4 4NP
Tel: 0706 226459

HEREFORD, Herefordshire
Herefordshire Waterworks Museum,
Broomy Hill, Hereford
Correspondence to Secretary,
44 Tower Road, Hereford HR4 0LF
Tel: 0432 273635

HOLYWOOD, Co Down
Ulster Folk & Transport Museum [see also Belfast],
Cultra Manor, Holywood BT18 0EU,
N Ireland
Tel: 0232 428428

HOVE, Sussex
The British Engineerium,
Nevill Road, Hove, E Sussex BN3 7QA
Tel: 0273 559583/554070

HULL, N Humberside
Town Docks Museum,
Queen Victoria Square, Hull HU1 3DX
Tel: 0482 222737
Hull Museum of Transport,
36 High Street, Hull
Tel: 0482 222737
Yorkshire Water Museum,
Springhead Avenue, Willerby Road, Hull HU5 5HZ
Tel: 0482 652283

HUTTON-LE-HOLE, N Yorks
Ryedale Folk Museum,
Hutton-le-Hole, N Yorks YO6 6UA
Tel: 07515 367

IRVINE, Ayrshire
Scottish Maritime Museum,
Gottries Road, Irvine, Ayrshire KA12 8QE
Tel: 0294 78283

KENDAL, Cumbria
Museum of Lakeland Life & Industry,
Abbot Hall, Kendal, Cumbria LA9 5AL
Tel: 0539 722464

KESWICK, Cumbria
Cumberland Pencil Museum,
Southey Works, Keswick, Cumbria
Tel: 07687 73626

KIDWELLY, Dyfed
Kidwelly Industrial Museum,
Kidwelly SA17 4LW
Tel: 0554 891078

KINGSBRIDGE, Devon
Cookworthy Museum,
The Old Grammar School, 108 Fore Street,
Kingsbridge, Devon
Tel: 0548 853235

LACOCK, Wilts
Fox Talbot Museum of Photography,
Lacock, nr Chippenham, Wilts SN15 2LG
Tel: 024-973 459
Lackham Agricultural Museum,
Lackham College of Agriculture, Lacock,
Chippenham, Wilts
Tel: 0249 443111

LANCASTER, Lancs
Maritime Museum,
Old Custom House, St George's Quay,
Lancaster LA1 1RB
Tel: 0524 64637

LEEDS, W Yorks
Leeds Industrial Museum,
Armley Mill, Canal Road, Armley, Leeds LS12 2QF
Tel: 0532 63786

LEEK, Staffs
Brindley Mill & James Brindley Museum,
Mill Street, Leek, Staffs
Tel: 0538 381446
Correspondence to Hon Secretary, 5 Daintry Street,
Leek, Staffs ST13 5PG
Tel: 0538 384195

LEICESTER, Leics
Leicestershire Museum of Technology,
Abbey Pumping Station, Corporation Road,
Abbey Lane, Leicester
Tel: 0533 616330
The John Doran Gas Museum,
Aylestone Road, Leicester LE2 7QH
Correspondence to British Gas, East Midlands,
De Montford Street, Leicester, LE1 9DB
Tel: 0533 535506

LINCOLN, Lincs
Museum of Lincolnshire Life,
The Old Barracks, Burton Road, Lincoln LN1 3LY
Tel: 0522 528448
National Cycle Museum,
Brayford Wharf, North Lincoln LN1 1YW
Tel: 0522 545091

LIVERPOOL, Merseyside
Liverpool Museum,
William Brown Street, Liverpool L3 8EN
Tel: 051-207 0001
Merseyside Maritime Museum, Albert Dock,
Liverpool L3 4AA
Tel: 051-207 0001

LLANBERIS, Gwynedd
The Welsh Slate Museum,
Gilfach Ddu, Llanberis, Gwynedd LL55 4TY
Tel: 0286 870630

LLANIDLOES, Powys
   Museum of Local History & Industry,
   Old Market Hall, Llanidloes SY18 6AD
   Correspondence to the Curator,
   Llandrindod Wells Museum,
   Temple Street, Llandrindod Wells,
   Powys LD1 5DL
   Tel: 0597 824513

LONDON
   British Motor Industry Heritage Trust,
   Syon Park, Brentford, Middx
   Tel: 081-560 1378
   Cutty Sark Clipper Ship,
   King William Walk, Greenwich SE10 9HT
   Tel: 081-858 3445
   Crossness Beam Engines,
   Thames Water, Crossness Works, Belvedere Road,
   Abbey Wood, London SE2 9AQ
   Correspondence to the Secretary,
   Crossness Engines Trust, 8 Yorkland Avenue,
   Welling, Kent DA16 2LF
   Tel: 081-303 6723
   Kew Bridge Steam Museum,
   Green Dragon Lane, Brentford, Middx TW8 0EN
   Tel: 081-568 4757
   London Transport Museum,
   Covent Garden, London WC2E 7BB
   Tel: 071-379 6344
   Museum of London,
   London Wall, London EC2Y 5HN
   Tel: 071-600 3699
   National Maritime Museum,
   Romney Road, Greenwich, London SE10 9NF
   Tel: 081-858 4422
   National Postal Museum,
   King Edward Building, King Edward Street,
   London EC1A 1LP
   Tel: 071-239 5420
   North Woolwich Old Station Museum,
   Pier Road, North Woolwich, London E16 2JJ
   Tel: 071-474 7244
   Science Museum,
   Exhibition Road, London SW7 2DD
   Tel: 071-938 8000
   Science Museum Library, London SW7 5NH
   Tel: 071-938 8000
   Telecom Technology Showcase,
   135 Queen Victoria Street, London EC4V 4AT
   Tel: 071-248 7444

LOUGHBOROUGH, Leics
   Great Central Museum,
   Great Central Railway, Central Station,
   Loughborough, Leics LE11 1RW
   Tel: 0509 230726

LOWESTOFT, Suffolk
   East Anglia Transport Museum,
   Chapel Road, Carlton Colville, Lowestoft,
   Suffolk NR33 8BL
   Tel: 0502 518459
   Lowestoft & East Suffolk Maritime Museum,
   Sparrows Nest Gardens,
   Lowestoft, Suffolk NR32 1XT
   Tel: 0502 561963

MACCLESFIELD, Cheshire
   Macclesfield Silk Museum,
   Roe Street, Macclesfield, Cheshire SK11 6UT
   Tel: 0625 613210

MAIDSTONE, Kent
   Tyrwhitt-Drake Museum of Carriages,
   Archbishop's Stables, Mill Street,
   Maidstone, Kent
   Tel: 0622 754497

MANCHESTER
   Manchester Museum of Science & Industry,
   Liverpool Road, Castlefield, Manchester M3 4JP
   Tel: 061-832 2244
   Museum of Transport – Greater Manchester,
   Boyle Street, Cheetham, Manchester M8 8UL
   Tel: 061-205 2122/061-205 1082
   National Museum of Labour History,
   103 Princess Street, Manchester M1 6DD
   Tel: 061-228 7212

MARYPORT, Cumbria
   Maryport Maritime Museum,
   1 Senhouse Street,
   Shipping Brow, Maryport,
   Cumbria CA15 6AB
   Tel: 090-081 3738

MATLOCK BATH, Derbys
   Peak District Mining Museum,
   The Pavilion, Matlock Bath, Derbyshire
   Tel: 0629 583834

MORWELLHAM, Devon
   Morwellham Quay Open Air Museum,
   Morwellham, Tavistock,
   Devon PL19 8JL
   Tel: 0822 832766

MURTON, N Yorks
   Yorkshire Museum of Farming,
   Murton, Yorks YO1 3UF
   Tel: 0904 489966

NAIRN, Highland
   Nairn Fishertown Museum,
   Laing Hall, King Street,
   Nairn IV12 4PP
   Tel: 0667 52064

NEWARK-ON-TRENT, Notts
   Newark Air Museum,
   Winthorpe Airfield,
   Newark-on-Trent NG24 2NY
   Tel: 0636 707170

NEWCASTLE UPON TYNE, Tyne & Wear
   Museum of Science & Engineering,
   Blandford House, Blandford Square,
   Newcastle upon Tyne, Tyne & Wear NE1 4JA
   Tel: 091-232 6789

NEWTONGRANGE, Midlothian
Scottish Mining Museum [see also Prestongrange],
Lady Victoria Colliery, Newtongrange,
Midlothian EH22 4QN
Tel: 031-663 7519

NEWTOWN, Powys
Newtown Textile Museum,
7 Commercial Street,
Newtown, Powys
Correspondence to Museums Officer,
County Library, Cefnllys Road, Llandrindod Wells,
Powys LD1 5LD
Tel: 0597 826060

NORTH BERWICK, E Lothian
Museum of Flight,
East Fortune Airfield,
North Berwick, East Lothian EH39 5LF
Tel: 062-088 308
Correspondence to Department of Science,
Technology & Working Life,
National Museums of Scotland, Chambers Street,
Edinburgh EH1 1JF
Tel: 031-225 7534

NORTHAMPTON, Northants
Museum of Leathercraft,
Bridge Street, Northampton
Tel: 0604 34881 Ext 5111 or 39415

NORTHWICH, Ches
The Salt Museum,
162 London Road,
Northwich CW9 8AB
Tel: 0606 41331

NOTTINGHAM, Notts
Canal Museum,
Canal Street, Nottingham
Tel: 0602 598835
Correspondence to The Curator,
Nottingham Industrial Museum,
Courtyard Buildings, Wollaton Park,
Nottingham NG8 2AE
Industrial Museum, Courtyard Buildings,
Wollaton Park, Nottingham NG8 2AE
Tel: 0602 284602
Green's Mill and Centre,
Windmill Lane, Sneinton,
Nottingham NG2 4QB
Tel: 0602 503635

OLD WARDEN, Beds
The Shuttleworth Collection,
Old Warden Aerodrome, Biggleswade,
Beds SG18 9ER
Tel: 076-727 288

OXENHOPE, W Yorks
Keighley & Worth Valley Railway,
Haworth Station, Haworth,
Keighley BD22 8NJ
Tel: 0535 645214

OXFORD, Oxon
British Telecom Museum,
35 Speedwell Street, Oxford OX1 1RH
Tel: 0865 246601
Museum of the History of Science,
Old Ashmolean Building, Broad Street,
Oxford OX1 3AZ
Tel: 0865 277280

PETERHEAD, Aberdeenshire
North East of Scotland Agricultural
Heritage Centre,
Aden Country Park, Mintlaw, by Peterhead,
Aberdeenshire AB42 8FQ
Tel: 0771 22857

PONTERWYD, Dyfed
Llywernog Silver-Lead Mine Museum,
Ponterwyd, nr Aberystwyth, Dyfed SY23 3AB
Tel: 0970 85620

PONTYPOOL, Gwent
Torfaen Museum Trust,
Park Buildings, Pontypool, Gwent NP4 6JH
Tel: 0495 752036

POOLE, Dorset
Waterfront Museum,
Paradise Street, The Quay, Poole BH15 1HJ
Tel: 0202 683138

PORT TALBOT, W Glam
The Welsh Miners' Museum,
Afan Argoed Country Park, Cynonville,
Port Talbot, W Glamorgan
Tel: 0639 850564
Correspondence to Director/Secretary,
Welsh Miners' Museum,
16 Percy Road, Cynonville, Port Talbot,
W Glamorgan
Tel: 0639 850875

PORTHMADOG, Gwynedd
Festiniog Railway Museum,
Harbour Station, Porthmadog, Gwynedd LL49 9NF
Tel: 0766 512340
Porthmadog Maritime Museum,
Greaves Wharf, Porthmadog,
Tel: 0766 513736
Correspondence to Eifion Davies, Gowerian,
Ralph Street, Borth y Gest, Porthmadog
Tel: 0766 512864

PORTSMOUTH, Hants
Eastney Industrial Museum,
Henderson Road, Eastney, Portsmouth PO4 9JF
Correspondence to Portsmouth City Museum &
Art Gallery, Museum Road,
Old Portsmouth PO1 2LJ
Tel: 0705 827261

PRESCOT, Merseyside
Prescot Museum of Clock & Watch Making,
34 Church Street, Prescot L34 3LA
Tel: 051-430 7787

PRESTON, Lancs
The British Commercial Vehicle Museum,
King Street, Leyland, Preston, Lancs PR5 1LE
Tel: 0772 451011

PRESTONGRANGE, E Lothian
Scottish Mining Museum [see also Newtongrange],
Prestongrange, East Lothian EH32 9RX
Tel: 031-663 7519
Correspondence to Director, Scottish Mining
Museum, Lady Victoria Colliery, Newtongrange,
Midlothian EH22 4QN

RAMSEY, Isle of Man
The Grove Rural Life Museum,
Andreas Road, Ramsey, Isle of Man
Correspondence to Manx Museum & National
Trust, Douglas, Isle of Man
Tel: 0624 675522

RAVENGLASS, Cumbria
Railway Museum,
The Ravenglass & Eskdale Railway Co Ltd,
Ravenglass, Cumbria CA18 1SW
Tel: 0229 717171

READING, Berks
Institute of Agricultural History & Museum of
English Rural Life,
The University, Whiteknights, PO Box 229,
Reading, Berkshire RG6 2AG
Tel: 0734 318660

REDDITCH, Hereford & Worcs
Forge Mill Museum,
Forge Mill, Needle Mill Lane, Redditch,
Hereford & Worcs
Tel: 0527 62509

REETH, N Yorks
Swaledale Folk Museum,
Reeth Green, Reeth, nr Richmond,
N Yorks DL11 6QT
Tel: 0748 84517

RHONDDA, Mid Glam
Rhondda Heritage Park,
Lewis Merthyr, Coed Cae Road, Trehafod,
Rhondda, Mid Glamorgan CF37 7NP
Tel: 0443 682036

RISELEY, Berks
National Dairy Museum,
Wellington Country Park, Riseley, Reading RG7 1SP
Tel: 0734 326444
Correspondence to National Dairy
Council, 5 John Princes Street, London W1M 0AP
Tel: 071-499 7822

ROCHDALE, Greater Manchester
Rochdale Pioneers Memorial Museum,
31 Toad Lane, Rochdale OL12 0NU
Tel: 061-832 4300
Correspondence to Co-operative Union,
Holyoake House, Hanover Street,
Manchester M60 0AS

RUDDINGTON, Notts
Ruddington Framework Knitters' Museum,
Chapel Street, Ruddington, Notts NG11 6HE
Tel: 0602 846914

ST AUSTELL, Cornwall
Wheal Martyn Museum,
Carthew, St Austell, Cornwall PL26 8XG
Tel: 0726 850362

ST DOMINICK, Cornwall
Cotehele Museum, Cotehele Quay,
St Dominick, Saltash PL12 6TA
Tel: 0579 50830

ST HELENS, Merseyside
Pilkington Glass Museum,
Prescot Road, St Helens, Merseyside WA10 3TT
Tel: 0744 692499

ST IVES, Cornwall
Barnes Museum of Cinematography,
Kino House, Victoria Place, St Ives TR26 1NZ
Tel: 0736 794080

SALFORD, Greater Manchester
Salford Mining Museum,
Buile Hill Park, Eccles Old Road, Salford M6 8GL
Tel: 061-736 1832

SETTLE, N Yorks
Museum of North Craven Life,
Chapel Street, Settle, N Yorks BD24 9HS

SHEFFIELD, S Yorks
Abbeydale Industrial Hamlet,
Abbeydale Road South, Sheffield S7 2QW
Tel: 0742 367731
Sheffield Industrial Museum,
Kelham Island, off Alma Street,
Sheffield S3 8RY
Tel: 0742 722106
Shepherd Wheel,
Whiteley Woods, off Hangingwater Road,
Sheffield 11, Tel: 0742 367731
Correspondence to
Abbeydale Industrial Hamlet,
Abbeydale Road South, Sheffield S7 2QW

SHILDON, Co Durham
Timothy Hackworth Railway Museum,
Soho Cottages, Shildon, Co Durham,
Tel: 0388 777999

SHREWSBURY, Shropshire
Coleham Pumping Station,
Longdon Coleham, Shrewsbury, Shropshire
Correspondence to
Rowley's House Museum,
Barker Street, Shrewsbury SY1 1QT
Tel: 0743 61196

SHUGBOROUGH, Staffs
Staffordshire County Museum,
Shugborough, Stafford ST17 0XB
Tel: 0889 881388

SINGLETON, W Sussex
  Weald & Downland Open Air Museum,
  Singleton, Chichester, W Sussex PO18 0EU
  Tel: 024363 348

SITTINGBOURNE, Kent
  Dolphin Sailing Barge Museum,
  Crown Quay Lane, Sittingbourne, Kent
  Correspondence to
  45 Park Road, Sittingbourne, Kent ME10 1DY
  Tel: 0795 423215

SKEGNESS, Lincs
  Church Farm Museum,
  Church Road South, Skegness, Lincs
  Tel: 0754 66658
  Correspondence to Museum of Lincolnshire Life,
  Burton Road, Lincoln
  Tel: 0522 28448

SKIDBY, Humberside
  Skidby Windmill & Mill Museum,
  Skidby, Cottingham, Humberside
  Tel: 0482 882255, ext 213

SKINNINGROVE, Cleveland
  Tom Leonard Mining Museum,
  Deepdale, Skinningrove, Saltburn, Cleveland
  Tel: 0287 42877
  Correspondence to the Secretary, South View,
  6 Wades Lane, East Barnby, Whitby
  Tel: 0947 83244

SOLIHULL, W Midlands
  National Motorcycle Museum,
  Coventry Road, Bickenhill, Solihull B92 0EJ
  Tel: 06755 3311

SOUTHAMPTON, Hants
  Southampton Maritime Museum,
  Bugle Street, Southampton
  Tel: 0703 223941/224216

SOUTHPORT, Merseyside
  Steamport Transport Museum,
  Derby Road, Southport, Merseyside
  Tel: 0704 530693

STAMFORD, Lincs
  Stamford Steam Brewery Museum,
  All Saints Street, Stamford, Lincs PE9 2PA
  Tel: 0780 52186

STEVINGTON, Beds
  Stevington Windmill,
  Stevington, Beds
  Correspondence to Director of Leisure Services,
  Bedfordshire County Council, County Library,
  County Hall, Bedford MK42 9AP
  Tel: 0234 228330

STICKLEPATH, Devon
  Finch Foundry Museum of Water Power,
  Sticklepath, Okehampton, Devon
  Tel: 0837 840046

STOKE BRUERNE, Northants
  The Canal Museum,
  Stoke Bruerne, nr Towcester, Northants NN12 7SE
  Tel: 0604 862229

STOKE-ON-TRENT, Staffs
  Chatterley Whitfield Mining Museum,
  Chatterley Whitfield Colliery, Tunstall,
  Stoke-on-Trent ST6 8UN
  Tel: 0782 813337
  City Museum & Art Gallery,
  Bethesda Street, Hanley, Stoke-on-Trent ST1 3DE
  Tel: 0782 202173
  Etruria Industrial Museum,
  Lower Bedford Street, Etruria, Stoke-on-Trent
  Tel: 0782 287557
  Gladstone Pottery Museum,
  26 Uttoxeter Road, Longton,
  Stoke-on-Trent ST3 1PQ
  Tel: 0782 311378/319232

STOWMARKET, Suffolk
  Museum of East Anglian Life,
  Stowmarket, Suffolk IP14 1DL
  Tel: 0449 612229

STREET, Somerset
  The Shoe Museum,
  C. & J. Clark Ltd, Street, Somerset BA16 0YA
  Tel: 0458 43131

STYAL, Ches
  Quarry Bank Mill,
  Styal, Cheshire SK9 4LA
  Tel: 0625 527468

SUNDERLAND, Tyne & Wear
  Ryhope Engines Museum,
  Ryhope, Sunderland, Tyne & Wear SR2 0ND
  Tel: 091-523 0235

SWANSEA, W Glam
  Swansea Maritime & Industrial Museum,
  Museum Square, Maritime Quarter,
  Swansea SA1 1SN
  Tel: 0792 650351/470371

SWINDON, Wilts
  Great Western Railway Museum,
  Faringdon Road, Swindon, Wilts SN1 5BJ
  Tel: 0793 526161, ext 4552
  Railway Village Museum,
  34 Faringdon Road, Swindon, Wilts SN1 5BJ
  Tel: 0793 526161, ext 4527

TELFORD, Shropshire
  Ironbridge Gorge Museum,
  Ironbridge, Telford, Shropshire TF8 7AW
  Tel: 0952 433522

TYWYN, Gwynedd
  Narrow Gauge Railway Museum,
  Wharf Station, Tywyn, Gwynedd LL36 9EY

UFFCULME, Devon
Coldharbour Mill Working Wool Museum,
Coldharbour Mill, Uffculme, Cullompton,
Devon EX15 3EE
Tel: 0884 840960

WAKEFIELD, West Yorks
Yorkshire Mining Museum,
Caphouse Colliery, New Road, Overton,
nr Wakefield WF4 4RF
Tel: 0924 848806

WALKERBURN, Peeblesshire
Scottish Museum of Woollen Textiles,
Tweedale Mills, Walkerburn EH43 6RH
Tel: 089-687 281

WALSALL, W Midlands
The Lock Museum,
54/56 New Road, Willenhall,
W Midlands WV13 2DA
Tel: 0902 634542

WANLOCKHEAD, Dumfriesshire
Museum of Scottish Lead Mining,
Goldscaur Row, Wanlockhead, Dumfriesshire
Tel: 0659 74387
Correspondence to Museum of Scottish
Leadmining, Biggar, Lanarkshire

WANTAGE, Oxon
Vale & Downland Museum Centre,
The Old Surgery, Church Street, Wantage, Oxon
Tel; 02357 66838

WARLEY, W Midlands
Avery Historical Museum,
GEC Avery Ltd, Foundry Lane, Smethwick,
Warley, West Midlands B66 2LP
Tel: 021-558 1112

WASHINGTON, Tyne & Wear
Washington 'F' Pit Museum,
Albany Way, Albany, Washington NE37 1BJ
Tel: 091-416 7640
Correspondence to Sunderland Museum &
Art Gallery, Borough Road, Sunderland,
Tyne & Wear SR1 1PP

WEYBRIDGE, Surrey
Brooklands Museum,
The Clubhouse, Brooklands Road, Weybridge,
Surrey KT13 0QN
Tel: 0932 857381

WIDNES, Cheshire
Catalyst: The Museum of the Chemical Industry,
Gossage Building, Mersey Road, Widnes,
Cheshire WA8 0DF
Tel: 051-420 1121

WIGAN, Greater Manchester
Wigan Pier Heritage Centre Trencherfield Mill,
Wigan Pier, Wigan WN3 4EU
Tel: 0942 323666

WINDERMERE, Cumbria
Windermere Steamboat Museum,
Rayrigg Road, Windermere, Cumbria LA23 1BN
Tel: 09662 5565

WORCESTER, Hereford & Worcs
Dyson Perrins Museum,
Severn Street, Worcester WR1 2NE
Tel: 0905 23221

WREXHAM, Clwyd
Bersham Industrial Heritage Centre,
Bersham, nr Wrexham, Clwyd LL14 4HT
Tel: 0978 261529

WYLAM, Northumb
Railway Museum,
Falcon Centre, Falcon Terrace, Wylam,
Northumberland
Tel: 0661 852174

YORK, N Yorks
National Railway Museum,
Leeman Road, York YO2 4XJ
Tel: 0904 621261

USEFUL ADDRESSES

The following are the names and addresses of mainly national bodies. Local and regional organisations have not been included as their addresses change frequently and the list would soon be out of date. The most complete index of industrial archaeological societies and preservation groups is maintained by the Association for Industrial Archaeology and may be consulted at the Ironbridge Institute, Ironbridge, Telford, Shropshire TF8 7AW (Tel: 0952 432751). Correspondence should be addressed to the Assistant Secretary. The Association of Independent Museums and the Museums Association (listed below) have current information on industrial museums, preservation projects and new museums.

ASSOCIATION FOR INDUSTRIAL ARCHAEOLOGY   ·
  Secretary: c/o Ironbridge Gorge Museum, Ironbridge, Telford, Shropshire TF8 7AW
  Tel: 0952 432751

ASSOCIATION OF BRITISH TRANSPORT MUSEUMS
  Secretary: Science Museum, London SW7 2DD
  Tel: 071-938 8000

ASSOCIATION OF COUNTY COUNCILS
  Secretary: 66a Eaton Square, London SW1W 9BH
  Tel: 071-235 1200

ASSOCIATION OF DISTRICT COUNCILS
  Secretary: 26 Chapel Street, London SW1P 4ND
  Tel: 071-233 6868

ASSOCIATION OF INDEPENDENT MUSEUMS
  Weald & Downland Museum,
  Singleton, Wesxt Sussex
  Tel: 024363 348

ASSOCIATION OF METROPOLITAN AUTHORITIES
  Secretary: 35 Great Smith Street, Westminster, London SW1P 3BJ
  Tel: 071-222 8100

BATH UNIVERSITY; CENTRE FOR THE STUDY OF THE HISTORY OF TECHNOLOGY, SCIENCE & SOCIETY
  Director: School of Humanities and Social Sciences, Claverton Down, Bath BA2 7AY

BRITISH LIBRARY BOARD
  Press Officer, Brill Place, London NW1 2DB
  Tel: 071-323 7116

BRITISH LIBRARY DOCUMENTS SUPPLY SERVICE
  Boston Spa, Wetherby, Yorkshire LS23 7BQ
  Tel: 0937 546000

BRITISH LIBRARY
  Newspaper Library,
  Colindale Avenue, London NW9 5HE
  Tel: 071-323 7353

BRITISH RAILWAYS BOARD
  24 Eversholt Street, PO Box 100, London NW1
  Tel: 071-928 5151

BRITISH RECORDS ASSOCIATION
  18 Padbury Court, London E2 7EH
  Tel: 071-729 1415

BRITISH SOCIETY FOR THE HISTORY OF SCIENCE
  Executive Secretary: 31 High Street,
  Stanford-in-the-Vale, Faringdon,
  Oxon SN7 8LH

BRITISH TOURIST AUTHORITY
  Head Office, Thames Tower, Black's Road,
  London W6 9EL
  Tel: 081-846 9000

BRUNEL SOCIETY
  Secretary: Brunel Technical College, Ashley Down,
  Bristol BS7 9BU
  Tel: 0272-41241

BUSINESS ARCHIVES COUNCIL
  185 Tower Bridge Road, London SE1 2UF
  Tel: 071-407 6110

CARNEGIE UNITED KINGDOM TRUST
  Secretary: Comely Park House,
  80 New Road, Dunfermline,
  Fife KY12 7EJ
  Tel: 0383 721445

CIVIC TRUST
  Director: 17 Carlton House Terrace,
  London SW1Y 5AW
  Tel: 071-930 0914

COUNCIL FOR BRITISH ARCHAEOLOGY
Director: 112 Kennington Road, London SE11 6RE
Tel: 071-582 0494

COUNCIL FOR NAUTICAL ARCHAEOLOGY
(Research Sub-Committee of the Council for British
Archaeology)
(Address above)

COUNTRYSIDE COMMISSION
Director: John Dower House, Crescent Place,
Cheltenham, Gloucestershire GL50 3RA
Tel: 0242 521381

COUNTRYSIDE COMMISSION FOR SCOTLAND
Director: Battleby, Redgorton, Perth PH1 3EW
Tel: 0738 27921

CRAFTS COUNCIL
Director: 12 Waterloo Place, London SW1Y 4AU
Tel: 071-930 4811

ENGLISH HERITAGE (Historic Buildings &
Monuments Commission for England)
Fortress House, 23 Savile Row, London W1X 1AB
Tel: 071-973 3000

ENGLISH TOURIST BOARD
Thames Tower, Black's Road, London W6 9EL
Tel: 081-846 9000

GEORGIAN GROUP
37 Spital Square, London E1 6DY
Tel: 071-377 1722

CALOUSTE GULBENKIAN FOUNDATION
United Kingdom Branch
Director: 98 Portland Place, London W1N 4ET
Tel: 071-636 5513-7

HIGHLANDS & ISLANDS ENTERPRISE
20 Bridge Street, Inverness
Tel: 0463 234171

HISTORIC COMMERCIAL VEHICLE CLUB
Secretary: Iden Grange, Cranbrook Road,
Staplehurst, Kent TN12 0ET

HISTORICAL ASSOCIATION
Secretary: 59A Kennington Park Road,
London SE11 4JH
Tel: 071-735 3901

HISTORICAL METALLURGY SOCIETY
Secretary: Dept of Economic History,
The University, Sheffield S10 2TN

INLAND WATERWAYS ASSOCIATION
Gen Secretary: General Office,
114 Regent's Park Road, London NW1
Tel: 071-586 2510

INSTITUTE OF ARCHAEOLOGY
Secretary & Registrar:
University of London,
31-4 Gordon Square, London WC1H 0PY
Tel: 071-387 7050

INSTITUTE OF CHEMICAL ENGINEERS
Secretary: The Davis Building,
165-71 Railway Terrace, Rugby CV21 3HQ
Tel: 0788 578214

INSTITUTE OF MARINE ENGINEERS
Secretary: Memorial Building, 76 Mark Lane,
London EC3
Tel: 071-481 8493

INSTITUTE OF PATENTEES & INVENTORS
Secretary: Triumph House,
189 Regent Street, London W1
Tel: 071-242 7812

INSTITUTION OF CIVIL ENGINEERS
Secretary: Great George Street, London SW1
Panel for Historic Engineering Works (PHEW):
189 Regent Street, London W1
Tel: 071-222 7722

INSTITUTION OF ELECTRICAL ENGINEERS
Secretary: Savoy Place, London WC2
Tel: 071-240 1871

INSTITUTION OF HIGHWAY &
TRANSPORTATION ENGINEERS
Secretary: 3 Lygon Place, London SW1
Tel: 071-730 5245

INSTITUTION OF MECHANICAL ENGINEERS
Secretary: 1 Birdcage Walk, London SW1
Tel: 071-222 7899

INSTITUTION OF METALLURGISTS
Secretary: 1 Carlton House Terrace, London SW1
Tel: 071-839 4071

INSTITUTION OF MINING ENGINEERS
Secretary: Hobart House, Grosvenor Place,
London SW1
Tel: 071-235 3691

INSTITUTION OF PRODUCTION ENGINEERS
Secretary: Rochester House, Little Ealing Lane,
London W5
Tel: 071-579 9411

INSTITUTION OF STRUCTURAL ENGINEERS
Secretary: 11 Upper Belgrave Street,
London SW1
Tel: 071-235 4535

INSTITUTION OF WATER ENGINEERS &
SCIENTISTS
Secretary: 31 High Holborn, London WC1
Tel: 071-831 6578

IRONBRIDGE GORGE MUSEUM TRUST
Chief Executive: Ironbridge, Telford, Shropshire
TF8 7AW
Tel: 0952 433522

IRONBRIDGE INSTITUTE
Ironbridge, Telford, Shropshire TF8 7AW
Tel: 0952 432751

LIBRARY ASSOCIATION
Chief Executive: 7 Ridgmount Street,
London WC1E 7AE
Tel: 071-636 7543

MARITIME TRUST
Director: 2 Greenwich Church Street,
London SE10 9BG
Tel: 081-858 2698

MUSEUMS ASSOCATION
Director: 42 Clerkenwell Close, London EC1R 0PA
Tel: 071-250 1929

MUSEUMS & GALLERIES COMMISSION
Director: 16 Queen Anne's Gate,
London SW1H 9AA
Tel: 071-233 4200

NATIONAL COUNCIL ON INLAND TRANSPORT
Secretary: 396 City Road, London EC1
Tel: 071-727 4689

NATIONAL FILM ARCHIVE
81 Dean Street, London W1V 6AA
Tel: 071-255 1444

NATIONAL HERITAGE MEMORIAL FUND
10 St James's Street, London SW1A 1EF
Tel: 071-930 0693

NATIONAL REFERENCE LIBRARY OF SCIENCE &
INVENTION
25 Southampton Buildings, London WC2
Tel: 071-323 7494/7288

NATIONAL REGISTER OF ARCHIVES
Quality House, Quality Court, Chancery Lane,
London WC2
Tel: 071-242 1198

NATIONAL SOUND ARCHIVE (BRITISH LIBRARY)
29 Exhibition Road, London SW7
Tel: 071-589 6603

NATIONAL TRUST
42 Queen Anne's Gate, London SW1H 9AS
Tel: 071-222 9251

NATIONAL TRUST FOR SCOTLAND
5 Charlotte Square, Edinburgh EH2 4DU
Tel: 031-226 5922

NEWCOMEN SOCIETY FOR THE STUDY OF THE
HISTORY OF ENGINEERING AND TECHNOLOGY
Secretary: Science Museum, London SW7 2DD
Tel: 071-589 1793
Midlands Branch
Secretary: 64 St Agnes Road, Moseley,
Birmingham B13 9PN
North Eastern Branch
Secretary: 25 Graham Park Road,
Newcastle upon Tyne NE3 4BH
North Western Branch
Secretary: Stamford Cottage, 47 Old Road,
Mottram-in-Longdendale, Hyde,
Cheshire SK14 6LW

NORTHERN MILL ENGINE SOCIETY
Secretary: Engine House, Atlas No 3 Mill,
Chorley Old Road, Bolton BL1 4EU
Tel: 02572-65003

PEAK DISTRICT MINES HISTORICAL SOCIETY
Secretary: Peak District Mining Museum,
The Pavilion, Matlock Bath, Derbys

PILGRIM TRUST
Secretary: Fielden House, Little College Street,
London SW1P 3SH
Tel: 071-222 4723

PUBLIC RECORD OFFICE
Ruskin Avenue, Kew, Richmond, Surrey TW9 4DU
Tel: 081-876 3444

RAILWAY & CANAL HISTORICAL SOCIETY
Secretary: 17 Clumber Crescent North, The Park,
Nottingham NG7 1EY
Tel: 0602 414844

ROYAL AERONAUTICAL SOCIETY
Secretary: 4 Hamilton Place, London W1V 0BQ
Tel: 071-499 3515

ROYAL COMMISSION ON HISTORICAL
MANUSCRIPTS
Secretary: Quality House, Quality Court,
Chancery Lane, London WC2A 1HP
Tel: 071-242 1198

ROYAL COMMISSION ON HISTORICAL
MONUMENTS OF ENGLAND
(Including the National Monuments Record and
Industrial Monuments Survey)
Secretary: Fortress House, 23 Savile Row,
London W1X 2JQ
Tel: 071-973 3500

ROYAL COMMISSION ON THE ANCIENT &
HISTORICAL MONUMENTS OF SCOTLAND
(Including the National Monuments Record of
Scotland)
54 Melville Street, Edinburgh EH3 7HF
Tel: 031-225 5994

ROYAL COMMISSION ON ANCIENT &
HISTORICAL MONUMENTS (WALES)
Secretary: Crown Building, Plas Crug,
Aberystwyth, Dyfed SY23 2HP
Tel: 0970 624381

SAVE
68 Battersea High Street,
London SW11 3HX
Tel: 071-938 8000

SCIENCE MUSEUM LIBRARY
Keeper: London SW7 5NH
Tel: 071-938 8000

SCOTTISH DEVELOPMENT DEPARTMENT
(HISTORIC BUILDINGS)
20 Brandon Street,
Edinburgh EH3 5DX
Tel: 031-556 3923

SCOTTISH RECORD OFFICE
General Register House, Edinburgh
Tel: 031-556 6585

SCOTTISH TOURIST BOARD
23 Ravelston Terrace, Edinburgh EH4 3EU
Tel: 031-332 2433

SHROPSHIRE CAVING & MINING CLUB
Secretary: S. Holding, 55 Briarwood, Brookside,
Telford, Shrops.
Tel: 0952 660087 (evenings)
0939 250383 (day)

SOCIETY FOR NAUTICAL RESEARCH
Secretary: National Maritime Museum,
Greenwich, London SE10 9NF
Tel: 081-858 4422

SOCIETY FOR POST-MEDIEVAL ARCHAEOLOGY
Secretary; Museum of London, London Wall,
London EC2Y 5HN
Tel: 071-600 3699

SOCIETY FOR THE PROTECTION OF ANCIENT
BUILDINGS
Secretary: 37 Spital Square, London E1 6DY
Tel: 071-377 1644

SOCIETY OF ARCHIVISTS
Secretary: Information House, 20-24 Old Street,
London EC1V 9NH
Tel: 071-253 5087

TOOL AND TRADES SOCIETY
Administrator: 60 Swanley, Swanley, Kent BR8 7JG
Tel: 0322 662271

VICTORIAN SOCIETY
Secretary: 1 Priory Gardens, London W4 1TT
Tel: 081-994 1019

WALES TOURIST BOARD
Brunel House, 2 Fitzalan Road, Cardiff CF2 1UY
Tel: 0222-499909

WELSH MINES PRESERVATION TRUST
Secretary: J. S. Bennett, 7 St John's Way,
Cuddington, Cheshire CW8 2LX
Tel: 0606 889325

WELSH MINES SOCIETY
Secretary: David Rowe, 14 Hillside Drive,
Yealmpton, Plymouth, Devon
Tel: 0752 881402

BIBLIOGRAPHY

The following is a selective list of books and pamphlets relevant to the general themes of industrial archaeology in Britain. The first sections relate to the chapter divisions of this book and are followed by regional works.

RAISTRICK, Arthur
Industrial Archaeology: An Historical Survey
(Eyre, Methuen, 1972).

TRINDER, B.S. (ed).
The Blackwell Encyclopedia of Industrial Archaeology
(Blackwell, 1993).
The most comprehensive and thorough work on world industrial archaeology

INDUSTRIAL ARCHAEOLOGY

BRACEGIRDLE, Brian etc
The Archaeology of the Industrial Revolution
(Heinemann, 1973).

BUCHANAN, R.A.
Industrial Archaeology in Britain
(Pelican, 1980).
Compact and comprehensive study of the subject

FALCONER, Keith
Guide to England's Industrial Heritage
(Batsford, 1980).
An excellent gazetteer

HARVEY, Nigel
The Industrial Archaeology of Farming in England and Wales
(Batsford, 1980).
Covers a neglected aspect of the subject

HUDSON, Kenneth
Industrial Archaeology
(John Baker, 1963).
The pioneer work on the subject
The Archaeology of the Consumer Society: the Second Industrial Revolution in Britain
(Heinemann, 1983).
Emphasis on the twentieth century
Industrial History from the Air
(Cambridge University Press, 1984).

PANNELL, J.P.M.
The Techniques of Industrial Archaeology
(David & Charles, 1966; new edition, J.K. Major, 1973).
Basic practical techniques of fieldwork

THE INDUSTRIAL REVOLUTION PERIOD

ASHTON, T.S.
The Industrial Revolution, 1760–1830
(Oxford University Press, first published 1948).
Still the standard text

BRIGGS, Asa
Iron Bridge to Crystal Palace
(Thames & Hudson, 1979).
Images of the Industrial Revolution

CHAMBERS, J.D. and MINGAY, G.E.
The Agricultural Revolution: 1750–1850
(Batsford, 1966).

CLAYRE, Alasdair
Nature and Industrialization
(Oxford University Press/Open University, 1977).

COSSONS, Neil (ed)
Rees's Manufacturing Industry, 1802–19, 5 volumes
(1819; edited version, David & Charles, 1973).
A five-volume condensation from Rees's *Cyclopedia* containing in alphabetical form the references on industry and technology

CROSSLEY, David
Post Medieval Archaeology in Britain
(Leicester University Press, 1990).

DERRY, T.K. and WILLIAMS T.I.
A Short History of Technology
(Oxford University Press, 1960).

HARTWELL, R.M.
Causes of the Industrial Revolution in England
(Methuen, 1967).

JONES, Edgar
Industrial Architecture in Britain 1750–1939
(Batsford, 1985).
Studies the influence of architectural styles on industrial buildings

KLINGENDER, Francis D.
Art and the Industrial Revolution, edited and revised by Sir Arthur Elton
(Adams and Mackay, 1968 and Paladin paperback, 1972).
The artists' point of view, admirably interpreted

LANDES, A.E.
The Unbound Prometheus: Technological Change and Industrial Development in Western Europe from 1750 to the Present
(Cambridge University Press, 1969).

MATHIAS, Peter
The First Industrial Nation: An Economic History of Britain, 1700–1914
(Methuen, 1969).
Reviews the economic and political progress of Britain through the Industrial Revolution

MUSSON, A.E.
The Growth of British Industry
(Batsford, 1978).

PAWSON, Eric
The Early Industrial Revolution: Britain in the Eighteenth Century
(Batsford, 1978).

PEVSNER, N.
Pioneers of Modern Design
(Pelican, 1960).
The birth and history of the Modern Movement in architecture and design

REES, W.
Industry Before the Industrial Revolution
(University of Wales Press, 1968).
An account of industrial activity in Britain before the Industrial Revolution with particular reference to the organisation of metal mining

RICHARDS, J.M.
The Functional Tradition in Early Industrial Buildings
(Architectural Press, 1958; reprinted 1968).
Still unsurpassed as the apotheosis of industrial architecture

ROYAL COMMISSION ON THE HISTORICAL MONUMENTS, ENGLAND
Industry and the Camera
(HMSO, 1985).
Photographic survey of industrial scenes from the RCHME archive

SINGER, C., HOLMYARD, E.J., HALL, A.R. and WILLIAMS, T.I. (eds)
A History of Technology, 7 volumes
(Oxford University Press, 1954–8), of which volumes 4, 5, 6 and 7 are the most relevant to the

industrial archaeologist.
The outstanding work on the development of technology available in a shortened single volume form is Derry, T.K. and Williams, T.I. *A Short History of Technology* (Oxford University Press, 1960).

TARN, J.N.
Working Class Housing in Nineteenth Century Britain
(Lund Humphries for the Architectural Association, 1971).

TRINDER, B.S.
The Making of the Industrial Landscape
(Dent, 1982).
Essential reading on this subject

WILLIAMS, T.I.
A Short History of Twentieth-Century Technology c.1900–c.1950
(Oxford University Press, 1982).

WIND AND WATER POWER

BROWN, R.J.
Windmills of England
(Hale, 1976).
A selective study of English windmills

FREESE, Stanley
Windmills and Millwrighting
(Cambridge University Press, 1957).
Contains useful information on construction techniques, etc, plus a detailed glossary of terms

REYNOLDS, John
Windmills and Watermills
(Hugh Evelyn, 1970).
An admirably illustrated review of wind- and watermills

SMITH, Arthur C.
This author has produced a series of studies of windmills, all published by Stevenage Museum; those counties covered to date include Shropshire, Hereford & Worcester, Sussex, Staffordshire, Bucks, Oxfordshire, Huntingdon and Norfolk

SOCIETY FOR THE PROTECTION OF ANCIENT BUILDINGS (Wind- & Watermill Section)
Windmills and Watermills Open to View
(SPAB, 37 Spital Square, London E1 6DY).
Essential handbook for those interested in mills to visit. Updated every few years

WAILES, Rex
The English Windmill
(Routledge & Kegan Paul, 1967).
A history of the development of windmills in England

STEAM AND INTERNAL COMBUSTION POWER

BARTON, D.B.
The Cornish Beam Engine: A Survey of Its History and Development . . . from 1800 to the Present Day
(D.B. Barton, Truro, 1965).

BUCHANAN, R.A. and WATKINS, George
The Industrial Archaeology of the Stationary Steam Engine
(Allen Lane, 1976).
Covers historical development, mechanical principles and construction details

DICKINSON, H.W.
James Watt – Craftsman and Engineer
(Cambridge, 1935).
Still the best of several works on Watt
A Short History of the Steam Engine (first published 1936, reprinted by Cass, 1963, with a new introduction by A.E. Musson).
The classic work on the evolution of the steam engine

HAYES, G.
A Guide to Stationary Steam Engines
(Moorland Publishing, 1981).
Pictorial guide to surviving engines

HILLS, Richard L.
Power from Steam
(Cambridge, 1989).

ROLT, L.T.C. and ALLEN, J.S.
The Steam Engine of Thomas Newcomen
(Moorland Publishing, 1977).
Biography of the steam engine pioneer

WATKINS, George
The Stationary Steam Engine
(David & Charles, 1968).
A well-illustrated review of steam engine types in Britain
Textile Mill Engines, two volumes
(David & Charles, 1970 and 1971).
A detailed study on this specialised species of engine
The Steam Engine in Industry
(Moorland Publishing, 1978/9).
Volume 1 covers the public services, and volume 2 mining and the metal trades

COAL

ATKINSON, F.
The Great Northern Coalfield 1700–1900
(Durham County Local History Society, 1966).
A brief history of the Durham and Northumberland Coalfield which provides an insight into the lives of the men who worked in it

FLINN, Michael W.
The History of the British Coal Industry. Volume 2 1700–1830 The Industrial Revolution
(Oxford University Press, 1984).
Most relevant of a series of volumes, covering coalmining from the earliest times to the present day

GALLOWAY, R.L.
A History of Coal Mining in Great Britain (originally published in 1882; reprinted, David & Charles, 1970).
The best easily accessible nineteenth-century view of the coal industry

GRIFFIN, A.R.
Coalmining
(Longman, 1971).
Reviews the development of mining technology

Guide to the Coalfields (published annually by the *Colliery Guardian*)
Contains an index with maps of every operational mine in Britain

NEF, J.U.
The Rise of the British Coal Industry, two volumes
(Routledge, 1932).
Still the classic work on the history of the industry, with plenty of statistics

TRUEMAN, A.
The Coalfields of Great Britain
(Arnold, 1954).
Account of the geology of the British coalfields

IRON AND STEEL

AGRICOLA, G.
De Re Metallica, English translation by J.C. and L.M. Hoover
(Dover, New York, 1950).
This sixteenth-century manual on mining and metallurgy provides an admirable background on the state of early technology

ALEXANDER, W. and STREET, A.
Metals in the Service of Man
(Pelican, first published 1944 but subsequent editions come up to date).
A review of the significance of metals, ferrous and non-ferrous, in the life of man

ASHTON, T.S.
Iron and Steel in the Industrial Revolution
(Manchester, 1924).
The standard general work on the economic history of the industry

BARRACLOUGH, K.C.
Sheffield Steel
(Moorland Publishing, 1976).
Steelmaking before Bessemer
(Metals Society, 1984).
In two volumes, the first covering blister steel, and the second crucible steel

Bulletin of the Historical Metallurgy Society
This contains excellent papers on all aspects of the history of metals, largely in Britain. The *Bulletin* and details of the membership of the Society may be obtained from The Secretary, Historical Metallurgy Society, Dept of Economic History, The University, Sheffield S10 27N

CLEERE, Henry and CROSSLEY, David
The Iron Industry of the Weald
(Leicester University Press, 1985).
An exemplary study showing what can be achieved from painstaking fieldwork and detailed documentary study

GALE, W.K.V.
The British Iron and Steel Industry
(David & Charles, 1967).
An account of the technology of the industry, largely in the Industrial Revolution period
The Black Country Iron Industry: a technical history
(Metals Society, 1979).
Chronicles the rise and eventual decline of one of the country's most important iron and steelmaking areas
Iron and Steel
(Moorland Publishing, 1977).
A useful volume in the Historic Industrial Scenes series, illustrating important developments in the industry

GLOAG, J. and BRIDGWATER, D.
A History of Cast Iron in Architecture
(Architectural Press, 1958).
Well-illustrated account of the architectural and some structural uses of cast iron

Griffith's Guide to the Iron Trade of Great Britain
(1873; with a new introduction by W.K.V.Gale David & Charles, 1968).

MOTT, R.A., edited by SINGER, Peter
Henry Cort: the Great Finer. Creator of Puddled Iron
(Metals Society, 1983).

RAISTRICK, A.
Dynasty of Ironfounders: The Darbys of Coalbrookdale
(Longman, 1953; reprinted David & Charles, 1970).
The standard work on the development of the Coalbrookdale Company

SCHUBERT, H.R.
History of the British Iron & Steel Industry from c 450 BC to AD 1775
(Routledge, 1957).
Covers the early history of the industry

TYLECOTE, R.F.
A History of Metallurgy
(Metals Society, 1976).

ENGINEERING

ARMYTAGE, W.H.G.
A Social History of Engineering
(Faber, 1970).
An account of technological developments, especially in Britain, and their interactions with society

BURSTALL, A.F.
A History of Mechanical Engineering
(Faber, 1963).
Mechanisms from earliest times to 1960

The Engineer: Highlights of 120 years
(Morgan-Grampian, 1976).
Extracts from issues of *The Engineer* covering many engineering topics; in 1981 there appeared a similar compendium entitled *The Innovative Engineer: 125 years of the Engineer* (Morgan-Grampian, 1981).

MOSS, Michael S. and HUME, John R.
Workshop of the British Empire: Engineering and Shipbuilding in the West of Scotland
(Heinemann, 1977).

PENDRED, L.St.L.
British Engineering Societies
(British Council, 1947).
A brief account of the Institutions of Civil, Mechanical and Electrical Engineers

ROLT, L.T.C.
Tools for the Job: a Short History of Machine Tools
(Science Museum, 1986).
A definitive work
Victorian Engineering
(Allen Lane, 1970).

STEEDS, W.
A History of Machine Tools 1700–1910
(Oxford University Press, 1969).

STRANDH, Sigvar
Machines: an Illustrated History
(Mitchell Beazley, 1979).
Thematic approach which brings the story up to the age of the computer

WESTCOTT, G. F. (comp)
Synopsis of Historical Events: Mechanical and Electrical Engineering etc, revised by H.P. Spratt
(Science Museum, London, 1960).

NON-FERROUS METALS

AITCHISON, L.
A History of Metals, 2 volumes
(Macdonald & Evans, 1960).
A wide-ranging survey of metals and their uses from earliest times

BARTON, D.B.
A History of Tin Mining and Smelting in Cornwall
(D.B. Barton, Truro, 1967).

and *A History of Copper Mining in Cornwall and Devon*, 2nd ed (1968) provide a detailed account of the most important non-ferrous metals area in Britain

BICK, David E.
The Old Metal Mines of Mid-Wales
Five (undated) volumes, published by the author at The Pound House, Newent, Glos, the result of many years of fieldwork and research

CLOUGH, R.T.
The Lead Smelting Mills of the Yorkshire Dales
(published by the author, Keighley, 1962).
A detailed survey, with numerous drawings, of the surviving remains of the industry

COCKS, E.J. and WALTERS, B.
A History of the Zinc Smelting Industry in Britain
(Harrap, 1968).
A brief historical background precedes a more detailed coverage of commercial and technical developments with particular reference to the Imperial Smelting Corporation

DAY, J.
Bristol Brass
(David & Charles, 1973).
The history of the most important brass-making area in Britain

FORD, Trevor D. and RIEUWERTS, J.H.
Lead Mining in the Peak District
(3rd ed, Peak Park Joint Planning Board, 1983).
Based on the work of members of the Peak District Mines Historical Society, this has an attractive guide-book format

GOUGH, J.W.
Mines of Mendip
(Oxford University Press, 1930; reprinted David & Charles, 1967).
One of the earliest regional works on lead mining and smelting

HAMILTON, H.
The English Brass and Copper Industries
(reprinted Cass, 1967).
The standard work on the industry

HEDGER, E.S.
Tin in Social and Economic History
(Arnold, 1964).
A general history of the tin industry

KIRKHAM, N.
Derbyshire Lead Mining Through the Centuries
(D.B. Barton, Truro, 1968).

MORGAN REES, D.
Mines, Mills and Furnaces
(National Museum of Wales, Cardiff, 1969).
Non-ferrous metal industries of Wales are covered with considerable reference to surviving remains

RAISTRICK, A.
Lead Mining in the Mid-Pennines
(D.B. Barton, Truro, 1973).
In effect a sequel to A. Raistrick and B. Jennings *A History of Lead in the Pennines* (Longman, 1966).

TROUNSON, J.H.
Mining in Cornwall 1850–1960
(Moorland Publishing, 1981).
Two volumes of pictures, published on behalf of the Trevithick Society

WILLIAMS, C.J.
Metal Mines of North Wales
(Charter Publications, Rhuddlan, Clwyd, 1980).
Mainly pictorial

STONE, CLAY AND GLASS

AUSTWICK, J. and B.
The Decorated Tile: an Illustrated History of English Tile-making and Design
(Pitman House, 1980).
Covers all the principal manufacturers

BAKER, Diane
Potworks
(RCHME, 1991).
A comprehensive survey of the potteries

BARKER, T.C.
The Glassmakers: Pilkington – the Rise of an International Company 1826–1976
(Weidenfeld & Nicolson, 1977).
Detailed history of one of the leading firms in the industry

BARTON, R.M.
A History of the Cornish China-Clay Industry
(D.B. Barton, Truro, 1966).

CLIFTON-TAYLOR, A.
The Pattern of English Building
(Batsford, 1962).
A classic on building materials

COX, Alan
Survey of Bedfordshire Brickmaking: a History and Gazetteer
(Bedfordshire County Council/RCHME, 1979).
Excellent account of surviving remains in the county

GUTTERY, D.R.
From Broad-glass to Cut Crystal: a History of the Stourbridge Glass Industry
(Leonard Hill, 1956).
One of the best regional studies on the glass industry

HILLIER, Richard
Clay that Burns: a History of the Fletton Brick Industry
(London Brick Company, 1981).
Account of brickmaking in the Peterborough area

HUDSON, K.
The History of English China Clays
(David & Charles, 1966).
Building Materials
(Longman, 1972).
Reviews the stone, slate, brick, tile and concrete industries with sections on minor building materials

LEWIS, M.J.T. and DENTON, J.H.
Rhosydd Slate Quarry
(Cottage Press, 1974).
Detailed record of one quarry in North Wales

LINDSAY, Jean
A History of the North Wales Slate Industry
(David & Charles, 1974).

PERKINS, J.W., BROOKS, A.T. and
PEARCE, A.E.McR.
Bath Stone: a Quarry History
(University College, Cardiff, 1979).
Brief, but useful account of extraction methods

TEXTILES

BISCHOFF, J.
A Comprehensive History of the Woollen and Worsted Manufacture
(1842; reprinted Cass, 1968).

CHAPMAN, S.D.
The Early Factory Masters
(David & Charles, 1967).
The development of the factory-based textile industry of the East Midlands

DICKINSON, T.C.
Lancashire under Steam: the Era of the Steam-driven Cotton Mill
(Lancashire County Council, 1984).
General coverage, but with special chapter devoted to Preston

ENGLISH, W.
The Textile Industry
(Longman, 1969).
An account of the evolution of textile manufacture in Britain

GILES, C. and GOODALL, I.
Yorkshire Textile Mills, 1770–1930
(HMSO, 1992).

HILLS, R.L.
Power in the Industrial Revolution
(Manchester University Press, 1970).
Concerned particularly with the use of power in the textile industry

JENKINS, J. Geraint
The Wool Textile Industry in Great Britain
(Routledge & Kegan Paul, 1972).
Good descriptions of processes and studies of the industry in several regions

MANTOUX, P.
The Industrial Revolution in the Eighteenth Century
(1928; revised edition, Cape, 1961).
Pays particular attention to the role of the textile industry in the Industrial Revolution

TANN, Jennifer
The Development of the Factory
(Cornmarket, 1970).
Well-illustrated history of textile mill development

WADSWORTH, Alfred P. and De LACY MANN, Julia
The Cotton Trade and Industrial Lancashire 1600–1780
(Manchester University Press, 1931, reprinted 1965).
Still essential reading

THE CHEMICAL INDUSTRIES

CAMPBELL, W.A.
The Chemical Industry
(Longman, 1971).
Reviews the whole range of chemical manufacturing, particularly during the nineteenth century

CLOW, A. and N.L.
The Chemical Revolution
(Batchworth, 1952).
A general work on the role of the chemical industry in the broader processes of industrialisation

HABER, L.F.
The Chemical Industry during the Nineteenth Century
(Oxford University Press, 1958).

HARDIE, D.W.F. and PRATT, J.D.
A History of the Modern British Chemical Industry
(Pergamon, 1966).
The development of chemical processes from the beginning of the Industrial Revolution to the present, including brief accounts of important chemical firms and trade associations

MIALL, S.
History of the British Chemical Industry
(Benn, 1931).

MULTHAUF, Robert P.
The History of Chemical Technology
(Garland Publishing, 1984).
Useful bibliography, with international coverage

MUSPRATT, Sheridan
Chemistry, Theoretical, Practical and Analytical, as applied and relating to the Arts and Manufactures
(William McKenzie, various editions 1850s–1870s).
Many useful descriptions of obsolete processes

TAYLOR, F.S.
A History of Industrial Chemistry, two volumes
(Heinemann, 1957).
Covers the rise of chemical industries up to 1780 in volume 1 and through the nineteenth century to today in volume 2

PUBLIC UTILITIES

BETT, W.H. and GILLHAM, J.C.
Great British Tramway Networks
(Light Railway Transport League, London, 1962).
Reviews the growth and decline of the street tramway in Britain

BINNIE, G.M.
Early Victorian Water Engineers
(Thomas Telford, 1981).
Chronicles the lives of ten such engineers

BOWERS, Brian
A History of Electric Light & Power
(Peter Peregrinus, 1982).

DUNSHEATH, P.
A History of Electrical Engineering
(Faber, 1962).

EVERARD, Stirling
The History of the Gas Light and Coke Company 1812–1949
(Benn, 1949).
The growth of gas supply to London

FARRUGIA, J.Y.
The Letter Box
(Centaur, Sussex, 1969).
A detailed history of letterboxes and their design

HANNAH, Leslie
Electricity Before Nationalisation: a Study of the Development of the Electricity Supply Industry in Britain to 1948
(Macmillan, 1979).
Concentrates more on business history

O'DEA, W.T.
The Social History of Lighting
(Routledge, 1958).

STEWARD, E.C.
Town Gas
(Science Museum, London, 1958).
A brief account of the introduction of town gas

WILLIAMS, T.I.
A History of the British Gas Industry
(Oxford University Press, 1981).

ROADS AND BRIDGES

BECKETT, D.
Bridges in Great Buildings of the World Series
(Hamlyn, 1969).
A general history of bridge building

BIRD, A.
Roads & Vehicles
(Longman, 1969).
Concerned mainly with vehicles rather than road development

COPELAND, J.
Roads and Their Traffic, 1750–1850
(David & Charles, 1968).

COSSONS, Neil and TRINDER, B.S.
The Iron Bridge: Symbol of the Industrial Revolution
(Ironbridge Gorge Museum Trust/Moonraker Press, 1979).
A study of the Iron Bridge and its influence on cast-iron bridge building generally

CROAD, Stephen
London's Bridges
(HMSO, 1983).
Mainly pictorial study of the 29 bridges between Tower Bridge and Teddington, drawn from the RCHME archive

HOPKINS, H.J.
A Span of Bridges
(David & Charles, 1970).
An engineering history of the bridge

JACKMAN, W.T.
The Development of Transportation in Modern England
(1916; reprinted, Cass, 1962).
Despite its age, Jackman's classic on transport development is still valuable

LAW, H.
Construction of Common Roads: A Rudimentary Treatise
(1855; reprinted Kingsmead, Bath, 1970).
A basic account of nineteenth-century road building methods

ROLT, L.T.C.
Thomas Telford
(Longman, 1958).
An admirable biography of the great engineer with good coverage of his road- and bridge-building activities

RUDDOCK, Ted
Arch Bridges and Their Builders 1735–1835
(Cambridge University Press, 1979).
Detailed study of the arch bridge at the height of its popularity

RIVERS AND CANALS

HADFIELD, C.
British Canals: An Illustrated History
(David & Charles, updated every few years).
The standard general history of British canals and the navigable rivers associated with them

HADFIELD, C. (ed)
Canals of the British Isles Series
(David & Charles, various dates).
The whole country is now covered by this excellent series of regional histories, many of which have been written by Charles Hadfield, who is also general editor for the series

HARRIS, Robert
Canals and Their Architecture
(Godfrey Cave, revised ed 1981).

McKNIGHT, Hugh
The Shell Book of Inland Waterways
(David & Charles, 2nd ed 1982).
Encyclopaedic coverage of all aspects of the British
waterways system

PAGET-TOMLINSON, Edward W.
The Complete Book of Canal & River Navigation
(Waine Research, 1978).
Includes fine drawings of inland-waterway and
coastal craft

ROLT, L.T.C.
Navigable Waterways
(Longman, 1969).
A general account of canal development with some
reference to surviving sites of significance

RUSSELL, Ronald
Lost Canals & Waterways of Britain
(David & Charles, 2nd ed 1982).
Concentrates on those canals no longer navigable

SQUIRES, Roger W.
*The New Navvies: a History of the Modern Water-
ways Restoration Movement*
(Phillimore, 1983).
Good summary of the achievements of the water-
way restoration movement since the early 1950s

RAILWAYS

AWDRY, W. and COOK, Chris
A Guide to the Steam Railways of Great Britain
(Pelham Books, 1979).
An informative guide to preserved lines

BAXTER, B.
Stone Blocks and Iron Rails
(David & Charles, 1966).
An account of the evolution of tramways in Britain,
with a gazetteer of sites

BIDDLE, Gordon and NOCK, O.S.
*The Railway Heritage of Britain: 150 Years of Railway
Architecture and Engineering*
(Michael Joseph, 1983).
Well-researched volume describing features of the
British Rail network

COLEMAN, T.
The Railway Navvies
(Pelican, 1968).
A highly readable account which brings alive the
men who built the railways

ELLIS, H.
British Railway History, two volumes
(Allen & Unwin, 1954 and 1959).
Volume 1 covers the period 1830 to 1876, volume 2
from 1877 to 1947. A most readable account of the
development of the British railway system

Journal of Transport History
Journal published twice a year by the University
of Manchester.
Covers all aspects of transport history

LEWIS, M.J.T.
Early Wooden Railways
(Routledge, 1970).
A detailed and comprehensive study of the earliest
type of railed transport

MARSHALL, C.F. Dendy
A History of British Railways Down to the Year 1830
(Oxford University Press, 1938).
Standard work which is still useful today

OTTLEY, G.
A Bibliography of British Railway History
(Allen & Unwin, 1965).

RANSOM, P.J.G.
The Archaeology of Railways
(World's Work, 1981).
Lavishly illustrated with useful information on the
early period

RICHARDS, Jeffrey and MacKENZIE, John M.
The Railway Station: a Social History
(Oxford University Press, 1986).
Goes beyond architecture, to look at the impact of
the railway station on society

ROLT, L.T.C.
Isambard Kingdom Brunel
(Longman, 1957, and Pelican, 1970).
Not only the life of a great engineer but an out-
standing biography in its own right

SIMMONS, J.
The Railways of Britain
(Guild Publishing, 1986).
A comprehensive general account of the develop-
ment of railways in Britain

THOMAS, D.St.J. (ed)
Regional History of the Railways of Great Britain
(David & Charles, various dates).
A new comprehensive series of regional histories
by various authors

WHITE, H.P.
Forgotten Railways
(David & Charles, 1986).
Companion and introduction to a series covering
the country in regional volumes

PORTS AND HARBOURS

BRACEGIRDLE, B. and MILES, P.H.
Thomas Telford
(David & Charles, 1973).
Illustrates a number of Telford's harbour works

CONWAY-JONES, Hugh
Gloucester Docks: an Illustrated History
(Alan Sutton/Gloucestershire County Library, 1984).
Good history of this inland port

DOCKLANDS HISTORY SURVEY
Dockland: An Illustrated Historical Survey of Life and Work in East London
Detailed study of all remaining features of interest in London's Docks. Preliminary report published 1984, and full report published in 1986, by the Greater London Council for the Docklands History Survey

GLYNN, J.
Construction of Cranes and Machinery: A Rudimentary Treatise
(1854; reprinted Kingsmead, Bath, 1970).
Useful work on small cranes frequently found on docks and canal wharves

GREEVES, Ivan S.
London Docks 1800–1980: a Civil Engineering History
(Thomas Telford, 1980).

LORD, John and SOUTHAM, Jem
The Floating Harbour: a Landscape History of Bristol City Docks
(Redcliffe Press, 1983).
Excellent account covering history and restoration

MCNEIL, I.
Hydraulic Power
(Longman, 1972).
Covers many applications of hydraulic power but with considerable emphasis on harbours

MOUNTFIELD, S.
Western Gateway
(Liverpool University Press, 1965).
A history of the Mersey Docks & Harbour Board

MURLESS, Brian J.
Bridgwater Docks and the River Parrett
(Somerset County Library, 1983).
Definitive history of this small West Country port

PORTEOUS, J. Douglas
Canal Ports: the Urban Achievement of the Canal Age
(Academic Press, 1978).
Studies of Runcorn, Stourport, Ellesmere Port and Goole

PUDNEY, John
London's Docks
(Thames & Hudson, 1975).
A good general history

RITCHIE-NOAKES, Nancy
Liverpool's Historic Waterfront: the World's First Mercantile Dock System
(HMSO, 1984).
Methodical study of the growth and decline of this great port

SENNETT, R. and ORAM, H.J.
The Marine Steam Engine
(Longman, 1915).
The standard work

REGIONAL PUBLICATIONS

Although some regional publications have been mentioned in the preceding subject bibliography, the following are concerned with industrial archaeology in specific regional or local areas of Britain. Many contain gazetteers of sites. The most comprehensive, although by no means complete, is the *Regional Industrial Archaeology* series published by David & Charles. There are numerous gazetteers published as pamphlets, of which a selected sample is included.

SCOTLAND

BRACEGIRDLE, B. and MILES, P.H.
Thomas Telford
(David & Charles, 1973).
Many Scottish illustrations

BUTT, J.
The Industrial Archaeology of Scotland
(David & Charles, 1967).

DONNACHIE, I.
The Industrial Archaeology of Galloway
(David & Charles, 1971).

HAY, Geoffrey D. and STELL, Geoffrey P.
Monuments of Industry: an Illustrated Historical Record
(HMSO, 1986).
Superb illustrations

HUME, John R.
The Industrial Archaeology of Glasgow
(Blackie, 1974).
The Industrial Archaeology of Scotland. Volume 1 The Lowlands and Borders
(Batsford, 1976).
The Industrial Archaeology of Scotland. Volume 2 The Highlands and Islands
(Batsford, 1977).

LINDSAY, J.
The Canals of Scotland
(David & Charles, 1968).

WATSON, Mark
Jute and Flax Mills in Dundee
(Hutton Press, 1990).

NORTH-WEST ENGLAND

ASHMORE, Owen
The Industrial Archaeology of Lancashire
(David & Charles, 1969).
The Industrial Archaeology of North-West England
(Manchester University Press, 1982).

BARBEY, M.F.
Civil Engineering Heritage: Northern England
(Thomas Telford, 1981).

CLARKE, M.
The Leeds and Liverpool Canal
(Carnegie Press, 1990).

DICKINSON, T.C.
Lancashire Under Steam
(Lancashire County Council, 1984).

HADFIELD, C. and BIDDLE, G.
The Canals of North-West England, two volumes
(David & Charles, 1970).

LANCASHIRE COUNTY COUNCIL
Lancashire's Early Industrial Heritage
(Lancashire County Council, 1983).

MARSHALL, J.D. and DAVIES-SHIEL, M.
The Industrial Archaeology of the Lake Counties
(David & Charles, 1969, 2nd ed Michael Moon, 1977).

PRICE, James W.A.
The Industrial Archaeology of the Lune Valley
(University of Lancaster, 1983).

REES, Paul
A Guide to Merseyside's Industrial Past
(North Western Society for Industrial Archaeology and History/Merseyside County Museums, 1984).

ROYAL COMMISSION ON THE HISTORICAL MONUMENTS, ENGLAND
Rural Houses of the Lancashire Pennines 1560–1760
(HMSO, 1985).

TIMMINS, J.G.
Handloom Weavers' Cottages in Central Lancashire
(University of Lancaster, 1977).

NORTH-EAST ENGLAND

ATKINSON, F.
The Great Northern Coalfield 1700–1900
(Durham County Local History Society, 1966).
The Industrial Archaeology of North-East England
(2 volumes)
(David & Charles, 1974).

CAFFYN, Lucy
Workers' Housing in West Yorkshire 1750–1920
(HMSO, 1986).

RAISTRICK, A.
Lead Mining in the Mid-Pennines
(D.B. Barton, Truro, 1973).

RAISTRICK, A. and JENNINGS, B.
A History of Lead in the Pennines
(Longman, 1966).

THOMPSON, W.J. (ed)
A Brief Guide to the Industrial Heritage of West Yorkshire
(Association for Industrial Archaeology, 1989).

THE WEST MIDLANDS

BROOK, Fred
The Industrial Archaeology of the British Isles.
Volume 1 The West Midlands
(Batsford, 1977).
Covers Hereford & Worcester, Shropshire, Warwickshire and West Midlands

BROOK, Fred and ALLBUTT, Martin
The Shropshire Lead Mines
(Moorland Publishing, 1973).

BROWN, Ivor J.
The Mines of Shropshire
(Moorland Publishing, 1976).

COSSONS, Neil and SOWDON, Harry
Ironbridge: Landscape of Industry
(Cassell, 1977).

CROMPTON, John
A Guide to the Industrial Archaeology of the West Midland Iron District
(Association for Industrial Archaeology, 1991).

HADFIELD, C.
The Canals of the West Midlands
(David & Charles, 1969).

RAISTRICK, A.
Dynasty of Ironfounders: The Darbys of Coalbrookdale
(Longman, 1953; reprinted David & Charles, 1970).

SHERLOCK, Robert
The Industrial Archaeology of Staffordshire
(David & Charles, 1976).

THOMPSON, W.J.
Industrial Archaeology of North Staffordshire
(Moorland Publishing, 1976).

TIMMINS, S. (ed)
The Resources, Products, and Industrial History of Birmingham and the Midland Hardware District
(1866; new edition, Cass, 1967).

TRINDER, B.
The Industrial Revolution in Shropshire
(Phillimore, 1981).
The Darbys of Coalbrookdale
(Phillimore, 1974).

THE EAST MIDLANDS

CHAPMAN, S.D.
The Early Factory Masters
(David & Charles, 1967).

COOPER, Brian
Transformation of a Valley: the Derbyshire Derwent
(Heinemann, 1983).

HADFIELD, C.
The Canals of the East Midlands
(David & Charles, 1966).

HARRIS, H.
The Industrial Archaeology of the Peak District
(David & Charles, 1971).

KIRKHAM, N.
Derbyshire Lead Mining Through the Centuries
(D.B. Barton, Truro, 1968).

NIXON, F.
The Industrial Archaeology of Derbyshire
(David & Charles, 1969).

PALMER, Marilyn and NEAVERSON, Peter
Industrial Landscapes of the East Midlands
(Phillimore, 1992).

PALMER, Marilyn and NEAVERSON, Peter
A Guide to the Industrial Archaeology of the East Midlands: Parts of Northamptonshire, Leicestershire, Derbyshire and Nottinghamshire
(Association for Industrial Archaeology, 1986).

SMITH, D.M.
The Industrial Archaeology of the East Midlands
(David & Charles, 1965).

WRIGHT, Neil R.
A Guide to the Industrial Archaeology of Lincolnshire, including South Humberside
(Association for Industrial Archaeology, 1983).
Lincolnshire Towns and Industry 1700–1914
(History of Lincolnshire Committee, 1982).

THE SOUTH-EAST

ALDERTON, David
Industrial Archaeology in and around Norfolk
(Association for Industrial Archaeology, 1982).

ALDERTON, David and BOOKER, John
The Batsford Guide to the Industrial Archaeology of East Anglia
(Batsford, 1980).
Covers Cambridgeshire, Essex, Norfolk and Suffolk

ASHDOWN, J., BUSSELL, M. and CARTER, P.
A Survey of Industrial Monuments in Greater London
(Thames Basin Archaeological Observers' Group, 1969).

AUSTEN, Brian, COX, Don and UPTON, John
Sussex Industrial Archaeology: a Field Guide
(Phillimore, 1985).

CROCKER, Glenys
A Guide to the Industrial Archaeology of Surrey
(Association for Industrial Archaeology, 1988).

HADFIELD, C.
The Canals of South & South East England
(David & Charles, 1969).

HALL, P.G.
The Industries of London
(Hutchinson, 1962).

HASELFOOT, A.J.
The Batsford Guide to the Industrial Archaeology of South-East England
(Batsford, 1978).
Covers Kent, Surrey, East and West Sussex

Industrial Archaeology in Enfield
(Enfield Archaeological Society, 1971).

INSOLE, Allan and PARKER, Alan
Industrial Archaeology in the Isle of Wight
(Isle of Wight County Council, 1979).

LAWS, P.
Industrial Archaeology in Bedfordshire
(Bedfordshire County Council, 1967).
A gazetteer of major sites in the county

MOORE, Pamela
A Guide to the Industrial Archaeology of Hampshire and the Isle of Wight
(Southampton University IA Group, 2nd ed 1984).

PAYNE, Gordon A.
Surrey Industrial Archaeology: a Field Guide
(Phillimore, 1977).

THE SOUTH-WEST

BARTON, D.B.
A History of Copper Mining in Cornwall and Devon
(D.B. Barton, Truro, 1966).
A History of Tin Mining and Smelting in Cornwall
(D.B. Barton, Truro, 1967).

BARTON, R.M.
A History of the Cornish China Clay Industry
(D.B. Barton, Truro, 1966).

BICK, David E.
The Old Industries of Dean
(The Pound House, 1980).

BOOKER, F.
The Industrial Archaeology of the Tamar Valley
(David & Charles, 1967).

BUCHANAN, C.A. and BUCHANAN, R.A.
The Batsford Guide to the Industrial Archaeology of Central Southern England
(Batsford, 1980).
Covers Avon, Gloucestershire, Somerset and Wiltshire

BUCHANAN, R.A. and COSSONS, Neil
The Industrial Archaeology of the Bristol Region
(David & Charles, 1969).

BUCHANAN, R.A. and COSSONS, Neil
Industrial History in Pictures: Bristol
(David & Charles, 1970).

DAY, Joan
A Guide to the Industrial Heritage of Avon
(Association for Industrial Archaeology, 1987).

GLOUCESTERSHIRE SOCIETY FOR INDUSTRIAL ARCHAEOLOGY
A Guide to the Industrial Archaeology of Gloucestershire
(Association for Industrial Archaeology, 1992).

HADFIELD, C.
The Canals of South-West England
(David & Charles, 1967).

HARRIS, H.
The Industrial Archaeology of Dartmoor
(David & Charles, 1968).

HART, C.E.
The Industrial History of Dean
(David & Charles, 1971).

HUDSON, K.
The Industrial Archaeology of Southern England
(David & Charles, 1965).
The History of English China Clays
(David & Charles, 1969).

MINCHINTON, W.E. (ed)
Industrial Archaeology in Devon
(Dartington Amenity Research Trust, 1976).
A comprehensive gazetteer of sites

TANN, J.
Gloucestershire Woollen Mills
(David & Charles, 1967).

TODD, A.C. and LAWS, Peter
The Industrial Archaeology of Cornwall
(David & Charles, 1972).

WALES

HADFIELD, C.
The Canals of South Wales and the Border
(David & Charles, 1967).

HAGUE, Douglas B.
A Guide to the Industrial Archaeology of Mid-Wales
(Association for Industrial Archaeology, 1984).

HUGHES, Stephen and REYNOLDS, Paul
A Guide to the Industrial Archaeology of the Swansea Region
(Association for Industrial Archaeology, 1988).

JENKINS, J.G.
The Welsh Woollen Indusry
(National Museum of Wales, Cardiff, 1969).

LEWIS, W.J.
Lead Mining in Wales
(University of Wales, 1967).

LOWE, J.B.
Welsh Industrial Workers' Housing
(National Museum of Wales, 1977).

REES, D. Morgan
Mines, Mills and Furnaces
(National Museum of Wales, Cardiff, 1969).
The Industrial Archaeology of Wales
(David & Charles, 1975).
Wales
(Moorland Publishing, 1979).
Historic Industrial Scenes series

SIVEWRIGHT, W.J.
Civil Engineering Heritage: Wales and Western England
(Thomas Telford, 1986).
Also covers the West Midlands

INDEX